FUNNY

The Life
and
Times
of
Fanny Brice

INDIANA UNIVERSITY PRESS BLOOMINGTON AND INDIANAPOLIS

F U N N Y

Barbara W. Grossman

W O M A N

First Midland Book Edition 1992

© 1991 by Barbara W. Grossman

The paper used in this publication meets the minimum requirements of American
National Standard for Information Sciences—Permanence of Paper for Printed
Library Materials, ANSI Z39.48–1984.

∞™

Manufactured in the United States of America

Library of Congress Cataloging-in-Publication Data

Grossman, Barbara Wallace, date.
    Funny woman : the life and times of Fanny Brice / Barbara Wallace
Grossman.
            p.   cm.
    Includes bibliographical references and index.
    ISBN 0-253-32653-2 (alk. paper)
    1. Brice, Fanny.   2. Comedians—United States—Biography.
3. Singers—United States—Biography.   4. Actors—United States—
Biography.   I. Title.
PN2287.B69G76   1991
792.7'028'092—dc20
[B]

ISBN 0-253-20762-2 (pbk.)   90–39331
                                                             CIP

3 4 5 6 7 96 95 94 93 92

To my parents,
Bernice and Joseph Wallace,
for inspiring my commitment to scholarship and to theatre

Contents

Illustrations follow Chapter Six.

Acknowledgments

Throughout the writing of this book, I received the support and encouragement of many people. I would like to express my sincere appreciation to all of them.

Special thanks to Laurence Senelick of Tufts University, my advisor on the dissertation which began this study, for suggesting that I focus on Fanny Brice. His thoughtful criticism was always incisive and his meticulous scholarly standards guided me in establishing my own.

The following curators, historians, and librarians were extremely helpful in locating and providing research material: Nancy Ciezki, Assistant Film Archivist, Wisconsin Center for Film and Theater Research; Rosemary L. Cullen, Special Collections Librarian, Harris Collection, John Hay Library, Brown University; Charles Cummings, Newark Public Library; Catherine Johnson and Robert Wright, Harvard Theatre Collection; Christine Karatnytsky, Billy Rose Theatre Collection, New York Public Library at Lincoln Center; Charles Longley, Microtext Division, Boston Public Library; Martha Mahard; Brooks McNamara, Director, Shubert Archive; Sharon Rivo, Director, National Center for Jewish Film at Brandeis University; Barbara Cohen Stratyner; Dorothy L. Swerdlove, Curator, Billy Rose Theatre Collection; Miriam Touba, New York Historical Society; Wendy Warnken, Associate Curator of the Theatre Collection, Museum of the City of New York.

I am indebted to Jeanne T. Newlin, Curator of the Harvard Theatre Collection, for her interest in this project and her willingness to contact William Brice on my behalf. The informative telephone interview he eventually granted resulted largely from her efforts.

I appreciate the kindness of Norman Katkov, who allowed me to quote from those portions of Brice's unpublished memoirs included in his book, *The Fabulous Fanny* (New York: Alfred A. Knopf, 1953), copyright 1952, 1953 by Alfred A. Knopf.

I want to thank my wonderful family and friends for their gentle prodding and constant support, especially Ronnie and Rob Bretholtz, Shirley and Edgar Grossman, Ellen and David Paushter, Sue and Joel Sherman, and Eleanor Wolff. To Christine Bodger, my thanks for typing the manuscript with such alacrity and care.

I am particularly grateful to my dear friend, Ruth Sidel, for the time she so generously spent evaluating the manuscript as well as for her constructive suggestions and enthusiastic encouragement; and to my parents, Bernice and Joseph Wallace, for advising me about both style and substance as my dissertation became a book.

Finally, to Steve, David, Ben, and Josh, for always being understanding, for helping me keep my sense of humor, for taking Swan Boat rides in the snow so graciously, my thanks and my love.

Introduction

Fanny Brice was a truly popular entertainer. Her manic mimicry and exuberant buffoonery won her a following in almost every branch of American show business. During her colorful four decades as a performer, she appeared in burlesque and vaudeville, drama and musical revues (including nine *Ziegfeld Follies* between 1910 and 1936), film, and radio. Toward the end of her long career, she became Baby Snooks, the precocious radio brat, and that is the characterization for which she is most often remembered. Yet Snooks was only one of Brice's many roles and, ironically, was not her most noteworthy. Prior to that narrowing of her comic range in the late 1930s, she had emerged as a gifted comedienne, capable of adroitly lampooning a variety of contemporary subjects. Brooks Atkinson, perceptive drama critic of the *New York Times* (1924–41, 1946–60), hailed her as "a burlesque comic of the rarest vintage," and film director George Cukor called her "one of the great, great clowns of all time."[1]

In a field where fame is especially ephemeral, Brice was a survivor. She made audiences laugh for forty years, and her longevity as a performer warrants analysis. Superficially, it may be attributed to her ability to adapt to different entertainment media, but there are more profound reasons for her success which must be considered. To understand the nature of her appeal, it is necessary to examine her stage career, for the stage is where she came into her own as a comedienne and did her most creative work. Between roughly 1910 and 1936, she discovered the material that best suited her talents and developed a distinctive comic style.

Reconstructing Brice's stage career, therefore, is crucial. It is also problematic because there is only fragmentary evidence with which to verify her activities. This is particularly true of the years before 1910 for which sheet music and comic sketches, production books and programs have almost completely vanished. In their absence, and this is the case for much of her life, one must turn to secondary sources such as newspaper and magazine articles, dramatic criticism, and the recollections of her friends, relatives, and colleagues. The very fact that such sources still exist exaggerates their importance and inflates the value of the information they provide. Their accounts, however, may be inaccurate, their insights unreliable. Although some of the errors are accidental, others are intentional, resulting from determined efforts to distort the truth.

With Brice, as with so many other famous people, separating myth from reality is exceedingly difficult. Facts mesh with fantasies in press releases, interviews, and articles. There is, not surprisingly, a rags-to-riches story in which a young, penniless Brice achieves Ziegfeld stardom overnight. Dressed in tattered clothes, she stands on street corners and sells newspapers. As she hollers out headlines, and strengthens her voice, she is discovered by a sharp-eyed, keen-eared talent scout who sends her at once to Ziegfeld. Astounded by her formidable talent, the impresario puts her on stage in the *Follies of 1910*, where she stops the show "cold" and knows only success ever after.

Other stories are less extreme, but may be equally dubious because they are selective in their presentation of Brice's biography. They emphasize certain aspects of it and eliminate others, sensationalizing or sentimentalizing her life in the process, in an attempt to make her career sound more impressive than it actually was. Such streamlining extends to the posthumous portrayal of Brice by Barbra Streisand in *Funny Girl*, the Broadway musical (1964) and Hollywood movie (1968), and *Funny Lady* (1975), its film sequel. Brice's family was intimately involved in these projects and clearly intended them as a loving tribute to her as a wonderful person and a brilliant performer. She may have been both, but the fictionalized life story each production presents should not be mistaken for reality.

Brice herself is not an unimpeachable source. She often demonstrates a breezy disregard for facts that renders her statements suspect and is inconsistent about many things, including the spelling of her own name. Throughout her life, she used both "Fannie" and "Fanny." Sometimes, both versions appeared in the course of one article or in the same playbill. Apparently she had no preference, although she said she liked to sign her checks with a "y" and wanted to call herself "Fanny" in the autobiography she planned but never lived to complete.[2] A number of the discrepancies in Brice's accounts may be attributed to carelessness; a few, when she had difficulty recalling details of distant events, to confusion. Others, however, seem to result from a deliberate attempt to distort the truth, to produce a version of her life that altered, embellished, or ignored what she had actually experienced. Consequently, interviews and retrospective articles must be approached cautiously because they portray a meteoric rise to stardom which bears little resemblance to the course Brice's career really took. As will be seen, she enjoyed many successes, but there were failures and disappointments as well, fallow periods in which she seemed to lose her sense of direction and identity as a performer, not to mention press coverage, critical acclaim, and enthusiastic audiences. To her credit, she persevered during these discouraging times. If she triumphed, it was because of her determination and tenacity as much as her talent.

Documenting Brice's career has required serious sleuthing in order to establish a plausible sequence of events. It is possible to reconstruct her activities based primarily on the hard evidence which does exist, on the recorded reminiscences of the people who knew her, and on the many articles, both "fiction" and "nonfiction," about her. Unfortunately, Brice's family was not particularly cooperative with this scholarly study. Although Brice's daughter, Frances Brice Stark, granted one telephone interview in May 1982, the family was unwilling to share additional recollections or memorabilia. Brice's son, William Brice, finally agreed to a telephone interview in August 1988. During that constructive one-hour conversation, he reminisced about his mother with candor and affection, but did not offer either to speak again or to reveal the personal documents still in the family's possession. He said he realized that he and his sister had been "difficult," but explained that painful past experiences with unscrupulous information-seekers had made them quite protective about their privacy.[3] As gracious as he was, he left no doubt that a particularly important source, the memoirs on which Brice was working when she died, was still unavailable for scrutiny. It is fortuitous that Norman Katkov, whom the Starks engaged as Brice's biographer after her death, did have access to those memoirs and quoted freely from them in *The Fabulous Fanny*. Whereas he seems to have taken liberties with his recreation of various episodes in Brice's life, Katkov apparently preserved the authenticity of the memoirs.

This study is based on a comprehensive review of the newspaper and magazine articles of the period, photographs, scrapbooks, sheet music, recordings, Brice's four extant films, and whatever script material has managed to survive the ravages of time. Many of the clippings are fragmentary, but since so little concrete documentation exists, even incomplete citations become important. *Variety*, the weekly newspaper about the entertainment industry, was a valuable source of information. Read issue by issue from its inception in 1905 until it printed Brice's obituary forty-six years later, *Variety* provided a record of her professional activities and a context within which to view her achievements.

Notwithstanding the recent mythologizing of her life and career, Brice was often a surprisingly minor player in the larger show business scene.

There were several years when she received very little critical attention and almost dropped out of sight. This initially disturbing discovery strongly suggested what further investigation eventually confirmed: that there was indeed a disparity between Brice's career as it actually took shape and that career as it was later portrayed.

Unlike so many of her contemporaries who have vanished into obscurity, Brice is still fairly well known. Whatever the association—whether it is with radio's Baby Snooks or Barbra Streisand's compelling interpretation of the character Fanny Brice—the mention of her name generally produces a flash of recognition. Why, then, should she be the subject of a scholarly study? It is my contention that Brice was a major American comedienne who deserves more substantial treatment than she has previously received. A unique talent with tremendous personal magnetism, she made an important contribution to the field of comedy. A consummate professional, her dedication and sense of artistic responsibility in many ways epitomized the spirit of her generation. The daughter of immigrants, Brice shared with many other new Americans the fervent ambition to succeed in this "golden land" and to be accepted, admired, and respected by its dominant culture. Her rise through the show business ranks—from burlesque chorine to featured *Follies* performer, from vaudeville headliner to Hollywood box office attraction (and disappointment), to superstar on the "airwaves" with a popular weekly radio show and an enthusiastic national following—not only indicates the extent of her achievement, but also reflects many of the changes in the American entertainment industry and provides a convenient way to trace its development.[4]

Yet, however typical of the times she may have been, Brice was also surprisingly contemporary. A single parent and a working mother long before either was common, she was adept at juggling the needs of her family with the demands of a successful career. She had a significant impact on a field—comedy—that had been predominantly male, proving that the term "funny woman" was not an oxymoron. Her good-humored clowning endeared her to audiences and her impressive artistry won critical acclaim. She demonstrated that talent, not gender, can be primary, and managed to reach her own remarkable goals without compromising either her femininity or her dignity. Through an analysis of her performances and a consideration of the major events in her life, this study will explore Fanny Brice's material and method, her uniqueness as an entertainer, and her important place in American theatre history.

FUNNY WOMAN

The Early Years:
Birth to Burlesque

The most precious thing in this world is talent; to be gifted.

—FANNY BRICE[1]

"Fanny was the one who made something of herself because she had ambition. Her ambition was the biggest part of Fanny."

—CAROLYN SAUL[2]

1.

Aside from her birth certificate, scattered city directory listings, and a few family photographs, all that remains of the sixteen formative years from 1891 to 1907 is Fanny Brice's own account of them, supported to some extent by the recollections of her older sister, Carolyn, and younger brother, Lew. Alternately humorous and nostalgic, peppered with slang and superlatives, the reminiscences Brice shared with press and public are remarkably vague and often contradictory. Yet these retrospective remarks do convey a vivid sense of the young Brice's irrepressible spirit, her enthusiasm for life, and her determination to become a stage performer. An indifferent student, she sought recognition, riches and acceptance in the glittering world of show business. For her, as for so many of her contemporaries and successors—Jack Benny, Milton Berle, George Burns, Eddie Cantor, George Jessel, Al Jolson, Sophie Tucker—the acclaim she achieved as a performer legitimized the aspirations of an immigrant generation and transformed the nature of American popular entertainment.

One autobiographical account appeared in an article called "Fannie of the Follies" in the February 1936 issue of *Cosmopolitan*. The first installment in a three-part confessional, it offered the magazine's faithful readers

something irresistible: "the hilarious life story" of America's "leading comedienne," Fanny Brice. "Here for the first time," its headlines proudly
proclaimed, "the funniest woman that the American stage has known"
would speak frankly about her life. Carefully timed to coincide with Brice's
appearance as the star of the *Ziegfeld Follies of 1936*, the six-page article
promised to reveal the real woman behind "the tinsel curtains." Complete
with caricatures and photographs, it would be a document "as amusing
as amazing."[3]

Then at the height of a stage career spanning more than thirty years,
the forty-five-year-old Brice expansively reminisced about her first foray
into show business. As she recreated it for attentive *Cosmopolitan* staff
writer Palma Wayne, her stage debut was a happy accident—the result
of fortuitous circumstances, the kindness of strangers, and sheer pluck.
Brice explained that she had always loved to sing popular songs and would
do so for hours "on the housetops" with her "newsboy friends." Eager
to make its music marketable, the enterprising group formed a band and
began singing for pennies "in backyards and poolrooms and alleyways—
anywhere that susceptible listeners would give us a chance."[4]

Impressed by her obvious talent, one of Fanny's friends urged her to
try her luck in an amateur night contest, at the time a popular weekly
event in most New York burlesque houses. Although she said she did not
even understand the meaning of the word "amateur," Brice set off for
Keeney's Fulton Street Theatre, Brooklyn, with "a little Irish girl" named
Hannah Ryan. Keeney's was actually a vaudeville house, the first one
to join the amateur circuit, having instituted an amateur night contest
at the end of December 1905. The new theatrical newspaper *Variety*,
founded earlier that year, noted with interest that Keeney's offered prizes
of up to twenty dollars "as an inducement for the budding genius to compete."[5]

"Untaught" and "illiterate," as she described herself in 1936, Brice
was unaware of Keeney's unique status. She simply wanted to see the
show and discover what amateur nights were really like. When she arrived
at the theatre, however, she was dismayed to find the gallery with its
inexpensive seats "jammed to overflowing." Too poor to sit anywhere else,
she was about to abandon her expedition when she met another newsboy
friend who suggested that she "shove around backstage" and pretend to
be "going on." That way, she could drift in with "the mass of performers
waiting their turns" and avoid paying any admission fee at all.[6]

She and Hannah took their experienced friend's advice and found
themselves backstage, where Brice quickly caught performance fever. She

was struck by the menace of the audience, "that hissing, booing mob" of "howling spectators" whose derisive cries cued the stage mechanic's large iron hook. She was impressed by the announcer who seemed "like a god on Olympus" and who could calm the screaming crowd with his temperate injunction, "Ah, don't frighten 'em. Give 'em an even break." Whether it was the mood of the tumultuous moment, brash self-confidence, or ignorance, Brice made the momentous decision to perform. "When do I go on?" she anxiously asked the omnipotent announcer. He reportedly responded, "I'll let you know."[7]

Finally, an unfortunate contestant "got the hook," and someone standing behind her whose name she "never knew" pushed her onstage. "That's what careers hinge on in greater New York," she said in 1936, musing on the vagaries of theatrical success. "A shove forward or a push downward and the rest is entirely up to you." She found herself suddenly facing a hostile audience whose cacophonous booing and shrieking rose to new heights at the sight of the latest victim, "a gawky, nondescript girl in a rumpled linen dress and a cheap sailor hat." Over the din, she managed to hear her newsboy claque shouting, "Stick it, Fan! Stick it!" Their encouragement led the skeptical announcer to quiet the raucous crowd and give Brice an opportunity to move closer to the piano player. As he "pounded out a routine accompaniment," she began to sing and, as she put it in 1936, "something clicked! The spectacle of a scrawny thirteen-year-old girl with a Jewish face singing a heartbreaking ballad" moved the audience.[8]

She was actually almost fifteen at the time, and her hazy recollection of such details as her age is typical of the pronouncements she made for the press throughout her career. Although it is possible that she honestly did not remember how old she was when she first performed onstage at Keeney's, it is more likely that she used thirteen intentionally, to heighten the effectiveness of the story she wanted to sell. Portraying herself as more youthful would suggest greater vulnerability and innocence, and would make her conquest of the Keeney's crowd all the more impressive. She had no trouble remembering that the audience showed its appreciation by showering her with money. "The coins rolled about me like hailstones," she confided to *Cosmopolitan*, as she exited, triumphant. At the end of the evening, she was ecstatic when the audience's applause marked her as the winner of the contest and she could claim her ten-dollar first prize. "Ten dollars!" she crowed in 1936. "What the Empire State Building is to New York, ten dollars was to me that night in Keeney's Theatre."[9]

Brice's victory at Keeney's in 1906 significantly altered the course of her life—a life which, until that time, had lacked direction and had come dangerously close to delinquency. Like so many successful entertainers of her generation, she was the child of Jewish immigrants living on New York's Lower East Side. Today, perhaps, the area conjures up nostalgic images of narrow streets, packed with people and pushcarts, chaotic yet colorful and, like old sepia-toned photographs, somehow appealing. For turn-of-the-century observers of Lower East Side immigrant life, however, reality meant the fetid squalor of airless tenements packed with as many as two hundred people to a six-story building. A typical block in these sprawling slums contained 2781 people and, as one astounded observer noted, not one bathtub.[10]

Social workers and journalists, shocked by the human misery, recorded their impressions:

> . . . the abominably crowded conditions, people living in cellars, in rooms without windows or light, sleeping in hallways, on roofs, on fire escapes, unbearable heat in the summer, unendurable cold in the winter, filth, noise, outdoor plumbing, endless hours of labor, smells, spectacles of vice flaunted for the children to see, bags of garbage flung with abandon out of tenement windows on to the hats of respectable citizens passing below, pushcarts, haggling, curses, quarrels, vermin of all kinds, mice, rats, beetles as big as half-dollars, street-fights, gang warfare.[11]

To that tragic litany, they could have added a chilling statistic: a death rate four times that of other parts of the city.[12] The grueling drudgery of the sweatshops and the laundries, the daily struggle against hunger and fear, drove many immigrants to despair, their dreams of dignity shattered by the degradation of poverty.

Brice's parents, Rose (Stern) and Charles Borach, were among the more fortunate. Rose had reluctantly left her family behind in a small village near Budapest, just as Charles had set off from Strasbourg, some time during the late 1870s or early 1880s. They were part of a great wave of immigration that would bring more than twenty-five million newcomers to the United States between 1870 and 1930. The population of New York City alone would swell from one million people in 1875 to three and a half million by 1900. Each day thousands streamed through the receiving stations at Castle Garden and, after January 1892, Ellis Island. Woefully inadequate when it opened because its architects mistakenly believed immigration had peaked, Ellis Island saw its daily traffic exceed eleven thousand by 1907.

Rose spent eight years alone in America, boarding with a series of families and working at a sewing machine in a fur factory. Charles was a bartender in a Bowery saloon when Rose met and married him. Fanny, their second daughter and the third of their four children, was born on October 29, 1891, following siblings Philip and Carolyn and preceding brother Lew. Brice's birth certificate and the Manhattan City Directories for 1891 and 1892 list her father as a bartender with a residence on Forsyth Street. Crossing such streets as Hester, Grand, and Delancey, Forsyth was close to the center of what one writer has called the "original heartland" of the Jewish section and another has labeled a "corridor to freedom."[13]

Those who could escape the area's congestion and crime did, and many families began moving west to the fertile and expansive territories opened by the railroads. Sometime between 1892 and 1895 the Borachs joined the westward migration. They went as far as Newark, the first city after New York, and the name of Charles Borach, bartender, with a home at 78 William Street, appears in the Newark City Directory for the year ending in May 1895. A thriving commercial and industrial center as early as 1806, Newark by the late nineteenth century had many big businesses supplying national markets. Among the most profitable were the breweries, attracted to the city by the purity of its water supply; in 1895, there were twenty-three listed in the City Directory. Their presence, as well as the thousands of factory workers eager for a drink at the end of a hard day, made Newark, a city with over fourteen hundred saloons by 1917, a logical choice for a bartender.[14]

Certain that owning his own business would be more rewarding than working in someone else's, Charles bought a saloon and promptly turned it over to his wife's efficient management. According to Brice's sister, Carolyn, Rose was illiterate, but "she could figure percentages like an adding machine" and "could tap a keg of beer better than any man."[15] While she waited on the customers in front, Charles (also known as "Pinochle Charlie") played cards in back, content to let his wife do all the work. Evidently she did it well, because Carolyn recalled that her family once owned seven saloons in Newark. Rose would go "from one to the other" working "from dark to dark," while Charles's compulsive gambling consumed his energy and the family's resources.[16]

That the business prospered at all was a tribute to Rose's industry, since the 1890s saw hard times settle over the country.[17] Contrary to the popular image of a "gay" decade with its red plush and gilt, its Gibson girls and Viennese operettas, its enthusiasm for baseball, boxing, and bicycling, the nineties were anything but carefree. In 1893 a grave financial crisis, caused by the federal gold reserves falling below one million dollars, triggered a panic. As investors rushed to convert their holdings into gold, banks and brokerage houses failed, factories shut down, railroads went into bankruptcy, creditors foreclosed their mortgages, trade declined, and unemployment skyrocketed.[18] The country entered a period of severe economic depression that continued for more than three years, bringing with it savage strikes and brutal labor repression, agricultural distress, and a national sense of frustration and foreboding.[19]

The Borachs, too, seem to have been affected by the disastrous economic events. Although Carolyn spoke of seven family-owned saloons, Newark directory listings do not confirm her claim. By 1898, however, when the depression had run its course and prosperity had returned to both agriculture and industry, Rose and Charles had at least one saloon operating in Newark.[20] Business was profitable enough for Rose to take her daughters to Europe, *circa* 1901, when Fanny was ten and Carolyn twelve. In her memoirs, many years later, Brice reminisced about traveling to Hungary to visit her mother's family. She recalled performing for her delighted relatives in Budapest and said she "sang songs and danced" for all the villagers in the "God-forsaken hole" where Rose was born.[21]

Brice's other retrospective glances at this period in her life include memories of her father. Although there is a somewhat disjointed quality to her recollections—"He liked his liquor. He said it made him feel good. He had asthma and he couldn't breathe sometimes. He never slept in bed. He used to put a pillow on the table and sleep on his arm . . ." —they indicate that Charles was an appreciative audience for his talented daughter.[22] After breakfast on Sunday mornings when the saloon was closed, he liked to have her sing and dance for him. She would climb up on the bar, over angry protestations from Rose, and wait for him to ask, "What are you going to do for us, my actress?" She would answer, "I'm a princess in a big castle. . . . The bad king has me locked up. I can't escape," and launch into her "routine." As she described it in her memoirs, "My father would applaud and throw me a nickel or a dime. Then I would sing a song and he would throw me another coin. It's funny, Mom made all the money and there he sat throwing nickels and dimes at me."[23]

It was during one of these Sunday morning sessions, in about 1903, after her return from Budapest, that Rose informed Charles she had sold the business.[24] Tired of the unequal partnership, she announced that she was leaving her indolent husband and moving to Brooklyn with her four children. As enterprising as ever, according to Carolyn, Rose had decided to go into real estate and had begun by buying an eight-family tenement.[25] Although Charles eventually followed his family to New York, the separation proved permanent. He drifted into a series of odd jobs and, as his sporadic visits became increasingly less frequent, eventually lost all contact with his children. It is unclear how, when, or where he died.

In Carolyn's words, Brice "adored" her mother and accepted the estrangement from her father as irrevocable. Except for the brief comments about him already quoted, written toward the end of her life, she never mentioned him publicly again and never spoke about the impact his loss undoubtedly had on her as an impressionable twelve-year-old. It is significant, however, that her own experience would be remarkably similar to her mother's. Like Rose, she would marry unwisely and unhappily. Like Rose, too, she would be a working mother, a single parent, whose relentless drive assuredly came from necessity as well as ambition.

In talking about her life, Brice virtually ignored her Newark experience. She did tell one reporter in 1925 that she had lived in that city "from the time she was a little tot until she was twelve years old" and claimed that "her first impressions of the stage were formed and her ambition to be an actress was fired [there]." She reminisced about "trotting down to Washington Street" to Blaney's Theatre where "the old blood-and-thunder" melodramas used to play and admitted that she could always find a way into the theatre without buying a ticket. "My favorite dodge," she confessed, "was to sneak into Blaney's Gallery while they were airing and cleaning the house in the morning at nine o'clock and hide until matinee time."[26] Not surprisingly, however, the interview in which these comments appeared ran in a Newark newspaper.

She preferred to emphasize her New York roots and her childhood in "the Ghetto." In "Fannie of the Follies" she rhapsodized, typically, "The Ghetto! It is so old and so strong; it is still carrying on all over the earth. It gave us a spirit I can tell you."[27] According to her nostalgic recollections, she was not oppressed by the crowded streets, the steaming clothes strung across the tenement kitchens, or the claustrophobic apartments. Her love for people kept her from finding her surroundings sordid. It was only the "relentless poverty" that "dogged" her steps and was still "on the warpath" when she moved to Brooklyn that made life unpleasant.[28]

By skipping directly from the Lower East Side to Brooklyn, Brice effectively erased the ten years she spent in rough but respectable Newark neighborhoods. In so doing she could create a romanticized view of herself as a child of the streets and claim, "I ran away from every school I ever went to or if I didn't I was thrown out." Untaught and illiterate, as her story went, she nevertheless received a special kind of education:

> I breathed and ate and drank and lived theatre—at home, on the streets, anywhere. In my neighborhood were the nationalities of all Europe. That is where I learned my accents: Salka's mother from Rostov; the Polish woman from Krasnik with her rising inflection like a chant.[29]

Brice portrayed the Ghetto as a vast theatrical training ground where she could learn by observation as well as by osmosis, where watching the characters around her could teach her everything she wanted to know. Since she was concerned with "what filled the heart" rather than "what filled the mind," a formal education was irrelevant. That was why, she explained, she never bothered with school. As she said in the Newark interview, she was much happier sneaking into the nearest theatre when it opened in the morning and hiding until the show started in the afternoon.

Not so, said younger brother Lew in conversations recorded after her death. While he recalled frequent truancy, he insisted that his sister went to school, although she hated it, until she was fourteen.[30] Unfortunately, municipal records are not available for any of the public schools that Brice might have attended in Newark or Brooklyn. Lew's statements, however, would indicate that she dropped out sometime during or after the eighth grade when she had a legitimate alternative: the prospect of a promising career in show business.

Lew remembered his sister as constantly performing and asserted that she found theatrical possibilities in almost every situation. Before she appeared on any stage, she was adept at creating and winning audiences. He described her "first act," a show she "conceived, produced, directed and starred in" for which "admission was a penny and the theatre was a shed beside the tenement."[31] Wearing a shawl draped over her head and shoulders, she played a penniless woman whose baby was dying of pneumonia. She stood on what she had announced was a bridge in torrential rain at midnight and lamented her lot until the audience responded with copious tears. As soon as it did, the performance was over, "the shawl folded carefully until her next appearance."

Lew suggested that she would often indulge in role-playing for the fun of it, enjoying the emotional response she could provoke. He mentioned frequent trips she engineered for both of them to Coney Island, the seaside resort and amusement complex directly south of Brooklyn and nine miles from Manhattan, accessible by nickel trolley ride after 1895. Called "Sodom by the Sea" in the 1880s and 1890s, Coney Island emphasized wholesome entertainment by 1900 and offered amusement on a scale unprecedented in American history.[32] With its bathing pavilions and arcades, its vendors and variety shows, and its three great amusement parks—Steeplechase Park (1897), Luna Park (1903), and Dreamland (1904)—Coney Island served as a summer resort for the masses, offering a welcome respite from oppressive city heat. Beyond that, as John F. Kasson observes in his important study, "for immigrants and especially for their children, notoriously eager to assimilate, Coney Island provided a means to participate in mainstream American culture on an equal footing."[33]

Often among the thousands of customers Coney Island drew each day were the adolescent Brice and her brother Lew. She fondly recalled the great "cunning" with which "one maneuvered for trips to Coney Island —baby streamers peddled from door to door, made from scraps of embroidery picked out of the alley refuse box of the lace factory; lemons stolen from the ice wagons for the lemonade one sold up at the ball games."[34] According to Lew, she had found an even more ingenious way to finance their frequent visits. On the trolley, she would have them pose as dutiful children on a visit to their grandmother. The two would be chatting happily, then Fanny would begin to cry when she discovered that she had accidentally "lost" all their money. Sympathetic passengers would come to their aid, enabling them to reach their real destination, Coney Island. Once there, Brice would repeat her routine many times and was convincing enough to supply them with food, amusement rides, and fare for the return trip.

Lew soon realized that, for Fanny, the thrill was less in going to Coney Island than in the performance she put on to get there. She was, to quote him, "in love with her act."[35] Others view such episodes less benignly, considering them delinquent rather than dramatic, like the Newark shoplifting incidents in which Carolyn said her sister had been involved.[36] Since these supposedly took place when the Borachs' saloon business was thriving, Brice did not need to steal to survive. If indeed she did, it must have been because, like singing for pennies, she enjoyed it.

However colorful these anecdotes may be, they cannot be verified. Role-playing and shoplifting do not constitute the beginning of a theatrical career and to regard them as a kind of apprenticeship is to exaggerate. Brice's first stage appearance was probably the one she described in "Fannie of the Follies," in the amateur night contest at Frank Keeney's Fulton Street Theatre sometime in 1906.[37] In January of that year, *Variety* had recorded manager Keeney's ebullient announcement that Brooklyn had a vast reservoir of undiscovered talent that he was pleased to put before the public.[38] His civic spirit was undoubtedly fueled by the shrewd realization that amateur nights provided highly entertaining evenings at minimal expense, and his weekly contests quickly became a neighborhood institution.

In the many interviews she granted over the years, Brice often glossed over various periods in her life and career. The night at Keeney's, however, was an episode she mentioned no less than three times. In addition to the 1936 *Cosmopolitan* article, she discussed it at length in 1914 and 1925, and actually recreated the event onstage in the *Ziegfeld Follies of 1923*. Although the details vary slightly from one version to another, all accounts indicate that she considered the Keeney's performance a turning point in her life. In April 1914, Brice told an interviewer for the *New York Dramatic Mirror*, an important theatrical newspaper, that Keeney himself had pushed her out on the stage. "Flustered at first," she sang well and "took it all as a good joke."[39] Keeney ordered her to "Get out there!" she recalled in 1925 in the November 11 *Saturday Evening Post*, but confronting her first real audience was so traumatic that she wanted to "sink through" the stage floor. Even with the encouragement of her newsboy friends, she "did not regain consciousness" until halfway through her first song.[40] Recovering her composure, she sang so successfully that the audience shrieked with delight, clapped wildly, and pelted her with coins.

The songs she performed were sensible choices for an ambitious amateur. The first was a sentimental ballad, "When You Know You're Not Forgotten by the Girl You Can't Forget" by Ed Gardenier and J. Fred Helf. With its maudlin lyrics and effusive emotionality, it was the kind of material that had reached new heights of popularity in the 1890s and that early twentieth century audiences still loved. Often called the "Golden Age of the Ballad," the troubled nineties sought escapist entertainment. Songwriters turned away from contemporary woes and churned out songs of romantic love and nostalgia, extolling the decade's cardinal virtues: morality, fidelity, and virginity.[41]

The sentimental ballad with its emphasis on unrequited love remained popular after the turn of the century and gave way only gradually to other song forms. Brice's selection, published in 1906, is typical of the genre. It is replete with sighs and tears and has the requisite pair of unhappy lovers taking reluctant leave of one another. As the "sweethearts" stroll alone at dawn, she hears him say that he must leave her. True to sentimental tradition, the woman is powerless to change the circumstances. She must accept her man's "roaming" and remain behind, hoping that he will return to her some day. He, too, finds the parting painful and fears that "his girl" will be unfaithful. She relieves his anxiety, assuring him that she will be true "thro' weary years, thro' smiles and tears."[42] The length of the separation and the reasons for it are never made explicit but, in keeping with sentimental standards, the pair's purity and constancy will be rewarded. The song's ending suggests the prospect of an eventual reunion and presumably makes their parting more palatable for a sympathetic audience.

Brice's audience loved her rendition of the popular favorite and demanded an encore. In 1925, she said it was another sentimental ballad: Bryan, Kendis, and Paley's "Cheer Up, Mary." Another paean to virtue and love, this song actually ends with Jack and Mary, its happy couple, eloping. At "break of day," they steal away, detected only by "the Man up in the Moon."[43] In 1914, however, the twenty-three-year-old Brice indicated that she had chosen a very different moon song for her Keeney's encore, another favorite of the day, Fred Fischer's racist and denigrating "If the Man in the Moon Were a Coon." Highly offensive today, "coon songs" had become a fad in the 1890s and were still acceptable in 1906.[44] They had not yet begun to provoke the rash of indignant outcries that would be heard within a few years, particularly after the formation of the NAACP in 1909. In singing one of them, Brice was giving her audience material she knew it would enjoy and with which it was familiar. After its publication in 1905, Fischer's composition proceeded to sell three million copies of sheet music. The cover of one of them proudly listed a total of forty-eight "professionals" then "singing the moon song."

Brice seems to have been as adept at coon-shouting as she was at ballad-singing and had found a winning combination for her stage debut. Encouraged by her great success at Keeney's, she quickly became a star on the amateur circuit, beginning with victories at two other Keeney's theatres. According to Lew, she had won twelve contests within a month and was earning as much as seventy dollars a week in prize money.[45] She was also accumulating valuable experience. As she stated in 1925:

> That first year I spent as a professional amateur, scanning the advertisements for notices and appearing at every theatre in Brooklyn, New York and Newark where amateur performances were given. I made out pretty well financially

—marvelously, I thought—but what I was getting, though I did not realize it, was wonderful training in the psychology of audiences.[46]

All audiences, she decided, were basically alike, but the amateur night audience was "primitive." She called it "a thing of large proportions," either "terribly cruel or vastly appreciative," and she quickly learned to play to it. "When it wanted sentiment," she said she "gave it tears by the bucketful" and "when it wanted funny stuff, I clowned to the best of my ability."[47] Although she was still far from developing any conscious technique or performance style, Brice was already demonstrating the sensitivity to audiences that would be one of her most outstanding characteristics as an entertainer. She often said that she loved performing on the stage because of the immediate rapport she could establish. Her responsiveness, as well as her great personal warmth and magnetism, would endear her to audiences throughout her career.

With the same repertoire she had relied on at Keeney's, "sentimental ballads and darky songs," the teenaged Brice earned enough money to convince her mother that she was serious about show business. Rose moved the family to 128th Street in Harlem and permitted Fanny to drop out of school in order to pursue her career. "I came out of school quick. They didn't want me anyway, because I'd upset the whole school," Brice stated bluntly in a 1938 interview. "I went to all the amateur nights for miles around and was soon making from $60 to $75 a week." Displaying an incipient fashion sense and eager to make a theatrical impression, she bought different colored willow plumes—"red, green, yellow, blue, chocolate, lavender, indigo—for every day of the week," to wear in her hair. Buoyed by her favorable reception as an amateur, Brice continued, she was ready to take her "art" seriously, confident that she would find equal success as a professional.[48]

Her optimism was in keeping with the spirit of the times. America in the early 1900s was a happier nation than it had been in the 1890s, enjoying new prosperity under a vigorous young president, Theodore Roosevelt. Sometimes called "the Cocksure Era," "a time of ebullience when spirits were high, humor was broad and heroines were winsome," the first years of the twentieth century saw great growth and progress.[49] America was once again a land of opportunity, and nowhere did opportunities seem as unlimited as they did in New York City, the largest city and the busiest port in the nation. Its millions of residents and frequent visitors included a large number of people whose appetite for amusement, and increased leisure time, sustained a thriving entertainment industry. With its thirty-three theatres for "legitimate" productions (five new ones would be built in 1903 alone), its seven vaudeville and six burlesque houses, its roof gardens and concert halls, New York was the nation's undisputed theatrical capital.[50] It also supplied other parts of the country with live entertainment, as most of the approximately one hundred burlesque troupes, twelve hundred vaudeville acts, and two thousand stock companies "on the road" originated in New York.

New York City certainly offered an aspiring performer many occasions for a theatrical debut. Realizing her professional ambitions, however, proved far more difficult than the fifteen-year-old Brice had anticipated. For a time, she told another interviewer in 1938, she worked for a dressmaker who paid her six dollars a week, until another job brought her closer to the world she hoped to enter.[51] For a weekly salary of only seven or eight dollars, she recalled in the February 1936 *Cosmopolitan*, she did a number of "chores" in a local nickelodeon, probably on the corner of 83rd Street and Third Avenue.[52]

By Brice's own account, her responsibilities included selling tickets, sweeping out the theatre, painting scenery, playing the piano "after a fashion," and singing for the screen slides which could be shown before or after the main attraction.[53] In 1907, such slides were an accepted means of illustrating and popularizing songs. As a number was performed, "scenes" from it would be flashed on the screen, presumably intensifying the impact and impelling the audience members to rush out and buy the sheet music. Screen slides first appeared in conjunction with Edward B. Marks and Joseph W. Stern's "The Little Lost Child," an 1894 sentimental sensation in which a tearful toddler reunited her estranged parents after an unfortunate separation. The enterprising Marks and Stern hired an electrician to photograph a series of pictures in order to dramatize their song, then introduced both ballad and slides at the Grand Opera House on 23rd Street and Eighth Avenue. The song's immediate success established the screen slide as a popular form of stage entertainment and an effective vehicle for song plugging.[54]

Brice remembered the slides as "highly colored affairs" and said that the nickelodeon would often send her to different publishing houses to learn new songs. At one of them, she recalled in 1936, she met "a brown-eyed, mild young man who generally came forward offering diffident suggestions" about the selections. It was Irving Berlin, then a struggling songwriter in Tin Pan Alley, an area covering two blocks of 28th Street between Fifth Avenue, Broadway, and Sixth Avenue, where music publishers clustered.[55] The colorful epithet, allegedly coined by composer Monroe H.

Rosenfeld, was not a mere geographical location. It acquired a pejorative connotation, to distinguish the Alley's tin-eared tunesmiths from composers for the theatre, its piano-thumping hacks from more accomplished musicians. Reminiscing almost thirty years later about her sessions with Berlin, Brice described his becoming "convulsed with laughter" when they sang one of the more saccharine offerings about "a moon, a girl, a boat, a float." As she sat there, trying to earn her eight dollars a week, the teenaged slide-singer could not have realized the profound impact he would soon have on her career.

That career seemed to take an auspicious turn when Brice decided to audition for a Broadway musical. According to her *Cosmopolitan* recollections, "the girl who sold tickets" at the nickelodeon handed her a theatrical newspaper and said, "Here's an ad—Cohan and Harris are calling for girls for their new show. Let's you and me try for it."[56] The show was *The Talk of New York*, the first of three musicals George M. Cohan wrote for the 1907–08 season and produced with Sam H. Harris. The son of vaudeville performers with whom he made his theatrical debut, Cohan had already secured his position as a leading figure on the American musical comedy stage. His fast-paced productions, brashly patriotic songs, and spirited performance style delighted New York audiences, and from 1904 until 1920 he formed a profitable partnership with producer Harris. *The Talk of New York* was one of their many successful collaborations.

Years later, Brice said she worried about leaving the nickelodeon before she had auditioned for Cohan and Harris. As she put it, "But I'm thinking to myself, if I don't get *that* job, I don't want to lose the job in the movie house." She decided to call in sick and asked her sister Carolyn to telephone the nickelodeon for her. When she refused, Fanny turned to Rose, who did not disappoint her daughter. "Mom did it," she recalled approvingly. "She had brains."[57] Then, Brice remembered, she and the box office girl went to see Harris:

> I told him that I would like to get in the show so he said, "All right" and made out a contract for twenty-three dollars a week. That was all. He didn't even ask me to sing. So I asked him if he would like me to do so. "I would like to sing for you," I said gratiatingly, because I thought that if he gave me twenty-three dollars without hearing me sing he'd give me much more if he knew how good I was.[58]

Harris declined her kind offer to audition and was not interested in hiring her co-worker at the nickelodeon. He did, however, offer the sixteen-year-old Brice a position in the chorus. She was elated at the prospect of being in a legitimate production. As she exclaimed in 1936 with unintentionally comic hyperbole, "To be in a Cohan and Harris play on Broadway! George M. Cohan was Broadway's fullest expression—an ejaculation, a vital exclamation of its mood, its pulse!"[59]

The Talk of New York would have been an important step for her as a young performer. Unfortunately, when the show opened at the Knickerbocker Theatre on December 3, 1907, the inexperienced Brice was not in the cast. She had been fired because she sang too well, danced too poorly, and was generally too conspicuous for the chorus. According to an explanation she provided many years later, she had reported for rehearsal "happy and excited" because she was sure that Cohan wanted her to sing. She was ready to oblige:

> When all the girls arrived, someone handed us copies of all the words of the opening chorus and told us to gather around the pianist and sing them. Mr. Cohan and Mr. Harris were sitting in the front row; so I pushed my chair down near the footlights so that they would be sure to hear me sing. Then, when we came to the last note, I kept on holding to it until Mr. Cohan yelled:
> "Hey, you—"
> "Yes," I said eagerly, thinking that I had at last been discovered.
> "Don't hold that note so long."[60]

Although Brice found the terse command disconcerting, she recalled that she continued "conscientiously and hopeful." The worst, however, was yet to come. After rehearsing for a week, Cohan began working on the dance numbers and Brice was completely at a loss. She did not know how to dance at all and, as she put it in 1936, "for once in that fresh overconfident life of mine, a note of fear entered."[61] Unable to distinguish between her left foot and her right, she could not possibly follow Cohan's directions. As soon as he saw her moving awkwardly about the stage, he stopped the rehearsal and fired her at once.

"Back to the kitchen," he barked to the disconsolate teenager. At sixteen, as she wrote many years later, "I had no place to go. At the nickelodeon they got another girl and at home they think I'm the new [Eleonora] Duse."[62] When that celebrated actress was Brice's age, she had already begun her conquest of the Italian theatre, playing Juliet to tumultuous applause in Verona.[63] Brice's unfortunate situation, as she knew all too well, was very different. Her dreams of Broadway stardom shattered by the reality of Cohan's harsh dismissal, she sat alone in her dressing room contemplating a suddenly gloomy future. After several solitary hours, she heard footsteps and, in her words, "I start crying quick. Well, in walks Cohan and I'm wailing like a funeral."

She recalled Cohan's soothing words, "'Now, now, little girl, you've never been on the stage. You can't dance.'" She replied, "'No, but I can sing,'" and continued "flooding the room with tears." Explaining that she simply could not be in the cast of *The Talk of New York* because he needed dancers, he suggested that she audition for another musical comedy currently in rehearsal nearby. When she arrived at the saloon in which the other company was working, however, she had misgivings about taking Cohan's advice. She remembered thinking, "'Uh-uh, not me,'" and instead of trying out for the show went home to her mother."[64]

Brice never identified that production and, although she has been linked with another musical, *The Time, the Place and the Girl*, it is most unlikely that she ever appeared in it. Fired from the cast of Cohan and Harris's show because she could not dance, she would have been equally out of place in the extravaganza created by Will M. Hough, Frank Adams, and Joseph F. Howard, with elaborate choreography by the talented Ned Wayburn. In its review of *The Time, the Place and the Girl*'s opening night performance at Wallack's Theatre on August 5, 1907, *Theatre Magazine* panned the trite story, absurd situations, and leaden humor, but praised the "uncommonly attractive girls" in the chorus for dancing "gracefully" and filling the stage "with gaiety, movement and color."[65] In 1907, the untrained Brice could not possibly have been among them. By her own admission, graceful dancing was beyond her.

Reminiscing about the Cohan and Harris fiasco almost fifty years later, Brice remembered telling her mother she had been fired because she looked too thin in the tights "all the girls" were supposed to wear. Rose "buys that," her daughter recalled, "and I'm looking to learn dancing." Painfully aware that her inexperience had cost her the coveted job, she knew she would never advance in the musical theatre if she could not keep up with her fellow chorines on the stage. "So in a few days," she was delighted when she heard "about a woman putting a new show on tour" because the woman was willing to "take beginners and teach them to dance."[66]

Brice provided a more detailed description of "the woman" and her show in a 1938 newspaper interview. She recalled consulting "a lady in diamond earrings at an Academy of Dramatic Technique that advertised it was turning out 'America's future stars.'" For a thirty-five dollar fee,

Brice was promised instruction in the technique guaranteed to ensure future triumphs. "I'm going to be a great actress," she announced to her mother, who responded by shouting, "You oughta be for thirty-five dollars." Then, Brice explained, "the theatrical agency—that's really what it was—sent me on the road in *The Royal Slave*." She played an alligator "that swallowed the villain" and "got 25 cents a day and board till the sheriff swallowed the show in Hazelton, Pa."[67]

In an earlier account, Brice labeled this experience one of those inevitable "halts in that exploring march people call a career." She recalled having had "two very sore arms" because she had to "lie on a hard stage and nab the leading man through oceans of green sailcloth." When the company suddenly disbanded, she added, she had to be rescued from the horrors of Hazelton by her mother, who was understandably upset about the outcome of her thirty-five dollar investment.[68]

In still another version, the 1914 *Dramatic Mirror* interview, Brice elaborated on this undoubtedly traumatic episode in her life. She identified "the woman" as Rachel Lewis and remembered that she had an assistant named James O'Neill. "If they read this," Brice explained, "they'll know for the first time that it was Fanny Brice they took in tow because I went under my own name [Borach] then."[69] Her zeal to impress her previous employers, however, produced biographical confusion. Mentioning Lewis and O'Neill in this context led to the erroneous assumption that Brice studied with James O'Neill, the actor famous for his interpretation of *The Count of Monte Cristo* and even more renowned as the father of celebrated American playwright Eugene O'Neill. Although a link to that illustrious family would have given her theatrical background the legitimacy it now lacks, there is absolutely no evidence to substantiate such a claim. With characteristic carelessness, Brice simply confused the names. An O'Neill did work for Rachel Lewis in the early 1900s, but it was Charles O'Neill, the company manager, not superstar James.[70]

Brice recalled that Lewis and O'Neill promised to teach her how to act and provide her with a costume for one hundred dollars. Rose paid fifty, but "the only thing the Lewis woman ever taught me," Brice stated, "was a Spanish dance and the nearest I ever got to costumes was a tape measure with which she was always marking off distances." Consequently, she had to wear one of her amateur night outfits in a "little production" the company staged, as well as in its major offering, *A Royal Slave*. She described that production for the *Dramatic Mirror* with almost deadpan humor:

The thing was staged, as before, without money. The Royal Slave was me. I pawned my rings to get costumes and did all the sewing for the company, putting fringe around all the big hats and so on. In one scene, I had to play a bride and I was at a loss for a bridal veil. The manager told me to take the curtains from the windows in the hotel. It worked fine, but the hotel proprietor happened to be in the audience, recognized the curtains, and wanted to have me arrested. I played the moving water under the canvas. Then I portrayed an alligator. That is, at the cue, I'd put up my two arms disguised with a property alligator jaw in each, and gobble up one of the characters when he dropped into the water. Twenty minutes always elapsed before that cue came while I lay almost flat on the stage supporting myself on my elbows. There is a scar now on each.[71]

The popular melodrama *A Royal Slave* would have been a likely offering for a traveling repertory company in the early 1900s. One of twenty-eight plays written by the prolific Clarence Bennett, *A Royal Slave* was full of the intrigue and suspense, the convolutions of plot and contortions of credibility characteristic of the genre. Although the exact dates of its composition and first production are unknown, it was performed almost continuously throughout the country between 1898 and 1915 by Eastern, Western, Northern, and Southern *Royal Slave* companies.[72] Early in 1907, when the sixteen-year-old Brice was a member of Lewis's ragtag troupe, the play would have been at the height of its popularity and Lewis must have hoped to capitalize on its success. Although the script's elaborate special effects would have been problematic for an insolvent company, Lewis may have believed that the plot's duels, disguises, and deaths, its love triangle and buried treasure, would compensate for shoddy scenery and inexperienced actors.

The company's tour, however, ended abruptly with Lewis's hasty exit from Hazelton. As Brice described it, concluding her 1914 recollections, she was busy sewing at the hotel when she "happened to glance up into a mirror" and saw Lewis and O'Neill "with their grips in hand, slipping out." Brice did not bother with hers, which "had only a toothbrush in it anyway," but "shadowed them out." She followed them to the train station and as they entered one car, she quickly got into another without being seen, then "went and sat down back of them in the same car." When the conductor asked for her fare, she "pointed to the others" who turned, saw her, and immediately "paid."[73]

Brice noted wryly that Rose "wasn't much taken with the acting business after that." Of her own feelings at the time, she said simply, "I put Lewis and O'Neill behind me for good and went back to amateur nights." Her pragmatic reaction typified the way she dealt with adversity throughout her life. Faced with personal or professional difficulties, she inevitably responded as she did at sixteen: by finding another job and returning to work. The years 1906–07 had been a trying time for her, as she struggled to become an actress. Flushed with her amateur successes, her initial failures must have been all the more painful, her disappointments so unexpected. With characteristic determination, however, she refused to abandon her dream. She was not yet ready for Broadway, the traveling stock company had been a disaster, but there were still other options for someone with her drive. Eager to learn, anxious to acquire valuable experience, she wisely turned to a less selective branch of the entertainment business: burlesque.

A "College Girl" on the Wheel

Burlesque was like a rocket that got off the ground in 1900 when Sam Scribner formed the Columbia Circuit. Along the way there were some of the brightest sparks ever seen in show business.

–Ann Corio[1]

In those days, if the audience was surprised at anything I did, they weren't any more so than I was, as I never had a routine or knew what I was going to do until I hit the stage.

–Fanny Brice[2]

2.

Fanny Brice spent three years in burlesque and that popular entertainment form had a profound impact on her development as a performer. Featuring variety acts and short comic sketches combined with musical numbers, the burlesque show offered its largely male audiences what they most enjoyed, women's bodies and bawdy humor.[3] Without the raffishness of its rowdy beginnings and the sleaziness which now unfortunately surrounds it, burlesque in the early 1900s was enjoying a period of growth, refinement, and acceptance. As *Variety* noted approvingly in its May 12, 1906, edition, the "clean show" had arrived and was attracting "the better classes" who no longer felt that attending burlesque was "a kind of slumming excursion."[4]

Competition between the Eastern and Western Burlesque Circuits, or Wheels, was generally thought to be the main reason for burlesque's marked improvement. The two circuits had been formed in 1905, with some theatre owners combining under the name of the Western Wheel, or Empire Circuit; the others, in the more prestigious Eastern or Columbia Wheel.[5] The intense rivalry between the two had helped burlesque advance. To produce quality shows, higher salaries were paid, better theatres and routes secured, and material more closely monitored. "'Clean' is the cry of the managers," reported *Variety*, predicting that burlesque would "never again reach the level of the long ago."[6]

However sanitized it was, burlesque never completely lost its stigma and Brice may have turned to it as a last resort. Later on, she said that she had originally considered herself too talented for burlesque but went into it because she realized she did not "know enough to get into a good show."[7] There was probably a good deal of truth to that harsh assessment. Burlesque was easier to break into than other kinds of entertainment; its "girls" did not have to meet Broadway's rigorous standards. Notorious for its "beef trust" chorines with legs like "stuffed black clubs," the burlesque show did not emphasize homogenized beauty.[8] All shapes and sizes found a place in its chorus line. Tall and, in her words, "skinny," Brice's would have been just one of many less than perfect forms. As a member of a burlesque troupe, moreover, her inexperience was not such a liability. She did not need the specialized skills demanded by vaudeville, and could simply learn the company routines along with everyone else.

At sixteen, without the insight she would have as a mature performer, Brice could not realize the effect burlesque would have on her career. She still aspired to stardom in drama or musical comedy and, given its rank in the hierarchy of entertainment forms, considered burlesque beneath her. Since she had not yet discovered her own wonderful flair for comedy, she did not appreciate the humor that was its essence. Nevertheless, the distinctive comic style that eventually became her trademark began to emerge during her three years on the Eastern Wheel in the *Transatlantic Burlesquers* (1907–08), *The Girls from Happyland* (1908–09), and *The College Girls* (1909–10).

In her 1914 *Dramatic Mirror* interview, Brice stated that she "drifted into burlesque with Hurtig and Seamon," a reputable New York firm with theatrical holdings "pretty much all over the United States."[9] She spent "two years in the chorus, beginning in the *Transatlantic Burlesquers*," one of the Wheel's better offerings. In later accounts of this period in her life, however, she portrayed herself as more resourceful, more decisive, and more immediately successful than she actually was. Instead of simply "drifting" into the *Transatlantics*, she said she went to see producer Joe Hurtig and asked him for a job. After hearing her sing and mistakenly assuming that she could dance, he gave her a contract for eighteen dollars a week. Hurtig soon discovered what she had tried to conceal: his new chorus girl was "a total loss as a dancer." He was about to fire her from the company when, either because she pleaded with him to keep her or because he realized that she was valuable as a singer, she was allowed to remain. Recognizing that she could "tear apart a song with that sentimental whine one heard in the vaudeville crooners of the day," she recalled, Hurtig and Seamon decided to use her to broadcast "unexpected second choruses" from different parts of the theatre. "I sang way up in the gallery, I sang behind the scenes backstage, I sang in the shadow of the boxes," she reminisced, "but the audience never got a glimpse of me because I never got a chance to sing on the stage as a regular member of the show."[10]

Undaunted, Brice was determined to join the company on stage as quickly as possible and proceeded to take dancing lessons from anyone willing to teach her. She bribed stage hands with quarters and chorus girls with clothes. Apparently Rose had given her daughter a trunkful of new dresses, stockings, and lingerie which Fanny bartered for dance steps. By the time she had depleted her wardrobe, she had learned to dance and, confident that she could keep up with the rest of the company, demanded to be admitted to the chorus. After demonstrating her dancing prowess, she was given a position in the chorus's third, and last, line. Intent on moving to the first, she practiced the routines diligently and was soon promoted to the second row. Then, after more work, "hour after hour in odd corners of the theatre," she was placed in the front but was not yet satisfied.[11] Hoping to become understudy to the company's female lead, the soubrette, she competed with the other chorus girls in special dance contests held at the end of certain performances. Designed to stimulate business, these talent nights also awarded prizes of up to ten dollars which Brice invariably won. When she had accumulated enough prize money, she was named understudy and resolved to become the soubrette's permanent replacement.

She realized that her chances were slim. In one account, she described the soubrette as not only the manager's wife, but also "a beautifully formed, graceful woman with a pleasing voice." In another, she remembered "a big, husky Italian girl" who was never sick and about whom she declared with typical hyperbole, "You couldn't knock her out."[12] In either case, it was unlikely that the lead would leave the show. Nevertheless, Brice waited and watched, ever hopeful that something unforeseen would happen and catapult her to the stardom she so clearly deserved.

In the best show business tradition, it did. In Chicago the soubrette began to complain of an abscess behind her ear, but continued to perform despite the pain. In Cincinnati, however, she grew increasingly uncomfortable and suddenly fainted in the wings. The seventeen-year-old Brice, as understudy, went on in her place. As she later recounted the momentous experience:

> When she started screaming with pain, I was singing out in front the first verse of "In the Land of the Buffalo." Her routine I didn't know, so I did the one I learned in the chorus—most of the time the same steps over, frontwards, backwards, and sidewards. Then the encores began. They wouldn't let me go. [13]

In another interview, given when she was thirty-four, she remembered how she had felt as a young performer doing a solo for the first time in a professional production:

> Now as the soubrette presented that song and dance, it did not suit my personality. She was voluptuous, I was not yet fully grown and weighed between seventy and eighty pounds. She was a graceful dancer. I was an awkward child with the knowledge of but a few steps. I was wildly excited, but I presented that song as I saw it, singing it rapidly and exaggerating the few steps I knew. [14]

The audience responded instantly to her. Sensing her "excitement" and the "feverish comedy" of her dancing, it reacted as the crowd had at Keeney's just two years before. Applauding wildly, people rose out of their seats and demanded six encores. Unfortunately for the soubrette, Hurtig was in the theatre that night and summarily sent her back to the chorus. Brice took her place for the rest of the season and, although earning only eighteen dollars a week, was delighted to be a principal in the company.

Brice's accounts captured her drive and dedication. They conveyed her determination to rise in the theatrical ranks and recorded the acclaim she so clearly deserved. The only problem with them is that they were all fabrications. The heroic struggle, the last-minute substitution, the overnight success—none of it took place as she described it. If it had, the event would have been a press agent's dream, a show business Cinderella story with the chorus girl making good. Nowhere along the route, however, did reviewers write about an unknown performer taking command of the stage and winning the audience with her incredible energy and skill. No one praised a bright young talent named Borach. In fact, no one mentioned Brice's name at all, not even in Cincinnati, where the understudy's wishes allegedly came true. Except for a notation in the December 7, 1907, *New York Clipper* that the chorus of sixteen included a Fannie Borach, her name did not appear in any publicity for the production, which made thirty-six stops between its August 1907 opening in Washington, D.C., and its May 1908 closing in Milwaukee.[15]

Perhaps Brice confused her tenure in the *Transatlantics* with a part she played in another burlesque show the following season and which, curiously, she never mentioned in any of her reminiscences. On August 30, 1908, she opened in Birmingham, Alabama, as a member of *The Girls from Happyland*, an inferior production headed by comedian Billy W. Watson and soubrette Lizzie Freligh. Whereas *Variety* had praised the *Transatlantics* as an extremely good burlesque show, it criticized *The Girls from Happyland* for being cheaply mounted and, with few exceptions, inadequately performed.[16]

That show was nevertheless a landmark in Brice's career because it marked her first appearance as Fanny Brice, the name she used for the rest of her life. She explained in a 1946 interview that she was tired of being called "Borax" and "Boreache" and selected Brice, the surname of a family friend, to prevent further teasing.[17] She was also, undoubtedly, trying to seem less ethnic, less foreign, less Jewish, and, by so doing, to broaden her appeal. In 1908 she did not know that she would shortly find fame as a performer by exploiting her Jewishness and caricaturing her ethnicity. Yet, although she would specialize in Yiddish-accented humor, she never lost her desire to be accepted by non-Jewish audiences. The resistance she encountered, the perception that she was "too New York," "too Jewish" would haunt her in Hollywood in the 1920s and would be a source of frustration throughout her career.

According to the September 19, 1908, *New York Clipper*, when *The Girls from Happyland* appeared at New Orleans's Greenwall Theater for the week of September 6–12, the company included "Fanny Brice." That was the way she was listed in the November 21 *Clipper*'s "Directory of Burlesquers" and it was the name *Variety* mentioned in its December 26 review of the production at New York's Murray Hill Theatre.[18] The citations are significant because there has previously been confusion about when the name change actually occurred. Some sources said that she chose Brice when she applied for the nickelodeon job. Others maintained that she did not begin using it until she had started in burlesque. From the above references, it is clear that Fanny was still Borach in the *Transatlantics*, but became Brice when she appeared in *The Girls from Happyland*.

Her role in the production is more ambiguous. The *Clipper* listed her as a chorus girl, but *Variety* indicated that she did something more. Sime, the paper's founder and longtime editor, observed, "There's another chorister from the mixed collection of twelve or fourteen who steps out of the line to take up a part, Fannie Brice as a maid." He added that, unlike some of her more corpulent colleagues, "Fannie at least looks good."[19] Was this the shining moment Brice chronicled over and over again in her reminiscences? Was this the source of the story about substituting for an ailing soubrette?

Apparently Lizzie Freligh became ill in early December and was absent from the cast for most of the month. The January 2, 1909, *Clipper* noted that she had rejoined the company, then in Philadelphia, and reviews of the show along its route indicated that she was again pleasing audiences with her performance. Although it is unclear exactly when she returned to the cast, she had resumed her role as female lead well before *The Girls from Happyland* closed in Brooklyn on May 29, 1909.

There is absolutely no evidence that Brice replaced Freligh during her illness. Newspaper reviews reveal that Freligh's numbers were divided among other women in the cast, but Brice was not one of them. According to *Variety*, a chorus girl named Mabel Leslie took over as "the leading woman." The *Springfield Daily News* confirmed this statement, reporting that Leslie was "advanced to the position of 'principal boy' in the absence of Lizzie Freligh."[20] Once again, the facts do not jibe with Brice's recollections. Her story of saving the show in Cincinnati was sheer fabrication, the fairy tale fulfillment of every understudy's dream. However innocent her motive, her accounts were untrue. They cannot be substantiated and that may be why Brice was so vague about the name of the show in which she was appearing when she allegedly became an overnight sensation.

In addition to selectively recreating her life, Brice also did her best to legitimize burlesque. By the mid-1920s, burlesque was becoming "dirty" once again. Rowdy humor grew raunchy, even scatological, as the striptease made shows salacious. Unwilling to tarnish her own image by an association with such an unsavory form of amusement, Brice carefully countered charges of indecency and impropriety. In order to make her own association with burlesque more acceptable, she stressed its innocuousness and validated its entertainment value. She defended its audiences as being much maligned by people who believed that "burlesque patrons saw off their hair two inches above their collars and appreciate broad jokes." "Nothing could be further from the truth," she said indignantly in 1925, because burlesque is "merely vaudeville performed by a whole company and interspersed with dancing and chorus numbers." She noted that "out of it have come many of our greatest actors and actresses" — including herself by implication — and concluded with the chauvinistic statement that "it is the branch of show business that most nearly approaches ideal democracy." As she was careful to explain, burlesque was egalitarian because "any difference between performers is determined by talent, and everyone with talent gets his or her chance."[21]

She clearly got "her chance" in Max Spiegel's *The College Girls*, a burlesque show she had read about in *Variety* and in which she really did have a sizeable part. She once said that she responded to an ad for it because she thought it was "a classy title" and it turned out to be "one of the best [shows] ever produced." *Variety* shared her opinion, calling *The College Girls* "one of the blue ribbon organizations of the circuit."[22] It was also, significantly, her first well-documented stage appearance. In its very favorable review of the production, the September 4, 1909, *Variety* predicted that it would be "one of the leaders in the Columbia Amusement Co.'s tour" because it had "splendid comedy values, a decidedly high average of novelty, clever people, new faces and bright dressing."[23] Among the new faces was Brice, who *Variety* acknowledged was a "substantial applause getter."

She was subsequently included in *Variety*'s "Variety Artists' Routes," beginning with the October 23, 1909, edition. (Her listing there as "Brice, Fanny *College Girls* BR" indicated that she was appearing in a burlesque show whose route could be found in the paper's weekly schedule.) The *Dramatic Mirror* referred to her by name in its September 18 "Vaudeville Correspondence" column as one of *The College Girl* Burlesquers then playing at Washington's Gayety Theatre and the *Clipper*, too, identified her as a member of Spiegel's company. In addition to the many reviews that praised her, two extant programs include her in the cast list. Both are from Brooklyn's Gayety Theatre and show that she played Josie McFadden, one of the soubrettes. Since one program is dated August 21, 1909, and the other May 9, 1910, she appears to have been with the production for its entire run.[24]

Newspaper critics noted approvingly that *The College Girls* had many spirited musical numbers, with nine "catchy songs" in the first act and eleven in the second, but said little either about the quality of the material or, specifically, how well Brice performed it. *Variety* stated simply that she and Grace Childress, the other soubrette, were not as effective as they might have been because, although "lively enough and undeniably pretty dressers," neither did "any dancing to speak of."[25] Apparently, in spite of the determined efforts Brice later described, dancing was still a problem for her.

Even less was said about her acting. Of all the reviews that mentioned her, only one observed that she interpreted her role as Josie McFadden, "rather sardonically."[26] In fact, what the critics praised was not Brice as soubrette, but the specialty act she offered in the second half of the show. Again and again, she was said to have "scored a hit" with her solo numbers.[27] According to one enthusiastic reviewer "Fannie Brice exhausted encores in the demand of the audience for more of her excellent character songs, a 'Yiddisher Salome' and a coon song."[28] Although the latter was familiar—albeit offensive—material, the "Yiddisher Salome" was a significant departure for her and one that would greatly influence her future as a performer.

According to Brice, Spiegel had hired her because she had lied to him. She had told him she had a specialty act, but as she admitted years later, she actually did not. When Spiegel announced to the cast that all "specialty people" were to appear in a Long Island benefit, she panicked. Realizing that she had better find some good material quickly, she turned to someone she knew from her days as a slide-singer: Irving Berlin. Although he had not yet produced "Alexander's Ragtime Band," the song that helped popularize ragtime and earned him the title "Ragtime King," Berlin was already winning recognition as a bright young songwriter. Seeking his advice was one of the wisest decisions Brice ever made in her long career.

She described their momentous meeting in her memoirs:

"Oh, Irving," I said, grabbing him. "I've got a job in a show, and when Spiegel signed me up he asked me if I did a specialty. I told him yes, thinking that was the way I could get the job. I never thought he really wanted me to do one. And I have to sing something because I've got to do this benefit . . . or I'm finished."[29]

As she reminisced about it forty years later, Berlin took her into a back room and played two songs. One was "Grizzly Bear," a spirited ragtime number already being performed by many singers. The other was "Sadie Salome, Go Home!"—in Brice's words, "a Jewish comedy song." Naturally, Berlin sang it for her with a Yiddish accent and Brice remembered her surprise: "I had never had any idea of doing a song with a Jewish accent. I didn't even understand Jewish, couldn't talk a word of it. But, I thought, if that's the way Irving sings it, that's the way I'll sing it."[30] With a Hungarian mother and a French father, neither of whom would necessarily have spoken Yiddish (the language Brice mistakenly calls "Jewish"), her disclaimers do not ring completely false. Although they certainly undermine her stories about a Ghetto childhood, they typify other statements she periodically made in which she tried to distance herself from anything ethnic, even as she was performing the most outrageous Yiddish-accented material. It was, she seemed to want her audiences to believe, just an act; the Jewishness, she implied, was as foreign to her as it was to them. Whether or not that pose ever caused her personal pain, the distancing she affected ultimately worked to her advantage as a performer as she developed her distinctive comic method.

Brice recalled learning both songs in an hour, an accomplishment she attributed to "youth and ambition," and always acknowledged the back room meeting with Berlin as a crucial moment in her life. Had he selected "an Irish song and done it with a brogue," she often asserted, she "would have been an Irish comedienne forever."[31] He could have, too, for that same year he had written, "I Wish That You Was My Gal, Molly," with an Irish theme, as well as "Dorando," a topical song in Italian dialect, and "Oh! How That German Could Love."[32] That he did not is testimony to his own perspicacity, if not to hers. However unaware Brice says she was of her affinity for Yiddish dialect comedy—and it is interesting to note that in *The College Girls* she was playing Irish Josie McFadden rather than Jewish Nanie Schmitz—Berlin must have recognized how well it would suit her. In "Sadie Salome, Go Home!" she had her first unmistakable success and one of the two songs she later said had the greatest impact on her career.

An outrageous spoof of Salome dancing, "Sadie Salome, Go Home!" was a timely selection. In 1909 New York was just beginning to recover from Salome fever, a phenomenon once described as "the phoniest craze of all to hit show business."[33] As a symbol of feminine decadence and depravity, Salome appealed to turn-of-the-century misogynists and became a familiar figure in European cultural circles. Salomes were painted in provocative poses, they tempted with serpentine dances in poetry and prose, but it was the one-act play written in French by Oscar Wilde and published in 1893 that provided the most vivid image of "the headhuntress's . . . pernicious sexual perversity."[34]

On July 8, 1907, aspiring impresario Florenz Ziegfeld renamed the New York Theatre's roof garden the "Jardin de Paris" and opened the first edition of his celebrated *Follies* there. The show included a spoof of the Richard Strauss opera, *Salomé*, with stout character singer Emma Carus and lithe dancer Mlle. Dazie costumed identically (and diaphanously) as Salome, despite their great difference in size.[35] Salome offered the right combination of sex and scandal and New York went "Salome mad."[36] By the following year, when women's clothing was practically protective armor and no upright female considered leaving the house without corset, long skirt, and hat, the craze was at its peak and many scantily dressed "Salomers" flocked to vaudeville and burlesque.

As the Salomes proliferated, so did the parodists. Theatres across the country were full of mock Salome dancers and, as early as August 1908, a satirical coon song called "De Sloamey Dance" appeared in *Variety*. By late 1909 when Brice was performing her "ethnic novelty version," the Salome fad had definitely fizzled. Iowa had even passed an austere "anti-Salome" law, *Variety* reported, under which the whole state was "barred from the seductive wriggle" and offenders were subject to fines and imprisonment.[37] But it was mediocrity rather than moral indignation that brought Salome dancing to an end. So many of the acts were "worthless trash," in the words of one hostile critic, that people were tired of them and receptive to spoofs such as Brice's. The prospect of a Sadie Cohen dancing suggestively was more than faintly ridiculous, and the sheer number of second-rate "Salomers" still gyrating made her doing so almost credible.

"Sadie Salome, Go Home!" with music by Berlin and lyrics by Edgar Leslie, is the saga of Sadie Cohen, a nice Jewish girl who has left her "happy home" and her sweetheart, Mose, in the hope of attaining Salome stardom. According to Sadie, Mose is distraught, not so much because of what she has taken on, but on account of what she is taking off. He admires her singing, but objects to her "funny motions," which Brice's antic clowning made truly ludicrous. Undeterred by Mose, Sadie launches into an encore and triggers another impassioned outburst:

> You better go and get your dresses
> Ev'ryone's got the op'ra glasses
> Oy, such a sad disgrace! No one looks in your face
> Sadie Salome, go home![38]

Adding to the comic effect of Brice's interpretation was the Yiddish accent she used. In 1909, ethnic humor was still very much in vogue as German, Irish, Jewish, Italian, and blackface comics, among others, cavorted in burlesque and vaudeville. Audiences continued to laugh at such sketches as "The Sport and the Jew," "Irish by Name, but Coons by Birth," "The Mick and the Policeman," "The Merry Wop," and "Two Funny Sauerkrauts." Although the reprehensible stereotypes were ultimately condemned, they were considered hilarious and appropriate entertainment from approximately 1880 to 1920.

In its reliance on ethnic humor, American popular entertainment reflected the nation's increasingly heterogeneous population. During the nineteenth century, when vast numbers of immigrants flocked to the United States, the country's population exploded as "potatoes, politics, and pogroms" created millions of new Americans.[39] Between 1830 and 1850, almost two and one-half million people, predominantly Irish and German, comprised the first great wave of immigration and, after 1878, Bismarck's anti-socialist legislation drove more disenchanted Germans across the ocean.[40]

Comedians in vaudeville and burlesque were quick to transform the traits of the new Americans into readily identifiable types. Irish and German (or Dutch) comics soon became stage favorites. The "Jew comics" appeared later because the great mass of Jewish immigrants did not arrive until the 1880s. There had been isolated clusters of Jews in the United States from colonial days and occasional settlements from the seventeenth century on. Even in New York City there was no large Jewish community before the 1870s, when one was formed by the Jewish immigrants beginning to arrive from Eastern Europe.[41] In the 1880s, however, the situation changed dramatically as a sudden influx of Jews began pouring into the country. In 1880, there were some eighty thousand Jews living in New York City; by 1910, a million and one-quarter. The total Jewish immigration to the United States between 1899 and 1914, most of which settled in or passed through the Lower East Side, was slightly over a million and one-half.[42]

Like the Irish and Germans, the Jews were parodied by the popular arts, and Jewish characters began to appear in the late 1870s. Jewish comics undoubtedly appealed to the audience's underlying hostility more than other ethnic clowns did. On account of their religion Jews were more alien than Irish, German, Swedes, Italians, or any other group portrayed—except blacks. Both blacks and Jews were so obviously different that they were objects of more intense contempt and ridicule, their crude caricatures designed to appeal to audiences' latent, or blatant, prejudice. Nevertheless, a skillful "Jew comic" could evoke sympathy as well as laughter.

By the 1900s, according to historian Irving Howe, the stage Jew and the "Jew comic" became "fixtures of the American theatre, straight, vaudeville, and burlesque."[43] In addition to some of the more familiar names such as Julian Rose with his "Levinsky at the Wedding" and Andy Rice with his monologue about Sadie's debut in society, there were literally hundreds of other Jewish acts listed in the weekly trade papers. Henry Frey as "a Jew Pawnbroker," James Mooney in a "Hebrew dance," Harry Steward's "Levinski and His Cloak Models," Gilday and Fox in "The

Hebrew Trainer and the Jockey," Biff Hall's "Melancholy Hebrew," and Fred Russell's "Jew with the Big Voice" were among the "Hebrew turns" winning favorable reviews.[44] There were even a few women—notably Sadie Fields, Belle Gold, Annie Goldie, Leah Russell, Lillian Shaw, and Fannie Woods—who amused audiences with "Hebraic comedy" and "Yiddish characterizations."[45]

In following Berlin's advice and performing "Sadie Salome" with a Yiddish accent, therefore, Fanny Brice was not doing anything novel. Although allegedly unable to speak Yiddish, she could join the many non-Jews who succeeded as Jewish comics by adopting the externals—the accent and the mannerisms—required for "Hebrew impersonation." Clearly Berlin must have believed that "Sadie Salome" would suit the tall, thin, ungainly teenager with the big nose and wide mouth. As soon as she heard him sing it "with all the intonation of Hester Street," she recalled many years later, she knew that he was right. Reminiscing in her "child of the Ghetto" mode, she said that the song conjured up familiar images which eliminated any reservations she might have had about using the accent:

> I saw Loscha of the Coney Island popcorn counter and Marta of the cheeses at Brodsky's Delicatessen, and the Sadies and the Rachels and the Birdies with the turnover heels at the Second Avenue dance halls. They all welded together and came out staggeringly true to type in one big authentic outline.[46]

Wearing a heavily starched white sailor suit, Brice performed both "Sadie Salome" and "Grizzly Bear" at the Long Island benefit as Spiegel had requested. From the description she provided in her memoirs, her specialty act was a spectacular success:

> Well I came out and did "Sadie Salome" for the first time ever doing a Jewish accent. And that starched sailor suit is killing me. And it's gathering you know where, and I'm trying to squirm it away, and singing and smiling and the audience is loving it. They think it's an act I'm doing, so as long as they're laughing, I keep it up. They start to throw roses at me. I did "Grizzly Bear" for them and I'm still with that creeping sailor. More roses. I was a hit, I guess.[47]

She "guessed" correctly, as both songs worked well. Like the chicken scratch, the bunny hug, the kangaroo dip, the camel walk, the crab step, the lame duck, and the turkey trot, "The Dance of the Grizzly Bear," with lyrics by Berlin and music by George Botsford, was one of the many new "animal" dances inspired by ragtime's fast tempo and exuberant rhythm.[48] A popular number performed by several singers, "Grizzly Bear" was most frequently associated with Sophie Tucker, who had already appeared as a blackfaced coon-shouter in vaudeville. Hers was the name that appeared on the cover of the sheet music published in 1910, but Brice's interpretation of the piece attracted favorable notices along *The College Girls'* route. A ragtime coon song, "Grizzly Bear" was the kind of material with which she was comfortable and anticipated "Lovie Joe," her first great *Follies* success.

Nevertheless, "Sadie Salome" was more important in the long run. With Sadie, Brice created the first of her many memorable characters and discovered the performance style that would eventually become her signature, a style based on parody, dialect, and physical humor.[49] "Sadie Salome" involved all three, but Brice was oblivious to any deliberate method at the time. She adopted dialect simply because Berlin suggested it and, in her memoirs, conveyed the impression that the physical humor was a happy accident. She wriggled and grimaced because her sailor suit was uncomfortably starched and her squirming just happened to amuse the audience, who thought it was intentional. In her 1936 *Cosmopolitan* interview, she remembered it somewhat differently. Ignoring the costume, she attributed her behavior to instinct.

Either way, the point is that the eighteen-year-old Brice did not plan her routine in advance. She did not consciously choose the actions she performed on stage, and it would be several years before she would develop the artistry and control necessary to do so. Yet, however haphazard her approach, the combination of the accent, costume, facial expressions, and "oblique, grotesque gestures" (her words) must have been very comical. All would have made the subject matter seem doubly ludicrous and would have enhanced the song's power as a parody of the Salome craze.

There may have been another kind of parody involved as well. In mocking Sadie, Brice could easily have been mocking herself, for each is a Jewish girl who wants to be an "actress lady" on the stage. While it would be a mistake to overemphasize Brice's identification with the subject of her song, she readily played the clown and the outrageous antics that helped to put the number across could have also said, "See how ridiculous I am." The buffoonery may have originally been accidental, but must have become part of the act very quickly and enabled the song to operate as a parody on three levels. Specifically, Brice's interpretation of "Sadie Salome" worked as a spoof of Salome dancing in general, of silly stagestruck girls like Sadie, and of her own dramatic aspirations.

"Sadie Salome" was a burlesque, as Brice's best performances would all be; the Yiddish accent she used so skillfully was a comic device. Like the blackface that so many other comedians wore and that Brice herself apparently adopted only once, it functioned as a kind of mask or persona, and allowed her to explore and debunk a variety of subjects. The fact that she was poking fun at herself, or appeared to be, would have made her seem both amusing and unthreatening. How could an audience take offense at the parody when the parodist was mocking herself so good-naturedly, too?

In "Sadie Salome," Fanny Brice had found the combination that would eventually serve her well and that critics would call "typically Bricean." In 1909, however, in her first solo performance as a professional, she lacked, the perception and the experience to understand why the number was so effective. It was not simply the dialect, nor was it the gesticulating, but she would not realize that for a long time and would not duplicate the success of "Sadie Salome" until 1916.

The Ziegfeld Connection:
The *Follies of 1910* and *1911*

My comedy to be successful must be spontaneous. Whenever it isn't, the feel of the audience tells me so and I throw out that particular piece of business and work out something to use in its stead.

—Fanny Brice[1]

When you made the *Follies*, you were king of the hill, all right.

—Eddie Cantor[2]

3.

"Sadie Salome, Go Home!" marked a turning point in Brice's career and she often acknowledged the impact the song had on her life. As she explained in 1925:

> I put my soul into Sadie Salome and she rewarded me three-fold. The first reward was a seven-year contract [with Spiegel] calling for eighty-five dollars a week for the first year, and providing for a ten-dollar weekly raise in every succeeding year. The second reward was the centering of Mr. Flo Ziegfeld's attention upon me and this resulted in a contract to appear in the *Follies of 1910*. . . . But the greatest reward of all was the habit of analyzing songs and the field of comedy that was forced on me by Sadie Salome's success.[3]

Although always reticent about technique, Brice believed that she learned a great deal from her experience in *The College Girls*. She said she improved substantially as a performer on the tour, "evolving into an artist" with "a rapidly growing instinct for feeling the audience." As she watched her fellow cast members, she remembered being surprised that the ones she considered most talented often went unheralded and unrecognized. She was especially impressed by Willie Weston, a pianist and dialect comedian, whose perfect timing and "impromptu business" made his routines incredibly funny. Unfortunately, Weston suffered from incurable stage fright, and audiences "paralyzed" him. The eighteen-year-old Brice, however, considered him a brillant comedian and observed him carefully. She adopted many of his "comedy methods," she recalled, of which the most valuable was his reliance on spontaneity. It soon became a "rule" for her, Brice asserted, "never to work out any routine business, but to depend instead on spontaneous gestures" as Weston did.[4]

Weston was a curious choice for a role model. In 1912, when he and Brice were touring in a Shubert production, *The Whirl of Society*, he was the subject of irate correspondence between producer J. J. Shubert and road manager Stanley Sharpe. One letter likened him to "absolutely excess baggage." Another called him the worst actor on the stage. A third ordered his release from the company and relegated him, apparently, to obscurity.[5] In 1925, six years after his death, when presumably few remembered his name, Brice recognized Weston's influence on her as a young performer and insisted that he had taught her how to be spontaneous on stage. As she explained then, using the elevated tone she often adopted in interviews:

> Every successful artist, no matter what his medium, has his own individual methods of getting his result, and anyone who attempts to borrow another's method becomes a mere impersonator. Some comedians work out every detail of their business in putting over a song or an act, and I think it is a most admirable method because it relieves one of the tyranny of moods. But I can't do it.[6]

To excel, she maintained, she could not feel locked into a set routine. She had to be free to improvise and to alter her performance on impulse. Although she would eventually develop a technique that would serve her well, her early years were more erratic because her method was so haphazard. She depended on her instinct and the reaction of her audiences. When handicapped by poor material, as increasingly she would be, she came to realize that spontaneity alone was insufficient to achieve the success she so desperately sought.

With "Sadie Salome," however, Weston's lessons combined effectively with Irving Berlin's instructions. Having accidentally discovered antics the audience found funny, Brice kept them as long as they continued to please —and they pleased audiences all along the show's route. While none of the reviews described her routines in detail, they indicated at least that the critics liked her. *Variety*'s Chicago correspondent wrote that her specialty "scored a solid hit."[7] In Washington, D.C., she received eight encores and New York audiences responded with frenzied delight to her "excellent character songs, a 'Yiddisher Salome' and a coon song."[8] There were more encores in Providence, Rhode Island, and Springfield, Massachusetts, where the February 15, 1910, *Daily News* called her "novel and meritorious Yiddish singing act" one of the "best applause getters of the entire bill."[9]

The same edition of the *Springfield Daily News* also reported an interesting personal item. It noted that Brice had married an Albany barber named Frank White the previous morning, on Valentine's Day. She had secured a license from the City Clerk and, according to the newspaper, seemed anxious to keep the matter secret. "It was quite easy to identify her, however," continued the account, "when she made her appearance at the Gilmore [Theatre] yesterday afternoon as she has a soubrette part and does a clever specialty." Not quite eighteen and a half, she was far less clever about love. Her motives for choosing White remained mysterious and the glib explanations she often gave were not very informative. She said that she married him because "he smelled so nice" or "to kill time." "When he proposed to me in Springfield," she told reporters, "I accepted because I had nothing else to do." Yet just "five minutes" after she became his wife, she explained, she realized she had made a serious mistake.[10]

Years later, recalling this brief entanglement in her memoirs, she wrote, "I can't get it through my head. I can't understand it. It was like a dream. I knew so little. I was never even out looking for guys. I wasn't looking for romance or anything."[11] Typically vague about specifics, Brice did not say where or when she had met him, nor did she attribute her impetuous action to strong emotional or physical needs. She simply said that she decided to end the relationship after three days and did not see Frank White again. She subsequently tried to have the marriage annulled, as it had never been consummated. When her appeal was rejected because she was over eighteen at the time of the wedding, her only alternative was to file for divorce. She did so in August 1912, her request was granted in February 1913, and she always insisted that she never even knew what happened to White. Her cavalier comments, however, strongly suggest that the short-lived Valentine's Day union was a publicity stunt designed both to bring her welcome media attention and to fill the theatre.

Whatever her motives in marrying Frank White, her work was unaffected by the escapade. She continued on tour with *The College Girls*, arriving at New York City's luxurious new Columbia Theatre on April 11, 1910, for a week's engagement. Showcase of the Eastern Wheel, the Columbia had opened in January on the corner of Broadway and 47th Street, a prime location. With its "Louis XVI interior decoration" in "old Roman Gold" and "French Gray," its upholstery and draperies in "Dubarry Rose," and its elaborate murals above the proscenium, the Columbia provided the better burlesque shows with an elegant setting and ample seating.[12] It was a good place to see and be seen, ideal for talent scouts looking for new faces and for promising performers eager to break out of burlesque. However respectable it may have become, burlesque was still burlesque. In its pay scale as well as its prestige, it was lower than the legitimate theatre and its performers were generally quite happy to move on to other more lucrative opportunities.

As early as March 5, 1910, the *Clipper* called Brice "one of the finds of the season" and predicted that she would soon be "snapped up" by some shrewd "Broadway manager." By April, she had been discovered by one of Broadway's brightest talents, Florenz Ziegfeld, Jr.[13] *Variety* announced in its April 30 edition that, Spiegel contract notwithstanding, she had been engaged for the fourth edition of Ziegfeld's *Follies*, scheduled to go into rehearsal the following week. The May 7 *Clipper* identified Brice as a "delineator of coon and Hebrew songs" and confirmed that she had signed a contract to appear in the *Follies of 1910* on the New York Roof.[14]

Then forty-three, the "fabulous Florenz" had already established his reputation as a charismatic and highly successful impresario.[15] Brice spoke many times about Ziegfeld's profound influence on her life and reminisced about how she came to appear in the *Follies*.[16] According to the story she frequently told, she hoped that someone would discover her in New York, take her out of *The College Girls*, and put her on Broadway. One night, she received a message backstage, probably a telegram containing a reference to Ziegfeld, who was notorious for barraging people with missives. Brice, however, pretended she had been summoned by the famous producer himself and proudly announced to everyone in the theatre that he wanted to meet her.[17]

Soon after her charade, Brice recalled, she really did get a telegram from Ziegfeld requesting that she see him at her earliest convenience. Convinced that someone in the company was trying to trick her, she ignored it until, according to one account, she met an agent named Bert Cooper on the street. Cooper supposedly had discussed Brice with Ziegfeld, who regretted that she had signed an eight-year contract with Max Spiegel. Cooper, however, knew Brice well and told Ziegfeld that the Spiegel agreement was invalid because she had been only seventeen, a minor, when she signed it. Upon learning that she had not taken the telegram seriously, Cooper urged her to speak with Ziegfeld at once. "He's crazy about you," he allegedly shouted, "I put that over. Don't forget about my commission."[18]

Although Cooper never reappeared in Brice's reminiscences, she took his advice and immediately raced down Broadway to Ziegfeld's office. In one story, it was a "warm autumn day" and she was nineteen. In 1936, she remembered that it was a July morning and that she was a "raw seventeen-year-old girl."[19] Actually, it was April, Brice was eighteen and a half, and her mother Rose accompanied her. In her *Cosmopolitan* article, she recalled that Ziegfeld seemed "mild-mannered and gentle beyond words to tell" and continued:

> He had a twangy, whiny voice—even I have never been able to imitate it. He spoke for a few minutes, telling me he thought there would be a place for me in the *Follies* and he asked me what salary I thought I ought to have.
> "Forty dollars a week," spoke up my mother who was with me.
> "Forty dollars?" replied Ziegfeld. "Forty dollars!" this as an exclamation. Then smilingly: "Let us make it seventy-five and we'll sign for a year."[20]

Brice often acknowledged this meeting with Ziegfeld as a crucial moment in her career. In a 1938 interview, she said it was "the thing I had in mind ever since I was six years old when I started giving imitations of people" and stated that "if the time had come to climb, I was willing to break my neck getting up there."[21] An article written in 1929 called it "the greatest turning point in her life" because "it not only lifted her out of burlesque for good, it took her into a completely different atmosphere." After "the long rough climb up the rocky road," it was now "ease and luxury and beautiful things and soft-speaking voices."[22] The same interviewer quoted Brice as saying:

> I owe everything to him. To me, he's a god. I'd rather work for him than for any other person in the world. If he's the only one in a room, I can sing for him as though I had an audience of ten thousand. He's worth ten thousand mentally—the greatest showman that ever lived![23]

At the time she made these fulsome statements in 1929, Brice had not worked for Ziegfeld for five years and was trying hard to further her flagging film career. Her devotion, therefore, seems somewhat suspect. Nevertheless, she must have been elated at the prospect of appearing in the *Follies of 1910*, just as Ziegfeld undoubtedly sensed that she had tremendous promise.

In an article called "Stars in the Making," published in *Theatre Magazine* in 1926, Ziegfeld discussed his discovery of new talent and declared that he could always detect a "potential star." "Stardust is immediately apparent to the seeking eye," he explained, adding that of the thousands of performers he saw, "there have been ten who were stardust."[24] Of that illustrious ten, he mentioned only Louise Brown, Eddie Cantor, Ray Dooley, and Marilyn Miller. If Brice were one of the other six, he did not say. Presumably, however, in 1910, she had "stardust," or what Ziegfeld defined as "an extraordinary power to draw humanity in streams to the playhouse." He produced a contract providing her with a weekly salary of seventy-five dollars for that year, with one hundred dollars per week promised for the following season. When he presented her with a copy of it, the ecstatic Brice sped off to announce her good fortune publicly.

Standing on the corner of Broadway and, depending on the account, either 42nd or 47th Street, she "displayed it to the world." As she recalled in *Cosmopolitan*, she showed it "to the cops on the beat, the professionals who passed, strangers." She "pulled it out" five times for Irving Berlin —a recurring image in her recollections—and "before long it was in ribbons."[25] Remembering this happy interlude in her memoirs, she said she wore out eight *Follies* contracts in all.[26] She also claimed she never returned to *The College Girls*, but probably performed in the show through its May 2–14 Brooklyn engagement. She was listed in the program for the second week, beginning on Monday, May 9, although this does not necessarily mean that she actually appeared on stage. She could not have been in Spiegel's company any longer than this, however, as she would have been involved in rehearsals for the *Follies*.

Once those rehearsals started, Brice was soon disappointed by how little she actually had to do. As the special numbers she envisioned did not materialize, she realized that she was indeed "an unimportant member of the 1910 *Follies* cast."[27] According to her account in *Cosmopolitan*, she decided to take action. She approached Will Marion Cook, the composer and lyricist for much of the score. "Coon songs were the influence of the hour," she recalled in 1936, and I asked Cook if he had anything on this order."[28] Cook told her that he had just written the chorus of a coon song called "Lovie Joe" and said that if she thought she could handle the material he would finish it overnight. He gave it to her in the morning as he had promised and she immediately began to rehearse it "in a corner of the stage," accompanied by a young pianist named George Gershwin, "who pounded hour after hour the music the choruses practiced by."[29]

"Lovie Joe" became Brice's hit song in the *Follies of 1910*, but was almost responsible for her being fired from the show before it reached New York. As she related the incident in 1936, she clashed with Abraham Lincoln Erlanger, a backer of the *Follies*, a partner in the producing firm of Klaw and Erlanger, and one of the most powerful men in the theatrical world at that time. He was head of "the Syndicate," an organization formed in 1896 by a group of businessmen as a means of booking shows more efficiently. Instead of allowing representatives of the many small theatre circuits to make their own often tentative arrangements with producers, the Syndicate created one national circuit and offered guaranteed bookings for both theatre owners and producers. By 1900, under Erlanger's aegis, it had established a powerful and rapacious monopoly; at its height, it controlled over seven hundred theatres in North America.[30] Sagacious critic Brooks Atkinson called the Syndicate in the early years of the century "the unseen monster that hovered over Broadway and preyed on theatre people" and portrayed Erlanger as a "fat, squat, greedy, crude egotist who had no interest in the theatre as an art or as a social institution."[31]

In Atkinson's words, Erlanger was a "dangerous enemy" and in June 1910, he was about to become Brice's. As she recreated their confrontation in 1936, he was sitting in the audience, "far back in the house like Jove in the heavens," the morning of the day before the dress rehearsal.[32] The show was in New Jersey in deference to the superstitious Ziegfeld's insistence on an Atlantic City opening and Erlanger had come from New York to inspect his investment. Brice's specialty was called and she sang the first verse with the chorus:

> Lovie Joe, that ever-lovin' man
> From 'way down home in Birmingham,
> He can do some lovin' an' some lovin' sho',
> An' when he starts to love me I jes' hollers "Mo'!"[33]

At that moment, Erlanger imperiously interrupted the rehearsal and objected to Brice's using black dialect in a *Follies* performance:

> "Stop! Stop! Just a minute! Will you please sing that chorus over and pronounce those words 'sure' and 'more'?"
> I knew instantly who was speaking, so I said to the darkness before me: "But this is a coon song."

"I know it's a coon song, but where do you think you are, in a burlesque show? The people who come to my theatre pay two-fifty a seat, and they want to know what you are singing about."[34]

Brice remembered walking down to the footlights where she could see Erlanger to justify her interpretation of the song. "I live on 128th Street. It's on the edge of Harlem," she shouted. "They all talk that way. No Negro would pronounce those words the way you did. I can't sing them any other way." To disagree with the autocratic Erlanger, however, meant automatic dismissal and it came "with the quickness of a pancake turner." She recalled his angry response, "Put something in place of that specialty! You're out! No one says 'No' to me on my stage when I say 'Yes.'"

With her ear for dialect, Brice knew she had to say "sho'" and "mo'" in order to be in character for the song and she was furious at Erlanger's outrageous action. "Fighting mad," she went back to her "cheap hotel room" where she later received a message to report to Ziegfeld. He told her that Erlanger had agreed to let her perform in the *Follies* in Atlantic City, but remained adamantly opposed to her appearing with the production in New York. She accepted his terms because she realized that she was powerless to do anything else. "Those first steps in the theatre," she reflected in 1936, "are like clutching at a bare wall, and until you obtain a hold, you can demand nothing."[35] Still determined to succeed, Brice made the most of the Atlantic City opening. She described her performance in considerable detail for *Cosmopolitan*:

> I appeared on the program at nine-thirty, the crux of the evening, when the audience was swimming in boredom because of the show's lack of rhythm and gait.
>
> I was sheathed in a white satin gown that fitted like a silk stocking—that was the fashion then. When the signal came for my appearance, it wasn't a stage I was on—it was a magic carpet! After about eight encores of "Lovie Joe" the audience was still so enchanted with me that I decided they should have all I had.
>
> I was painfully thin and my dress fitted like a vise. The last roar that met my ears came when I pulled my skirt up over my knees and then, peering down on legs that looked like two slats, put my hand over my eyes in one despairing gesture and stalked off.
>
> As I left the stage, Erlanger was standing in the wings. He had his straw hat in his hands, the rim broken. He was beaming as he held it out to me.
>
> "See, I broke this applauding you."
>
> When the tumult and the shouting died, nothing further was said about my not going to New York.[36]

Given Brice's tendency to rewrite her life, it is possible that the "Lovie Joe" story did not happen as she remembered it and that the dramatic argument with Erlanger never actually occurred. However apocryphal the account may in fact be, it succeeded admirably in conveying her indomitable spirit as a young performer. Having realized that she would be lost in Ziegfeld's lavish production without a good song, she was resourceful enough to find one she knew she could sing well. In defying Erlanger, she was not simply being cantankerous. She was defending the interpretation she believed was artistically valid. As a coon song, "Lovie Joe" demanded appropriate dialect. Although "blacking up" was optional for coon shouters, and there is no evidence that Brice ever performed "Lovie Joe" in blackface, adopting the accent was imperative. Her characterization depended on it, just as the Yiddish accent had been crucial to "Sadie Salome." For someone who was beginning to be identified as a "character comedienne," creating those characters as fully as possible was essential.[37]

In hiring Brice, Ziegfeld was not adding another beautiful showgirl to his stable. He had lured her away from Max Spiegel because she was funny and there was always a place for a good comedian in the *Follies*. It was often said of Ziegfeld that he did not have a quick sense of humor and, consequently, did not really appreciate the clowns in his show. Supposedly he never laughed at their routines and was always willing to sacrifice a comic sketch for an elaborate production number. His glorified girls were always supreme; as dramatic critic George Jean Nathan observed, "He can dramatize girls the way no other producer can. . . . He can create the illusion of feminine beauty even where beauty isn't."[38]

Yet Ziegfeld himself recognized the need for buffoonery as well as beauty. In an article in the April 16, 1911, *San Francisco Examiner*, he declared that the public wanted "girls and laughter." He expressed his belief that there was a place in the theatre for a "good little story play with or without music," but insisted that "the great big show" was "the thing." In order to hold the audience's interest, a production had to move quickly. "Let the acts and the stunts and the features follow one another as swiftly as the cars of a train," he advised. "We're living in a rapid transit age and your show has got to be a rapid transit show to make good." Even more important than speed, however, was humor. As he put it, "Above all, it's got to amuse. It simply has to make you laugh. If it doesn't make you laugh—good night."[39]

Like Eddie Cantor, Ray Dooley, Leon Errol, W. C. Fields, and Will Rogers, who helped bring levity to subsequent editions of Ziegfeld's musical extravaganza, Brice soon demonstrated her ability to make audiences laugh throughout the run of the *Follies of 1910*. She was praised as an "eccentric young singing comedienne" whose "exuberant extravagances of song and mirth" made her one of the hits of the show.[40] Much of her comedy depended on physical humor and audiences found her funny as soon as she appeared on stage. Before she even opened her mouth, she convulsed them because she looked so comical. She was a sight gag and she knew it.

The description she gave of herself in 1936 as being "painfully thin" with slatlike legs was typical of the self-deprecating comments she frequently made about her appearance. In 1938, she spoke of her first Ziegfeld contract and said that "Ziggy must have been wearing blinders. I look like all my relations from way back," she continued, "and every time a photographer took their picture he was taking a big chance of changing his gallery into a chamber of horrors."[41] Similarly, in 1946, she declared that "if they had put me in front of a camera thirty-five years ago when I was starting out, I had such a kisser the camera would have stood up and walked away in disgust."[42]

Such statements seem particularly ironic because Brice was far from unattractive. Tall and thin with long, slender legs, beautiful hands, and an expressive face, she would be considered "interesting" at the very least today. In 1929, *Moving Picture Stories* admired her appearance. Admitting that she was not "pretty" in a conventional sense, the magazine asserted that she had "so much more than prettiness":

> That . . . slim lankiness of hers was a delight to watch, so supple and swift it was, so subtly transformed on the instant, from grotesque laughter-raising mimicry to lines of brooding beauty. Her hair was a wavy mass, light brown and abundant; her narrow face, rather pale, showing up in contrast the deep-set green eyes.[43]

Notwithstanding the fact that the article was part of a publicity campaign for Brice's first film, the above description suggests that she was anything but unappealing.

In 1910, however, Brice did not conform to the prevailing notion of female beauty and, more specifically, to the Ziegfeldian definition of it. She stated flatly in 1938 that "Ziegfeld thought I was funny, but positively not good-looking."[44] It is easy to understand why in view of the opinion he expressed in the *San Francisco Examiner* when he declared: "This is the era of the cute little girl on the stage and in the street and in the ballroom and down the middle aisle when the organ is playing the wedding march."[45] Brice was neither "cute" nor "little," and in publicity photographs she did not look like the other "girls." She did not have the requisite rosebud mouth, pert upturned nose, and halo of curls. She could not compete with fellow *Follies* performers such as Lillian Lorraine, modestly billed as the "prettiest Girl on the Stage," and Ziegfeld's chorus line of "long-stemmed American beauties" must have made her appear (and feel) less attractive than she actually was. Whereas in burlesque she looked fine because there were so many sizes and shapes around her, Ziegfeld's elevated and homogenized standard of beauty exaggerated her difference from the norm. Yet, paradoxically, in so doing, Ziegfeld provided the setting that would show her off to best advantage. If she could not be the prettiest girl, she could be the funniest, as she soon realized. She was literally built for comedy.

After a successful week in Atlantic City where it played nightly to capacity houses, the *Follies* moved on to New York City and, as Brice put it in 1936, "that swift-moving, glittering, dizzy world known as Broadway."[46] The fourth *Follies* to premiere at the Jardin de Paris, the show opened on Monday night, June 10, 1910. Since 1882, roof gardens had been popular spots for summer entertainment in New York. In the days before air conditioning, they offered welcome relief from oppressive city heat, and there were several operating along Broadway in 1910. Nevertheless, on opening night, the enclosed Jardin de Paris was stifling. *Variety* reported that "on top of the New York Theatre, with its packed humanity, it was red hot" and "no one felt much like applauding."[47]

Whether or not the heat was responsible, the *Follies of 1910* received decidedly mixed reviews. The show was overlong by thirty to forty minutes, and overdone. "Everything," Sime wrote, "seemed a little too much," including the novel staging which made half the numbers take place in the orchestra. He admired Lorraine's swing scene but considered this "one-time novelty" too time-consuming, requiring ten minutes to set the stage and ten to strike it. The delay destroyed the act's momentum and irreparably damaged the pace of the production. "After that," he asserted, the *Follies* "just about flopped."[48]

The featured performers in particular were handicapped by the length of the show. Sime noted that several seemed to "strike the house wrongly at a late hour." Among these was Bert Williams, usually an audience favorite, whose songs were not well received. Another was Brice, about whom Sime wrote:

> Also around eleven o'clock, Fanny Brice, who had previously made a big hit with her own style of singing a "coon" song, tempted the fates again with

a "Yiddish" number that couldn't get over. Miss Brice entered the *Follies* from burlesque. She left a good impression and will safely be continued a member of the organization if merit counts.[49]

The "Yiddish number" was most likely Irving Berlin's "Goodbye Becky Cohen" which, further on in the same review, Sime included in a group of songs that failed at the first performance.[50] About the coon song he mentioned, however, there is no doubt. It was "Lovie Joe."

Other reviews commented favorably on Brice's opening night performance. In a backhanded compliment the *Times* noted that "Fannie Brice, not especially prepossessing elsewhere, scored a hit with 'Lovie Joe,' for which her eccentric facial expression and queer vocal interpolations were largely responsible." The *Dramatic Mirror* considered her one of the few principals able to salvage the show and lift it above the "plane of boredom." Observing that she "scored one of the biggest hits of the performance" with "Lovie Joe," the review continued: "Her facial expression is amusing and her method of handling the song stamps her as an artist of decided individuality." The *Clipper*'s critic devoted a relatively large portion of his review to Brice. She "scored a pronounced hit" with "Lovie Joe," he wrote; he had been particularly struck by her "odd expression" and "queer semi-intelligible style of delivery of the patter text of the song."[51]

Brice's unusual and distinctive interpretation of "Lovie Joe" impressed the critics, but it is difficult to determine exactly what she did. No detailed record of her performance exists and the lyrics of the song are not particularly helpful because they are similar to so many others. The singer is "mad about" her "lovin' man." He is "so neat" and "sweet as the berry that grows on the vine." Joe, her "beau," has got her "goin' so" that she is "mos' crazy." His love drives her "wil'." He can kiss and squeeze, he knows how to please. The obvious course, which she takes, is to bring a wedding band to the "preacher man" who will then join her "han' in han'" to Lovie Joe.[52]

In singing this song, Brice could have been bold and brassy in blackface as so many other coon shouters were or, eschewing blackface as she did, still could have been loud and boisterous. Judging from the reviews cited, however, she chose another approach. The papers mentioned her "amusing" and "eccentric" facial expressions, her "queer" and "odd" vocal interpolations. In addition, there is her own description of the Atlantic City performance. Wearing a tight satin sheath, she drew the skirt up, probably struck a knock-kneed pose, and glanced in mock horror at her thin legs. With one hand shielding her eyes from the offending limbs, she marched offstage.

All of these observations suggest that Brice must have injected as much humor as possible into her interpretation. She kept it "catchy," according to the *Daily Tribune*, but she assumed a comic character for it as she had for "Sadie Salome." Some of the lines such as "I'm sad, I'm glad, I'm mad" would have easily lent themselves to a variety of facial expressions and Brice undoubtedly used herself as a comic target. Beyond the "eccentricities" suggested by the lyrics, her singing must have conveyed a sense of disbelief that "a master of them ever-lovin' arts" like Joe could be in love with someone so funny-looking. Yet the implication is clearly that, even though she has skinny legs, she has other attributes that might interest a man like him. Through the wiggling in a tight gown as well as through the verses she sang, she could have projected a kind of sexuality that would not have been threatening because it was so comical. As in "Sadie Salome," the self-mockery made the singer safe—she, after all, not he, goes off in pursuit of wedding band and preacher—and would have produced a most entertaining number.

Another clue to Brice's interpretation of "Lovie Joe" is a cryptic comment she made in her *Cosmopolitan* interview. According to her reminiscences, Ziegfeld was so pleased with her work that he added to her specialty and gave her "a new Irving Berlin song" called "The Grizzly Bear." Apparently confusing her memories of the *Follies of 1910* with *The College Girls*, Brice nevertheless provided an interesting glimpse of her performance style by stating that she embellished the song with "grotesque Yiddish steps."[53] Although it is difficult to know exactly what she meant by this phrase, she was probably referring to the stock comic gait and physical "business" typically used by Jewish comedians in burlesque and vaudeville. If this is the case, then Brice was bringing the gestures and mannerisms of "Hebrew impersonation" to the coon song, superimposing the conventions of one genre upon the performance of another. Instead of wearing blackface and singing raucously, as coon-shouters commonly did, she relied on the eccentric movements and facial expressions associated with Yiddish dialect comedy. She had used these successfully in "Sadie Salome," combining them, of course, with the Yiddish accent. For her coon songs, naturally, she imitated black speech patterns, but she retained the same "Jewish" physical behavior. The resulting incongruity would have made her innovative interpretation instantly amusing for an audience expecting the customary coon song delivery. Unfortunately, Brice did not elaborate on her method, so the tantalizing suggestion that she was combining the tech-

nique of "Jew comics" with the material of coon-shouters cannot b
stantiated. It may not even have been something of which she was
in 1910, but a retrospective consideration of her work makes that brilliant
melding seem to be precisely what she was doing in "Lovie Joe." It certainly would have marked her, as the *Dramatic Mirror* put it, as a performer
of "decided individuality."[54]

In January 1911, *Variety* ran its first photograph of Brice with the heading, "This is the girl that became an overnight sensation in Ziegfeld's
revue *Follies of 1910* singing 'Lovie Joe.'"[55] In the picture, she wears a
long satin gown with wide vertical stripes accentuating her lanky figure.
Her chin tucked down, she gazes demurely out at the camera but her
body position suggests great comic potential. She stands slightly pigeon-
toed, torso bending to one side, arms held away from the body as if to
keep her from falling. A ruffled collar frames her face, a wide belt with
an enormous rhinestone buckle cinches her waist and a satin band encircles
her knees, pushing them together. Such a costume would have forced
Brice to move awkwardly about the stage in a manner consistent with
the comic character she was creating.

The caption beneath the *Variety* photograph called her "one of the
most promising character comediennes we have."[56] Another photograph
of Brice in the same costume makes that character more clear. Whereas
Variety's shot showed her in a state of suspended animation with the humorous possibilities suggested but not explicit, this one catches her in a moment of obvious mimicry. It is as if the two pictures were part of a film
and this one is several frames beyond *Variety*'s in the sequence. Here Brice
stares directly at the camera. Her wide-open eyes are slightly crossed and
her lips are pursed in a leer, if that is possible, forming an expression
that would certainly qualify as eccentric. She leans forward as if she would
like to run, but is inhibited by her absurdly tight dress. Her left leg extends
in front of her, her right leg reaches back, both with the toes turned
sharply in. Her left arm hangs straight down with the index finger pointing
to her knees. Her right arm is bent at the elbow and the index finger
seems to be pointing at the camera. Her shoulders slope to the left, her
hips face the right, creating the impression that the top part of her body
is moving in a different direction from the bottom half. Even the costume
in this photograph—the dark ruffled collar, the oversized belt, the bold
stripes—looks clownlike.

A caricature of Brice in the *Follies of 1910* is still more successful
in capturing her distinctive performance style, a seemingly paradoxical
combination of graceful angularity and dynamic awkwardness. Drawn in

a double "S" curve with head jutting forward and back arched, she strides determinedly on tiny feet. Taut arms stretch back from the shoulders as if to propel her and, bent at both wrists and elbows, mirror the curve of her body. Simple slashes represent her strong features and indicate that, with eyes slanting down and mouth turning up, she grins as she advances towards her appreciative audience.[57]

Given Brice's comical appearance in these images, it is not difficult to understand why critics considered her rendition of "Lovie Joe" so entertaining. Calling it "one of the few real treats of the year," *Variety* said that she "easily placed that song in a class by itself as a coon number."[58] She also placed herself in a special class as a performer. One New York newspaper declared that she could present a song better than "most anyone else" and asserted that she was the "real star" of the *Follies of 1910*. Another reported that the seven or eight encores she received nightly were a tribute to her talent since she performed against a simple velvet curtain without benefit of elaborate scenic effects. She had been given a chance, the paper observed, and had "made good" by combining "a certain genius for pantomime work" with "distinct enunciation" that carried "to every corner of the roof.[59]

Brice continued to receive very favorable reviews when the revamped *Follies* ended its New York run on September 3. The show had been restructured during the summer so that it was now in three acts and sixteen scenes. According to extant programs, Brice only appeared in Acts I and II.[60] At the beginning of the first act, in a scene that was supposed to be a *Follies* dress rehearsal, she played "Miss Pansy Perkins" and sang "Goodbye Becky Cohen." This was the number *Variety* said did not work on opening night when it was presented late in the evening. Ziegfeld must have decided that the solution was to sing it earlier, hence its new position at the beginning of the show. The only clue to Brice's performance is the *Washington Post's* statement that she "bids a gleeful farewell to a Yiddish lady." Nevertheless, both comment and title strongly suggest that Brice interpreted this song as she had "Sadie Salome," with a heavy Yiddish accent and exaggerated mannerisms.[61]

Later in the first act, Brice appeared in a sketch called "Office of a Musical Publisher." She played one of the "Dotty Sisters," spoofing the Dolly Sisters, then the most popular sister act in vaudeville. In addition to the laughs she occasioned at the expense of that singing and dancing pair, she pleased audiences with her rendition of "Lovie Joe." Act II, evidently, offered more of the same. Brice performed two songs, "Riskey Issey" and "Wild Cherry Rag." The first certainly sounds like another

Yiddish dialect number; the second, a coon song. The absence of sheet music for either of them, however, precludes definitive analysis.

Years later, Brice asserted that audiences so enjoyed her in the *Follies of 1910* that they always kept her onstage for repeated encores. When the ever pragmatic Rose saw her daughter's great success, Brice remembered, "she decided the time was ripe to ask for a salary raise." Both women met with a beaming Ziegfeld, whose swift response was, "All right—bring down the old contract; I'll make out a new one for a hundred dollars a week." As Brice recalled in 1936, "This was the last contract made between Ziegfeld and me, though I was with him over a period of sixteen years and my last salary was three thousand a week."[62] However amicable they sound, these unspoken agreements would result in a spectacular misunderstanding following the *Follies of 1911*.

In 1910, one hundred dollars a week was an investment Ziegfeld could well afford. On its nine month tour, the *Follies* took in average weekly receipts of about fifteen thousand dollars and Brice impressed critics from Chicago to Omaha with her songs. When the *Follies* arrived in Washington, D.C., at the end of December, the *Washington Star*'s drama critic trumpeted, "Fanny Brice looks like a discovery, a comic star of the first magnitude. She does not create laughter, she is laughter itself, with every grotesque trick of speech or gesture in the clown's repertoire at natural command."[63]

The Washington newspapers also supplied some interesting biographical information about Brice, identifying her as a former newsgirl. Similar statements appeared in other cities as part of the publicity for the show, indicating that Ziegfeld, always ready to boost the box office any way he could, was making the most of his new leading comedienne. In the same spirit as he had staged milk baths for Anna Held and invented a lollipop diet for Nora Bayes, he told the press that he had discovered Brice singing as she sold her papers on a corner underneath the Brooklyn Bridge.

Newspapers across the country picked up the story and began producing articles such as the following piece of creative journalism:

> From Brooklyn, New York, newsgirl to a stellar position with one of the largest musical shows in America is an unusual advancement. Nevertheless, this distinction has been attained by Miss Fanny Brice, who, up to three years ago, sold papers at the corner of Bergen Street and Vanderbilt Avenue, Brooklyn.
>
> F. Ziegfeld, Jr.'s attention was attracted to the girl's singing ability and he engaged her for a part in the *Follies of 1910*. . . . Despite the fact that in the organization there were a number of stars, the former newsgirl on the opening night captivated the entire audience and scored the real individual success of the evening.[64]

The article went on to describe Brice's "unique" theatrical experience which it said began when a customer suggested she enter an amateur night contest at Keeney's. "She rendered a Yiddish song and made the hit of the entertainment, and the management awarded her the prize—fifty cents." Encouraged by this success, she joined "*A Real Slave* company a few weeks later." When this troupe "did not do a self-sustaining business" and "disbanded abruptly," Brice "later" became a member of the *Follies*.[65] Nothing was said about the *Transatlantic Burlesquers*, *The Girls from Happyland*, or *The College Girls* and the omission suggests that Ziegfeld did not want to sully her stardom with the stigma of burlesque. He created an American success story for her—from rags to riches, from obscurity to overnight acclaim—as much a tribute to his discerning judgment as to her obvious talent.

Brice may have felt that in joining the *Follies* she was leaving burlesque behind her. In fact, just the opposite was true. She brought burlesque, or what was emerging as her own style of burlesquing, with her and that is what the critics loved. According to Julian Johnson of the *Los Angeles Times*, commenting on the absence of Lillian Lorraine who had left the show, the *Follies* was fine without its advertised star. He preferred watching "a superlative young comedienne like Fannie Brice—barely nineteen years of age and one of the most ridiculous mimics who ever pranced before the footlights." As he so perceptively observed, "There are plenty more Lillian Lorraines in New York; there are indeed some with this company, but there are mighty few Fannie Brices anywhere."[66] His sentiments were remarkably prophetic.

After its Los Angeles engagement in early May the *Follies* traveled to Utah, Colorado, and Iowa, concluding its highly successful tour in Omaha, Nebraska, on June 3. It had played a season of almost fifty-one weeks and, according to the *Dramatic Mirror*, had made an "excellent impression" to the very end. The paper also noted that some of the principals had left their parts to understudies after the opening performance in order to return to New York and rehearsals for the *Follies of 1911*. Brice was one of them.

Recalling her experience in the *Follies of 1910*, Brice stated in *Cosmopolitan* that she "had always been a beaver for work" but it was not until this first Ziegfeld show that she started "to feel a purpose" in what she did. As she saw it in 1936:

> It began to take form; I found early in my career what some actors take years
> to discover—that it is the audience that does the directing. It gives you your

rhythm, your timing and your beat. You have to see what you do through the response of your public.[67]

Brice often returned to this theme and nostalgia may well have colored her reminiscences. In 1911, however, the response she would receive from her public was to be disappointing and ultimately caused her to break from Ziegfeld.

The *Follies of 1911* began auspiciously enough. *Variety* reviewed the show's June 20 opening in Atlantic City very favorably. From the headline, "Follies Look Big," to the concluding statement that "the show points to a big success," *Variety* was quite positive about the production. With lyrics by George V. Hobart, music by Maurice Levi and Raymond Hubbell, staging by Julian Mitchell, musical arrangements by Gus Sohlke and Jack Mason, "reinforced by a cast of unusual merit," *Variety* believed there was "small chance for the launching of anything but a brilliant show."[68]

Variety reviewed the *Follies* again in its July 1 edition and was more critical of it. According to Sime, it was fine for a road show but was too draggy and lifeless for New York with only "two big applause moments."[69] Although Sime was less severe with Brice, he was unhappy with her performance. Poor acoustics were partly to blame. The large size of the Roof made it difficult for all the singers to be heard and she was greatly affected. Beyond this, however, she was handicapped by weak material. As he observed:

> Fanny Brice seemed to be hit the hardest, or else she has given up coon-shouting. Both her songs needed that style of singing, particularly "Ephraim [*sic*]." Neither got over very well. "That Chilly Man," Miss Brice's first number, had little to recommend it. Fanny's best was a "Yiddisha" speaking part in *Pinafore*.[70]

Sime's comments indicate that, with two songs and one speaking part, Brice appeared three times in the production. The other reviews concur and, in the absence of an opening night program, help to clarify her role in the *Follies*. Near the end of Act I, just before Lorraine's aerial "Pony Ballet," she sang Berlin's "Doggone That Chilly Man." In the *Pinafore* spoof which opened the second act, she played Rachel Rosenstein, the Little Buttercup character, on the H.M.S. *Vaudeveel*. She sang "Ephraham Played upon the Piano," with lyrics and music by Berlin and Vincent Bryan, in the much ballyhooed third act cabaret, "New Year's Eve on the Barbary Coast."

Without a script or production book for the show, it is difficult to discuss Brice's performance with any certainty. Sime's reference to the "Yiddisha" speaking part as well as the character's obviously Jewish name make it clear that Brice played Rachel with a Yiddish accent. One critic, reviewing her work far more favorably than Sime, liked her very much in this sketch. Praising her as "one of the brightest lights in the *Follies of 1911*," he noted that she introduced a song, "I'm Called Rachel Rosenstein" (which Sime did not mention), and observed that "it was for the presentation of this song that she sought color and atmosphere" on the Lower East Side.[71] Brice must have burlesqued Rachel with the same broad comic style she had used for Sadie Salome.

Dealing with the other songs is less difficult because at least there is sheet music for both the titles Sime cited. The music itself, however, cannot provide information about Brice's interpretation, and Sime's criticism indicates that he did not find her performance effective. His statement that she seemed to have given up coon-shouting suggests that she presented both songs in a more subdued style than she had used for "Lovie Joe" the previous season. She may have deliberately chosen a modulated delivery as a way of showing that she had achieved greater sophistication and subtlety as a performer. Yet such conscious decision-making on her part would have been unlikely, given the nature of the songs. In both cases, they were supposed to be humorous and really were not. "Doggone That Chilly Man" was particularly unfunny, combining an undistinguished melody with leaden lyrics. In an attempt, perhaps, to duplicate the success of "Lovie Joe," Berlin has Brice sing about her man, but this one is different. He is a "bonehead, a stoneheaded man," a lover who does not know "that the lights a-burning low" mean that he should be lovable. "A dove with no heart," he wants "to part" when he should hug, "snug like a bug within a rug." He refuses to kiss her, reads the newspaper when she wants to talk about love, and makes faces at the moon when she is "all fussed up for an ever-lovin' spoon." He is as cold as "the pole that Cook discovered" and the singer despairs that she has fallen in love with such a "chilly man."[72]

As Sime tersely observed, the song had "little to recommend it." The music was not very good, the lyrics were terrible, and there was probably little Brice could have done with it. She could not have treated it as a ballad because the use of words like "bonehead" spoiled the mood and undercut whatever sympathy she might have aroused. Similarly, the deliberate attempt to get a laugh with a line such as "overboard I'd shove him, just because he made me love him" failed because the humor seemed so forced.

"Ephraham Played upon the Piano" was better. Although there was nothing special about the music and lyrics, at least it allowed Brice to use the exuberance and energy she had brought to "Sadie Salome" and "Lovie Joe." In it, she sang the praises of Ephraham, "a lovin' piano player" who lived "down below the Dixie line in Alabam'." The gist of the song is simply that Ephraham is a wonderful pianist. Even though he "never took a lesson," everyone who hears him marvels at his skill because he makes any "upright sound like a Baby Grand" and turns every piano into "an instrument of joy."[73] The number is upbeat, good-humored, and would have permitted Brice to present it with warmth and enthusiasm. What it lacked, however, was the comic potential of "Sadie Salome" or "Lovie Joe."

"Sadie Salome" involved parody on several levels. "Lovie Joe" did not, but allowed Brice to poke fun at herself as Joe's awkward but adoring woman. With "Ephraham," she did not have such comic latitude because she could not really involve herself in the action of the song. Whereas in "Sadie Salome" and "Lovie Joe" she was a participant, in "Ephraham" she was simply an animated observer. Whatever physical business she used must have come through her acting out different parts, such as a "certain lady" who asks, "Can you play a fiddle, mister?" and Ephraham who responds, "Sister, I don't know because I've never tried." Brice probably used different accents and many gestures, but could not have sustained any of them long enough to create distinct comic characters. If, therefore, she seemed subdued to Sime, it may have been because her songs did not suit her as well as she would have liked.

Although it is impossible to prove that Brice's material inhibited her performance, there is evidence that it greatly disappointed her. While the *Follies of 1911* was playing a month-long engagement in Chicago, an interview with Brice appeared in the *Tribune*. Written by Thyra Samter, the article had a title worthy of the most maudlin sentimental ballad, "Listen if You Would Hear the Sad Story of Fanny's Life," and contained some strong statements by Brice about her role in the Ziegfeld production. When Samter asked her if she liked her part, Brice responded with a vehement "No!" According to Samter:

> It sounded like an explosion the way Miss Brice said it. "I haven't a good song. 'Ephraham' is funny enough but the words are bad. I want a new song. I want a new song." It was almost a wail this time. . . .

> Miss Brice smiled the sad sweet smile one uses when talking of the dead, "I'm getting to be a fiend on song-hunting. I hunt and hunt and hunt. I've got a couple of songs now. I may spring them some day." Another sad, sweet smile. "But I want a really funny song."[74]

Brice's obvious displeasure and her efforts to find better songs show that she was, at least, trying to do something constructive to change her unhappy situation. Her inability to obtain more appropriate material suggests, however, that she may not have known exactly what she was looking for. She might have sensed what did not work for her, but apparently did not have the insight into herself as a performer to recognize what she could handle effectively. As she explained in the same interview, she did not have any particular method of working and still approached each number in a totally arbitrary fashion. Responding to Samter's query about the origin of some of her dances, she stated:

> "I don't get them. I haven't even a routine of work. Why, I never do the same thing twice. I just get out on the stage and act natural. I'm funny enough natural. When I plan ahead of time what I want to do it falls flat. When I get a laugh for something and try to do the same thing the next night not a soul even grins. I simply do the first thing that comes into my head and I usually get away with it.
> But I've got to feel like being funny or I'm a frost. I've got to get in a mood for it"—business of funny poses—"like this"—more poses—"in the wings before my cue. Then I just run on and keep on trying to be funny."[75]

Such statements imply that Brice used her "funny poses" and expressions, whether or not they were appropriate to the particular song, because that was the only way she knew of getting a laugh. Yet such antics would not have worked for material like "Ephraham" or "That Chilly Man"; because the singer's eccentricity would have exceeded the subject's, they would have seemed incongruous.

The *Tribune* interview is interesting for another important reason. It is the first example of Brice's penchant for discussing her life candidly but inaccurately. Described by Samter as "friendly, clever, magnetic, and self-satisfied," she spoke freely about her experiences but gave a selective "life history." She discussed the amateur night at Keeney's. She recalled her part in the *Royal Slave* company, which finally "went broke." She admitted joining a burlesque troupe and described her efforts to learn to dance. Unable to distinguish between left and right, she explained, she pinched her left leg until it was black and blue. Whenever the manager said "left foot," she put out the one that hurt and "got along fine" after that. Yet she mentioned absolutely no specifics about any of the burlesque shows in which she appeared. As Samter noted, "Offstage, Miss Brice accompanies her conversations with comical gestures and weird and angular poses, quite as funny as her unlovely and eccentric dances."[76] The observation suggests that, in granting an interview, Brice was giving another bravura performance. Her nonchalance about names and dates was part of the persona she was trying to create.

In spite of mediocre reviews and oppressive heat, the *Follies of 1911* had a successful summer run in New York City. *Variety* reported that it was "doing the biggest business in town" and was filling the New York Roof nearly to capacity every night.[77] Capacity business continued in Chicago, the first stop on the *Follies* tour, probably because the show had been substantially reworked during its ten weeks in New York. In two acts now, rather than three, the streamlined *Follies* presented its scenes in a tighter sequence and had cut several numbers entirely. These included the elaborate pony ballet with Lillian Lorraine, who had left the cast sometime in July, and "That Chilly Man." With the elimination of that song, Brice had only two parts of any consequence in the *Follies*: singing "Ephraham" in the Barbary Coast scene, now at the end of Act I; and playing Rachel Rosenstein, renamed Becky Butternut, at the beginning of Act II.

Although her role had been reduced, her performances were well received on the road. The *Chicago Tribune*'s Percy Hammond described her as "looking like a caricature of something female on an obelisk" and awarded her the "lyric honors" of the evening. In St. Louis, where the *Follies* played in early November, Ripley Saunders of the *Post-Dispatch* shared his colleague's enthusiasm. Calling the show "an up-to-date spectacular and musical revue," he named "the unfailingly diverting Fanny Brice" as one of its stars and said that she "made a memorable hit with her new songs." The drama critic for the *Cleveland Press* disagreed, dismissing her with one disparaging sentence: "Fannie Brice is lost in the show, singing an old song and a parody on 'Little Buttercup.'" Yet, when the *Follies* played in Detroit the following week, the *Detroit News* reported that her "Ephraham" stimulated so many calls for encores, the management almost had to stop the performance.[78]

The *Follies of 1911* toured until the end of March and, according to the newspapers, continued to draw capacity houses. After month-long engagements in Philadelphia and Boston, the show made brief stops in cities throughout the northeast: Providence, Portland, Springfield, Hartford, Washington, Baltimore, Syracuse, Rochester, Toronto, Buffalo, Ithaca, and

Elmira. Reports from the road indicated that the box office was doing well. The *Dramatic Mirror*'s Baltimore correspondent wrote that "receipts registering close to the $18,000 mark" had come in.[79]

The *Springfield Daily News* reported that the *Follies* gave three successful performances in which "Fannie Brice's Yiddish facial grimaces" were "grotesquely humorous."[80] The paper had included pictures of them the week before as part of the pre-show publicity campaign under the heading, "Some funny faces portrayed by one of the comediennes of Ziegfeld's *Follies* . . . Fanny Brice." There were six shots of Brice's face, which leered, sneered, twisted, and stretched with remarkable elasticity. Eyes turned up, sideways, down, and crossed. Lips seemed to push and pull in different directions. Even Brice's nose appeared to change its angle in the various poses. She did look comical in these photographs, and they illustrate how important such physical business was to her work. The fact that the grimaces were called "Yiddish," moreover, suggests that this sort of clowning was typical of the "Jew comics." The rubber-faced Brice for whom Protestant prettiness was clearly unattainable was performing very much in the dialect comedy tradition.[81]

Brice had demonstrated her "business of funny poses" during the *Chicago Tribune* interview and had expressed her frustration at being unable to find a good song. In spite of her efforts, a new hit never materialized and her solution was to return to an old one. In its favorable review of the *Follies* at Washington's National Theatre, the *Post* described the rowdy Barbary Coast scene and Brice's part in it. Noting that she made her first appearance with "Ephraham," the paper reported that she "score[d] the personal triumph of the evening with her old reliable 'Lovie Joe.'"[82] Singers constantly perform their big hits and there is nothing unique about Brice's reviving "Lovie Joe." Yet she seemed to have returned to it as a last resort and that was disturbing. Unable to find a new song comparable to it, desperate for new material, she went back to one she knew worked well. To have done so at this point in her career indicates that she may well have lost her identity and direction as a performer. In the *Tribune* interview she blithely stated, "I've been with the *Follies* two years. I haven't the least idea what I'll do next." There was far more truth to that seemingly offhand remark than she realized when she made it in September 1911. When the *Follies* closed on March 31, 1912, in Elmira and plans were underway for the fifth edition of the show, the twenty-one-year-old Brice had not been offered a Ziegfeld contract. There was to be a Brice in the cast, but it was Elizabeth—a demure singer—not Fanny.

According to Brice in 1936, she did not appear in the *Ziegfeld Follies of 1912* as a result of a misunderstanding. "It was Ziegfeld's habit," she recalled in *Cosmopolitan*, "to relay to those he wanted for his next year's cast this message: 'After you arrive in town, Ziegfeld wants to see you.'"[83] When she had not heard from him at the end of the 1911–12 season, she assumed that he did not want her in the new show and decided to see his rival, producer Lee Shubert. A friend suggested that she ask Shubert for five hundred dollars a week and she readily agreed, hoping to impress Ziegfeld with the amount. "Much as I loved money," she explained, "it meant more to me to have that sum in black and white on a contract so I could show Ziegfeld what other managers thought of me." Even after she had signed with the Shuberts, however, she stayed away from him "like a little hound pup licking its wounds."[84]

Ziegfeld finally sent for her and, as Brice described it, the meeting was traumatic for both:

> "Come here and sit down," he said. "What did you do it for?"
> "You never sent for me. I thought you had lost confidence in me."
> He called me ungrateful. I have cried many times since but never in quite the way I did then. Gratitude laced my veins where Ziegfeld was concerned and I thought his remark unjust.
> "Was there so little friendship between us that I had to send for you like any actor?" he asked.
> Here was the most scornful reference he had it in his mind to make. For actors as a whole he had a biting contempt.
> "You belong here. You'll always belong here," he said gently. I didn't see him again for two years.[85]

She did not work for him again for four years and her nostalgic recollections lack credibility. Although the misunderstanding she described may have occurred, it seems unlikely, given the tremendous frustration she said she felt during the run of the 1911 *Follies*. She may have found herself lost in the show, as the Cleveland critic charged, and believed that she would do better elsewhere. She may have thought that another manager and a different kind of production would provide her with a better opportunity to display her talents. She may have decided, therefore, not to appear in the next edition of the *Follies*. On the other hand, Ziegfeld may have been so displeased with her work that he chose not to renew her contract for the *Ziegfeld Follies of 1912*. He must have sensed her dissatisfaction and, since she was unable to find songs that suited her, could have easily become disenchanted with her. Acclaimed in 1910, she was often ignored in 1911, and he may have opted to exclude her from the cast of the first *Follies* to bear the name "Ziegfeld" in its title.

Whatever the reasons for the breach, Brice was about to enter a difficult period in her professional life. During the next four years she would appear in a variety of productions, but the reviews she received would grow increasingly negative. She would continue to be handicapped by poor material or, more specifically, by material for which her extremely physical style was inappropriate. She would clown outrageously to win laughs from her audiences, yet the grimaces and gestures would become tiresome as they began to seem totally unrelated to the songs she performed. What made "Sadie Salome" and "Lovie Joe" so entertaining was that the eccentricity of singer and subject coincided. The spontaneous gestures worked well because they complemented the character Brice created. With "That Chilly Man" and "Ephraham," the same technique was less effective because, while still amusing, it had little relevance to the subject of the song. The funny movements and expressions were done primarily for their own sake, imposed on the material rather than arising organically from it. Brice seems not to have had enough insight to understand that as a performer, she had to create the character first, then find the ways to make that character comical. Until she resolved this serious problem, her work would seem unfocused, even monotonous, and the success she knew in *The College Girls* and the *Follies of 1910* would elude her. Within two years she would become so discouraged, she would announce her retirement from the stage.

Dramatic Doldrums: 1912–1916

> I was never happier in my life. I didn't know what the word happy meant until I saw Nicky in that deck chair.
>
> —FANNY BRICE[1]

> If Fanny Brice will go right to it, the girl is going to make a big name for herself yet.
>
> —SIME, *Variety*, 27 June 1913[2]

4.

From 1912 to 1917, American culture flourished with a vitality not seen since the mid-nineteenth century. The period was known as "the little renaissance" or "the joyous season."[3] It was a time of creative ferment when American writers, artists, reformers, and intellectuals were turning away from established conventions and looking at the world from new perspectives. According to historian Eric F. Goldman, it was a time "to be free of all arbitrary yardsticks, progressive or conservative, to be free of everything that smacked of the old America." When Woodrow Wilson became the twenty-eighth President in 1913, succeeding William Howard Taft, he caught the reform mood in his call for a New Freedom. "The New Freedom," as Goldman so effectively described it, "spawned a hundred other shimmering escapes from the past—the New Poetry, the New History, the New Democracy, the New Art, the New Woman, the new anything so long as it was new and gave an intoxicating sense of freedom."[4]

Artistic turbulence was everywhere. Ezra Pound edited the first anthology of the Imagist poets in 1912, the same year that the little theatre movement made its debut in Chicago.[5] In 1913, New Yorkers were shocked by the Armory Show, a daring exhibition organized by the "Ashcan School" to expose American viewers to modern art. (Of all the works in the show, Marcel Duchamp's "Nude Descending a Staircase" evoked the most vituperative response, including one hostile critic's comment that it looked like "an explosion in a shingle factory.")[6]

The quest for newness and freedom was matched by exhilarating technological accomplishments. By 1915, as Henry Ford made his millionth automobile, the Wright Brothers had already patented and flown their airplane.[7] Transcontinental telephone service facilitated communication and luxurious ocean liners enhanced transportation although, as the *Titanic* disaster reminded a horrified world in 1912, transatlantic crossings were still perilous. Even the dance craze which swept the country after Vernon and Irene Castle's rapid rise to stardom in 1913 was appropriate to the swiftly accelerating pace and the revolutionary spirit of American life. As women began "storming the colleges and the professions, raising their skirts a daring few inches above the shoe, winning the vote in state after state," social dancing became commonplace and made public propinquity acceptable.[8]

Ironically, this buoyant epoch in American life was Brice's least successful period as a performer. She left Ziegfeld in the spring of 1912, after the *Follies of 1911* had closed. She rejoined him in the spring of 1916, at twenty-five, when she signed a contract to appear in that year's edition of the show. During the intervening four years, she did not perform under the Ziegfeld banner at all but worked almost constantly in musical comedy and vaudeville. She took part in seven revues, three of them in London, and had vaudeville bookings in over thirty cities. Yet, in spite of her tremendous activity, her efforts for much of this time were curiously undistinguished, and later on she had little to say about this segment of her professional life. In interviews where she reminisced about her past, the period of 1912–1916 was almost a blank, notable for only one Bricean achievement: meeting Jules Arnstein.

The momentous encounter took place in November 1912 in Baltimore, after a performance of *The Whirl of Society*, the Shubert production in which Brice was then appearing. She was twenty-one and the handsome thirty-three-year-old Arnstein impressed her with his elegance and sophistication. As she described it in her 1936 *Cosmopolitan* series:

> Nothing of importance affected my career at this time and it is significant in my life but for one thing.
> In Baltimore, one Saturday afternoon . . . I was introduced to a man

who stood then and forever after for everything that had been left out of my life—manners, good breeding, education and an extraordinary gift for dreaming.

The following day in Philadelphia, two members of the cast and I had dinner with him. He occupied what was called the gold suite in the old Bellevue Hotel. Everything in that room—piano, furniture, taffeta, draperies—was golden. In its blaze of light and color it might have been an exclamation of his life.

His name was Jules Arnstein, but his friends called him Nick.[9]

They also called him John Wilson Adair, James Wilford Adair, and J. W. Arnold—aliases under which Arnstein, born Julius Wilford Arndt-Stein (or Arndstein), also operated.[10] Contrary to Brice's glowing portrait and perception of him, Arnstein was a gambler, a con man, and a criminal. His impressive appearance and impeccable taste belied his dishonesty and ineffectuality. Brice's "golden boy" failed at everything he attempted, including the wire-tapping that sent him to Sing Sing in 1915 and the bond theft that led him to Leavenworth in 1924. Brice, however, was oblivious to his flaws and fell in love with him immediately. On one occasion she claimed that it happened the moment she saw his seven toothbrushes and monogrammed silk pajamas in the bathroom of the Baltimore hotel suite.[11] Although already married, he returned with her to New York and moved into the apartment she shared with Rose on the corner of Broadway and 52nd Street. According to Brice's sister, Carolyn, her mother "hated Nick from the beginning" and tried to convince her daughter to end the ill-fated relationship.[12] Fanny refused and enjoyed almost fifteen tempestuous years with Arnstein, financing his abortive ventures and ignoring his indifference.

After living together for six years, two of which Arnstein spent in Sing Sing, he divorced his first wife and married Brice in 1918. They had two children, Frances, born in 1919, and William, born in 1921. Their life was far from idyllic. In 1920, "Nicky" was accused of orchestrating a five million dollar Wall Street bond robbery. (When Brice heard the charge, she supposedly remarked, "Master Mind. . . . He couldn't Master Mind an electric bulb into a socket.")[13] Arnstein fled from New York but quickly tired of living as a fugitive and surrendered to the authorities two months after he had disappeared. "For the next six years," according to one observer, "Fanny devoted all her money and most of her energy to her miscreant husband's defense."[14] Convinced of his innocence, she remained loyal to him throughout the ordeal of a long trial, with considerable notoriety, and a two and one-half year prison term. Shortly after his release from Leavenworth, however, they were divorced because of his flagrant infidelity.

Although others could not comprehend her devotion to such a reprobate, Brice always maintained that Arnstein was the only man she ever loved. She wrote once, "All my life, I was afraid I was going to get stuck on some little guy who played the piano in a joint filled with smoke." Instead, she met "this tall handsome guy with the beautiful hands and thin ankles" and decided "this is the guy" she wanted "to have children with."[15] Insecure about her own appearance, she fell in love with his, oblivious to his obvious character flaws and callous behavior. Even after she filed for divorce in 1927, she hoped he would atone for past infidelities and return, repentant, to her. Years later she reminisced, "I didn't believe what was happening. I didn't believe we were through . . . I knew I was just as much in love with Nick that day as the day I first saw him."[16] He did nothing to stop the divorce or to contest the decree awarding her sole custody of their two children. He disappeared from their lives more abruptly than Charles Borach had vanished from Brice's some twenty-five years before. According to Nicky in an interview granted after Fanny's death, he never saw Frances and William again. As he put it, "I didn't even go back to the New York house for my clothes. She auctioned them off with her furniture later. I was through."[17]

Although Arnstein caused Brice much pain, he did encourage her in her career—however inadvertently. Throughout her life, the willingness to work hard and steadily was one of her most striking characteristics. There were few gaps of any consequence in her professional activities and, if relentless ambition was one explanation for her diligence, there was another more practical reason. Since Arnstein never worked productively at anything during their years together, "somebody," she explained, "had to pay the rent."[18] In times of emotional stress, moreover, performing may have served as a much-needed escape, enabling her to concentrate on something other than personal problems. She even exploited her unhappiness on the stage and achieved one of her greatest professional successes. In 1921, when she had been back in the Ziegfeld fold for five years and Arnstein's indictment for bond theft was front-page news, she sang "My Man," a mawkish ballad about a cad and the faithful woman who loves him in spite of his brutal treatment. Audiences automatically assumed that the stormy relationship it chronicled was Brice's and were moved by the poignant correspondence they perceived between singer and subject. Indelibly hers, "My Man" became Brice's signature, the title of her first film and, with the exception of "Sadie Salome," the song she always said had the greatest impact on her career.

For a good part of the period from 1912 to 1916, however, Brice's career suffered as a result of her tumultuous private life. Preoccupied by her affair with Arnstein, she did not bring to her work the concentration and enthusiasm she had previously demonstrated. Her material often seemed stale, her performances increasingly forced. It is not surprising that Arnstein's trial and sentencing early in 1915 coincided with her professional nadir: several months during which she received poor notices, lost top billing, was fired from a show, and almost dropped completely out of sight. Fortunately, she was able to bounce back and reverse the disastrous downturn her career had taken. With Arnstein in prison—the one place, friends believed, she could be assured of his fidelity—she could focus once again on her work, on giving her creative energy and talent a more appropriate outlet.

Less than a month after leaving the *Follies of 1911*, Brice made her debut in vaudeville. It was an auspicious occasion as vaudeville then was the nation's leading entertainment form. For roughly two decades, from 1895 to 1915, vaudeville was at the height of its popularity. With its big-time and its small-time circuits, thousands of theatres and performers, and millions of fans, vaudeville was a nationwide industry—according to one disgruntled observer, as "cut-throat" as any other.

Until it was eclipsed by film and radio in the 1920s, vaudeville dominated American show business and Brice must have welcomed the opportunity to perform in it. From April to August 1912, she played at least nine vaudeville engagements in the New York area, beginning with a week at Hammerstein's Victoria Theatre, then the most prestigious vaudeville house in the city. Her initial efforts, however, resulted in only mediocre reviews. Both the *Clipper* and *Variety* acknowledged her innate ability and future promise, but expressed reservations about her performance. Although she ended with "the big audience in her lap," the *Clipper* considered her delivery awkward and her mannerisms intrusive. *Variety*'s Jolo discussed the thirteen-minute act's structure and content more explicitly:

> She starts slowly with two songs, out of which she gets comparatively little, then puts over a "wallop" with a "Yiddish" ditty, . . . and finally spoils it all by changing to a silly costume consisting of white satin trousers of eccentric design with an equally inconsistent red coat. Had the young woman confined herself to a single gown and sung just one more number of consequence either before or after the "Yiddish" ditty (preferably before) she would have landed

with both feet. . . . But the last two numbers are inane and the first two not worthy of her talents as comedienne.[19]

Brice was still plagued by poor material and the "silly costume" she selected suggests that she relied too heavily on sight gags to put her songs across.

At New York City's Colonial Theatre the following week, Brice was billed as "America's best singing comedienne." Once again, however, the *Clipper* found her disappointing. Observing that she had the "ability and personality to secure rapid advancement on the vaudeville stage," the paper urged her to find more suitable material. A week-long appearance at Brooklyn's Orpheum Theatre in May and a return engagement at Hammerstein's in June received an equally tepid critical response.

In July and August, she performed as the headliner in five different vaudeville bills: at the New Brighton, Brighton Beach; Keith's Union Square; Morrison's, Rockaway Beach; Proctor's Fifth Avenue; and Proctor's, Newark.[20] The fact that she was the star attraction in her very first vaudeville season was less a tribute to her talent than an example of vaudeville's ability to snare successful performers from other entertainment media. The caption, "Late Feature *Ziegfeld Follies*," gave Brice special status and made her a valuable addition to a vaudeville bill. Yet the cachet of the Ziegfeld name alone would not have ensured the warm reception that she apparently received at all five houses. As the *Clipper* put it, reviewing her at Proctor's Fifth Avenue, she quickly "won herself into the favor of the audience" before her first song was finished and "had the house" until she closed.[21]

Brice seems to have literally gotten her act together, streamlining it so that it better suited vaudeville where speed and showmanship were practically synonymous. Judging from the reviews, the major problem with her initial appearances was that her act did not build properly. It lacked what the best vaudeville "turns" were supposed to have: a fast pace and, as Sime put it, "a wallop." By summertime, however, she had greatly improved. Reporting on her successful appearance at Keith's Union Square, the *Clipper* called her "exceptionally clever" with "a mannerism of her own which is attractive." By the time she played Proctor's in August, she had progressed still further. *Variety* awarded her "the biggest individual honors of the evening" and the *Clipper* said that the six songs she performed "left the audience wanting more."[22]

Brice was able to use the skills she was developing as a vaudeville performer in *The Whirl of Society*, the Shubert musical in which she made her next stage appearance. Ads for the show billed it as a "musical satire of up-to-date society," a "musical mélange" full of "maids, mirth and melody."[23] Most critics, however, found the satire minimal and considered the production just an evening of glorified vaudeville. It qualified as vaudeville because its many principals had a chance to perform their own specialties and followed one another in quick succession. It was glorified because, unlike the acts in a regular vaudeville show, these were loosely connected by a plot which revolved around the efforts of "an aspiring parvenu" to break into London society. Both features, the fast pace and the plot, also distinguished the show from a Ziegfeld revue where the elaborate staging tended to create long delays between production numbers and made the whole evening move much more slowly.

With a book by Harrison Rhodes, lyrics by Harold Atteridge, and music by Louis A. Hirsch, *The Whirl of Society* opened on March 5, 1912, at New York's Winter Garden Theatre, the Shuberts' new "gold-encrusted palace."[24] Brice was not a member of the original cast, which starred Al Jolson, in his trademark blackface, as a butler named Gus. The show ran fairly successfully until June 29 when it closed for the summer. On September 1, a revised *Whirl* opened at Chicago's Lyric Theatre and began a five-month tour. Jolson again headed the cast, which included several of the New York principals and a chorus of sixty.[25] It also featured Brice in the role of a Jewish maid named Sadie: the comic counterpart to Jolson's butler, Gus. The role had been created expressly for her and had not been part of the original production. The story itself, however, remained the same, clearly secondary to the singing, dancing, and special features such as a runway down which the entire company trooped to the footlights at frequent intervals, over the heads of the audience.[26]

Ads for the show in the Chicago newspapers hailed Jolson as "the fellow who put 'The Whirl' in *The Whirl of Society*." He was the undisputed star, yet other performers were also applauded, among them Brice. The *Post* praised her as being "singular in her comic abilities." The *Examiner* gave her "a position of special prominence in the honor column" because "her impersonation of a Yiddish maid carried with it the hearts and laughter of the audience." Two reviews, however, suggested that Brice may have overdone it, trying so hard to be funny that her performance seemed forced and, to some, offensive. According to the *Record Herald*, "Miss Brice has an inimitable knack for exaggerated mimicry in song, but some kind restraining person should tell her what not to do." Similarly, the *Evening American* praised her "hard and earnest" work as "a Yiddish servant maid," but added that "she need not labor so arduously." Not only was she "funny and pleasant without such honest exertion," but "once she went so far for a laugh that she transcended politeness in a song chorus." The critic found this "deplorable" as neither she nor the show needed to be "over-frank" to please.[27]

The number with which Brice shocked the Chicago critics—and which the *Tribune*'s Percy Hammond called "septic"—was probably "Fol de Rol dol Doi."[28] With lyrics by Edward Madden and music by Jean Schwartz, the song is reminiscent of "Sadie Salome," but only because both require a Yiddish accent. "Fol de Rol" presents Brice as a Jewish Juliet passionately entreating her "Hebrew Romemo" [sic], Ignatz, to sing the song that makes her "skid-did-dish" when she hears that Yiddish, "Fol de rol dol, dol de rol dol, dol de rol dol doi."[29] The verses are embellished with comical imagery, as when the lovesick singer urges her "Yiddisher turtle dove" to flap his wings and "crow mit love," but the basic idea is simple: she wants Ignatz to sing the song because it stimulates her. That, presumably, is what some critics found objectionable and lines like "Grab me, grab me, baby nab me, darlink treat me rough" and "Kiss me, kiss me, don't you miss me?" must have qualified as "overfrank." Combined with a lively pseudo-Semitic melody, Brice's heavy Yiddish accent, and undoubtedly outrageous actions, it also must have been very funny.

The *Examiner* noted that "Fol de Rol" was done "with such pleasing abandon that she amused herself" and the *Sunday Tribune* carried a caricature of Brice in an angular, loose-jointed pose reminiscent of her earlier work.[30] Nothing more specific was said about her songs or about her actual performance as Sadie, the "little Jewish maid." In Chicago and other cities along the show's route, however, newspapers did run articles presenting Brice as a "fine delineator of Yiddish types" and questioning her about the method she used to create a character such as Sadie.[31] In all of them she maintained that her work was based on deep and earnest study of the "Ghetto types" she actively sought out. A Chicago paper reported that she lived in "daily terror" of forgetting her accent and speaking "the way everyone else does"—an interesting comment given Brice's subsequent claim that she never used a Yiddish accent until Irving Berlin suggested she do so. According to the Chicago account, however, she spent "two or three weeks every summer in the Ghetto—listening, bargaining, quarreling—using every opportunity for a new trick."[32]

A Cincinnati article took the idea even further, trailing Brice "through back streets and dingy tenements to the heart of the Jewish quarter in

New York." There she endured countless hardships in her search for authenticity. As she explained in an informative interview.

> It is the only way I can keep in touch with the character I play. . . .
> I rent a back room and I bargain for the room rent, too. During the day I
> wander through the markets. Heavens, I have bought more stuff than I could
> ever use in the world, needless things that are of no use to me. I buy them
> mostly to get into conversations with the dealer or other customers. During
> these debates on prices I pick up true characters. . . .
>
>   I go to their dances and outings and eat in their restaurants. I do not
> bother with the Jewish types who have been in this country long enough to
> become Americanized. I nearly ruined my digestion at a restaurant because
> I found the waiters there to be a fund of study.[33]

Such comments succeed admirably in conveying Brice's enormous commitment to her career, her selfless dedication as a performer. Unfortunately, they were all spurious, merely part of a massive Shubert publicity campaign.

To generate interest in her and, more importantly, in the production, Brice was to play up her identity as a Yiddish dialect singer and the energy she expended in creating her colorful stage characters. These accounts of going back to the Ghetto recall Ziegfeld's stories about the poor little newsgirl selling papers beneath the Brooklyn Bridge and arose from a similar impulse. If Ziegfeld sought to impress readers with Brice's talent by portraying her rise as meteoric, the Shubert articles tried to confer a greater legitimacy on her work by showing that it was based on serious study. They also suggested that Brice was trying to distance herself from the "Jewish types" she represented, to make it clear that they were also foreign to her. She had to observe them carefully because she was unfamiliar with their manners and customs—a curious stance for someone who would later portray herself as a child of the Ghetto. Evidently at this stage in her career Brice thought it advantageous to stress her separateness from such a world and its alien characters.

That spectacular fabrication was extremely successful, as Nellie Revell, one of J. J. Shubert's press agents on the road, was eager to inform her "Boss." She wrote that the syndicated story "went over for Fanny Brice" and would be carried in eighty papers in towns along the show's route. Inventing such stories was an important part of Revell's job and she said she had dictated so many she was "blue in the face." She was equally busy organizing publicity stunts, all designed to stimulate ticket sales. She had rejected Brice for one of them involving an aviator because, as she explained to J. J., "Fanny had a divorce case on" against Frank White "and could not lend enough romance to it."

Revell did, however, include Brice in another scheme she described in a letter sent to J. J. from Kansas City in mid-September. It involved various members of the company who were to write newspaper articles compatible with their onstage characters. Al Jolson was to cover sports in "Negro dialect." Lawrence D'Orsay, who played the British Earl of Pawtuckett in the show, was to report on society "in his dialect." Ada Lewis, the social-climbing Mrs. Dean, was assigned a "Police Court trial in slang." And Brice would, of course, discuss "the Ghetto district in Yiddish dialect." "That ought to make a wonderful stunt," Revell crowed, "and something that I could use all along the line if I can get the cooperation of the company."[34]

The Shubert correspondence provides a fascinating glimpse behind the scenes of an increasingly troubled show. From New York, J.J. barraged Revell and road manager Stanley Sharpe with daily missives detailing his disgust at the disappointing box office and mounting expenses. The letters and telegrams they sent in response revealed a backstage melodrama far more compelling than the production onstage. Defending themselves against charges of mismanagement and incompetence, they described heat so intense in Chicago it almost closed the theatre. They chronicled the health problems of various cast members. Melville Ellis, one of the featured performers, had fainting spells. Jolson, the star, had a severe sore throat (possibly diphtheria, speculated Sharpe) and had to cut several songs. Brice, too, was indisposed with an undisclosed illness of such severity she had to be hospitalized for five days and missed almost a full week of performances. There is some evidence suggesting that she had an abortion at this time. Sharpe reassured the anxious J.J., concerned more about the health of his ticket sales than of Brice, that he had found "a little Jewish girl by the name of Gussie White" to perform her numbers. She was "great," Sharpe wired, and even "went as big as Brice."[35]

A variety of illnesses continued to plague the company along the route, but there were other problems as well. The cast was upset because Shubert, furious about unauthorized expenses and "rotten business," had cut salaries. Brice, now singing for just half the money she had expected to receive, was desperately searching for new material. Shubert complained to Sharpe that her songs were not working well and ordered him to "see that she gets a couple of good numbers." Sharpe evidently gave her a coon song, thereby infuriating Jolson who considered them his property in the show. The temperamental star, still dropping songs on account of his sore throat, promised J.J. he would work tirelessly for the remainder of the run if Brice found another vehicle. He explained that he was frustrated because he thought everyone in the cast was copying him and trying to steal his material. For Brice to have a coon song was especially "unwise" and he urged J.J. to replace it with a "Yiddish song." Shubert instructed Sharpe to tell Jolson he would have Brice "put in a straight song or a Jewish character song" on one condition—that Jolson "goes on every single night and gives the same performance and attends strictly to business."[36]

The squabbling company soon had greater complications to contend with. *The Whirl of Society* was on its way to Washington, D.C., when it received a wire to go to Baltimore instead. There, on November 18, it merged with *Vera Violetta*, a Shubert production starring Gaby Deslys, a French dancer, singer, and pantomimist noted for her flamboyant costumes. The new three-hour show featured Deslys, Jolson, and Ada Lewis, all of whom received favorable reviews. Brice, however, did not fare as well. According to Revell, "Everything but Fannie Brice went enormously. Think you can spare her and save that money."[37]

J.J. did not act on Revell's suggestion; he kept Brice in the show. She continued to play Sadie, although several of her songs were dropped. The Shubert correspondence indicates that she was still searching unsuccessfully for better material and that the production itself was not free of problems. Jolson was still sick, he and Deslys were feuding, and the publicity campaign promising the public a naughty Deslys backfired. As Sharpe explained, defending himself against J.J.'s constant carping, audiences expected her to do "something risqué" and were disappointed when she did not.

Nevertheless, the production completed its scheduled tour with stops in several northeastern and Canadian cities. After playing in Boston, the show went on to Montreal, but it opened there without Brice. An exasperated Sharpe wrote to J.J. that she had missed the train from New York, to which Shubert angrily responded, "I do not like the idea of her disappointing us in this manner and she had no right to leave for New York."[38]

Neither man commented further on Brice's unprofessional behavior, nor did she explain what she was doing in New York when the company was in Boston and about to leave for Canada. It is quite possible, however, that she had gone there to see Arnstein. After their cataclysmic meeting in Baltimore the previous month, they had decided to live together in the New York apartment Brice shared with Rose. Arnstein had probably moved in while she was in Boston, and she must have wanted to spend time with him before leaving for Canada. However emotional the reunion, she managed to rejoin the company in Montreal in time for the New Year's Day matinee and continued on with the show, which finally closed in Brooklyn on January 25, 1913.

Less than two weeks later, Brice opened at the Winter Garden in *The Honeymoon Express*, another fast-paced musical with Jolson, Deslys, and many other *Whirl* cast members. With book and lyrics by Joseph W. Herbert and Harold Atteridge, music by Jean Schwartz, and staging by Ned Wayburn, *The Honeymoon Express* was billed as a "spectactular farce with music in two acts and six scenes."[39] It was, according to the *New York Times*, another extravagant "musical mélange," the kind of "big show" with which the Winter Garden had come to be identified.[40]

As usual the plot was minimal, centering on the desperate attempts of Yvonne (Deslys) to win back her husband, Henri, from whom she has just been divorced and who is on his way to Paris by train. Yvonne's butler, Gus (Jolson), gallantly offers to drive his mistress to Rouen where she can take another train to Paris and have the divorce decree revoked. That leads directly to the show's most sensational feature, a thrilling night-time race between Yvonne's car and the train. Beginning with a film clip showing Jolson at the wheel in mad pursuit, the scene created striking visual effects. Using one line of moving lights to represent the train and another for the car as they twisted and turned down a mountain, around corners and through tunnels, the chase ended with both vehicles roaring onstage to the audience's amazement.

Brice was not involved in that startling scene, about which the *Clipper* raved, "Cold type cannot do it justice." She played Marcelle, Yvonne's maid, and the reviews of her performance were extremely negative. Sime, writing in *Variety*, delivered the most unfavorable assessment of her work to date, observing, "It was almost pitiful to see the state of Fanny Brice. She did not recover herself until the second act when [she] led 'My Raggyadore' with a good swing to her swaggering walk."[41] Neither the *Times* nor the *Dramatic Mirror* mentioned her at all. The *New York Evening Post* called her "an acquired taste" and the *Evening Sun* asserted that "for reasons for which she had only herself to blame," she "did not hit it off any too well with her audience." The one voice in her favor was the *Clipper's*: she had "a small role, but scored heavily with her songs."[42]

No other notices about Brice in *The Honeymoon Express* appeared in the newspapers. Her name did surface in *Variety* in conjunction with the Sunday evening Winter Garden vaudeville programs in which she frequently participated, but the reviews did not make her work sound impressive. In commenting on her March 30 performance, Sime stated that Brice led "My Raggyadore" with the chorus after singing two of her "former songs." With more than a hint of dissatisfaction he added, "If Fanny won't change her numbers for any Sunday show, she might at least wear a new dress now and then."[43] The implication was that the twenty-one-year-old Brice was committing one of vaudeville's cardinal sins: she was getting stale. Worse than that, in the April 27 program, she was sloppy. Sime noted that, once again, Brice sang "My Raggyadore" and that "on looks," she "just made the stage in time, leading the number in her street clothes."[44]

One explanation for such an unprofessional lapse was carelessness. Another was that she did not wear the costume because she no longer had it. She had left *The Honeymoon Express* the day before. When the spring edition of the show opened on Monday, April 28, Marcelle was being played by Ina Claire, who won far more glowing reviews for her performance than Brice had for hers. The newspapers did not mention Brice at all and her leaving the show, along with Deslys, was never explained.[45]

It is unclear whether Brice was fired from *The Honeymoon Express* or withdrew from it voluntarily. What is apparent, however, is that she was no longer in great demand as a performer. An article in the May 9 *Variety* reported that producers Lew Fields, Ziegfeld, and the Shuberts were all involved in a "mad scramble for players."[46] In the list of people mentioned, Brice's name was conspicuously absent. Unlike Jolson, who had recently signed a lucrative seven-year contract with the Shuberts, she did not receive any offers. No one clamored for her services and it is not surprising that the May 16 *Variety* reported, "Fanny Brice is taking a vacation, the first in seven years. Fanny has so much leisure she goes to all the musical shows in town."[47]

Brice's vacation lasted until June 9 when she returned to vaudeville and once again received favorable notices. Commenting on her June 23 appearance at Proctor's Fifth Avenue, Sime wrote in *Variety* that her thirteen-minute performance "cleaned up on the show." On the page devoted to new acts, he discussed her at some length, tempering his admiration for her innate ability with some helpful criticism:

> Fanny Brice is always around with a new act and Fanny Brice is always growing better. Some day if Fanny will take care of herself she is going to be a great comedienne for Fanny has a naturally humorous streak in her composition. Even if vaudeville does not get it altogether, it is there. And Fanny can originate or create a song.[48]

He acknowledged that she was "the hit of the bill," but added that she had one serious problem as a performer. "She's careless," he wrote, "doesn't care whether school keeps or not," and advised her to become much more disciplined about her work.[49] In the coming months, as Brice became increasingly undiscerning and unfocused, his observation would seem particularly prescient.

She performed next at the Brighton Beach Music Hall from July 7 to 12 and was subsequently scheduled to open at the Temple in Detroit on July 28, followed by a week at Shea's in Toronto beginning August 11. According to reviews of both shows, however, she was not part of either bill. For a month, she dropped out of sight. She was not mentioned in any newspaper articles, her vaudeville route listings were inaccurate, and she ran no ads announcing her current activities or future plans. Unlike other performers such as Eva Tanguay who bombarded the papers with publicity, Brice was remarkably reticent. There was no clue to her whereabouts until August 15, when *Variety* published a special cable from London. Dated August 13, it reported that Brice was working at the London Opera House at "$650 weekly" and was "getting over."[50]

The August 16 *Clipper* printed a brief statement from its London correspondent corroborating *Variety's* cable and, in its August 23 edition, explained how that engagement had materialized. Brice had come to London "just for a holiday," but decided that she wanted to "do a stunt" at the London Opera House. The managers let her audition, but were unaware of "her status and ability." Brice convinced them to "give her a chance" and was "slipped into the revue all unannounced" on Monday evening, August 4. She was an immediate success and was rewarded with a "very nice" contract.[51] According to the August 30 *Clipper*, she was "promptly accepted as a London favorite." Audiences enjoyed her two scenes in the revue. In the first, she sang a duet with "the versatile Mr. Schwartz." Toward the end of the show, she performed several coon songs "with characteristic business." It was all "very charming," the correspondent concluded.[52]

England at the time was in the throes of ragtime fever, which *Variety* announced was about to spread over the continent, and American performers were in great demand for British productions.[53] In its January 24, 1913, edition, *Variety* reported that 150 American acts had been booked to appear in England with "almost as many more being negotiated for," so Brice's presence at the London Opera House would not have been unusual.[54] In addition, the new theatre, billed as "the most beautiful in the world," had been built by American impresario Oscar Hammerstein who certainly would have been familiar with her work. Brice freely admitted, however, that she did not sail to England because she had a job waiting for her. She went because Arnstein had business there that would take him away for several months. In her *Cosmopolitan* series, she described her momentous decision to go with him:

> Youth in torment. Youth at grips with destiny—what won't it do! No one would want to forget that young girl whose pulse was beating wildly as she knocked on a cabin door of the ocean liner *Homeric* an hour after it had put to sea. My salary was always handed over to my mother intact and only the courage to pawn all the jewelry I possessed had made possible this timid knock and the low whisper to Nick:
> "I'm here. Did you think you could leave me behind?"
> A week later we were in England.[55]

Brice asserted that there was "nothing remarkable about this period except a complete happiness." Reality, however, intruded. In England as at home, she had to finance Nicky's purchases and projects. In her 1925 *Post* interview, she remembered returning to performing after only one week, although she attributed it to a sudden desire "to be behind the footlights."[56] According to her 1936 recollections, she received her first engagement in London from Sir Alfred Butt, manager of several large theatres. "He had never heard of me," she admitted, but hired her "to oblige Gaby Deslys."

Whatever fears Butt may have had were soon allayed by her performances. British audiences loved her. Brice attributed her success to the universality of her comedy. England, she wrote, was "not hard to win: humanity is the same the world over, and humor an elemental thing. The week's trial turned into a long engagement at the Palace at five hundred dollars a week."[57] First, however, as the reports in *Variety* and the *Clipper* have already indicated, Brice played at the London Opera House. She appeared in *Come Over Here*, a revue which the British newspaper *Era* praised as one of the best of the year's productions. The *Era* reported that her character songs were "specialties" and that she was "a particular favorite of the company," which also included "fancy skaters," "capital fun-makers," "expert dancers," an accomplished soprano, a masterly flutist, and, as the star attraction, Mademoiselle Mado Minty's impersonation of a spider in its web.[58]

Brice remained in *Come Over Here* for four weeks through the end of August and did not perform again until late October. On the twenty-seventh of that month, she opened a two-week engagement at the Palace in *A La Carte*, a revue starring Deslys. The *London Times* identified "Miss Fanny Bryce" as "an American eccentric comedienne" and announced that she would be singing "new rag-time songs."[59] Both *Variety* and the *Clipper* published special cables from London attesting to the enthusiastic welcome Brice received. *Variety*'s correspondent noted that "the audience liked her eccentric ways" and the *Clipper*'s said that "her Jewish song, 'Fol de Rol' was especially admired."[60]

Brice had equally favorable notices at Butt's Victoria Palace, where she performed from November 24 to 29. From there she moved to the Palladium, where she made her fourth and last London appearance in another revue called *Hullo Ragtime*. In its December 3 review, the *Era* credited Brice and the male lead for much of the production's effectiveness and noted that both "accomplished artistes" immediately "won the favor of the audiences." Elaborating on Brice, the paper reminded its readers that she had first "made good with her clever and original sketches and songs and mimicry" at the London Opera House. In her Palladium appearance, she was displaying "her versatility and popularity" even further.[61]

British audiences may have responded warmly to Brice, but she did not receive much publicity. Aside from the notices mentioned, there were no articles about her in the newspapers and it is unclear when she left *Hullo Ragtime*. The show itself ran for two weeks through December 13, but the cast lists published in the *London Times* did not include her name. Although Arnstein asserted in an interview that he "had her name on every bus in London," he is an unreliable source and there is no indication that Brice was very well known in 1913. Arnstein also recalled that they stayed in England until war was declared in the summer of 1914 but that, too, is incorrect. According to *Variety*, Brice sailed for the United States on Saturday, January 31, 1914, on the *Mauretania*.[62]

On January 16, an ad in *Variety* announced that Brice would be "returning to America soon after a successful eight months' tour of England."[63] Since vaudeville performers constantly paid to publicize themselves in the trade papers, there was nothing unusual about Brice's calling attention to her imminent arrival. What is curious, however, is the amount of time she claimed to have spent in England. Since she left for London in July 1913 and returned in January 1914, she was actually away for only six months. The two-month discrepancy is peculiar. Did she deliberately misrepresent the length of time she was away, believing that an eight-month tour sounded more impressive than a six-month? Or did she simply lose track of time and say eight months by mistake?

Attributing the distortion to an innocent error might be credible were it not for an even more disturbing bit of publicity. The February 25 *Dramatic Mirror* ran a photograph with a caption announcing "Fannie Brice, in Vaudeville Again after English Tour."[64] She is shown in profile, gazing demurely away from the camera. Her lovely hair is gathered in a chignon at the nape of her slender neck. A long strand of pearls rests against the soft folds of her silk blouse. She looks elegant and refined, the essence of propriety. The only problem with the photograph is that Brice is not the woman in it. Or if she is, the photograph has been doctored to significantly alter her appearance. The rosebud mouth, the dark eyelashes, the masses of wavy hair are close enough to Brice's to pass inspection, but the nose is dramatically different. It is smaller, straighter, and much less Semitic—designed to conform to the norm of feminine prettiness in America circa 1914 when little Mary Pickford with her porcelain skin and golden curls was the most popular female screen star.

Did the *Dramatic Mirror* publish the wrong photograph by mistake? This is unlikely, since the same one appeared in at least two other Brice advertisements from the same period so that its use had to be intentional. One of the ads merely prints Brice's name to the right of the picture. The other, however, has more extensive copy which seems particularly incongruous in view of the accompanying image. Brice, "The Character Comedienne," is touted as "Somebody who will wake you up!" "She's a typical New York girl, as flip and smart and fly and fresh as they make 'em in this man's town and just as foolish as a fox. . . . Oh, such a Funny Fannie! Oh, How She Mugs!" screams the boldface type, informing readers that Brice is at the "corner of 42nd Street and Broadway doing a snappy single."[65] The woman pictured, however, looks ethereal, almost somber, not like someone who could "mug" very well at all.

Did Brice think that people wanted a pretty face? Did she feel that she had to be beautiful to attract audiences initially, but that once they were in the theatre she could win them over with her comedy? Was the picture a joke, aimed at those who did not know what she really looked like and would be surprised when they saw her? Was it a gibe at those who liked ethnic humor but not ethnic looks? Was it a jab at herself, another instance of her tendency toward self-deprecation, her insecurity about her appearance? Or was it simply a short-lived publicity stunt? Brice never discussed these photographs so that it is impossible to determine what her real motivation was. Nevertheless, their use strongly suggests that she felt the need to distort the truth, to portray herself as different than she actually was. Evidently being funny was not enough. At twenty-two, she believed a woman also had to be pretty to please.

1914 began well for Brice. On February 23, she made her debut at New York's Palace Theatre. Although it was not immediately successful when it opened on March 24 of the previous year, the Palace soon replaced Hammerstein's Victoria as the most prestigious vaudeville house in New York. For virtually two decades, as one observer put it, it was "the throne room of the kings of Vaudeville" and Brice's weeklong engagement was auspicious for her.[66] The *New York Mail* proclaimed, "From nothing theatrically to a vaudeville headliner in the brief period of four years is a record for stage celebrities" and advised its readers to see Brice at the Palace as an example of this "high-leaping stunt." *Variety* reported with more restrained enthusiasm that she started with a song "in which she displayed a perceptible English accent, but soon dropped it" and was a "bigger hit than ever" with her "Fol de Rol" and "Yiddish kidding."[67]

From the Palace, Brice went to the Colonial (March 2–7) and Hammerstein's (March 9–14). She did not headline at either theatre but, as the *Clipper* noted, held an important program position as a "character comedienne." The review did not discuss her act specifically, but described Brice in glowing generalities as "perennially bright, an entertainer to her fingertips," a woman who "brings warmth and gladsome laughter to her audiences on all occasions."[68] Another newspaper called her a "true humorist" and observed that "few women have the broad low-comedy gift that makes Miss Fannie Brice an international laughing success." The review praised her dedication and continued: "The young comedienne really studies comedy effects and the few books she carries with her on the road are devoted to studies of clowns, comedians and mirthmakers. She also has a scrapbook filled with criticisms of famous comedies and comedians."[69]

Such comments sound as specious as other examples of skillful press agentry and its creations: Brice the Brooklyn newsgirl and Brice the serious observer of Ghetto types on the Lower East Side. They suggest that she still wanted to legitimize her work by emphasizing how seriously she prepared for her performances. In addition, she may have been trying to change the public's perception of her as primarily a Yiddish dialect comedienne. Aiming at a broader audience, she has left her immigrant subjects behind and has become a student of comedy itself. The same desire to escape from ethnicity may have led her to straighten her nose in her publicity shots.

Brice's obvious talent won her a contract with the United Booking Office, the conglomerate created in the early 1900s by vaudeville magnates B. F. Keith and E. F. Albee in partnership with other powerful theatre owners. Ostensibly designed to limit competition within the industry and to reduce the chaos of booking thousands of acts across the country, the UBO under Keith and Albee's dictatorial management soon became a monopoly, jealously protecting its customer circuits and contracted performers.[70] However ruthless the organization could be, a UBO contract ensured each recipient steady engagements in better vaudeville theatres throughout the United States.

Brice worked until the end of June at UBO houses in various northeastern and midwestern cities. Available reviews indicate that she headlined and that audiences were very pleased with her performances. Critics praised her unmistakable artistry and irrepressible comic flair. As *Variety* put it, commenting on her May appearance at New York's Colonial Theatre, she succeeded admirably in "facial expression, gesture making and doing nut stuff."[71] At this point in her career, however, she seems to have confined her "nut stuff" to the stage. Publicity shots for the UBO tour present a very different image. They show her standing in a ladylike pose. Her hair is neatly styled and she wears an elegant evening gown. She gazes out at the camera pensively, seriously, without the suggestion of a leer. Yet, this time at least, there has been no attempt to retouch the pictures. Unlike the "false Fanny" who appeared several months earlier, these photographs are unmistakably Brice. Whatever the reason—whether the earlier campaign produced a negative response, or whether Brice, buoyed by favorable reviews and UBO bookings, had the confidence to be herself—she abandoned the spurious shots.

After a triumphant vaudeville debut in Boston (the *Globe* called her "one of those rare comediennes who knows how to be genuinely funny every instant"), Brice returned to New York for appearances at the Palace and Hammerstein's Roof. Although she received generally favorable notices for both engagements, *Variety* was more critical than the other theatrical newspapers. Acknowledging that her eighteen-minute Palace act "corralled a lot of applause," *Variety* tempered its praise with the suggestion that she stop billing herself as a "late star of *Follies of 1912*" [sic] because that line was "too antedated to use any longer."[72] Ignoring the cavil, she kept the Ziegfeld label at Hammerstein's, where her performance inspired *Variety*'s laconic observation that "Fannie Brice can thank her stars the Roof was enclosed."[73] The implication was clearly that, had it been open, she would have been inaudible.

The *Clipper* reported that Brice was scheduled to play three more vaudeville engagements in July and August: Morrison's, Rockaway Beach (July 13–18), the New Brighton, Brighton Beach (July 20–25), and Shea's, Toronto (August 3–8). In the paper's review of the New Brighton show, however, Brice was not among the performers listed and there is no evidence that she appeared in either of the other two bills. According to *Variety*, there was a good explanation for her absence: she had decided on another European tour. In its July 17 issue, *Variety* announced that she would sail for England on the *Aquitania*, leaving New York on the twenty-first.[74]

This trip would be very different from the one she had enjoyed the previous year. On July 28, exactly one month after Austrian archduke Francis Ferdinand and his morganatic wife, Sophie, duchess of Hohenberg, were assassinated by a Serbian nationalist, Austria-Hungary declared war against Serbia. Two days later, Russia ordered general mobilization against Austria-Hungary. On August 1, Germany declared war against Russia and, on August 3, against France. On August 4, after German forces invaded Belgium, Great Britain declared war against Germany. By the end of the month the conflicts had erupted into World War I, sweeping across Europe and into Japan. As early as August 7, under the headline "American Players Abroad Held There by the Battle," *Variety* printed an admittedly incomplete list of American performers trapped in the war zone. Brice's name was not included, but it did appear in a *Clipper* article the following week. According to that paper, Americans were "in distress from Moscow to Paris," even "in London itself" and Brice was among the acts the UBO planned to help "as far as needed." It is uncertain when or how she returned to the United States. *Variety* reported that many "show people" sailed in steerage on the *Adriatic*, due in New York on August 28 or 30. Brice, however, must have managed to book an earlier passage because on August 31 she began a week's engagement at Brooklyn's Orpheum Theatre.[75]

Whether it can be attributed to bad timing, bad judgment, or bad luck, Brice's second transatlantic crossing marked the beginning of an increasingly unsuccessful season for her. It started well enough with four solid weeks in New York at the Orpheum, Colonial, Bushwick (Brooklyn), and Alhambra. Although not the headliner, she was warmly received by critics and audiences. The *Clipper* responded favorably both to her "mannerisms" and her material, noting that she sang five songs well. At least one of them was new. According to the *Brooklyn Eagle*, her last number was "one glorifying President Wilson" and the timely selection was "a decided hit."[76]

"We Take Our Hats Off to You, Mr. Wilson" was one of the many patriotic songs produced during World War I. Although it never became as popular as "Over There," sung most successfully by Nora Bayes, "Mr.

Wilson" was a sprightly mixture of chauvinism and sentimentality. It made
the appropriate references to Uncle Sammy, Yankee hearts, Washington,
Lincoln, and the American flag. Wilson, the world's "big mediator," is
"greater than a gladiator." He is the "right kind of man in the right kind
of place," steering "the greatest land on earth. . . . At home and abroad,"
people know that his "pen is greater than the sword." A paean in march
tempo to the President and his commitment to peace, "Mr. Wilson" was
an audience favorite and remained in Brice's repertoire for the 1914–15
season. More significant than the song itself, however, is the fact that
it was the first composition she performed by Blanche Merrill, a young
songwriter who would soon have a profound influence on her career.[77]

That career was about to take a downturn. Brice was scheduled to
play the Palace again from September 28 to October 3. She appeared
in the Monday matinee but left, according to *Variety*, "after a cold grabbed
her."[78] There was more to the story, however, as *Variety*'s next issue indicated. Under the heading "Fannie Brice's Escape," the paper reported
that Brice had come very close to losing her UBO route when an ad she
placed in a local newspaper caused a furor in the Jewish community. An
"overzealous advertising solicitor" had "induced her to part with $1000
for publicity":

> He then gave a comparatively small space in his paper to advertise that
> she would appear at the Palace all last week, including Yom Kippur, the most
> holy of the Hebrew reverences.
> Several Jewish societies wrote, protesting against the wording of the adver-
> tisement and the United Booking Office men are reported to have taken Miss
> Brice's name off their sheets for the affront.[79]

It is unclear whether "the affront" was the Yom Kippur performance
itself or Brice's brazen announcement that she intended to ignore the religious holiday and appear onstage as usual. Her motives for placing the
ad are equally obscure. It is possible that she did so because she no longer
wanted to be classified as a Jewish comedienne specializing in Yiddish
dialect comedy. She may have hoped that her outrageous statement would
win her a greater following as a comedienne unlimited by ties to any particular ethnic group. She may have run the ad as a publicity stunt, in which
case it was simply a bad joke that backfired. If so, Brice went too far
for a laugh. Under the stringent code of the Keith-Albee empire, vaudeville
performers were often penalized for seemingly minor infractions. Losing
one's route or having it changed to one of the so-called "death trails"
was not uncommon, for pleasing the audience was paramount. By announc-

ing that she would be seen at the Palace "twice daily, including Yom Kippur," Brice had offended too many patrons and her abrupt exit from the bill was probably not on account of poor health.

The controversy must have ended quickly because Brice was back on the circuit the following week, appearing at Poli's in Scranton and, after that, at New York's Royal Theatre. From October 19 to 24, she returned to the Palace where, presumably, she avoided controversial advertisements. This time, however, she had a different problem. She was not very good. The reviews indicated that she was "handicapped by wretched songs" and a monotonous presentation.

Brice still relied on clowning to carry her and compensate for mediocre material, but her routines had come to seem increasingly one-dimensional because she kept playing the same part. She regularly appeared as an eccentric ingenue, the persona she had created with "Lovie Joe" and sustained, with only slight variations, through countless numbers. In doing what the *Dramatic Mirror* called her "ingenuish specialty," she became a goofy, gawky girl whose grotesque grimaces, awkward gestures, and "loose-jointed" movements delighted audiences and brought her recognition as a "character comedienne." Yet, whether she sang about Joe or Mose, in coon or Yiddish dialect, it was her only fully developed character and it was really just a cartoon version of herself, funny as well as funny-looking. Now, audiences were beginning to tire of the characterization. The material was getting stale; the "vein of comedy" growing thin. These were serious problems for any performer and they would plague Brice throughout the year.

She had no bookings for the next four weeks and there are clear indications that this was a very difficult time for her. Her vaudeville salary was cut twice, as she told a *Variety* reporter after appearing in an act at the Winter Garden with brother Lew. Teaming with Lew in itself was unusual and suggests that, in her desperate search for better material, Brice may have even turned to a brother-sister routine as a new gimmick. Although she said she "balked at the second clipping," she was unable to do anything about it.[80] Rather than accept it, she decided to retire. According to the account given by one New York newspaper, she planned to leave show business and open a "millinery establishment" on Fifth Avenue.[81]

Was the announced retirement another publicity stunt? Was Brice's intention to unleash such a public outcry that the UBO would boost her salary once again? She never offered an explanation and no other newspaper carried the report so that it is impossible to determine its authenticity. Yet the very fact that the article used those terms suggests that she was discouraged and that she had lost whatever "star status" she had achieved. Another indication of such a diminution is the way *Theatre Magazine* described her in a piece called "Browsing for Vaudeville Talent." There was no reference to her as a great comedienne in the *Ziegfeld Follies* or as a vaudeville headliner. Instead, she was simply "happy Fannie Brice, the coon singer," recently discovered "singing in the streets . . . on the east side" by a vaudeville scout.[82]

Brice must have used the four week hiatus well, for her next appearances received more favorable reviews. After a week at Keith's in Louisville (November 23–28) where she was an "instant favorite," she returned to the Colonial.[83] There *Variety* noted that she used some new songs, among them a "Yiddish number in which a stage hand figured" called "Such a Suit." The *Dramatic Mirror* thought it was effective as a "new bit of comedy" and observed:

> With a stage hand in a baggy suit of second hand clothing posing as a customer, Miss Brice gives a travesty of a Jewish old clothes man. It is amusing —and characteristic—with its refrain—
>
> "Put it on—take it off,
> Wrap it up—take it home."[84]

Brice had obviously decided not to abandon dialect comedy and turned to a familiar stereotype. Although the character and the accent would have suited her, such an impersonation did not show much imagination or taste. Long a fixture on the vaudeville stage, the Jewish peddler by 1914 seemed old-fashioned and increasingly offensive. Moreover, the *Dramatic Mirror* still found her monotonous. Acknowledging that she was trying to vary her songs, the paper insisted that there was still "too much of the familiar ingenue specialty."

Brice saw 1914 out with appearances in Brooklyn and Washington, D.C., to encouraging reviews. And 1915 began auspiciously with a successful engagement at the Harlem Alhambra. There, according to the *New York Star*'s "Weekly Laugh Bulletin," Brice received a "good" reception, including "good" applause and nineteen laughs. She played for eighteen minutes, pleased the audiences with a "new Yiddish song," and finished "fine."[85]

In its January 9 issue, *Variety* reported that Brice was trying out with the William Fox Picture Company for comedy films.[86] Although vaudeville was still the nation's most popular—and profitable—entertainment form, movie-making was emerging as a viable industry in its own right, providing potentially lucrative opportunities for aspiring talent. By 1915, the movie business had attracted such outstanding directors as D. W. Griffith and Mack Sennett and had produced its first stars: "Little Mary" Pickford, "the little tramp" Charlie Chaplin, coy comedienne Mabel Normand, and sultry siren Theda Bara. Given her recent disappointments on stage, Brice must have decided to try a different field where she might find greater success. The screen test went poorly, however, and she would not appear in a film until 1928.

She continued in vaudeville, playing in Brooklyn, Pittsburgh, and Baltimore. After returning to New York, she opened at the Palace on February 1. It was a dismal performance. Although the *Clipper* found her "without a superior in her line," *Variety* and the *Dramatic Mirror* reacted very differently. *Variety* stated that she worked "in a manner that seemed to be only for the first few rows," implying that she was inaudible, and considered her first two numbers ("Show a Little Love" and "'S Too High") "too old for the Palace." Of the two new songs, "Mosha from Nova Scotia" and "By Heck," the first "got over because it was done by Brice"; the second was "a flop as she forgot the lyrics." In *Variety*'s opinion, it was only by means of "her foolery" that she "won out."[87]

Brice's new songs were terrible. "By Heck," a "rube" number about a yokel who comes to the big city to sell his cow, was an especially poor choice. It is not surprising that Brice forgot the lyrics; they are inane and repetitious, liberally sprinkled with quaint expletives. As old Uncle Josh reacts to the new sights and sounds around him, he exclaims "By Heck," "By Gosh," "By Gum," "Wow," and wishes he had put a "half-dollar" in his "jeans."[88] "Mosha from Nova Scotia" was not much better, although it would seem to have been perfect for her. It was obviously meant to be sung in dialect because it was the saga of Moses Cohen, the "kosher kid from Nova Scotia." This "Jewish Eskimo" goes to dances every night at Snowball Hall and is so charming he has won Becky Klein away from Max (who has been sent to Halifax). Like so many of her more successful dialect songs, "Mosha" mixes ethnic jokes with innuendoes but does not do it very cleverly. (For example, Mosha goes out fishing practically every morning and catches "mostly eel," because he "always keeps his hands in his pockets.")[89] The song may have been written for Brice, but she should have sensed that, with its unpleasant melody and unfunny lyrics, she would have had a hard time doing it well.

Brice now virtually disappeared from the newspapers. There were no articles about her, no interviews, no mention of her in news of society or the stage. She did not even surface in the gossip columns or the advertisements, with the exception of two ads which appeared at the end of December 1914. One, in the December 16 *Dramatic Mirror*, read: "Fannie Brice in Vaudeville, Direction, Max Hart." The other, in *Variety*'s Christmas issue, conveyed greetings from "Fanny Brice, Direction Max Hart."[90] Hart was a New York agent and it is unclear exactly when she engaged his services. It may have been sometime in November, during her contract dispute. Early in 1915, however, Hart was not doing much to advance her career. To find information about her, one has to really search, and then it is usually just a line or two in a newspaper review of a vaudeville appearance.

Billed as "the Funniest Girl on the Stage" and still linked with the *Follies*, Brice toured in vaudeville throughout the spring of 1915. Some critics expressed surprise that she was still singing the same songs as at her last appearance in their cities, but none criticized her as harshly as *Variety* and the *Dramatic Mirror*. Most reacted favorably to her act, although their comments indicated that she was in a creative rut. Some, in fact, damned her unwittingly through their praise. For example, the critic for the *Detroit News* stated categorically that "any variety program" which included "the name of Fanny Brice among its performers" was "far from a failure" and continued:

> There aren't many women in vaudeville as successful as Miss Brice. Her act from year to year differs little. There is always the eccentric dancing, the badinage with the director, the comic songs. All of these things she does this year and does all of them funnier than ever before.[91]

To a certain extent, every vaudeville performer perfected an act and then made a career out of doing it at different stops along his route. Yet that act needed variety. A performer might present the same persona each time, but could not go on telling the same jokes or singing the same songs year after year. As Sophie Tucker put it in her autobiography, *Some of These Days*, "Show business is constantly changing and to stay with it, you have to change with it. . . . Something new is what counted with audiences."[92] Brice was still relying on familiar material and a predictable presentation. Ironically, when she did select "something new," it was often totally wrong for her. She had extremely poor judgment about what would work well and was unable to distinguish between effective comedy and what she later labeled as "mediocre clowning." Without any clear comic method or a sense of her own strengths as a performer, increasingly distracted by her personal problems with the incorrigible Arnstein, Brice at twenty-three was floundering.

Following her New Orleans engagement, Brice was supposed to continue her tour and appear in Atlanta. Instead, she went into rehearsal for a new musical revue called *Hands Up*, scheduled to preview in New Haven on June 3 and to open in New York four days later. A Shubert production conceived by Lew Fields, *Hands Up* was to star Fields and the dancers Maurice Mouvet and Florence Walton, a team whose popularity was second only to the Castles' during America's dance mania. Among the thirteen cast members listed as "supporting the stars" were Brice, her brother Lew, and dialect comedian Bobby North.[93] The show played in New Haven June 7–9 and was supposed to move on to New York the next day. It did not, and the numerous postponements announced by the trade papers suggested that the production was in trouble. On June 14, *Hands Up* did open in New York, but in Albany, not Manhattan. The *Clipper* reported that producers Lee and J. J. Shubert came up to see a preview and, greatly displeased, decided the show had to be "entirely rewritten" because it was "not in shape for a New York presentation."[94]

Hands Up finally arrived in New York City on July 22, after weeks of rehearsals, several postponements, and many cast changes. Lew Fields was among the casualties; so was Fanny Brice. The only explanation for her being dropped appeared in the June 25 *Variety* which noted that the "reorganized" show did not include "Fanny and Lew Brice and Bobby North," whose places were "to be refilled." According to *Variety*, each used a "Hebrew accent" and sounded so similar onstage that audiences at the out-of-town tryouts became confused.[95] None of the other trade papers commented on the incident and as Brice herself never mentioned *Hands Up* in her reminiscences, it is impossible to reconstruct either her part in the show or the decision to let her go.

The last two weeks of June must have been deeply troubling for her. In addition to losing *Hands Up*, she also lost Arnstein, sentenced to two years in Sing Sing on June 28. Working must have been difficult and it is not surprising that she practically disappeared from view. *Variety* did not mention her at all until September. The *Clipper* listed her as making three vaudeville appearances, one in July and two in August, but reviews of those shows indicate that she did not take part in them.[96] In its July 7 edition, the *Dramatic Mirror* ran a photograph of a pensive Brice with the caption, "The Comedienne Will Soon Be Seen in the Beach Theaters" and announced under "Vaudeville Gossip" that she would be at the Palace from July 12 to 17.[97] None of these engagements materialized and, during the summer, only three other items about Brice appeared. They were, however, particularly significant. On July 21, the *Dramatic Mirror* reported that songwriter Blanche Merrill was "writing an act for Fannie Brice"; on August 11, it referred to Brice as one of several performers actively seeking new vaudeville material; and on August 18, it stated that Brice would bring her new act "with special songs by Blanche Merrill" to the Palace on September 6.[98]

Brice's collaboration with Blanche Merrill marked a turning point in her career and the beginning of a productive professional relationship. During their long association, Merrill created some of Brice's most distinctive material and freed her from the problem that had always plagued her: finding songs that really suited her. At last, with someone who could supply her with those songs, Brice could develop into the character comedienne she had promised to be with "Sadie Salome." Although she could not have known then what an important influence Merrill would have on her life, Brice made a wise decision in seeking her help. Desperate for a new act, she had already performed one of Merrill's songs, "We Take Our Hats Off to You, Mr. Wilson," fairly successfully. As one of the few women working as a professional songwriter, moreover, Merrill had already established a reputation as someone who catered to individual performers— particularly women.

Reminiscing in 1925 about their work together, Brice described Merrill as "a song modiste who builds to fit her customers." By 1915, they included well known vaudeville singers Rita Boland, Stella Mayhew, Rae Samuels, Lillian Shaw, and stellar Eva Tanguay. It was Tanguay, actually, who brought Merrill her billing as the "Star Writer." According to Brice's account, Merrill was still in school when she saw Tanguay in vaudeville and "went home and wrote a song she thought would fit her."[99] The song was "Give an Imitation of Me" (1910) which Merrill mailed and Tanguay accepted, launching the fifteen-year-old songwriter on her career. "Before I realized where I was headed for," Merrill recalled in a 1917 interview, "I was writing all Miss Tanguay's songs." Work for other vaudeville performers soon followed. The same article reported that within "two or three years, she was not only writing songs—words and melody both— for all the headliners but she was getting up entire novelty acts for them."[100] Another interviewer later that year called her "a sort of efficiency expert in songwriting" and described her method as being "based on careful observation of each performer." She studied each client's "personality," as well as her "range" on the stage, before creating the appropriate vehicle.[101]

The reviews soon confirmed that Merrill, who left teacher training school in New York to become a songwriter, had done her homework well. Brice presented her new act at the Palace on September 6 and, in contrast to her February debacle, was enthusiastically received. The *Clipper* reported that her "new songs and stories went over big." The *Dramatic Mirror* congratulated her for dropping her "old eccentric ingenuish specialty" and "invading new comedy fields." "She is working with more humorous delicacy and less low-comedy buffoonery," editor Smith noted approvingly. "Her work shows that she can think for herself."[102]

Variety's Jolo agreed with his colleagues, declaring her fifteen minutes of "songs, dancing and patter" a resounding success. He considered "The Hat" Merrill's "cleverest" creation and especially enjoyed the second verse in which Brice posed as a Jewish mother praising her infant prodigy. His favorite number, though, was "Becky Is Back in the Ballet." Jolo loved Brice's "ludicrous impersonation of a ballet dancer graduated from Hester St. or that neighborhood." He noted that she wore a short "ballerini skirt" with "pink fleshings" and tried "some toe pirouettes with disastrous results." In his opinion, it was "by far her strongest bit." The first song Brice could act since "Sadie Salome," "Becky" quickly became a staple of her repertoire.[103]

Brice had an effective vaudeville act once again but, after a week at New York's Colonial Theatre, had no bookings. There were no listings for her in the *Clipper* or the *Dramatic Mirror*. *Variety* did not mention her until October when she turned up in Philadelphia in the production from which she had been fired in June: *Hands Up*. In spite of the Shuberts' best efforts, the revue had received mixed notices. The critical consensus was that Irene Franklin, who had been brought in relatively late in the rehearsal period, saved the show. A popular vaudeville singer known for her fiery red hair and feisty characterizations, Franklin was making her acting debut in *Hands Up*. *Variety* praised her lavishly and contrasted her performance with that of Maurice and Walton, the purported stars. According to Sime, Maurice and Walton could "dance in several styles" but were terrible actors and singers who looked even worse next to the talented Franklin.

Such unflattering comparisons only exacerbated the "internal differences" between Maurice and Walton, on the one hand, and Franklin and Green, her accompanist-husband, on the other. After *Hands Up* closed in New York on September 4, it began a tour, but was rumored to suffer from "constant battling" between Franklin and Walton. When the show opened in Philadelphia on Monday, October 11, *Variety* reported that

Franklin refused to go on. After negotiating for an hour, she agreed to remain with the company for another week. She fainted during the performance, however, and left the cast.[104]

Although *Variety* never mentioned Brice in its coverage of the show, she stepped in as Franklin's replacement, beginning with the Tuesday evening performance. The *Dramatic Mirror*'s Philadelphia correspondent announced that she was "taking the part as best she can. Her gowns are new, her songs took and to make a long story short, Fanny has become the hit of the show."[105] Nevertheless, in spite of her efforts, "the musico-comico-filmo-melo-drama" closed less than two weeks later on October 23. *Variety* explained that "the punch" departed with Franklin and resulted in such disappointing business that the tour could not continue.

Brice's performance brought her little acclaim, but won her a job in another touring production, *Noboby Home*. A musical comedy by Guy Bolton and Paul Rubens with music by Jerome Kern, *Nobody Home* had opened on April 20 in New York where it was considered one of the more enjoyable shows of the season. The *Dramatic Mirror* praised the "delightful musical numbers," the "artistic" sets and costumes, and the performances by principals and chorus alike.[106] These more than compensated for the ludicrous book, which chronicled the adventures of a visiting Englishman in America. Frederick ("Freddy") Popple has come to see his brother, a professional dancer, and is dismayed to find that the hotel in which he planned to stay is too full to accommodate him. According to a program note for the show, Popple is "wondering what to do" when Miss Tony Miller, "a Winter Garden prima donna," graciously offers him the use of her apartment on Central Park West. "Then the complications start and last through two acts of splendid singing, real comedy and most fascinating dancing."[107]

The *Dramatic Mirror* applauded Lawrence Grossmith in the "silly ass" role of Freddy Popple and Adele Rowland as Tony Miller. They remained in the cast after *Nobody Home* concluded its successful New York engagement and went on to Boston where it played from August 28 until October 30, then moved to Washington, D.C. for the week of November 1–6. The next stop on the tour was Baltimore where the *Dramatic Mirror* informed its readers that "Fanny Brice has taken the Adele Rowland part."[108] Brice played Tony Miller in Pittsburgh, Cleveland, and Chicago until she left the company on December 29.

Although she was in the show for only seven and a half weeks, *Nobody Home* was significant in her career because it was her first relatively straight, as opposed to broadly comic, role. A publicity shot of her for the tour is appropriately serious, almost somber. Brice takes her characteristic pensive pose, head cocked slightly back, eyes gazing off in the distance. She wears a broad-brimmed hat and a sophisticated dark outfit with a plunging neckline that sets off her luminous white skin. She has a glossy fur draped artfully over her shoulders, giving her an air of studied elegance. She looks refined, remote, and much older than twenty-four—perfect for a Winter Garden prima donna.

Her performance received mixed reviews. Of her appearance in Baltimore, the *Dramatic Mirror*'s critic had no comment except to say that Adele Rowland was "greatly missed." The *Baltimore Sun*, however, found her very pleasing, declaring that Brice as Tony Miller was "in a class wholly by herself and quite able to keep any audience sitting up and taking notice whenever her magnetic smile beams upon the stage." The *Pittsburgh Leader* was equally kind. Its reviewer called Brice "inimitable," insisted that her "unique methods, her natural drollery and her personality" always made her one of the most popular entertainers in Pittsburgh, and asserted that she delighted the audience "every second she was on the stage." Yet according to the *Chicago Tribune*'s Percy Hammond, that "natural drollery" made her inappropriate for the part. Although he acknowledged her efforts to subdue "her comic eccentricities of expression and locomotion," he thought she was "scarcely the romantic figure called for by those who take their musical comedy plots seriously."[109] He did, however, admire her singing and felt that she had performed two songs, "Any Old Night" and "The Magic Melody," very effectively. Sheet music for both numbers indicates that she could have handled them nicely. Although they were far more melodic than some of the other songs she had recently done, they were well within her vocal range. Both required the kind of warmth she could readily project, but would not have given her much room for comedy. Certainly, neither was anything like "Becky."[110]

Was Brice uncomfortable in her role as Tony Miller? Did she decide to leave the show on account of the tepid critical response she received? She made no public statements in 1915 and never discussed the show in her reminiscences, so one can only guess as to why she abruptly quit the company in mid-week. *Variety* reported that she "handed in her notice" on December 29; the *Clipper* announced that "she would shortly make her return to vaudeville."[111] It is possible that she received a more lucrative vaudeville contract and dropped out of *Nobody Home* simply on account of salary, always an important consideration for her. Or she may have decided that, having started moving in the right direction with her new vaudeville act, she ought to continue with it before trying something different.

Whatever her reasons, Brice returned to the Palace on February 7, 1916, and as the *Clipper* put it, "walked away with the show."[112] The *Dramatic Mirror* asserted that "Fannie Brice, who seemed a season ago to have slipped into a rut, has safely rehabilitated herself."[113] She performed two old songs, "The Hat" and "Becky," which *Variety*'s Sime found even more pronounced as a burlesque because interpretive dancer Ruth St. Denis had appeared at the Palace the previous week. She also had two new ones, "When Priscilla Hits High C" about an aspiring opera singer, and "The Yiddish Bride."

Brice opened her sixteen-minute act with "Priscilla," the number Sime thought least effective and, significantly, the only one not written by Blanche Merrill. He considered "The Yiddish Bride" a "gem" and loved the way Brice, "costumed in bridal outfit and holding flowers," soliloquized "lyrically and melodiously" about her chances of getting married. All the songs had a "Yiddish tinge" and appropriate physical "business." Combined with her "apt delivery" and "highly cultivated sense of stage humor," they put her "right to the front" as a "real singing comedienne."[114] On a negative note, however, Sime disapproved of the banter Brice exchanged with the audience at the conclusion of her performance. She approached the footlights and shouted over the tumultuous applause, "I ain't got no more material. What do you want of my young Jewish life?"— lines that did nothing to enhance her act. He also objected to the Palace program's calling her "the funniest woman in vaudeville," a title he believed she did not yet deserve.

At the end of February, Brice left New York on an Orpheum Circuit tour which took her to Omaha, Kansas City, Calgary, Seattle, Portland, San Francisco, Sacramento, Stockton, and Fresno. Sime's criticism may have had nothing to do with it but, on the tour, she was more modestly billed as "Fannie Brice, the well known comedienne, in character songs and creations." West Coast audiences enjoyed her as much as those in the East had. The *San Francisco Examiner* observed, "She sings and acts in her own distinctive way, her pleasant personal peculiarities dominating everything she does," and reported that the audience would have liked to have kept her on stage for "two hours instead of twenty minutes."[115]

With Blanche Merrill's help, Brice had rediscovered "her own distinctive way." She had returned to the kind of song she did so well and was beginning to build her repertoire of unique comic characterizations. Relieved of the constant pressure to find appropriate material, she could concentrate on performing the wonderful songs Merrill created for her, refining her natural instincts into a more polished and deliberate comic style. Increasingly comfortable as a comedienne, confident of her ability to succeed on stage, she would finally develop the technique she needed to serve her talent and make her artistry seem effortless. At twenty-five, she would be a Ziegfeld star once again and would enjoy even greater acclaim than she had in 1910.

"A Cartoonist Working
in the Flesh":
The *Ziegfeld Follies of
1916* and *1917*

In point of subtlety and genuine humor as well as artistic merit, nothing could have surpassed the finished performance of Fanny Brice. Every word, every gesture is perfect and it is doubtful if anyone can equal her in her Jewish types.

–The BALTIMORE SUN, 27 March 1917[1]

There is good taste in humor like there is good taste in clothes or furniture. It is okay for one Irishman to call another Irishman anything, any kind of name. But if you are not an Irishman, keep the mouth shut. The same with all people.

–FANNY BRICE[2]

5.

The May 5, 1916, *Variety* contained two items about Fanny Brice. One of them noted that she would be finishing her Orpheum Circuit route in Fresno, California, the following day "to return east for a production engagement."[3] The other identified that engagement as none other than the tenth anniversary edition of the *Ziegfeld Follies*, a booking which would explain Brice's abrupt termination of a successful vaudeville tour. The details of that contract are unclear, although the *New York Telegraph* related the following canard:

In negotiating for Fannie Brice's services for next season's *Follies*, Florenz Ziegfeld, Jr. sent her a telegram in which he offered her two hundred dollars a week. He received this telegram in reply:

"Fannie Brice found dead in her room in the hotel. The only clue is a telegram, signed by Florenz Ziegfeld, Jr. which was clutched in her hand."[4]

Brice must have been delighted at the prospect of returning to the *Follies*. As she put it in *Cosmopolitan*, after the years of "marking time," it was "back to the fierce undertone of the greatest city on earth; back once more under the symphony of light over Manhattan called the Great White Way. Best of all, back in the old jeweled setting of a *Ziegfeld Follies*."[5] According to her rhapsodic recollections:

> Look—look at the comet in the sky! Some pieces of its tail have dropped down over the roaring Forties. Tonight's the opening night of the *Follies*, and ticket speculators are asking—and getting—seventy-five dollars a seat.
>
> High-powered imported cars, broughams, hansom cabs in one grand crush. The foyer seethes in a cauldron of excitement. Backstage is vibrating like an enormous dynamo. Everyone is drunk with the spirit of the moment! . . .
>
> Electricians adjust lights. The girls are grouped in the flies.
>
> The orchestra bursts into the overture. The curtain rises. Here they come, the girls all walking like a salute, and another deluxe edition of the *Follies* is in circulation.[6]

The *Ziegfeld Follies of 1916* opened on June 6 in Atlantic City. *Billboard* echoed Brice in its enthusiastic appreciation of the "gorgeous, indescribably kaleidoscopic revue" and the excitement it generated in the "big first-night audience." E. Edmund Foster, the newspaper's man in Atlantic City, admired Ned Wayburn's staging, Joseph Urban's "exquisite settings," George V. Hobart and Gene Buck's book and lyrics, and the "bright, tuneful songs" by Louis Hirsch, Jerome Kern, and Dave Stamper. The "dazzling array of pulchritude" on view for two acts and twenty-one scenes convinced the correspondent that Ziegfeld had "out-Ziegfelded Ziegfeld," making it impossible for him to single out one cast member as the star, since all excelled in their particular specialties.[7] He did, however, praise several by name, among them Fanny Brice. According to Foster, she had "a great deal to do in the production for which the audience was glad."

When the opulent show opened at New York's New Amsterdam Theatre on June 12, the critical consensus was that Fanny Brice dominated the second and stronger act. Under the headline "The 1916 *Follies* full of splendor," the *New York Times* declared that Brice, along with Ina Claire, won "the First Honors in a sumptuous revue." Although the paper mistakenly identified Brice as a "newcomer to the *Follies*"—revealing how quickly

her earlier success had been forgotten—it praised her "uproariously amusing" character songs.[8] According to *Variety*'s Sime, she was one of "the
personalities to stand out" (along with Claire, Bernard Granville, Ann
Pennington, Carl Randall, and Frances White) and the second act gave
her "almost a clear field" for her "funnyisms." In Sime's view, "she caught
the house from her first entrance of the evening" with a song about Nijinsky, the brilliant Russian dancer, and "later walked off with the comedy
hit of the show while singing two songs in one, 'The Hat' and 'The Dying
Swan.'"[9] The *New York Herald* reported that "her songs and impersonations
set the audience roaring" to such an extent that "it almost spoiled the
act of the sensational slack wire dancer, Miss Bird Millman, who followed."[10] The *New York Clipper* observed that not only had this "clever
comedienne" captured "the lion's share of the laughter," but that she had
never been funnier.[11]

Like its predecessors, the *Ziegfeld Follies of 1916* was an elaborate musical revue in which visual spectacle took precedence over thematic unity.
The *New York Times* stated that it was a revue "in the sense that it pilfer[ed]
its music from everywhere" and, more important, because it dealt "gently
with the passing show, making use for its material of such more or less
time-honored, familiar and varied institutions as Preparedness, George M.
Cohan, the Shakespeare Tercentenary, Billie Burke and the Russian Ballet."[12] The key word in this description is "gently." Like the lovely stage
pictures it created, the show's spoofs were intended to delight, not debunk,
to amuse rather than offend. Serious satire was as alien as discordant notes
or clashing colors. It was, after all, the *Follies*, not the Vices, *of 1916*
and the mood was jovial, not juvenalian. Topics could be timely, but should
be innocuous and always entertaining.

The *Follies* opened with a series of Shakespearean travesties in honor
of the three hundredth anniversary of the playwright's death. Brice did
not appear in these scenes, about which the *Times* sniffed, "the less said
the better." Nor did she take part in the "Somnambulistic Melody" number where white-clad "Sparkling Girls" danced in semidarkness as sparks
of electricity came from their shoes. She was absent from the stage until
Act II, when she quickly took over as "the real funmaker of the evening."[13]
The act began with an elaborate scene called "The Blushing Ballet,"
which parodied the most famous male dancer of the time, Vaslav Nijinsky.
Then in America as the star of Diaghilev's Ballets Russes, Nijinsky had
opened with the troupe at the Metropolitan Opera on April 12. The tremendous publicity surrounding his appearances, coupled with the disappointment many New York critics expressed about the company's reper-

toire, made him appropriate material for a *Follies* spoof. Like the celebrated Russian ballerina Anna Pavlova, who had already made several appearances on the vaudeville stage, Nijinsky was someone with whom more than just balletomanes were familiar.

As staged by Ned Wayburn, and characteristic of his style, several specialty acts burlesqued works and roles associated with Nijinsky. The scene began with Emma Haig and the "'Sylphides' Girls" dancing a *Follies* version of *Les Sylphides*, the work which traditionally opened the Ballets Russes' programs. It was followed by "A Suggestion of 'Le Spectre de la Rose'" with Carl Randall, a talented dancer, as Nijinsky. Next came a satire on *Scheherazade*. The work which had dazzled Paris in its 1910 premiere at the Opera had not pleased New York audiences in 1916. The *Follies* version presented a comic quintet: Sam B. Hardy as the Sultan, eccentric dancer Don Barclay as Zobeide (the female lead), Norman Blume as the Eunuch, W. C. Fields as O. Shaw (a pun on "bashaw" or "pasha" as well as the old-fashioned colloquialism, "Oh, Pshaw!"), and Bert Williams in Nijinsky's role of "Le Nègre," the Golden Slave. Without a script, it is difficult to discuss the *Follies* scene, but it probably included burlesques of Nijinsky's astounding leaps and banter about the ballet's harem setting.[14]

"And then," as the *Times* put it, "Fannie Brice takes a whack at him with an unblushing song that makes capital out of certain inescapable mannerisms."[15] In the original, Nijinsky flew to Zobeide's couch in a single leap and became the center of an orgiastic dance with the Sultan's harem. Brice entered wearing a costume reminiscent of Nijinsky's in the original, except that she substituted an absurd conical hat for his close-fitting bandanna. Instead of seeming exotic, as he had, she looked funny and undoubtedly made the audience laugh before she opened her mouth. When she did, it was to sing Gene Buck and Dave Stamper's "Nijinsky," a number the *Brooklyn Citizen* found "screamingly funny" and the *New York Press* called a "clever burlesque." The lyrics themselves, however, are not really satirical. They make statements about the enigmatic star which are factual and, in themselves, not particularly humorous. For example:

> There's a dancing man, who at prancing can, outdo any man today
> He's a guiding star, owns a motor car, pals with the Czar they say.
> His gymnastical style, beats the Castles a mile
> His fantastical smile, has won my heart away.[16]

The song continues with "ski" suffixes—a technique commonly used by vaudeville's "Jew comics"—russianizing references to Nijinsky's other attributes. He "leaps right upski in the air," he is a "bearski beyond compareski," "his Russian styleski is so rare." It concludes with the singer's confession that "his ballet wayski's won [her] love." She is "goneski" when he does the "Faunski" because "he's airy like and fairy like and very like a Dove."

These lyrics are not clever, witty, biting, or acerbic. There is nothing inherently critical or judgmental about them, but they are comical because the "ski" endings sound so silly. In combination with the Yiddish accent Brice assuredly used, they served as an effective means of mocking Nijinsky and minimizing his achievements. Although none of the reviews mentioned it specifically, dialect was Brice's signature in 1916 and a sure way of getting a laugh. A Yiddish accent was certainly not associated with the star of the Ballets Russes and the incongruity would have contributed substantially to the comedy. In "Nijinsky" as in "Sadie Salome," it was the disjunction between the audience's expectations and what they actually heard that helped make the song so funny.

Brice's actions were even more ludicrous than her accent. According to *Variety*, she "made" the song with "her mugging and gestures."[17] Her actions turned "Nijinsky" into a parody because they were so different from the behavior the lyrics described. Brice undoubtedly appeared as a character totally unlike the real Nijinsky. Instead of his grace and "gymnastical style," she was clumsy and uncoordinated. Where he could leap to astonishing heights and seemed almost to hang in the air, she must have remained rooted to the ground. Her attempts to soar as he did probably produced awkward jumps and convulsive little starts with knock knees, wayward elbows, and pigeon toes. Even the "fantastical smile" as Brice conveyed it could have become an outrageous leer. The result would have been a hilarious parody because Brice would have undermined each line of the song with her antics. The disparity would have created the satire and would have rendered the great Nijinsky suitably ridiculous for an American audience still uncomfortable with classical ballet. It was, concluded the *Times*, an "uproariously amusing" performance, which ended with Brice surrounded by a stage full of Nijinskys.

When she next appeared, it was as a totally different character in "Puck's Pictorial Palace" where the *Follies* invaded "the moving picture field." Ina Claire delighted audiences with her impersonation of film stars Jane Cowl, Geraldine Farrar, and Ziegfeld's second wife, Billie Burke. Diminutive dancer Ann Pennington played winsome waif Mary Pickford in overalls and corkscrew curls, and Brice became movie vamp Theda Bara. Once again, she was dealing with someone whose name was a household word. Beginning with *A Fool There Was* in 1915, Bara had soared to short-lived stardom as the leading lady of exotic horror. With her waist-length black hair and darkly kohled eyes, the Cincinnati-born Theodosia Goodman had been transformed by movie publicists into an Arabian beauty who epitomized depravity and wanton lust.[18] In all her films, she played a sexual vampire ("the vamp") who eagerly devoured her victims. By 1916, she was well into her second year of vamping and was already becoming absurd as a predatory mankiller. The type was ripe for parody and Brice was ready to oblige in her Bara burlesque, "I'm Bad."

In her 1925 *Post* interview, Brice reminisced about the origin of the song. She said that her vamp character was inspired less by Bara herself than by the foolish women who emulated her. As she put it, "a stream of amateur vampires" at that time had "descended upon us" and had "suggested a song so obviously that, in the language of Tin Pan Alley, 'it leaped out and hit me in the eye.'"[19] She wanted to satirize these incompetent imitators, the young girls who took Bara's example to ridiculous extremes, who insisted on covering their lovely natural "color" with "cheap cosmetics" and were happy to "dye and friz their hair." They raised their skirts to a scandalous eighteen inches above the ground, adopted "a slouch which eventually would ruin their lungs and warp their shapes," and "otherwise" acted "as women will if given little brainpower they set out to follow fashion."[20] Far from being mysterious and seductive, Brice found these self-styled "man destroyers" "funny," "pathetic," and perfect for a song. Intent on finding the perfect vehicle for her social commentary, she "brought the idea" to Blanche Merrill who developed it with her usual skill and humor.

Brice recalled playing her vamp routine "quietly," but this statement is at odds with the colorful description provided by an enthusiastic reviewer from Cleveland who was present at the New York opening of the *Follies*. According to John De Koven, writing for the *Cleveland Leader*:

> Alas for Theda Bara when Miss Brice is done. Theda is thrown, eyes and all, to the lions to make a Ziegfeld holiday. It is a symphony of so many snaky maneuvers, so staggering an assortment of amorous wiggles, so luscious a collection of lip-twisting and eye-rolling—in fine, so gorgeous and grim a grotesquerie that it is almost libel and the original Theda might well be ill over it.[21]

De Koven found nothing subtle about Brice's Bara. He called the impersonation "an irresistible rib-tickler" and described her hilarious vamping in considerable detail for his Cleveland readers. Wearing "a few yards of black something—something that clings to her like a wet bathing suit," Brice proclaimed "herself a six cylinder 1916 model of Sappho" ready to take on all challengers in a "flapping contest to be had then and there." After demonstrating "her expert and accomplished slinking ability" and securing her position as "the vampiest vamp you'll ever know," she succeeded in finally wiggling herself off the stage, leaving an almost hysterical audience.[22]

De Koven's comments suggest both that Brice was at her comic best when she mimicked someone her audience immediately recognized and that her burlesques were based on broad physical humor. Obviously, the lyrics of the song helped create the character, but the gestures and movements created the comedy. In each number, what Brice did was much funnier than what she said. In "Nijinsky," her actions did not conform to the audience's image of the great dancer and that incongruity produced laughter. In the case of "I'm Bad," her behavior was consistent with one's expectations of a movie vamp, except that it was more extreme. She wiggled and wriggled so outrageously that Bara, all would-be Baras, and vamping itself became ridiculous.

She obtained similar results with the other "character" numbers she performed in the second act, "Becky Is Back in the Ballet" and "The Hat." The songs Blanche Merrill had created for her successful vaudeville tour earlier in the year continued to work well in the more opulent *Follies* setting. As envisioned by Merrill and enacted by Brice, Becky was hopelessly clumsy and the song chronicled her hapless attempts to become a ballerina. Brice stated in 1925 that Merrill had indicated the places where she was supposed to perform dance steps, but it really was unnecessary for her to have done so. The actions were implicit in the lyrics and gave her ample opportunity to indulge in comic business.

Although she said she memorized Merrill's instructions, Brice insisted that there was always an improvisational element to her work: "I never have any set ideas of what I am going to do and when a piece of business occurs to me, I do it instinctively. If it is successful, I keep it until it is stale, if it is not, I discard it for something else."[23] She recalled that her dance steps in "Becky" changed nightly and some of the specific ones probably did. Yet this emphasis on spontaneity seems exaggerated and makes her comic method sound much more haphazard than it could possibly have been. Brice developed her characterizations carefully and, as shall be seen, retained them for a long time. At this point in her career, she was skilled enough as a comedienne to sense when her "comedy stuff" (her words) was working and probably did not change her routines as much as she implied she had later on.

In her performance of "Becky," however, Brice did have a major new "piece of business" which she did not mention in the *Post* article. As part of the number, she now did a burlesque of Anna Pavlova in "The Dying Swan." Created for the ballerina by Fokine, this dance was her most celebrated solo. She invariably included it on her programs and the *Follies* audience would undoubtedly have been familiar with it. There is no evidence that Brice did a "Dying Swan" spoof when she sang "Becky" in vaudeville. The reviews said only that she performed in pink tutu and tights as an inept ballerina, not that she parodied Pavlova. The reviews of the *Follies*, on the other hand, specifically mentioned the Russian ballerina. The *New York Evening Journal* referred to the song as "The Swan." The *Evening Sun* said, "Her dying swan dance in pink ballet skirts was so funny that Elsie Janis [a popular vaudeville singer known for her celebrity imitations] laughed so hard that she nearly had hysterics." The *Brooklyn Citizen* maintained that "her burlesque of Pavlova in the Swan Dance was worth the price of admission alone" and the *New York Herald* exhorted its readers "by all means" to "see her imitation of Pavlova."[24]

Brice parodied dancing throughout her career and the point here is not that she had a new routine with which to enliven old material. Rather, it is to suggest that her "Dying Swan" expanded the song's satirical range because it permitted "Becky" to operate on another level. Just as "I'm Bad" succeeded in burlesquing Bara, the legions of Bara-worshippers, and the idea of vamping in general, "Becky" now poked fun at Pavlova, graceless girls like Becky, and the pretentiousness of classical dance. Brice was debunking culture for her largely middle class audiences, reassuring them that their ignorance of ballet was acceptable because it was such a ridiculous art form. The Yiddish accent completed the process, reducing dancer and dancing to total absurdity. It provided a hearty dose of ethnic humor —crude, unsophisticated, the antithesis of "culture," and always good for a laugh.

"The Hat," and Brice's impersonation of a Jewish mother extolling the wonders of her child's singing, was a hit in the *Follies* as it had been the previous season in vaudeville, According to the *Evening Journal*, her "demonstration of the manner in which the vocalization failed to measure up to the promised excellence literally stopped the show." The *Tribune* declared her "beyond the suspicion of a doubt, the funniest woman on the stage today." *Variety* asserted that the *Ziegfeld Follies of 1916* would place her "where she has belonged for a long while since, without the proper recognition, as one of America's real comediennes."[25]

Not quite twenty-five, after struggling to establish her identity as a performer, Brice had finally come into her own. The four distinct characters she created were greeted with the acclaim her best work would always receive. At this point, it is worthwhile to consider the nature of that work more specifically because it would remain essentially unchanged for the remainder of her stage career. Brice would expand her comic repertoire and, beginning in 1921, would broaden her range by dealing with pathos as well as humor. She would eventually abandon her Yiddish accent. Yet, regardless of the subjects she lampooned, her future forays into comedy would not differ substantially from what she did in the *Ziegfeld Follies of 1916*.

What distinguished Fanny Brice as a performer and made her, as critics would come increasingly to say, "inimitable"? Brice was still a "character comedienne," as she had been called in 1910. The success of her comedy depended on how vividly she brought her gallery of characters to life. In 1925, with tremendous self-perception, she described herself as "a cartoonist working in the flesh." She explained that in "working out a comedy offering," she always thought of it as "legitimate" and tried "to do it as legitimately—or straight—as possible." In a cartoon, she asserted, "there must first be a likeness and then an exaggeration." By creating a "likeness," she created a character; with her "exaggeration," she burlesqued it.[26] It was a funhouse mirror she held up to nature: the reality she presented was always skewed.

Brice stated that the inspiration for most of her songs came from people she saw about her "every day, especially people of a pronounced type" because "their activities, though serious and important and many times beautiful" could easily be "broadened into comedy."[27] Sometimes that broadening began with the lyrics themselves, but the real broadening took place more typically through Brice's behavior, through her performing the actions implicit or explicit in the text. Her comic songs were all very physical. Many of them were inspired by dance, but even the ones that were not depended on a great deal of movement.[28] Blanche Merrill perceptively described Brice as "an action artist," meaning, the artist explained, that "I push my comedy home to an audience by a gesture that accentuates a comedy point."[29] Merrill understood that Brice needed to act out her songs. She could not simply sing them. It is not surprising that the collaboration between the two women produced some of Brice's most successful material.

In the *Post* interview, Brice elaborated on the nature of their working relationship. She explained the process by which they created songs together and referred to her song, "Spring" as an example. It was yet another number in which Brice played an ungainly ballerina in order to mock the acknowledged affectations of an upper class art form. It was "snob appeal" in reverse and, not surprisingly, Brice recalled that she was in a theatre watching a "beautiful ballet" when the nonsensical aspects of the performance struck her. She remembered seeing "thirteen girls" who "postured and flitted about the stage" as the orchestra played "a spring song." She thought it ludicrous that "they get up on their toes and chase madly after nobody. Then they flee where no man pursueth, while the little birds sing." As she watched the laughable scene, "silly words" came to mind, "Oh, would I were a bird! Oh, would I were a bird! I would fly in the spring!"[30]

That night, she asserted, the lines kept "recurring" to her. She summoned Merrill the next morning because she knew she had a "song idea." As she explained it to the attentive songwriter, she would "come out" wearing oversized pink tights "and the rest of the regulation costume." She would "work very hard and very seriously and execute the difficult steps" as well as she could. "We worked it out that way," Brice told her *Post* interviewer, emphasizing her role in the creative process, "I giving my conception of the character and she making a suggestion now and then and writing a line that might go with some movement of the ballet." Merrill produced saccharine lyrics and the music was appropriately "full of the sweet caroling of the birds."

"There remained," as Brice put it, "the characterization and the audience." They were clearly her responsibility and she concentrated on developing her "ballet girl." First she memorized the lyrics and "practiced them to the music" until she knew them so well she "would not have to think of it." Next, she "outlined in general the movements a ballet goes through," but decided on "no particular business." Then she took her character "out on the stage" and, recalling the experience in 1925, found that "she worked for me." In an unusually detailed description of the performance, Brice explained how she interpreted this ballerina. As she remembered the character:

> She danced lightly to the music. She pursued—nobody. She turned and fled when no man pursued. She danced and posed gracefully, and if she tripped, she caught herself quickly and went on with the dance. Business occurred spontaneously. One night she decided to execute the difficult twirl that calls for such poise and muscular control. She raised herself on her toes to do it. Fear struck her and she suddenly decided not to try it. Then she wagged her finger at the audience, pretending she had fooled them and intended to all along. This particular piece of business brought a howl and she used it night after night. But one night it brought no reponse. She found she was doing it mechani-

cally. All the spontaneity had gone from it, and the audience knew it and resented it. She discarded the whole twirl and pursued a phantom bird instead, almost catching it, but losing it at the last minute. As long as any piece of business brought a laugh, she used it. When it ceased to be funny and became mechanical, she discarded it.[31]

This lengthy passage in the *Post* interview is apparently the only instance on record when Brice discussed the method she used to create her characters. Her comments are important, for they show how she brought her material to life. The collaborative process with Merrill produced songs to act, and the behavior grew out of Brice's conception of the characters. Unlike much of her early work which seemed mechanical because the mugging was being done for its own sake, Brice's interpretation of someone like Becky allowed the "business" to develop more naturally. The actions came from a clear sense of who that character was and were not imposed arbitrarily on it. That is why Brice placed so much emphasis on spontaneity. It was not so much that she appeared on stage each evening and moved randomly about according to whim. Rather, it was that she became the person of her song and was able to act out a variety of funny gestures. She may have twirled one night and abandoned it the next, but whatever she did was consistent with the character she was playing. By exaggerating behavior subtly or outrageously, she broadened the song into a burlesque.

Contributing to that broadening was the Yiddish accent which heightened the lunacy because it sounded so funny and made the characters seem more ludicrous than they already were. Rather than emphasizing Brice's ethnic identification, the accent served as a comic contrast to the parts she played and enabled her to reduce each subject to the same absurd level. The idea of a Jewish Nijinsky, vamp, or ballerina was apparently so incongruous that it made Brice's outrageous actions even funnier. The accent, together with the antics, became her signature and the principal means by which she created her cartoons.

Another important aspect of Brice's comic technique was the rapport she worked hard to establish with the audience. She spoke many times about how crucial it was for a performer to gauge "the feel of the audience" and ascribed much of her own success on stage to that skill. Brice's eagerness to please made her a warm, open, and ebullient entertainer. It also made her completely safe. She never deliberately did anything on stage to disturb her audience. She avoided controversial subjects and tried to choose topical material that would not be offensive. She could occasionally be raunchy, but she was never cruel and she knew when she had gone

too far. As a popular entertainer, her career depended on winning a large
and enthusiastic following. The more universal her appeal, the greater her
chances of success. Whether she lampooned the ludicrous or spoofed something serious, therefore, she could not risk antagonizing her audience. She
had to keep the target of a song separate from the people for whom she
was performing it.

The Yiddish accent she affected was not considered objectionable.
Like blackface, it was accepted as a comic convention, but Brice was careful not to vex her Jewish fans. She insisted that she did not base her
work on a sense of her own superiority. She said she "never did a Jewish
song that would offend the race"—an offensive term in its own right—
because she identified with her subjects and did not hesitate to poke fun
at herself when she performed. "In anything Jewish I ever did, I wasn't
standing apart, making fun of the race," she explained in her memoirs,
"I *was* the race, and what happened to me on the stage is what could
happen to them." "They identified with me," she continued, "and then
it was all right to get a laugh, because they were laughing at me as much
as at themselves."[32] Brice sounds somewhat defensive here. Nevertheless,
her great personal warmth onstage softened her subsequent caricatures and
diffused whatever displeasure they might have produced.

Brice's desire to establish a rapport with the audience gave her what
was perhaps her most distinctive trait as a performer: the ability to be
a character and, at the same time, to comment on that character. When
Brice performed a song such as "Becky," she became the awkward "ballet
girl" she sang about and selected appropriate behavior for that character.
When the dancer leapt ungracefully or walked with bowed legs and flat
feet, those actions immediately showed the audience that Becky was totally talentless. Like theatrical asides, Brice's actions and gestures would
have created a feeling of camaraderie between the actress and her audience
because it would have been clear that both held the same opinion of hapless Becky.

As critics applauded Brice's various characterizations, they often mentioned her "sly winks," "knowing glances," and "conspiratorial grimaces."
These phrases suggest that some kind of direct communication was taking
place between performer and audience. In the absence of conclusive documentation for Brice's stage work, an example from her 1930 movie, *Be
Yourself*, helps clarify the nature of this exchange.[33] One of the highpoints
of this undistinguished film was "The Dying Swan," a later version of
the number Brice had done so successfully in the *Ziegfeld Follies of 1916*.

After looking pointedly at the audience, Brice dances sorrowfully to

Swan Lake. She is all fluttery hands and soulful eyes as she tiptoes daintily around the floor to lugubrious music. Suddenly, an old hunter pops up from behind the rock cluster. He is a dwarf and the ludicrous Tyrolean costume he wears makes him look very peculiar. The "Swan" does not see him. He takes aim and shoots her with a large arrow. She starts, eyes and mouth wide open, then clasps her hand over her stomach. The orchestra plays "How Dry I Am" as she wipes a tear from her nose and exits with head down, chest in, stomach out. Her arms are bent at the elbow and held out to the side, her hands droop limply, her knees are bowed. She holds this position as she ambles slowly off.

Brice's mannerisms and movements make it obvious that this "denser" is anything but "appilling." She may think she is gorgeous and graceful, but the audience knows differently. So does the actress. Just as actions throughout the song (such as sticking her stomach out on "slim") succeed in immediately conveying the opposite meaning, the winks and smiles that punctuate the performance instantly tell the audience members that she knows what they think and agrees with them.

Such communication was an important part of Brice's comic technique because it enabled her to stand apart from the character she was playing and comment on it. However brief the flashes, they signaled that she shared the audience's awareness of the character's silliness because she was separate from that character. The distance that existed between the two, between the actress and her comic creation, made Brice's portraits burlesques. She parodied her subject by calling attention to the disparity between the character's perception of herself and the way others viewed her. To use her own terms, Brice was both the cartoon and the cartoonist. She created the cartoon, then framed it through her animated commentary, most of which was unspoken. The feeling of fellowship she fostered, as well as the warmth and energy with which she played the clown, kept that commentary from ever becoming cruel and characterized her best work.

Brice's outstanding performance in the *Ziegfeld Follies of 1916* continued when the successful production began its annual tour in September. Although she did not figure prominently in any advance publicity, critics applauded her on the road as they had in New York. She was favorably mentioned in notices from Boston to Baltimore, where the *Follies* concluded its run at the end of March. The *Baltimore Sun*'s reviewer considered her performance the strongest in the show and her efforts were rewarded with another Ziegfeld contract.[34] In May, *Variety* announced that the principals for the 1917 edition had been called to rehearsal. According to an item in the May 4 issue, the men included "newcomers" Eddie Cantor and Walter Catlett, as well as George Baldwin, Don Barclay, Will Rogers, and Bert Williams. Among the women mentioned, *Variety* said that only two were definite, Fanny Brice and Ann Pennington.[35] When the *Ziegfeld Follies of 1917* opened at the New Amsterdam on June 12, Baldwin and Pennington were out. W. C. Fields, Irving Fisher, Tom Richards, and Russell Vokes had joined the men, while the female principals now included Marion and Madeline Fairbanks, Peggy Hopkins, and Allyn King.

The eleventh edition of the *Follies* had book and lyrics by George V. Hobart and Gene Buck, with music by Raymond Hubbell, Dave Stamper, Victor Herbert, and Jerome Kern. Once again, Ned Wayburn provided the staging and Joseph Urban the dazzling "scenic backgrounds." *Variety* speculated that "Ziegfeld must have told [Urban] to go the limit which he did."[36] The *Clipper* summarized the opinions of the dailies as follows:

> *Times*—never been surpassed on New York Stage
> *World*—reaches new pinnacle of splendor
> *Tribune*—one of the most gorgeous productions ever revealed
> *Sun*—the best ever
> *Herald*—appears to be the best
> *American*—lavish and startling.[37]

The *Clipper* itself announced that the *Ziegfeld Follies of 1917* had surpassed "all its predecessors . . . in the manner of its almost unprecedented appeal to the eye."

The whole elaborate construct was based on a ten thousand dollar wager that a prospective son-in-law could show his future father-in-law more in three hours around New York than had been described in the *Arabian Nights*. "Then," Sime reported, "everyone, including the audience, forgets all about it until the final scene of the evening when the lost plot is recalled through seeing the opening setting once again."[38] The two acts and twenty scenes (eleven in the first act, nine in the second) began and ended in an "Arabian Nights" atmosphere, with lovely Allyn King presiding as Scheherazade in diaphanous gown and conical headdress. Each scene was an "Episode" which had no relation whatsoever to the one preceding it. The most spectacular was the first act finale involving "The Episode of Patriotism" and "The Episode of the American Eagle," supported by "OUR FLAG" and "OUR NAVY."[39]

The timely chauvinistic display coincided with America's entry into World War I. On April 6, 1917, the United States had joined Britain,

France, Russia, and their allies in declaring war on the forces of Germany, Austria-Hungary, and the Ottoman Empire. In June, as the *Ziegfeld Follies of 1917* opened in New York, the first troops of the American Expeditionary Force, commanded by General John J. Pershing, sailed for France. Although they would not decisively affect the fighting until the spring of 1918, American soldiers had been sent overseas to help keep an entire generation of Europeans from being exterminated.[40] President Wilson had declared that "the world must be made safe for democracy," a war message that seems to have inspired Ziegfeld to create his first act finale.

According to the *New York Times*, his opulent paean to patriotism began with a tableau representing the ride of Paul Revere, with Revere and his white horse racing feverishly on a treadmill. George Washington and Abraham Lincoln appeared next, followed by "a troop of maidens in costumes more artistic then historic." They marched in formation "before a painted eagle that fairly screamed" and were "reviewed" by "a frock-coated President Wilson." The audience stood as the orchestra played "The Star Spangled Banner" and "a huge American flag that canopied the auditorium was unfolded." The stirring spectacle ended with a "scenic tableau" in which a fleet of American battleships "seemed to stream through the night up to the very breakwater of the footlights, growing in size with their approach."[41]

Variety observed that it was extremely difficult for the "people" to compete with the impressive "production," but several managed to attract favorable attention. The *Times* reported that "Rogers, Williams, Cantor, and Brice" excelled. In *Variety*'s estimation, it was Brice, Cantor, and Catlett. The *New York Evening Sun* narrowed the field to Brice and Cantor, judging them "the most entertaining of the principals." For the *New York Telegraph*, however, there was only one winner of the night's "first honors" and that was Brice. The *Times* declared that she was "as funny as last year" and the *Tribune* was delighted to discover that "the eyes of Fannie Brice roll(ed) as of yore."[42]

Brice's material in this edition was not as strong as it had been the previous year and it is a tribute to her skill as a performer that she managed, nonetheless, to win accolades. She made three appearances in the show: "The Episode of the Ziegfeld Follies Rag" (I. vi), "The Episode of the Mississippi Levee" with Eddie Cantor (II. iv), and "The Episode of the Fannybriceisms" (II. vi).[43] Of the first, little can be said with certainty other than that Brice performed with her customary zest and enthusiasm. The second was noteworthy because it marked the only time that she appeared in blackface or, as the *Evening Telegram* put it, "colored makeup."[44] She and Cantor sang "Just You and Me," a ragtime number which received favorable comments. In the third, the "Fannybriceisms" were songs written by Blanche Merrill. Of these, the number called "Egyptian" was Brice's personal triumph in the production and the song *Variety* labeled "the real riot of the evening."[45]

"Egyptian" was the kind of material she did so well: in dialect, about another inept dancer, with satirical references to a real person. This time the oblique target was Ruth St. Denis. A pioneer of American modern dance well known to theatregoers through her frequent concert and vaudeville tours, St. Denis favored exotic subjects redolent with spirituality. One of the staples in her repertoire was "Egypta," an Egyptian ballet first staged in New York in 1910. She often excerpted segments from this composition for popular performances throughout the country.

In her *Follies* number, Brice posed as a "Yiddish-Egyptian maid" (*Variety*'s words) called Sahara. Actually, several reviewers referred to her as "Sara," and it may be that the heavy Yiddish accent made "Sahara" sound like an elongated version of that name. Either one would have been appropriate for the character who, like Sadie Salome, is a Jewish girl who yearns to be an exotic dancer. According to the lyrics of the song, "the only thing she knows about Egypt is how to smoke Egyptian cigarets"—an allusion to St. Denis who was inspired to create her Egyptian dance allegedly after seeing a picture of the goddess Isis on a poster advertising "Egyptian Deities" cigarettes.[46] Nevertheless, Sahara manages to orientalize her origins and make "improvements upon her Yiddisher movements."

Merrill's "Egyptian" allows Brice to combine deft jabs at St. Denis ("Up goes the foot, she holds it there / It's bare, it's bare but she don't care!") with amusing self-parody ("All dressed up in Egyptian clothes, / She's all Egyptian but her nose!"). In addition to the bars where dance steps are indicated, the lyrics suggest the kind of movement with which Brice liked to animate a song.[47] That she did so seems clear from the critical response "Egyptian" received. The *New York Globe and Commercial Advertiser* found her "excruciatingly funny" and complained that she did not have enough to do in the show.[48] The most astute (and pithy) observation, however, came from the *Times*. Although critical of the "essentially lowbrow comedy" in the *Follies*, the paper acknowledged the brilliance of the "artists" who supplied their own material and did not rely on the forgettable script. They were Fields, Rogers, Williams, and "the droll Fanny Brice whose sense of travesty amounts to genius."[49]

Brice received similar praise on tour with the *Ziegfeld Follies of 1917* which left New York on September 15 and opened two days later in Boston.

After a successful six-week engagement there, the show played in Philadelphia, Pittsburgh, Washington, D.C., Detroit, Chicago, Cincinnati, Indianapolis, Columbus, Buffalo, and Toronto before closing in Montreal on April 20, 1918. When the twelfth edition opened at the New Amsterdam in June, however, Brice was not a member of the cast. No explanation for her absence appeared in any contemporary article, nor did she discuss it in her reminiscences. It is possible that having been an outstanding performer in two successive *Follies*, she demanded a higher salary than even the extravagant Ziegfeld was willing to pay and he decided to dispense with her services. Yet it is more likely that Brice parted with him for artistic reasons, rather than over a contractual dispute. On August 23, she would open in New York as the star of a legitimate drama, *Why Worry?*, produced by A. H. Woods. In so doing, she thought she was about to fulfill an ambition that would impel her for almost a decade: the desire to be accepted as a serious actress in her own stage show. When Woods's production and her much-ballyhooed leading role proved disappointing, she would return to Ziegfeld, though not to the *Follies*, in December. She would enjoy many more triumphs as a Ziegfeld performer, but would also experience considerable frustration as the impresario's repeated promises to provide her with an appropriate vehicle never materialized and led to their final, irrevocable break.

Disappointments, Debacles, and "That Immortal Song"

In my mind, I think of Nick leaving and the tears just come.

–FANNY BRICE[1]

Miss Brice is a consummate artist. Each year she achieves her effects by more subtle and delicate means. . . . Her sense of the comic is unfailing.

–NEW YORK WORLD, reviewing the Ziegfeld Follies of 1921[2]

6.

From 1918 until 1927, Fanny Brice worked hard and steadily on the stage. She appeared in two "legitimate" plays, three *Follies*, four other Ziegfeld productions, and two non-Ziegfeld revues. She made her first records, produced two shows, and filled the remaining time with lucrative vaudeville engagements. During this nine-year period, she took only one extended vacation and worked into the seventh month of both her pregnancies, returning to rehearsals very soon after the birth of daughter Frances in 1919 and son William in 1921. Her drive and energy, her singleminded dedication to her career were formidable, yet she failed to fulfill the one ambition that was most important to her: to be recognized as more than "just a comic."[3] More than anything else, she wanted to be respected as a serious actress, and believed that to achieve this aim she needed her own starring vehicle. She was promised several, but they either failed to materialize or flopped.

To her credit, she remained undaunted and dealt with disappointment in her own characteristic way: by working. When her beloved Nicky ran afoul of the law once again in 1920 and went into hiding, she performed indefatigably for Ziegfeld, even though her weight dropped alarmingly and she was on the verge of collapse. She recalled later that "life had turned into a grim reality," but remembered that she managed nevertheless "to go on the stage night after night and make people laugh."[4] When Ziegfeld kept her on tenterhooks for an entire season with repeated announcements of a forthcoming new musical created expressly for her, she did not sit around waiting for a script. Instead, she booked herself into a cross-country vaudeville tour that took her from New York's Palace in October 1922 to the Orpheum Theatre in Los Angeles in June 1923. She worked throughout the years in which Arnstein's trials, sentencing, and appeals dragged on, and just as steadily during his stay at Leavenworth.[5]

In part, her dedication was pragmatic. She worked hard because she had no choice. She needed her salary to cover the enormous legal expenses Arnstein had incurred. In part, her diligence was therapeutic. Working undoubtedly offered an escape, albeit temporary, from personal unhappiness. While she was clowning for an audience, she could forget that the man she loved was a criminal. Ultimately, however, Brice performed as tirelessly as she did because she was driven to succeed on her own terms. She wanted to star in her own show and be accepted as a legitimate actress. This desire far outweighed the financial and emotional considerations.

It also produced a curious side effect. Brice's self-absorption verged on myopia. She was so preoccupied with her own career that she often seemed out of touch with the rest of the world. During World War I, for example, when hundreds of performers offered to help the war effort by performing overseas, her name never appeared on the honor roll published weekly in *Variety*. She recalled selling doughnuts on the steps of the New York Public Library for Liberty Bonds, but that may well have been the extent of her wartime volunteer work.[6] Although she played in occasional benefits throughout her life, she never lent her talent and energy to philanthropy in the same way that Eddie Cantor, Elsie Janis, Al Jolson, or Sophie Tucker did. Unlike them, Brice never championed a cause (other than Nicky) or volunteered her services to a pet charity. She was devoted to her family and generous to her friends, but seemed oblivious to any situation in which she was not immediately involved. An interviewer writing about her in 1946 observed:

> She is an excellent fortune teller, working from tea leaves or the palm. She also can hypnotize people and compel them to perform in obedience to posthypnotic suggestions. Outside of these fields, Miss Brice can hardly be called an intellectual. She is completely absorbed in her little world of show business

and reads nothing, not even newspapers, and knows almost nothing about world affairs or weighty questions of the day.[7]

There is something childlike about such egocentricity which suggests that Brice may not have had to stretch very far to play Baby Snooks, her most enduring comic character.

When the March 15, 1918, *Variety* reported that she was under contract to A. H. Woods for a dramatic production, Brice must have believed that she was about to fulfill her professional aspirations. An item in the May 3 edition, however, indicated that a serious acting debut was unlikely. Woods, whose tastes ran to lurid melodrama and ethnic comedy, announced that she would be appearing in a comedy written by Montague Glass and Jules Eckert Goodman, the team responsible for *Business before Pleasure* the previous year.[8] The third in the successful *Potash and Perlmutter* series, the play presented Abe Potash and Mawruss Perlmutter, "two harried Hebraic merchants" and partners in a New York "cloak and suit" business.[9] Historians have dismissed the popular pair as twentieth century specimens of the offensive "stage Jew" with "hooked nose, flapping hands, singsong English and Yiddish expletives," but that is much too harsh an assessment.[10] Although their accent and mannerisms placed them squarely in the dialect comedy tradition, Abe and Mawruss moved beyond its stereotypes. Beginning with *Potash and Perlmutter* in 1913, they emerged as more fully developed characters than the two-dimensional caricatures burlesque and vaudeville's "Jew comics" perpetually paraded before their audiences. Abe and Mawruss were fractious, volatile, and, occasionally, too anxious to succeed in business, yet they were also kind, loyal, honest, and compassionate, ethical in their dealings with their customers, as well as with one another, and devoted to their families.

According to Alexander Carr (Mawruss), reflecting on the partners in 1914, *Potash and Perlmutter* was significant because it marked "the first time that the real Jew, with all his faults and failings, and with all his good qualities as well, has ever been shown in a play."[11] By 1913, however, the stereotyped image of the Jew was fast becoming intolerable. Vaudeville houses across the country were beginning to succumb to pressure from organized Jewish groups such as the Anti-Stage Jew Ridicule Committee in Chicago, the Anti-Defamation League of B'nai B'rith, and the Associated Rabbis of America to remove the objectionable caricatures from their stages. The *Potash and Perlmutter* series was consistent with this movement toward a more realistic and humane handling of Jews because, in its four plays, the old stereotypes were rounded into more believable characterizations.

Nevertheless, for all that was positive about them, the *Potash and Perlmutter* plays hardly qualified as great drama. Looking back at them more than seventy years later, observers have called them "good-natured, unpretentious" comedies and "harum scarum Jewish dialect farces," comments that do not differ significantly from critical opinion in 1917.[12] Then, one reviewer described *Business before Pleasure* as "a nice friendly old comic strip." Another noted "the cartoon's infinite lack of variety."[13] Both remarks suggest that the kind of play Glass and Goodman would produce for Brice would capitalize on what she could already do well and would not enable her to develop her talents as a dramatic actress.

By June 9, 1918, the play had a title, *Why Worry?*, and by June 21, Brice indicated that she had a good reason. Under the heading "Fannie Brice Wants to Act," *Variety* quoted her as saying that the production had "so much comedy," it gave her "but little chance" to display her skills.[14] In spite of her reservations, she began rehearsing early in July, and on July 29 *Why Worry?* opened a week-long engagement at Washington's Belasco Theatre. According to *Variety*, the show received "the worst panning" given "in many a month." The *Star* said it was "not so bad," but the *Post* review was scathing. Calling it a "theatrical hodgepodge that defies classification," the *Post* went on to describe it as wavering between "slapstick burlesque, deleted vaudeville, crude melodrama, and a cheap trading on patriotic emotions." The story was dismissed as "uninteresting as well as unimportant," the writing uninspired, the acting insincere. The "players" tried to "overcome defects of authorship by reading their lines in a roar," but failed to salvage the "three act curiosity." In her role as a waitress named Dora Harris, Brice received the most damning criticism of all. She was completely ignored. As *Variety* put it, "If Fanny Brice has anything to do in the performance, you would never know it from reading the *Post* review."[15]

After a second disastrous week, this one in Atlantic City, *Why Worry?* closed for repairs. *Variety* reported that the show had been found "deficient in 'class'" and explained that the illness of Glass's wife had kept him from doing the extensive rewriting A. H. Woods thought the script needed. Now, however, revisions had been made and *Why Worry?* was slated to reopen on August 23 at New York's Harris Theatre. Among the additions were two songs written for Brice by Blanche Merrill. One was called "I'm an Indian." The other was the Theda Bara vamp song, "I'm Bad."[16] "I'm an Indian" quickly became one of Brice's most popular songs. Like so many of her other numbers, the concept was not novel. For years, vaudeville had its Jewish Cowboys and Indians such as the "Yiddish Cowboy, Tough Guy Levi" and "Solomon Cohen, Indian Chief."[17] Brice portrayed little Rosie Rosenstein, now a "terrible squaw," and as always, made the song unmistakably hers by means of parody, dialect, and broad physical humor. According to *Variety*, the lyrics were especially suited to her style of clowning.

> Down at the feet is the moccasins for the shoes
> Up in the back is a little fat papoose.
> Up in the head is the feathers from a goose.
> It's a goose, it's a goose, but I'm an Indian . . .
> Oi Oi Oi Oi! I'm a terrible squaw.[18]

It is not difficult to imagine the exaggerated expressions and animated gestures with which Brice amused the audience, or the war dance with which the *Evening World* said she won deserved laughter. The *Tribune* applauded both songs and admired "her curious mixture of ungainliness and grace, a sort of ungainliness under perfect control."[19]

The songs, however, could not compensate for the rest of the show which received negative reviews from all but one of the New York newspapers.[20] The critical consensus was that *Why Worry?* was dreadful. The script was the major problem. The dialogue was lifeless, there was no suspense, and the complicated plot moved very slowly. As the *Herald* put it, "though described as a melodramatic farce by Montague Glass and Jules Eckert Goodman," the three interminable acts "proved to be an unfortunate succession of incoherent situations made endurable by Miss Fannie Brice and the Avon Comedy Four."[21]

A popular vaudeville group that included the legendary Smith and Dale among its members, the Avon Comedy Four had made the "school act" or "kid scene" famous early in the twentieth century. The group had also developed a Hungarian restaurant sketch with Smith as the chef, Dale as "the boss," and the other half of the foursome (Harry Goodwin and Irving Kaufman) as singing waiters.[22] *Why Worry?* incorporated this routine, with the Avon Comedy Four as bumbling musical waiters providing moments of hilarity amid the plot's convolutions.

Their antics could not save the show. *Why Worry?*'s tortuous plot lacked credibility and its banal dialogue often sounded nonsensical. Other equally serious problems emerged in performance. *Variety* found the excessive reliance on Yiddish expressions annoying and stated that there was so much Yiddish in the script "as to be absolutely unintelligible to any but orthodox Hebrews." Jolo was particularly disappointed in Brice's performance, partly because the play gave her no opportunity to display her talent. "The little she revealed in *Why Worry?*," he observed, "was comedy responses in a series of crossfire duologs." Yet he also expressed reservations about her acting ability and suggested that, even with a better script, she would have done badly. "Given anything more legitimate," he speculated, "she would prove unequal to the task."[23]

The *Evening World* thought the twenty-six-year-old Brice seemed "quite lost in the shuffle until she found her way into comic songs."[24] The *Tribune*'s Heywood Broun admired her as an entertainer but admitted that she still "sings better than she acts." Although he acknowledged her "distinct . . . comic gift," he found that she had "lapses in which she pounds her points too hard." He noted that "this is chiefly emphasized by a tendency to make a line a little funnier than it is written by looking cross-eyed while saying it"—precisely the technique that she used so successfully with her musical numbers.[25]

Brice was approaching a script as she did a song, but the exaggerated comic movements did not work for her in the same way. Her mannerisms became monotonous and failed to amuse. She was unable to create a believable character, in part because the play was so absurd, but also because she simply did not know how to act. According to the Avon Comedy Four's Joe Smith, reminiscing about the *Why Worry?* experience years later, Brice "was a very funny girl, but a good actress for only about fifteen minutes." He recalled a sketch in which "one of the fellows played her lover." Brice, mugging outrageously, "put her arms around his neck and with her face to the audience she stuck out her tongue." "Of course," he stated bluntly, "the scene fell apart."[26]

The combination of unsuitable vehicle and untrained star made for a disastrous dramatic debut. The September 20 *Variety* announced that the "unfortunate attraction" had closed the previous Saturday (September 14) at a loss of $1,400.[27] *Why Worry?* had won the title of "the season's most terrible play thus far," an accomplishment that must have pained Brice. Undaunted, however, she proceeded to find another project. *Variety*'s October 6 edition announced her imminent return to vaudeville for a seven-week engagement in New York houses at a weekly salary of $1,000.[28] Yet her name did not appear in any of the vaudeville reviews or route lists for October and November 1918. One explanation for its absence was that her private life had temporarily taken precedence over her career. Nicky had been released from Sing Sing and, after a six-year relationship, he and Brice were finally married in a quiet Brooklyn ceremony on October 18.[29] By November, moreover, she was sick, one of the thousands of victims of a virulent form of influenza then ravaging the country.[30] The epidemic had broken out at Fort Devens near Boston in mid-September and soon spread throughout the world. Before it abated, the Spanish influenza took twenty million lives, more than even World War I's carnage had claimed. The war had ended on November 11, but the death toll from the virus continued to mount. In New York City, it reached forty-five hundred a week; in Philadelphia, it passed one thousand a day. In nine months, at least five hundred and fifty thousand Americans—many times the number of American casualties in the war—died from the Spanish flu.[31]

Brice was one of the lucky ones. She recovered, and by December was well enough to return to work. On the ninth, she appeared on the New Amsterdam Roof in the latest edition of the *Ziegfeld Midnight Frolic* and the first of his *Nine O'Clock Revues*. Both productions were fast-paced musical variety shows in a luxurious nightclub setting, designed by Joseph Urban and modestly billed as "the meeting place of the world."[32] Ziegfeld had staged the first *Midnight Frolic* in 1915 with characteristic extravagance and care. Buoyed by its success and the euphoric postwar spirit, he added the *Nine O'Clock Revue* three years later. Most of these cabaret shows were written by *Follies* regulars Gene Buck and Dave Stamper, choreographed by Ned Wayburn, with "decorations and scenic investiture" provided by Urban, and featured favorite *Follies* performers.[33] The productions changed periodically and, as *Variety* observed, "drew the classiest after-theatre patronage ever known to nightclubs then or since."[34] Offering polished performances in an intimate setting, excellent food, and alcohol in abundance, the New Amsterdam Roof was a popular late supper spot until Prohibition effectively killed it in 1920.[35]

Brice had actually taken part in the *Midnight Frolic* earlier in the year, between the completion of her *Follies* tour and her ill-fated debut in *Why Worry?* She had performed in the midnight show for six weeks from the end of May until the beginning of July, and sang two of her best numbers, "Becky" and "Egyptian."[36] Now she was engaged for the first *Nine O'Clock Revue*, as well as the new *Midnight Frolic*, along with dancers Evan Burrows Fontaine, Hal Hixon, and Bessie McCoy Davis; singers Lillian Lorraine and Bea Palmer; Lillian Leitzel, "the greatest woman gymnast in the world"; Bird Millman, "the bird on a wire"; comedian Bert Williams;

and a chorus of thirty-six. *Variety*'s Sime described the two shows as "numbers and songs, songs and numbers, clothes and women"—or, as another critic put it, "short on wit, long on leg"—with most of the principals appearing in both productions.[37]

Variety identified Brice as "one of the old favorites" and reported that each of the three Blanche Merrill songs she performed was "a corker": "I'm Bad," a "French soubret (travesty) number," and "an Indian number during which Fannie said they could tell she was an eagle by her beak."[38] The "French soubret number" remains unidentified, but the first and third songs were the ones she had just used in *Why Worry? Variety*'s The Skirt called "I'm Bad" the bright spot of the first part and noted that "her gown was of course the inevitable black." *Theatre Magazine* ran a sketch and described it as "a striking black satin princess gown that has these graceful black lace sleeves, weighted with jet tassels."[39] A newspaper caricature showed Brice dressed comically for "I'm an Indian" in a short flounced dress, black tights, high heels, and feather headdress.

Although *Variety* attributed Brice's success more to the clever material Blanche Merrill had created than to her own skills as a performer, it declared her "a laughing riot."[40] Ziegfeld, ever adept at "knowing the value of women and how to select them for the stage," quickly recognized her value to the production. By January 1919, she had been given three additional songs and a raise. By the end of June, however, she was out of the show, not because Ziegfeld was displeased with her work, but because she was pregnant. Her disgruntled employer allegedly sent the following telegram: "You should have more respect for your contract than to allow yourself to get in a position where you are forced to quit any time you see fit."[41] *Variety* reacted more objectively. Under the heading, "Fannie Brice's Expected Event," the July 25 edition reported that she had left the *Midnight Frolic* "some weeks ago," had taken up residence in Long Island with her husband "Nick Arnold," and was expecting "an addition to the Arnold household."[42]

As well as a large apartment on Central Park West at 83rd Street, Brice and Nicky had a house in Huntington, Long Island. "It was," she wrote years later, "the one thing Nick ever bought. He made some money gambling and he paid $14,000 for it." She spent an additional $25,000 on remodeling, which included building mahogany-lined stables for Nicky, who envisioned a new career as a racehorse owner. Like the rest of his schemes, this fantasy never materialized and the mahogany stables remained empty. Brice, however, was happy to indulge him and eagerly awaited the birth of their first child, disappointed only that he did not share her enthusiasm. "That made me sad," she recalled, "because I had waited so long to have this baby."[43]

Frances Brice Arnstein was born on August 12, 1919, just six days before both Roof shows closed on account of a stagehands' strike which affected twenty-six plays in New York, in addition to theatres in Boston, Chicago, and Los Angeles. Since the strike was settled within four weeks, the *Nine O'Clock Revue* resumed on September 10 and ran until a new *Midnight Frolic* featuring Brice opened on October 2. *Variety* applauded the production stating, "if possible, it is even more gorgeous than all previous seasons." It combined elaborate visual spectacle with ingenious choral numbers in which the "showgirls" interacted alluringly with members of the audience. In one naughty song called "Tea Time," they lifted their skirts, dipped down into their silk stockings, and, with the enforcement of Prohibition only three months away, boldly brought forth flasks, "the contents of which," observed *Variety*, they poured "into the glasses of those fortunate enough to have ringside tables."[44] In "The Surprise Package," they produced a huge candy box trailing long satin ribbons which they handed to various members of the audience. At a given signal, the audience tugged on the ribbons and opened the lid, revealing one of the specialty performers who serenaded them with "The Midnight Maid." *Variety* considered the song mediocre, but seemed impressed that those audience members holding ribbons were rewarded for their efforts with one-pound boxes of candy.[45]

Brice appeared next and, as she had in the *Follies*, provided ample comic relief. She and Eddie Cantor performed a "travesty apache song and dance" which *Variety* found "excruciatingly funny in a burlesque way." "Miss Brice sacrifices all sense of dignity," reported Jolo, "permitting Cantor to administer kicks upon her posterior."[46] Without sheet music, one can only speculate about the song, but it is not too difficult to imagine a saucer-eyed Cantor listening to Brice's Yiddish-accented lament before joining her in a comical dance. Her buffoonery continued in the second act, amid the show's elaborate tableaux and extravagant stage pictures, as she sang Blanche Merrill's "Spring" for the first time with great success. Jolo called it a "screamingly ludicrous burlesque," and other reviewers noted the "remarkable reception" she received.[47]

Brice remained in the *Midnight Frolic* for its twenty-two-week run until the end of February 1920, when it closed in preparation for the next edition. The new production would do well in spite of Prohibition, largely through her efforts. By 1918, a Prohibition Act outlawed the sale of all intoxicating beverages and in January 1919, the Eighteenth Amendment was ratified and ultimately approved by every state except Connecticut, Rhode Island, and New Jersey.[48] When it took effect on January 16, 1920, America was officially dry. Although its enforcement was virtually impossible from the beginning, Prohibition was the law of the land until its rather anticlimactic repeal in 1933.

By December 1919, intoxicating beverages were no longer being sold on the Roof and *Variety* was quick to comment on Prohibition's deleterious effect on the late-night show. Although initial reports indicated that the *Midnight Frolic* was profitable despite the absence of alcohol, losses were recorded as early as February 1. As Ziegfeld struggled to prove that lemonade could successfully replace liquor, moreover, Brice had to deal with serious personal problems. Nicky had fled from New York in mid-month and a front page story in the *Times* on February 21 explained his sudden disappearance. The sensational article identified "Nicky" Arnstein as head of a plot to steal $5 million in a Wall Street Bond deal.[49]

Arnstein was eventually convicted, but Brice always maintained his innocence. Years later, she recorded her version of the distressing events:

> There were a couple of messenger boys, runners in Wall Street, who used to deliver bonds to people's houses. The bonds were in different names and some guy in the gang that Nick hung around with, some stupid guy somehow got the idea that he could get rid of them. He got to the messenger boys and told them he knew a banker in Washington who could get rid of the bonds for them. The boys told the man they would like to meet the banker and talk to him, but the guy said that this was impossible; they could see him, but he was too important a guy to talk to punks like them. So the fellow arranges for them to be in a restaurant on 86th Street and Broadway. He then called Nick and said: "How about a drink? I want to talk to you." So Nick meets him for a drink in this restaurant, the two messenger boys see the guy with this tall, handsome, well-dressed man, and they go in on the deal. In those days, Nick looked more like a banker than J. P. Morgan.
>
> After the kids got caught, they told all about the banker from Washington. They were asked: "Did you meet the banker?" They said: "No, but we saw him." So they were shown a lot of pictures and when they saw Nick's picture, they said: "That's the banker."[50]

According to her glib explanation, it was simply a question of mistaken identity. The perennially dapper Arnstein looked like a banker and easily became the helpless victim of an unscrupulous fellow gang member's scheme.

Whether she was unable to come to terms with Arnstein's criminal activities or unwilling to be publicly and permanently linked with a gangster, Brice said she never questioned her husband's integrity. Whatever doubts she may have actually had, preserving the image of Nicky's innocence was obviously important to her. As she maintained that he had not committed a crime, she found the succeeding months extremely difficult. While Arnstein remained in hiding she was hounded by police and press, but she refused to allow her anguish to interfere with her career and seemed resolved to carry on in spite of personal distress. Whereas, five years earlier, Nicky's incarceration in Sing Sing had coincided with her professional nadir, in 1920 she plunged into performing with a vengeance.

On March 8, the new *Nine O'Clock Revue*, called *Ziegfeld Girls of 1920*, opened on the Amsterdam Roof; on the 16th, the latest *Midnight Frolic* premiered. Brice was prominently featured in both productions, which were written by Stamper and Buck, staged by Wayburn, and mounted with typical Ziegfeld "smartness and artistic attractiveness." *Variety* reported that the Roof, newly decorated in gold and buff, was now serving an elegant pre-show dinner. "Minus booze," the paper explained, Ziegfeld was "trying to fill the void of percentage profits . . . by running his own cafe."[51] *Variety* wrote that "the most humorous bit of the early show came with Fannie Brice dolled up in antebellum frock doing 'Don't You Remember Me?'" In red coat and cap, she also amused in a hunting number by Blanche Merrill, most likely the song she recalled performing with disastrous results for a predominantly Jewish vaudeville audience. Apparently, the sophisticated Roof crowd did not object to the characterization of a *nouveau riche* Jewish girl in hunting garb.

Brice's third song was "Rose of Washington Square," a number songwriters Ballard MacDonald and James F. Hanley had created expressly for her after hearing about a Jewish art model in the Bronx.[52] They transferred the subject of the song by poetic license to Greenwich Village and provided two sets of lyrics, one serious and one comic.[53] The former uses lugubrious generalities to describe the short-lived love affair between a "gay butterfly" and a "beautiful rose." It could have been sung by anyone and probably was, but there is no indication that Brice ever performed it that way. She certainly did not in the *Nine O'Clock Revue* where *Variety* stated that she "drew fresh laughter." The comic version supplied her with the kind of material she handled so beautifully, giving her ample room for parody. She could not dance as she did in "Becky," "I'm an Indian," and "Spring," but portraying Rosie, "the queen of models," allowed her to strike a variety of supposedly artistic poses which must have been very funny. As she sang in dialect, she boasted about her bohemian beaux, acknowledged her Roman nose, admitted that she had no future, and gloated, "but Oh what a past!"[54]

In the *Midnight Frolic*, well received despite the fact that several numbers were carried over from the October edition, Brice performed two songs. One of them was "Spring," in *Variety*'s words, a "repeater." The other was Ballard MacDonald's "Rockaway Baby," in which Brice, dressed as a little girl, sat in a rocking chair with her doll. The comical costume and amusing lyrics contrasted effectively with the show's "beautiful girls," "sumptuous costumes," and elaborate pictorial effects. These pleased the "Roofians," as did specialty acts by a variety of performers. The one disappointment was Ziegfeld's latest Parisian import, Mademoiselle Spinelly. She specialized in bizarre costumes, including one crystal bodice "so cut that very little is left to the imagination." According to *Variety* she had returned "too recently from Paris" and her numbers failed because "nobody seemed to know what" they were all "about."[55]

Although both productions were initially successful, business was dismal by the end of May. Ziegfeld closed the *Nine O'Clock Revue* and announced that the *Midnight Frolic* would only continue until the next edition of the *Follies* arrived in New York. After the customary preview in Atlantic City, the *Ziegfeld Follies of 1920* opened at the New Amsterdam Theatre on June 22.

Brice was one of the show's outstanding performers. As the *Times* saw it, she was "working harder and more often than she ever did before in her life" and was "quite at her most comical" in the three sketches that featured her.[56] The first was Act I's "The Family Ford" in which she played Mrs. Fliverton, wife to W. C. Fields's irascible George Fliverton and mother to Ray Dooley's cantankerous Baby Rose. In the opening scene of the second act, she and Fields played another comical husband and wife in "The Little Follies Theatre during Intermission." She had a "laughing moment" here, *Variety* reported, when she accused Fields of flirting with a chorus girl and proceeded to drag him from the theatre. In the third scene, "The Dancing School—Her First Lesson," Brice was able to perform another of the burlesque ballet numbers she did so well. She was the new pupil and looked especially clumsy next to graceful Mary Eaton, "whose toes twinkled like stars of the first magnitude." In contrast, Brice danced in "her inimitably ludicrous way."[57]

Brice also had two extremely successful songs. The first was another "vamp" number, "I'm a Vamp from East Broadway" by Irving Berlin, Bert Kalmar, and Harry Ruby. According to one enthusiastic observer, it was a "corker" and Brice, praised as a "really brilliant travesty artist," performed it "with telling effect."[58] *Variety* described the end of the song in which she held an imaginary conversation with one of her East Side victims. She smirked as he detailed the ruin her vamping had brought him. When he had concluded his tale of woe, she said, "You look terrible, thank God!" and flounced triumphantly offstage.[59]

In the second act, Brice sang Ballard MacDonald and Harry Carroll's "I was a Florodora Baby," an amusing parody of *Florodora*, one of the most successful musical comedies of the 1900-01 Broadway season. Originally produced in London, *Florodora* opened in New York at the Casino Theatre in November 1900 and proceeded to run for more than five hundred performances. The improbable story, which concerned an attempt to cheat a beautiful heiress out of her rights to a famous perfume, did not account for the show's unexpected popularity. What brought crowds to the theatre night after night was a scene in the second act in which six fashionably dressed young women sang a duet with six equally attractive young men. To her partner's polite query, "Tell me, pretty maiden, are there any more at home like you?" each chorus girl responded demurely, "There are a few, kind sir, but simple girls and proper too." The charming song continued through several coquettish verses, as the handsome couples glided around the stage to the delight of the audience.[60]

The six Florodora girls, known as the Florodora sextette, became phenomenally—and tangibly—successful. Deluged with expensive gifts from wealthy admirers, escorted to glittering after-theatre suppers at New York's most glamorous nightspots, all six of the original sextette fulfilled every chorus girl's dream and married millionaires. They were immediately replaced by new Florodora girls, eager for similar fame and fortune. There was continual turnover in the sextette, as individual members left for marriage or more lucrative theatrical opportunities.[61]

The popular musical was frequently revived and had just enjoyed another profitable New York run during the 1919–20 season. It was, therefore, a logical choice for a *Follies* spoof. Brice obliged with a timely Yiddish-accented lament in which she posed as a Florodora girl who has not shared her fellow chorines' success. Unlike her five friends who quickly found rich husbands, she married for love twenty years earlier when she decided on Abie, a drummer. Now the "other girls are living fancy," but her address is strictly Lower East Side: Seventeen Delancey. Her friends go to the best restaurants and dine on steak, while she has to settle for cakes at local delicatessens. They enjoy high society; she remains in the chorus, "a disgrace to the whole sextette." Yet she really is not unhappy. Although she chides herself for supposedly having made the wrong choice, she has a husband she loves and her own sextette at home—or, as she puts it, "Five I've got, the other one I'll get yet."[62] Such lyrics must have allowed Brice to indulge in some gentle self-mockery as the perpetual chorine, with the gestures and grimaces in which she specialized. Combined with her great personal warmth and her amusing accent, "I Was a Florodora Baby" must have been extremely entertaining.

Brice contributed substantially to the success of the *Ziegfeld Follies of 1920*, which did well over the summer in spite of generally poor Broadway business. On October 22, *Variety* noted that the show had averaged $31,000 weekly, a higher figure than in previous seasons, and predicted a "road cleanup." The first stop was Boston, where critics applauded Brice and the production drew enthusiastic audiences into November. From there, it traveled to Cleveland, Detroit, and Chicago, doing capacity business until midway in its ten-week run when *Variety* reported it did not hold up to its "whirlwind start."[63] The returns were also disappointing in Cincinnati, Columbus, and Philadelphia, the last city on the *Follies* route. When the show opened there at the beginning of April, critics commented on the "lack of humor this year" and noted that profits were "distinctly under last year's average."[64]

Such remarks seem surprising in view of the favorable response the *Ziegfeld Follies of 1920* initially received. There was, however, an explanation for the lackluster conclusion to a promising run: Fanny Brice was no longer in the show. She had dropped out during the week of February 10 in Chicago and box office receipts immediately declined. The *Follies* managed to run without her until April 16, but it is no wonder that the Philadelphia critics noted a "lack of humor." Although Fields and Dooley were still in the cast, the production had lost much of its comic clout with Brice's departure.

Variety said nothing about Brice's leaving, nor did critics along the route, but the February 19, 1921, *Billboard* carried an item announcing, under the heading "Fanny Brice Quits," that she had canceled her contract for the rest of the engagement, "owing to ill health."[65] Brice, however, was not sick; she was almost seven months pregnant. She was also preoccupied with her husband's continuing legal problems. Arnstein's lawyer had succeeded in having his trial transferred to Washington, D.C., because, if found guilty there, Nicky faced a maximum of only two years in prison; in New York, he could be sentenced to as many as twenty-five for the same offense.[66] On April 23, 1921, one week after the *Follies* closed in

Philadelphia, with Nicky in Washington, Brice gave birth to their son, William—supposedly named after Arnstein's lawyer, William Fallon—in New York.

Convicted of transporting stolen Wall Street securities, Arnstein proceeded to initiate a lengthy appeal funded, of course, by Brice. However difficult the ordeal was for her, she recalled years later that he seemed to revel in the attendant publicity. "When he was out on bail, everyone would want to meet him. When someone sat down at our table in a restaurant and I would tell them Nick had nothing to do with it, he would shut me up," she reminisced. "He enjoyed all that stuff and the headlines. He wanted people to think of him as the Master Mind."[67] If anyone was masterful, it was Brice. Juggling the demands of family and career, concerned about her husband's complicated legal affairs and impending incarceration, she resolutely returned to work. Within weeks after William's birth, she was rehearsing for the *Ziegfeld Follies of 1921.*

The October 1920 *Vanity Fair* had called the twenty-nine-year-old Brice "the most finished artist of them all." A glowing article in the popular magazine had asserted that "no one in America is so sure of her audience, so subtle in her burlesque, so much a mistress of expression, so skillful in turning the vulgar to artistic account."[68] In the fifteenth *Follies*, she would surprise that audience by demonstrating her ability to handle serious material as well. Whereas the *Ziegfeld Follies of 1920* had called upon her to present variations on familiar themes (the ballerina and the vamp) and exploited her talent as a comedienne, the *Ziegfeld Follies of 1921* would reveal her unexpected range as an entertainer. In addition to performing "her usual dialect songs," as *Theatre Magazine* put it, "with her inimitable sense of character," she would sing "My Man," one of the two songs (the other being "Sadie Salome") she later said had had the greatest impact on her career.[69]

After previewing in Atlantic City, the *Ziegfeld Follies of 1921* opened at New York's Globe Theatre on June 21. With two acts and twenty-nine scenes, the lavish production was not without its detractors. A few critics suggested that it was overdone and at least one voiced the dangerous opinion that it was boring. Most reviewers, though, were enthusiastic. Among the performers, several won praise, including W. C. Fields, Raymond Hitchcock, Ray Dooley, Charles O'Donnell, Mary Eaton, Florence O'Denishawn, Germaine Mitti, and Fanny Brice.

"If there is one figure above all the others who stands out as the chief bright light of the *Follies* this season, it is Fannie Brice," wrote an enthusiastic critic, expressing an opinion that many shared.[70] As *Variety*'s Lait observed, using some picturesque imagery to describe her versatile performance:

> Miss Brice easily qualified as principal comic, despite the distinguished competition. She was all over the *Follies*. She appeared no less than a dozen times and her repertoire ran through typical Brice songs, Barrymore burlesque, hoakum prize fighting with Ray Dooley, housewife-character, serious song-drama, satire and ludicrous Dainty Marie stuff. She had the fattest lines and the skinniest legs in the troupe and thus she guzzled the gravy and gobbled the apple sauce. It is by far the most conspicuous work this veteran funner has ever offered.[71]

In calculating her "dozen" appearances, *Variety* must have included those numbers in which Brice participated but did not figure prominently (such as the first and second act finales). Excluding these, she had seven major parts in the show, four in the first act and three in the second. Her first came in the production's seventh scene when she performed Grant Clarke and James Hanley's "Second Hand Rose."[72] One critic stated she had never been more amusing, and she always considered the song one of her most successful pieces.

In addition to being perfect for Brice's brand of comedy, "Second Hand Rose" was better written than many of her other songs so that it not only created an interesting character, but told her story very well. Brice as Rose wails that she has never had "a thing that ain't been used." It is not just the secondhand hats and pearls, not just the piano in the parlor that her father bought "for ten cents on the dollar," not just the pajamas with "somebody else's 'nitials on 'em" that bother her. It is the girl who got her "goat" one day at the Ritz by nudging her friend, pointing to Rose, and exclaiming, "Look, there's my old fur coat." Even worse, it is Jake the plumber, the man she adores, who "had the nerve to tell" her "he's been married before." As performed by Brice with animated accent and gestures, Rose's lament must have been funny indeed.

Brice returned five scenes later to sing Blanche Merrill and Leo Edwards's "I'm a Hieland Lassie," for which she created an amusing combination of Scottish and Yiddish accents.[73] Originally called "My Scotch Jewbell," the number spoofed music-hall and vaudeville superstar Sir Harry Lauder, one of whose songs was "My Scotch Bluebell." Although the tasteless title was soon dropped, Brice's hilarious parody of the perennially popular Lauder was one of the highlights of the first act. She appeared as a Lauder lookalike in tartan kilt and socks so that her knees, often her most expressive appendage, were in full view, then sang:

I'm a Hieland Lassie. Get the quilts, I'm classy.
I don't care about a thing. Hoot mon, Hoot mon, Hoot mon, Hoot mon!
No one would have known my Christian name was Cohen
'Cause look! I'm a regular Hieland fling![74]

In scene fourteen, Brice appeared with Raymond Hitchcock and W. C. Fields in a spoof of the theatrical Barrymores, playing Ethel to Hitchcock's Lionel and Fields's Jack. Brice's Ethel was performing her favorite role, the tubercular courtesan Marguerite Gautier in *Camille* or *The Lady of the Camellias*. Brice remembered the scene fondly as "great." In her March 1936 *Cosmopolitan* reminiscences, she recalled lying on her bed, coughing terribly, and finally speaking: "'Yes, yes, Armand, I know— I know I have been a bad, bad voman'—this in Yiddish accent—with a delicious leer—'but awfully good company, *nu?*'"[75] The idea of the imperiously beautiful Barrymore speaking with a Yiddish accent must have been so improbable that it alone could have assured the scene's success. The cartoon concluded with a song called "Lionel, Ethel and Jack" which one observer said "poked good-natured fun" at the threesome's well-known eccentricities.[76]

Brice continued to capitalize on her wonderful flair for burlesque in her next appearance as boxer George Carpentier in a bout with Ray Dooley's Jack Dempsey. Hitchcock announced, Fields refereed, and the *Follies* Girls followed the fight as frantic fans. The sketch was certainly timely as the then-unpopular Dempsey was about to defend his heavyweight title against European champion Carpentier in a 60,000-seat stadium near Jersey City on July 2, 1921. The first important sports event ever broadcast by radio, the fight, according to one source, "was listened to eagerly in thousands of speakeasies, pool rooms, lodge halls, barns and living rooms up and down the East Coast."[77] Dempsey held the title with a fourth-round knockout. In the *Follies*, after lanky Brice had exchanged blows and grimaces with tiny Dooley, the fight ended in a knockout for everyone on stage, including the referee, the announcer, and the chorus girls seated at ringside.[78]

In the second act, Brice perched on a web to sing Ballard MacDonald and James Hanley's "Allay Up," an acrobatic spoof one opening night observer found "screamingly funny." She cavorted with Fields, Hitchcock, and Dooley in "Off to the Country," a subway sketch which Woollcott called "hilarious." But her most memorable appearance was in "The Bridge on the Seine," when she presented an uncharacteristically serious selection, "My Man." As Brice acknowledged in 1936, it was a song with which she would be "inescapably connected," although she often maintained that she was surprised at the emotional impact it always had on her audiences. She recalled how she had come to sing it:

> Flo brought it to me soon after Nick's departure with these words: "Listen, Fannie, I've got a song for you. It is so great I've commissioned Channing Pollock to write the English words. Don't try to get funny—it's supposed to be sad."
>
> To be honest, no one thought of connecting this song of the forlorn apache girl with my personal life. It was a fine number, sung all over Paris. Ziegfeld and I never dreamed what it would do to an audience at just this time.[79]

It is difficult to take this seriously. The naivete she attributes to Ziegfeld and herself is ludicrous; "My Man" obviously capitalized on her relationship with Arnstein. By 1921, anyone who read newspapers would have recognized the connection of life and lyrics. If Ziegfeld had simply wanted the maudlin song in his show, there were more likely candidates to perform it. Surely he deliberately chose Brice because he knew what an impact her singing it would have. Moreover, he did not offer it to her "soon after Nick's departure," as Brice said, in 1920. He gave it to her a year later, when the pain was not so fresh and she had come to terms with the reality of her complicated situation. In 1920, when Arnstein was still in hiding, she probably could not have performed it.

Further undermining Brice's credibility is Channing Pollock's claim that he suggested the "remarkable ballad" to "Flo" after hearing Mistinguett, a popular French music-hall performer, sing it at the Casino de Paris. "Because of it," Pollock stated in his autobiography, Ziegfeld "engaged Fannie Brice."[80] The implication is that both men were very much aware of the reciprocity between song and singer. The number that became Brice's signature began as Mistinguett's, but the two versions were actually very different. In adapting Albert Willemetz, Jacques Charles, and Maurice Yvain's composition for Brice, Pollock did more than change the lyrics from French into English. As he readily admitted, he had made "an almost literal translation" on his return from Paris and, "finding it impossible," had written "completely new verses with the original theme."[81]

Both as it was written and as it was sung by Mistinguett, "Mon Homme" was much tougher, harsher, and earthier than "My Man." The singer in the original knows that her "demon man" is going to be her undoing, but she is unable to suppress the profound physical attraction she feels for him. He controls her to such an extent that, as she unhappily admits, she would even kill if he demanded it. She is willing to endure his terrible abuse because she feels so passionately about him. Their relationship is dangerous, destructive, even diabolical, but it is all-consuming and she is powerless to end it.

"Mon Homme" may have been acceptable in Paris, but it was unsuitable for New York. As Pollock realized, the predominantly middle class crowds that flocked to the *Follies* would not have tolerated the song's sadomasochistic overtones and intimations of immorality. *Follies* audiences did not go to a Ziegfeld production for a slice of grim reality, nor did "Flo" consider anything sordid the province of his elaborate productions. Glorifying the American Girl, and presenting the beautiful, was the Ziegfeld credo. "Mon Homme" did not qualify. It was too brutal, too ugly.

As Brice interpreted it in the *Ziegfeld Follies of 1921*, "My Man" was cleansed of its unappetizing implications. As Pollock explained, he retained the song's "original theme," but removed any glimpse it afforded of unsavory Parisian street life. The overwhelming impression the English version creates is very different from the French. The refrain, "Oh my God, I love him so," conveys despair, but it lacks the intensity of "I'm going crazy because he's under my skin." Although Pollock's lyrics acknowledge the man's brutality with "he beats me too," the detail that he takes the singer's money is omitted, altering the nature of their relationship. In the English, he is her lover, however callous; in the French, he is her pimp. That change is significant because it makes "My Man"'s singer more sympathetic. Though weak, she is not a whore. In addition, the reference to "demon homme" is eliminated, as is the important admission that she would kill for him.

In Pollock's translation, "Mon Homme" has been sanitized and turned into a sentimental ballad. With its presentation of woman as victim and its prospect of a possible reconciliation for the two lovers, "My Man" is similar to so many turn-of-the-century sentimental songs which audiences loved and with which Brice began her career. In performing it, she was returning to a genre with which she was comfortable, but that alone would not have accounted for "My Man"'s tremendous success. What made it a sensation in 1921, and ever after, was the illusion Brice created of singing about herself. She convinced audiences that they were hearing a musical true confessions, that she was sharing her own painful experience with them. They were seeing a facet of Fanny that she had not previously revealed, they believed, and found it very moving. Regardless of her statements in *Cosmopolitan*, she could not have been oblivious to the strong parallel between the song and her own life. She must have known that people would see "My Man" as autobiographical and that this perception would lend poignancy and resonance to an already effective vehicle.

Whether the idea was originally Pollock's or Ziegfeld's, Brice had agreed to perform a song that was totally different from the material with which she was normally associated. Unlike all her other big hits, "My Man" was not a burlesque. It involved no dialect, no parody, no outrageous physical humor. Whereas her successful comic songs allowed her to mimic and debunk her subjects through hilarious movements and gestures, "My Man" was surprisingly static. Members of an audience expecting a typical Brice spoof would have been shocked to see her standing almost motionless, to hear her singing without a funny accent, to find themselves crying at her pain instead of howling with delight at her ridiculous behavior. If her other songs were designed to produce laughter, "My Man" was clearly intended to inspire tears. The emotional effect was as carefully calculated as the ludicrous dance steps she habitually choreographed. With "My Man," Brice greatly expanded her artistic range, but she did so by consciously manipulating the feelings of her audiences. She had consented to participate in the exploitation of her personal life and misfortunes for profit.

Brice sang "My Man" on opening night in a torn costume smeared with ashes, underneath the flickering glare of a streetlight.[82] When she finished, she received tumultuous applause. As she recalled in 1936, "It wasn't a theater I was standing in, it was pandemonium. I can feel my body shake now with the thunder of it," she continued, trying to explain the intensity of her own reaction to the piece. "That immortal song! It was not my song—it was every woman's song."[83] Yet, in spite of her disclaimer, "My Man" was undeniably Brice's song. Even her young daughter, Frances, responded to the obvious emotion which her mother showed in performing it. Years later, discussing one of the many occasions on which she sang it, Brice remembered seeing Frances crying in the wings. As she came off stage, she wondered why her daughter was so upset. "She was so young and what could the words mean to her?" Brice wrote. "I picked her up and I carried her to the dressing-room and I wiped her tears. 'Why are you crying?' I asked her. 'Because you looked so sad,' Frances said."[84] If the feelings were not genuine, it was a brilliant performance.

Ziegfeld was at his entrepreneurial best when he gave "My Man" to Brice. The decision was fortuitous for the *Ziegfeld Follies of 1921* and for her career. As reviewers praised her artistry and genius, Ziegfeld responded to the critical acclaim by raising her weekly salary from $1,000 to $2,500. She had succeeded beyond even his expectations and had demonstrated that she was capable of interpreting serious material as well as comic. Unfortunately, however, Brice would never be able to put "My Man" behind her. It became her signature. Although she could not have realized it in 1921, she would never again have a song with so much emotional power.

Largely because of Brice, the *Ziegfeld Follies of 1921* did well despite an unprecedented heat wave, which almost caused the collapse of the Broadway summer season. The show remained in New York until the end of September, when it began its tour with a five-week stop in Boston. The *Globe*'s critic appreciated the production and admired Brice's work, especially "Second Hand Rose" and "My Man," which he described inexplicably as a "Scotch ditty," probably having confused it with her Harry Lauder impersonation.[85] From there, the *Follies* went to Philadelphia, Pittsburgh, and Chicago, where a contract dispute with a member of the chorus threatened to close the show. The Chicago newspapers portrayed Brice as the ringleader of the proposed strike but she denied any knowledge of it in a telephone call to Ziegfeld. After a prosperous eight-week engagement, the *Follies* continued on the road until its mid-April closing in Washington, D.C.

When it did, Brice's plans were uncertain. As early as January 1922, Ziegfeld had announced his intention of starring her in a new musical production. In March, *Variety* announced that she would appear in the next edition of the *Follies* instead. In April, however, *Variety* informed its readers that she would "not go with the *Follies* this summer," but would "later be starred by Ziegfeld in a Rida Johnson Young play." On May 5, the paper relayed Ziegfeld's plan to "star her in a new musical comedy next season."[86] In the meantime, Brice would return to vaudeville, opening at the Palace on June 12.

She actually made her vaudeville debut one week earlier in Washington, D.C., playing there June 5–10. On Friday of that week, a poem appeared in *Variety* called "When I Was with the *Follies*." It was signed "Fanny Brice," but had been written by Blanche Merrill and presented a wistful Brice remembering her many happy years in the musical extravaganza:

> This week I'm playing vaudeville—first time in seven years.
> This week the *Follies* opened and ringing in my ears
> Are the applause and the excitement that thrills those opening nights
> And makes the *Ziegfeld Follies* the greatest of theatrical flights.

I've been with the *Follies* so long that tonight I'm kinda blue
Thinking of all the fun I've had and now all the fun is through.
I can hear Flo say in his drawly way: "Now Fanny, listen here.
You better get some good songs or you'll be a flop this year."[87]

She must have felt considerably better after reading the reviews. Washington audiences appreciated her act and the New York critics were even more enthusiastic. Sime reviewed the Palace bill and Brice's part in it at length in *Variety*. She was on next-to-closing, the headliner's slot, and showed that she deserved that program position as she "whanged them for thirty minutes with songs and fun." Sime was impressed with her new act which wasted "not a second" and succeeded in putting her "delectable comedy and self . . . entirely over."[88]

Brice treated her audience to an international songfest called "Around the World." As she performed her songs, placards on an easel indicated the country represented with Brice appearing in a different costume, as a distinct character, for each one. She began with an introductory number called "I'm Back Again," full of amusing personal references. According to Sime, the combination of Blanche Merrill's clever lyrics and Brice's delightful delivery made the song "an act in itself." The globe-trotting began with a "Scotch number," which must have been "I'm a Hieland Lassie." Next came "I'm an Indian." It was followed by what Sime called the "Grecian travestied dance number" (probably "Spring"), then "My Man" as the Parisian entry, and a recitation. New York squeaked in with an encore, "Second Hand Rose."[89]

Only the opening song was new, but Sime did not seem to mind and approved of the selection. He thought that it showed Brice's "pleasing singing voice to good advantage" and admired her interpretation of "Second Hand Rose," in which a "certain plaintiveness" gave "added force to this comic ballad." As it had in the *Follies*, her sensitive treatment of "My Man" showed that she could be serious, while her comic skills made her "one of the best clowns among the women." Sime praised the skillful means by which she amused, noting that "an expression or gesture or movement, if intended for comedy by Miss Brice will bring a laugh," and added that her act was "a succession of laughs." He also acknowledged the considerable part Blanche Merrill played in Brice's success. She understood Brice so well and could "so fit her personality and style" that the best songs "Fanny Brice has had and those she has now brought into vaudeville were written by that brilliant young woman." He remarked that few vaudeville acts could sustain the consistently high level of amusement that Brice offered in over thirty minutes of "clean entertainment," and concluded, "She may have been away from vaudeville for a long while, but it was worth the wait to see how she came back to it."[90]

For her second week at the Palace, Brice moved to the middle of the bill, closing the first half. She performed the same act and Bell, this edition's *Variety* reviewer, said it placed her "quite in a class by herself in vaudeville" as a "finished artiste—and that most rare of human beings —a funny woman." In the twenties, that was indeed a rarity. The Jazz Age may have been the era of "flappers and bathtub gin and 'necking,' of rumble-seat romance, of women who 'shingled' their hair and for the first time smoked in public."[91] It may have been a spirited time of rebellion and frivolity in which women enjoyed a new freedom. But it was also a period in which women were still supposed to be glamorous, when sex appeal was called "It" and movie star Clara Bow would soon become "It's" personification, when the Miss America pageant—established in 1921— reinforced the American ideal of feminine beauty.[92] For a woman to play the clown so freely was indeed unusual and Brice undoubtedly endeared herself to audiences by doing so. Yet it was ultimately her great skill as a performer that made her work so memorable. Bell observed that one of her strongest assets was "the ease and repressed method by which she marks the delivery of her numbers."[93] Such a comment contrasts with many of the notices Brice received early in her career. Then she was often criticized for trying too hard, for straining to be funny, for "pushing" as it is called in contemporary stage jargon. As a mature and confident artist, she did not need to do that any longer. Comfortable with her onstage persona, she had refined her comic technique. She could concentrate on creating a variety of amusing characters through increasingly subtle means —as one appreciative reviewer put it, "the slightest movement of her hands, the merest glance of her eyes."

Brice played two more weeks at the Palace, adding "I was a Florodora Baby" to her act, and was just as well received. On August 19, she sailed to Europe for a vacation, after having spent most of July negotiating with Ziegfeld. *Variety* reported that upon returning to New York she expected to appear "in a new play Flo Ziegfeld has promised her, written by Rida Johnson Young."[94] Before he left, however, unexpected complications had arisen. Ziegfeld also wanted Ann Pennington to appear in the production. Pennington had just starred in George White's *Scandals*, a musical competitor of the *Follies*, and named terms identical to Brice's: "ten percent of the gross," reported *Variety*, "and a guarantee to be featured." Ziegfeld balked at the prospect of two "ten percenters in one show" and refused to capitulate to either woman's demands.

Brice remained abroad through September, hoping perhaps that the uncertain situation would be resolved in her absence. When she returned from London on October 3, she found that Ziegfeld and Pennington had been unable to come to terms and that Pennington had been engaged by rival producer Charles Dillingham. *Variety* had already reported that Ziegfeld was preparing "the new Fannie Brice musical piece by Rida Johnson Young and Jerome Kern due to open in November."[95] Yet on October 30, Brice headlined at the Palace and remained in vaudeville for the next seven weeks. She was obviously not involved in rehearsals for Ziegfeld.

Brice must have been terribly disappointed that, once again, Ziegfeld had not kept his promise to her, but at least her vaudeville reviews were raves. After having seen her in the October 30 matinee, *Billboard* critic Mark Henry rated her at one hundred percent entertainment value and emphatically stated that she stopped the show. From his description of her performance, it is clear that she was doing the act Sime had loved in June, with one change. She had added a song, "Dancing Shoes," which she sang in "male attire" and which Henry considered weak. She subsequently removed the number, substituting "Egyptian" for the unsuccessful male impersonation. Henry applauded the decision, declaring that it showed great wisdom on her part, and observed that her "big luminating artistry" was "outstanding in the wonderful conception of 'Mon Homme.'"[96]

On December 15, *Variety* reported encouraging news: Ziegfeld was about to cast "the new Fannie Brice show."[97] For three weeks, there were no vaudeville listings for her, as she was presumably preparing for her long-awaited starring role. On January 8, 1923, however, she was again headlining at the Palace. It was her third appearance in a seven-month period, and an item in the January 19 *Variety* provided the explanation. Ziegfeld was in Palm Beach, recuperating from an undisclosed illness, and Brice's show, tentatively called *Rebecca*, was now slated for a spring production in New York. *Variety* added that it might be "held up for a few weeks" pending Ziegfeld's return to work. It was delayed, but for several months. The next announcement about the on-again off-again show came in the June 30 *Billboard*, according to which Brice was supposed to begin rehearsing the following week for the production, now called *Laughing Lena.*[98]

In the interim, Brice remained in vaudeville. Between her January Palace engagement and her concluding week at the Orpheum Theatre in

Los Angeles from June 18 to 23, she worked steadily, appearing in Washington, D.C., Providence, Manhattan, Brooklyn, Kansas City, Chicago, St. Louis, Milwaukee, Minneapolis, and San Francisco. She played the Palace again in late February and the *Times* review made the disturbing observation that the audience might actually be tiring of her songs, "some new and some not so new, all delivered in her familiar manner." *Billboard* disagreed, stating that she "did nothing new" because "she doesn't have to." According to the enthusiastic Henry, "her song characterizations are classics," she "clowns delightfully, and has her own inimitable way of putting over numbers."[99] In April at Chicago's Palace, she stopped the show three times with her "rare sense of romping fun." In St. Louis, the audience demanded six encores. In San Francisco, *Billboard*'s correspondent called her a "song characterization genius" and noted that the Orpheum audiences welcomed her warmly after an eight-year absence. They enjoyed her "brilliant impersonations" and clamored for "My Man," which she finally performed. Wearing "the apachian black and red, leaning against a lamp post, with great pathos," she gave a moving "portrayal of the abused companion of some slum brute singing of her love."[100]

Brice returned to New York to begin work on *Laughing Lena* but once again the phantom production never materialized. The last mention of it came in the July 26 *Variety*, where an item on Blanche Merrill noted that she was preparing some material for "the Ziegfeld-Brice show."[101] By the end of August, however, Ziegfeld's plans had changed. The August 30 *Variety* reported that Ziegfeld had "definitely decided on the musical which will star Fannie Brice." It had no title, but its authors were now Ring Lardner and Rudolf Friml. Yet, less than a month later, the newspaper informed its readers that Brice would instead be featured as a principal in the forthcoming edition of Ziegfeld's *Follies*, "notwithstanding the many stories of a starring piece for Miss Brice by the same producer."[102] In spite of all the changes and postponements, the promises and press releases, none of the plans had come to fruition.

Ziegfeld never explained his decision to abandon Brice's show. It was not the first time one of his much-ballyhooed productions had been junked in the planning stage, nor would it be the last. In the coming years as his career declined, more and more of his announced projects would share the fate of *Rebecca/Laughing Lena*.

Although Brice must have been frustrated at the eighteen months of deliberations and delays, she had kept characteristically busy. In addition to her vaudeville engagements, she had also made a successful debut as a "canned" vocalist for the Victor Talking Machine Company. In February

1922, she had recorded two of her best numbers, "Second Hand Rose" and "My Man," for Victor and received a very favorable response from *Variety*. In November, the newspaper enthusiastically reviewed her two latest Victor releases, "Becky Is Back in the Ballet" and "The Sheik of Avenue B," a new song spoofing movie star Rudolph Valentino. The "Great Lover" of the 1920s had made his sensational silent film *The Sheik* in 1921 and its spectacular success inspired Brice's amusing parody. Her sheik lived on the Lower East Side and she recounted his exploits with an appropriately heavy Yiddish accent. "He treats the girls rough / His hugs and kisses scare 'em," she gleefully sang, "He don't spare 'em / You should see his Hebrew harem." Her Jewish sheik "acts like a real Arabian lord / Since he bought a brand-new, second-hand Ford." As *Variety* succinctly put it, "two typical Fanny Brice numbers are aptly fannybriced by the inimitable comedienne."[103]

Nevertheless, the disappointments of 1922–23 must have been extremely difficult for her to accept. In addition, there was her ongoing concern about Nicky, whose precarious legal situation remained unresolved. The thirty-two-year-old Brice responded by taking a drastic step, one that would have serious consequences for both her marriage and her career. In August, she decided to have cosmetic surgery on her nose. Always dissatisfied with her appearance, she probably felt that if she were prettier she would be more likely to realize her dramatic ambitions. She may also have wanted to look less ethnic, believing that her obviously Semitic nose was keeping her from being accepted as a serious actress. The public display which surrounded her rhinoplasty, however, suggests a certain desperation on Brice's part, a desire to take control of her life and work with one decisive act. Her plastic surgery in 1923 was to have disastrous repercussions in the coming years, years in which her marriage failed and her career threatened to founder.

Will Rapport portrait drawing of Brice, probably in the *Ziegfeld Follies of 1936* (Harvard
Theatre Collection)

Undated publicity shot of a young Brice (Billy Rose Theatre Collection,
New York Public Library at Lincoln Center, Astor, Lenox and Tilden
Foundations)

Brice in the *Follies of 1910* (Billy Rose Theatre Collection, New York Public Library at Lincoln Center, Astor, Lenox and Tilden Foundations)

FANNIE BRICE IN "FOLLIES OF 1910"

Caricature of Brice in the *Follies of 1910* (Harvard Theatre Collection)

Brice as Nijinsky in the *Ziegfeld Follies of 1916* (Harvard Theatre Collection)

Brice in characteristic "My Man" pose, in about 1921 (Harvard Theatre Collection)

FANNIE BRICE SAYS A FEW THINGS ABOUT HER NOSE
Provided by the FAMOUS FACIAL SURGEON, DR. HENRY J. SCHIRESON, of Chicago.

"I am making this statement of my own free will and spending my own money to correct a wrong that I believe has been done a veritable genius in his specialization in surgery, because I personally feel I am indebted to Dr. Henry J. Schireson to that extent for the splendid work that he has done for me in operating on my nose.

"Prior to consulting Dr. Schireson I satisfied myself of his surgical abilities in facial corrections through viewing the physical miracles that he performed for the Brill Sisters, Frankie James, Minnie Allen, Stepanoff the dancer, Senator Murphy, Rubini Sisters, Ben Burd of Bard and Pearl, and Weston and Elaine, all of whom he successfully operated on and who are to my own personal knowledge not only entirely satisfied with his work, but also feel deeply indebted to him for what he accomplished for them.

"I believe that the greatest expression of undoubted faith that I have in Dr. Schireson is shown in the fact that I insisted that my brother, Lew Brice, have his nose operated on by him, and now, despite all disclosures regarding the doctor, I am having my second brother undergo an operation as soon as the doctor returns to his offices at the State Lake Bldg. in Chicago.

"My principal reason for making this statement, in addition to public expression of my faith in the doctor, is to assure well-meaning friends, who have been incessantly telephoning me and expressing their condolences—while I thank them for their interest, I wish to assure them that I have no need for expressions of sympathy—that I'm satisfied, and I believe that is sufficient."

(Signed) FANNIE BRICE.

Brice, supposedly "before" and "after" plastic surgery (*Billboard*, 5 January 1924, p. 18)

Publicity shots for *Fanny*, including one with a doctored nose, 1926 (Billy Rose Theatre Collection, New York Public Library at Lincoln Center, Astor, Lenox and Tilden Foundations)

Brice in the *Ziegfeld Follies of 1934*, "Countess Dubinsky" striptease and fan dance (*Stage*, January 1934, pp. 26–27)

Brice as Zuleika and Bob Hope as Sir Robert in "Fancy, Fancy," *Ziegfeld Follies of 1936* (*Stage*, March 1936, p. 51)

Brice helps her daughter, Frances, apply makeup for a onetime appearance in the opening number of the *Ziegfeld Follies of 1936* (Harvard Theatre Collection)

Brice and her son, William, in New York, April 1938 (Harvard Theatre Collection)

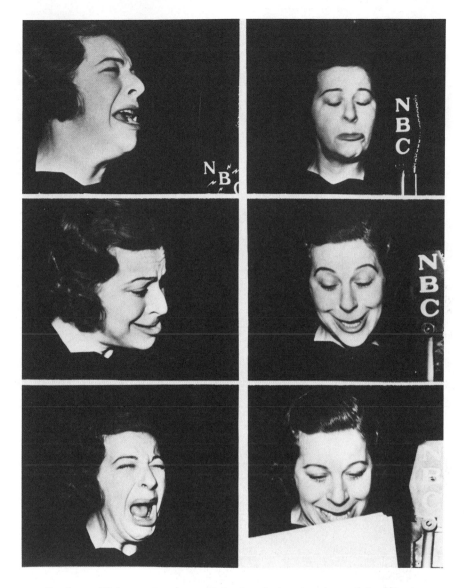

Six shots of Brice performing as Baby Snooks in a broadcast of the "Good News of 1938" radio show, NBC photograph, 13 April 1938 (Billy Rose Theatre Collection, New York Public Library at Lincoln Center, Astor, Lenox and Tilden Foundations)

Publicity shot of Brice as Baby Snooks for the "Maxwell House Coffee Time" radio show, NBC photograph, 1944 (Harvard Theatre Collection)

Publicity shot of Brice for radio, 1943 (Harvard Theatre Collection)

Plastic Surgery for the Stage

7.

No woman on the stage today can afford to have a nose that is likely to keep on growing until she can swallow it.

—FANNY BRICE, *New York Times*, 15 August 1923[1]

The Thursday, August 2, 1923, *New York Times* devoted many of its pages to detailed reports of the sudden illness of the country's twenty-ninth President, Warren G. Harding, while traveling in California. The amiable Republican had won a landslide victory in the presidential election of 1920 and had not yet been tainted by evidence of rampant corruption within his administration. The nation would subsequently learn of the many scandals Harding sanctioned, including the illegal leasing of naval oil reserves at Teapot Dome, Wyoming, but in the summer of 1923 the former farm boy, newspaper editor, and Senator from Ohio was at the height of his popularity, and his precarious health was a matter of grave concern.

Although articles on the state of Harding's health took up much of the *Times*'s front section, there were other newsworthy items—among them, in the "Amusements" section, a report that Fanny Brice planned to alter her nose through "facial sculpture." "It is now declared possible to change one's face to suit the season or to suit the latest role, if one is in the theatrical profession," the account began. Explaining that an actor named Ben Bard had just had his nose "taken up" by a Chicago surgeon as fascinated reporters watched, the story went on to state that the same doctor would be coming to New York the following week to "work on the face of Miss Fanny Brice." According to the newspaper, Brice "feels she has got all she can out of her nose and mouth and wants new ones to fit her for the comedy roles to which she aspires."[2]

Whatever interest the Brice announcement generated was obliterated by Friday's headline: "PRESIDENT HARDING DIES SUDDENLY OF STROKE OF APOPLEXY AT 7:30 P.M. CALVIN COOLIDGE IS PRESIDENT." In spite of encouraging signs reported earlier, Harding had collapsed on Thursday evening as his wife read aloud to him. "That's good. Go on, read some more," he said, then succumbed "instantaneously" to the "death stroke." The sixth President to die in office, he was immediately succeeded by a somber Coolidge, who took the oath of office in his Vermont living room early Friday morning and pledged to uphold Harding's policies. Mrs. Harding remained brave to the end, even as expressions of sympathy and tributes to her late husband began pouring in.[3]

For the next nine days newspaper coverage was devoted almost exclusively to Harding. Retrospective articles such as "Harding a Farm Boy Who Rose by Work" and "Harding—From Childhood to President" appeared alongside a variety of related stories providing details of the funeral arrangements. The train carrying Harding's body had left San Francisco on Saturday, August 4. After its arrival in Washington, D.C., the flag-draped coffin lay in state in the East Room of the White House. Crowds saw the funeral train as it returned to Marion, Ohio, where Harding was buried on Friday, August 10, following a simple, private service.

The homages to Harding continued through the weekend. By Monday, however, the subject had been exhausted and journalists could concentrate on other events: communist agitation in postwar Germany, a disastrous Wyoming mine explosion that entombed 138, and Fanny Brice's plastic surgery. Contrary to her initial public statement, Brice had not had her operation the previous week. Instead she waited until August 15. It is likely that the delay was not due to her respect for the dead President, but to maximize the amount of attention her rhinoplasty would receive.

Brice was by no means the first to undergo such an operation, nor was she alone in sharing her experience with the public. Plastic surgery was a topic of great interest, and *Variety* often regaled its readers with graphic accounts of celebrity medical procedures. Yet the carnival atmosphere surrounding the Brice nose job was unusual in that it appears to have been deliberately created, indicating that she saw her surgery as another publicity stunt—albeit one with tangible and permanent results. On August 15, the day of the operation, the *New York Times* ran an article under the headline, "FANNIE BRICE'S NOSE TO BE SCALED DOWN." The announcement was dated August 14, issued from Atlantic City, and appeared in newspapers throughout the country:

"Everything about me has stopped growing except my nose," is the explanation offered by Fanny Brice, vaudeville actress, who is to undergo an operation tomorrow to have that conspicuous feature made over into what the plastic surgeons term a "normal" nose. Miss Brice is at the Ritz-Carlton here and the operation will be performed in her apartments at that hotel . . . [by] Dr. Henry J. Schireson, an expert in "recontouring" at 11 o'clock tomorrow morning. . . .

Miss Brice said that she did not fear the operation and that she is willing to undergo the ordeal in order that her nose may return to normalcy. . . . "I have all kinds of faith in Dr. Schireson and I am coming out with a nose which I hope will not detract from if it does not add to my stage appearance."[4]

On August 16, the *New York Times* reported that the operation to change the Brice nose from "prominent" to "merely decorative" had lasted for one hour and forty minutes and had been called a success by the surgical team.[5]

An editorial appeared in the same issue under the heading, "Plastic Surgery for the Stage." It discussed the procedure in the language of a real estate transaction and, although its tone was humorous, stated clearly that "the real reason for the reconstruction of the nose" was Brice's desire "to act in plays of a different type":

Miss Brice, already successful in homely comedy for which the old nose was an asset, now wants to branch out. In the drama of the drawing room the nose might distract attention from the play. . . . Other artists would accept the limitation and go on doing comedy; Miss Brice boldly decides to abolish the inhibitory nose. It is a perilous undertaking, artistically if not surgically. Yet everybody will hope that the purpose which its owner has in mind will be attained. Certainly no great harm can be done, for unlike some other comedians, Miss Brice carries her talent inside her head and not on the frontal elevation.[6]

Since Brice had already expressed her hopes of becoming a serious actress, the *Times*'s observations simply confirmed her previous statements. She thought that a smaller nose would help her gain acceptance on the legitimate stage because, with a less comical appearance, she would seem more appropriate for a wide variety of roles. If she were no longer so funny-looking, she would be believable in drama and would not have to be restricted to comedy.

There was probably another reason why Brice decided to alter her nose. Although she never publicly admitted it, she must have hoped that the operation would make her look less Jewish. Ethnicity was definitely not fashionable in the 1920s, a decade that began with the Justice Department's wholesale deportation of suspicious aliens, a decade that witnessed the execution of anarchists Nicola Sacco and Bartolomeo Vanzetti amid great controversy, a decade tortured by chauvinism, xenophobia, and racism. The Bolshevik revolution abroad and the activities of radicals in the United States triggered a great "Red scare" and created widespread hostility to foreigners. American disillusionment with the Treaty of Versailles led to an increasingly isolationist foreign policy, based on the belief that it was best to sever all ties with Europe and sharply curtail the volume of immigration into this country.[7] Laws passed in 1921 and 1924 established strict quotas that had disastrous consequences during the next World War for Jews trying desperately to escape the Nazi death machine. Within the borders of the United States, millions of Americans donned hoods and terrorized minorities in the name of Aryan supremacy. Fueled by fear and ignorance, the noxious Ku Klux Klan reached the peak of its influence by 1924.[8]

It would be wrong to exaggerate the extent and depth of this intolerance and to overlook the strong current of dissent and protest which also characterized the period.[9] Nevertheless, it is important to recognize that the 1920s was more than simply a carefree time when women threw away their corsets, shortened their skirts, and bobbed their hair. Nostalgia may color our perception of the period as a decade of get-rich-quick schemes, speakeasies, and bathtub gin, but the era was far more complex than such simplistic observations suggest. Prejudice against ethnic groups was very real and produced, among many members of those groups, a desire to assimilate and blend inconspicuously into predominantly Protestant America. Name changes and nose straightenings made the process so much simpler. Brice had escaped from Borach fifteen years earlier; at thirty-two, thanks to medical advances made during World War I, she was ready for plastic surgery.

Algonquin wit Dorothy Parker quipped that Brice had "cut off her nose to spite her race" and there was probably far more truth to that acerbic statement than Brice ever acknowledged. However legitimate her ambition to become a serious actress, it was motivated in part by her wish to escape from the ethnicity of her comedy. She seemed to have decided that her Yiddish-accented routines had become too limiting, and sought acceptance from a broader audience for which, as she saw it, her Jewish mannerisms and appearance were inappropriate.

The August 30 *Variety* reported that Brice was still recuperating in Atlantic City and added, "Just what the operation was, no one seems to be certain although the tip of her nose was reduced."[10] After two months of silence, she went public with her reaction to the surgery. In its November

8 issue, *Variety* ran a large picture of her with the caption. "Fanny Brice says a few things about her nose provided by Dr. Henry J. Schireson." The accompanying text praised his surgical skills, but concluded with the following revealing paragraph:

> My principal reason for making this statement, in addition to public expression of my faith in the doctor is to assure well-meaning friends who have been incessantly telephoning me and expressed their condolences—while I thank them for their interest I wish to assure them that I have no need for expressions of sympathy—that I'm satisfied and I believe that is sufficient.[11]

The same declaration appeared in the January 5, 1924, *Billboard* with different photographs.[12] Brice was shown in profile, before and after the operation, but the noses were not authentic. "He made a big nose on the 'before' picture. He was crazy," she explained years later.[13] In the "after" picture, she appeared with a much smaller nose than she ever obtained surgically and, in spite of Schireson's attempts to make the results look impressive, the text suggested that she was disappointed. Legitimate photographs indicated that the new nose was not only less shapely than she might have hoped it would be, but also managed to rob her face of its distinctive character. She still looked like Fanny Brice, but Brice with a much less interesting expression, and the change may have had a significant impact on her as a performer.

After the operation, many Broadway observers shared Dorothy Parker's view and believed that Brice had disastrously altered the course of her career. The consensus was that she was not as funny as she used to be, partly because she was no longer such an obvious sight gag, and partly because, in aspiring to play more serious roles, she was deliberately eschewing comedy. In a February 3, 1924, newspaper article, a journalist named Karl K. Kitchen argued that "Miss Brice, since she has had her nose bobbed, no longer provides the laughs she used to," a "predicament" of which Ziegfeld was acutely aware. Kitchen interviewed the disgruntled producer during the run of the *Ziegfeld Follies of 1923* and recorded his reaction to the new Brice:

> "I want Fanny to make 'em laugh—that's what I pay her for," said Mr. Ziegfeld the other day as he watched her performance in the *Follies*. "But you can see for yourself that she doesn't do it. She's become serious and that's fatal for a funny woman. . . ."
>
> "It's the old story of the clown who wants to play Hamlet," [he] said as the curtain came down without applause on one of Miss Brice's scenes. "Before Fanny got this foolish idea of having her nose straightened, she was the funniest

woman on the stage. Now, because her nose is straight, she wants to act in
A Doll's House, one of those highbrow Ibsen things. Can you beat it?"[14]

Kitchen spoke to Brice after the performance "to get her side of the
story." She admitted that she probably did not look as funny as she did
with her "old beak" and acknowledged that it might take "a couple of
seasons" for the public to get used to her new nose. She explained, however, that it was extremely important to her to prove that she could succeed
in serious roles:

> I want to do more pretentious things than I have done. I'm ambitious, like
> every actress. I know I can act, and I want to show the public what I can
> do. It's a more difficult matter, for the public doesn't want to accept me in
> any other role than a comic one. If I can give a matinee performance of *A
> Doll's House*, I'll convince the most skeptical.[15]

She concluded her remarks as she had in 1911 by chastising Ziegfeld for
failing to supply her with good material. She called hers "unfortunate"
and stated, "If Mr. Ziegfeld wants me to be as funny as I used to be,
let him provide me with some funny songs. Don't blame it all on my
nose."[16]

It is difficult to know how seriously to take Brice's statements. Given
the problems she encountered as Dora in *Why Worry?*, her desire to play
Ibsen's Nora seems highly unrealistic at best. Assuming that she meant
what she said to the inquisitive Kitchen, however, her comments strongly
suggest that she had once again lost her identity as a performer. At this
juncture in her career, she revealed the same lack of self-awareness she
had shown earlier when she was unable to find material that suited her.
Before Blanche Merrill helped her find her comic way, she inevitably made
the wrong choices, selecting songs that did not work and failing to capitalize on her own unique abilities. Although presumably Merrill was available
to help her in 1923, the talented songwriter may have been unable to
compete with Brice's insecurities at this difficult time in her life and career.
Her dismay at the prospect of Nicky's imprisonment, her failure to receive
a starring vehicle from Ziegfeld, and her desire to be more conventionally
beautiful, combined with the social pressures and prejudices of the times,
may have led Brice astray as an entertainer. When she said she wanted
to do "more pretentious things" than she had previously done, she probably
did not realize how much she sounded like one of her own comic creations.
So many of the characters she had effectively portrayed on stage were
girls who were trying to be something they were not, from Sadie Salome

to the succession of inept ballerinas and comic vamps. Brice's buffoonery involved putting down their pretentions to culture, spoofing their attempts to mimic their far more skillful models, mocking the efforts for which they were obviously so ill-suited. In expressing her aspirations about Ibsen, Brice revealed a serious conflict between her comic instinct and her vanity, one that she would not resolve for several years. She was dangerously close to becoming a caricature of her own best work.

However blind she may have been to her own motivation, Brice's comments do reveal her awareness that the *Ziegfeld Follies of 1923* was not as successful as its predecessors. When the show opened at the New Amsterdam Theatre on Saturday, October 20, it was over five hours long and, according to the *Times*, "the good portions . . . were so conspicuously good and the bad portions so incredibly bad that almost any member of the first audience could do Mr. Ziegfeld's cutting for him."[17] By Tuesday night, it had been reduced to two hours and fifty-seven minutes, but *Variety* found that it still left "much to be desired." A disgusted Arthur Hornblow, writing in *Theatre Magazine*, called it "the most dreary, stupid, pointless, unbeautiful, unfunny show that Broadway had ever seen." He did praise Brice, noting that her "exuberant humor acted like a tonic amid the general gloom."[18]

The eighteenth edition of the *Ziegfeld Follies*, advertised as the last of an illustrious series, was created by Ziegfeld regulars Gene Buck (lyrics); Rudolph Friml, Victor Herbert, and Dave Stamper (music); Joseph Urban (scenery); and Ned Wayburn (staging and choreography). This time, however, the talented production staff had failed to meet its own high standards. *Variety's* Skig expressed his disappointment with the sets and costumes. Unlike the lavish displays of other years, the *Ziegfeld Follies of 1923* had only one impressive visual effect, the first act's "Shadowgraph" number. When members of the audience put on their special "*Follies* Scope Glasses," shadows from the stage seemed to leap across the footlights, but this novel effect was the only part of the show to generate any excitement. The fact that there was "no book whatsoever" and "a deplorable lack of comedy" made for a dull evening. Although the seventy-seven *Follies* Girls compared favorably to those in previous editions, the specialty performers were surprisingly undistinguished. The *Times* mentioned Brice and Bert Wheeler, a transplant from vaudeville, as the production's only stars. As Skig saw it, Brice alone deserved "laurels," both on account of "the amount of work" she did and her obvious "ability."[19]

Brice's first appearance in Act I was to sing Eddie Cantor's "South

Sea Island." A photograph shows a grass-skirted Brice in a characteristic pose, standing on her toes in a semi-plié, with arms bent at the elbow and held out to the side. She wears a low-slung flower belt, some necklaces decorated with shells, and several bangle bracelets from her wrists to her elbows. The position is "typically Bricean," but the expression is not. It lacks the zany exuberance she usually exhibited in her comic songs. Instead of the familiar leer, her lips are pursed and she actually seems prim. It may just be the photograph, but it may also be Brice's unwillingness to look funny with her new nose. Later in the act, she played Pocahontas and Queen Isabella in another Cantor composition, "Snappy Stories of History." Heywood Broun disliked the sketch, which he described as "low and yet dull," but Skig thought it was one of the evening's two really humorous moments.[20]

In the second act, Brice offered a selection of songs. Neither the programs nor the reviews indicated which ones she performed, but there are two likely candidates. "The Fool" and "Lonesome Cinderella." The covers of both pieces of sheet music note that they were "written for and featured with great success by Fannie Brice in the *Ziegfeld Follies of 1923*."[21] Both were dreadful. "The Fool," with words by Benton Ley and music by Lee David, was a maudlin piece straining to be another "My Man." Lew Brown and James F. Hanley's "Lonesome Cinderella" was better, but not much. Brice is the title character, looking for a "nice young feller," and asks plaintively, "Where can he be?" Unlike the real Cinderella, her forlorn namesake cannot find a man and all her efforts seem to backfire. When the real Cinderella loses her glass slipper at the ball, she ends up with a handsome prince. Brice's character, on the other hand, has to go out and buy a new pair because nobody cares about her or her shoes. Whereas the real Cinderella finds her prince at midnight, all this unhappy character catches as a result of her late night foray is a cold.

In spite of its attempts at humor, the overwhelming feeling of the song is melancholy. This Cinderella is far more pathetic than someone like "Second Hand Rose," another Hanley creation. For all her grumbling about hand-me-downs, plucky Rose has a lover and a fur coat. "Lonesome Cinderella" ends with the sorry statement, "I'll never get a feller, zipping my life away," and even a Yiddish accent—if indeed Brice used one in performance—could not have done much with that line. Brice may have considered the song a more serious piece consistent with her new image, but it came across as a hybrid, neither comic nor dramatic, and not at all effective.

Fortunately, Brice had an opportunity to redeem herself. She appeared as an "old time amateur night" contestant in a sketch the *Times* considered "the highpoint of the evening."[22] According to one observer, "she came on in a brown-skirt-and-coat suit of the vintage, with high brown shoes, and her hair in a braid tied with a huge black bow."[23] In character as a nervous neophyte, she offered the hostile audience "When You Know You're Not Forgotten by the Girl You Can't Forget," the song she had originally performed at Keeney's. In a *Herald Tribune* interview, she reminisced about that real amateur night and explained how her experience had been incorporated into the *Follies* scene:

> My real name is Fannie Borach and I was announced under that name. The stage manager announced it as "Borax" and a gallery boy up in the "seventh heaven" yelled out to me, "Go ahead, washing soda." I mentioned this incident to Gene Buck who arranged the act for Mr. Ziegfeld, and he put the line in so that now every night at the New Amsterdam, I am announced as Fannie Borax and Arthur West who plays the gallery god yells just as some unknown person did seventeen years ago: "Go ahead, washing soda."[24]

She recalled her anxiety "that first night" and how she "broke down" as she sang "two or three times," something she was currently using in her *Follies* act. She remembered the "great big hook" that hovered over her head and threatened to pull her offstage. She "ducked" in time, to the delight of the crowd which then came to her aid. "Shut up, fellers," she heard "someone in the gallery" cry. "Give the kid a chance." The obvious feeling with which she recreated her experience made the sketch a great success throughout the run of the show.

The same cannot be said of Brice's other material and it is not surprising that some selections were eventually dropped in favor of better offerings. One of them was "Russian Art," a character song in dialect written by Blanche Merrill and Leo Edwards.[25] It may not have been the "pretentious" piece Brice sought, but it was the type of material she did well. This time she became "Luba Rockamonanoffsky," starring in the *Chauve-Souris*, a "Russian vaudeville" show which had just left New York after a profitable engagement.

As Luba explained, she was riding on the streetcar one day when she "bumped right into Morris Gest." A Ziegfeld rival and enterprising showman in his own right, Gest had brought the Moscow Art Theatre to America for the 1923–24 season and had imported the *Chauve-Souris* and its creator, Nikita Bailieff, the previous year. In addition to enabling her to poke fun at the competition, "Russian Art" brought Brice back to familiar ground. Returning to dialect and to debunking "culture," she could also indulge in the physical behavior with which she animated so many of her successful comic songs.

Brice had another new piece called "Mary Rose." With lyrics by Gene Buck and music by Maurice Yvain, the composer of "My Man," it was a serious attempt to provide her with the dramatic material she sought. The program actually describes it as a "song scene" in which Brice plays "an outcast" on "a side street in New York." Presumably there was dialogue between the outcast and the other two characters, Mary Rose and a policeman, but the lugubrious song belonged to Brice. She warns the young and beautiful Mary Rose to be careful because "like the twilight shade ev'ry flow'r must fade." Youth "drifts away," tears follow lights and laughter, and "some must grieve" because others "deceive." It is a musical cautionary tale and the outcast serves as a moral *exemplum*. She admonishes her young listener to hesitate "before it's late" and sighs, "I've played the game, don't do the same, my Mary Rose."[26]

Reviewer Kitchen wrote that "Mary Rose" was her most effective serious song and caused "tears instead of laughs—to the obvious discomfort of Mr. Ziegfeld." He could not have felt too badly, though, because the *Follies* managed to stay on Broadway for twenty-nine weeks until the end of the season. It closed on Saturday, May 10, 1924, and *Variety* reported that Brice was in Washington, D.C., the following Monday to see her husband before his departure for Leavenworth. On February 5, 1924, Arnstein's 1920 conviction for bringing stolen Wall Street securities to Washington had been upheld by the District of Columbia Court of Appeals. According to the February 6, 1924, *New York Times*, Arnstein and his accomplice, Isadore Cohn of New York, were sentenced to two years in the penitentiary and a $10,000 fine. Three other men involved in the scheme—two New York stockbrokers and a Washington attorney—received identical prison terms but lesser fines.[27]

As always, Brice kept working. The same *Variety* article noted that, once again, Ziegfeld was "said to be preparing a new revue for Fannie Brice, to go into rehearsal the latter part of June."[28] Like the rest of the Brice revues Ziegfeld announced, this one also failed to materialize. On June 25, with another edition of the *Follies* about to open in New York, *Variety* reported that Brice and Ziegfeld were involved in a contract dispute. He planned to send the *Ziegfeld Follies of 1923* on a national tour and was anxious to feature Brice prominently in the production. She was apparently willing to oblige, for a weekly salary of $2,500. When Ziegfeld rejected her terms, she refused his offer and defected to a rival camp, that of producer Sam Harris.

Formerly of Cohan and Harris, the enterprising Harris continued in show business when his long association with Cohan ended in 1920. Beginning in 1921, he joined Irving Berlin in creating a series of musical revues for their new Music Box Theatre, built specifically as a showcase for Berlin's songs. The 1924 *Music Box Revue* was slated to open in November, and the August 20 *Variety* reported that Brice "expected" to be one of its principals. In its next issue, the newspaper announced that Harris and Brice had "closed negotiations" and that she was to receive a "run of the play contract at $2,500 a week," the terms Ziegfeld had refused to meet. The same article also noted that Brice had not initially accepted Harris's offer because she had "become interested in a script" he showed her in July "which was intended to star" her.[29] In other words, Harris had wooed her with the promise of her own show which, like so many others, did not work out. Whether or not his offer had been genuine, Brice had again been disappointed. She could at least console herself with the knowledge that she had gotten the salary she wanted.

The fourth and final *Music Box Revue* opened behind schedule on December 1, 1924. *Variety*'s Skig called it "the weakling of the series," largely because of the "absence of comedy and the thinness of the score." Brice suffered on both counts from inadequate material and, in his view, fell short of expectations. Most of the reviews, however, were favorable. The *New York Times* dubbed the show "a worthy successor" to "the gorgeous and tuneful spectacles" that had preceded it and noted approvingly that Brice had been "dissuaded from being tragic for more than a few seconds at a time."[30]

Brice was back to broad comedy in a variety of songs and sketches. Her opening number was a ballad called "Don't Send Me Back to Petrograd," in which she appeared as an immigrant on Ellis Island who begs to remain in the United States. ("I promise to work the best I can / I'll even wash the sheets of the Ku Klux Klan.")[31] It was supposed to be a comic lament, but *Variety* thought it "fell short of the objective." She was much more effective playing Eve to Bobby Clark's Adam, in a sketch one critic described as a "racy and joyous . . . collection of all the Adam and Eve stories from the days of the first serpent."[32] Photographs show the two in ludicrous caveman costumes which, for Clark, included fur slippers and a wooden club, as well as his trademark cigar and greasepaint glasses. Brice wore enormous fig leaves in strategic locations

on her tunic and had oversized "splay-toed feet."[33] The leers she exchanged with Clark indicate that she could still look funny, in spite of
fears to the contrary.

Later on in the act, she performed Blanche Merrill and Leo Edwards's
"Moving Picture Baby," a song she had originally done in vaudeville as
a spoof on popular child star "Baby Peggy." Her "hair was all curled and
bleached, and she was always in pink or blue. She always looked like
an ice cream soda or something," Brice recalled. "I thought I could be
very funny with it."[34] The travesty was timely, as child stars were making
a successful transition from stage to screen and Shirley Temple, the most
famous movie moppet, was still to come. Like Sadie and Becky and the
rest of Brice's endearing incompetents, this "little moving picture baby"
goes "from studio to studio" and does not realize how futile her efforts
are. She will never make it "on the screen," but that is the point of the
amusing parody. Brice's impersonation, complete with lisping baby talk,
kinky hair, and abbreviated pastel pinafore, must have been very comical
and anticipated her future work as Baby Snooks.

Brice appeared with the rest of the cast in "Bandanna Ball," an unimpressive number at the end of Act I. She returned to more congenial material in Act II and performed "I Want to Be a Ballet Dancer," another
of her series of ballet burlesques. After a forgettable sketch called "Another
Good Girl Gone Wrong," she joined Clark in "The King's Gal" in which
she played an elaborately coiffed and gowned Mme. Pompadour to his
Louis XV. Although her work was not as distinguished as it had been
in the *Ziegfeld Follies of 1921*, it still classed her along with Clark as "just
about the best of the revue comedians," and kept the *Music Box Revue*
running in New York until May 6, 1925.[35]

While she was in the show, moreover, Brice began a short-lived producing career. The January 14 *Variety* reported that she was involved in a
show called *Is Zat So?* at the 39th Street Theatre. She recalled that she
had invested $9,000 in the project but, fearing that it would not do well,
decided to cover her potential losses by selling some of her shares. As
she later remembered it, Lee Shubert bought forty percent, "somebody
else" took five percent, "and so on," leaving twenty-five percent for herself.
According to her reminiscences:

> Well, the show comes into New York. *Is Zat So?* is a big hit, sensational. And
> we sell the moving picture rights for a pile of money. I got checks from that
> show for years and years. I made a hundred and some thousand. If I had any
> brains, I would have owned one hundred percent instead of twenty-five percent.

I would have been rich from that show alone. But me and business—oogly-boogly—that's my big trouble.[36]

Variety intimated that her business sense was even worse than she admitted. Although she had been one of the initial seven investors, she had sold all her stock in the *Is Zat So?* corporation by March.[37] Subsequent articles about the long-running production, which spun off several touring companies and eventually became a successful film, never mentioned Brice as being at all involved with the enterprise.

Her second and last producing venture was even less rewarding. It was a musical comedy called *The Brown Derby* starring fellow *Ziegfeld Follies of 1923* cast members, Bert and Betty Wheeler. The May 6 *Variety* reported that Brice would join the show for its Boston premiere at the end of the month. It opened on May 25 and received a favorable review from the *Boston Globe*, which predicted a successful run after some second act "tinkering."[38] An interview with a busy Brice appeared in another Boston newspaper four days later. "No one asked me to be a producer," she said. "It just fascinated me so I elected myself. I have to be doing a lot of things at one time, otherwise I get all nerved up." When asked if she would give up acting for producing, she responded, "Never! I'm always going to act and what's more," she noted, revealing an apparent revaluation of her career goals, "I'm always going to be a comedienne. I know my business too well to give up the one thing in the world that brought me success—comedy." She added that she planned to do "producing and acting, both."[39]

In spite of her enthusiasm, *The Brown Derby* closed after its week in Boston and did not reopen. It subsequently became a movie, but Brice had nothing to do with that project, nor was she involved in the lawsuit the Wheelers filed against her coproducer, Charles K. Gordon, for the premature termination of their contract. Although she had just stated her commitment to producing, she must have changed her mind on the basis of her experience with *The Brown Derby* and abandoned her new career as abruptly as she undertook it.

She had other exciting prospects to contemplate. She was scheduled for a fall tour with the *Music Box Revue* and, after that, had an offer that promised to let her display her talents as a dramatic actress. On May 2, 1925, the *New York Times* reported that veteran producer David Belasco had taken Brice under his management and planned to "star her in a play without music." Definite arrangements had not yet been made, but it was understood that Brice would "be seen in a semiserious play containing emotional possibilities."[40] The May 6 *Variety* provided additional details: she had signed a three-year contract beginning with the 1926–27 season when she would receive a weekly salary of $2,000; by the third year, the amount would increase to $2,500. According to *Variety*, "D.B." planned to "exploit the erstwhile comedienne as 'a female Warfield,' in comedy dramas of his own writing, with nary a song in the plays."[41]

Belasco had successfully transplanted David Warfield from a Weber and Fields burlesque to the legitimate stage when he starred him in *The Auctioneer* in 1901. Their long association had ended only recently. Warfield thought Belasco had misdirected him as Shylock in his 1922 production of *The Merchant of Venice* and broke with him immediately afterward.[42] Brice was probably never aware of that relationship's acrimonious conclusion or that she was dealing with a Belasco well past his prime. The man whom George Jean Nathan called "the Broadway Rasputin" and Brooks Atkinson considered "the master of mediocrity," was, to her, "the white-haired dean of the American drama." That was how she described him in an obviously ghost-written article published after his death in 1931, when she reminisced about him:

> Some years ago—a lady never mentions exact figures —the theatrical world was startled when David Belasco took the funny Fannie Brice under his tutelage to produce her in a play, an honest to goodness play, not a revue or a musical comedy. If any other producer had attempted to lift a *diseuse*, comedienne, or whatever you care to call me from the vaudeville stage to the most exciting stage of America, the Belasco stage, and make out of her a dramatic actress, there would have been a shout of derision, a shrugging of shoulders. Broadway is skeptical. As a matter of fact it remained skeptical even after the Fannie Brice production by Belasco . . . but still Broadway received the announcement with respect, the respect which Belasco's personality always commanded.[43]

Still denigrating her accomplishments as a comedienne, in spite of other statements to the contrary, she believed that the opportunity she had been waiting for and working toward had finally arrived. Belasco was going to enable her to become a serious actress who would soon impress the Broadway skeptics with her versatility.[44]

She first had to fulfill her obligations to Sam Harris and left New York with the *Music Box Revue*. Stops included a six-week engagement in Chicago and a week in Milwaukee, where a delighted Brice learned that her beloved Nicky was to be released from prison seventy-two days early for good behavior. That unexpected event must have compensated for a disappointing tour and, after the show closed in Philadelphia on March 6, the Arnsteins were able to return to New York, their children, and the promise of a more normal family life.

On March 31, *Variety* informed its readers that Brice would begin rehearsing for her Belasco production at the end of April. Although it did not yet have a title, the script was finished and the newspaper predicted a New York opening "about June 1."[45] On April 21, *Variety* reported that Belasco had a collaborator, actor-playwright Willard Mack. The show, now called *Fanny*, a "new comedy with songs," would go into rehearsal in early May. The next edition of the popular weekly provided more specifics. Brice would appear in her play for only two weeks out of town, after which she would be going into vaudeville with a new act written by Ballard MacDonald. In *Fanny*, now slated for a New York opening after Labor Day, she would "sing one song, incidental" and would "play a Jewish girl out West among the Cowboys." Any doubts as to the merit of the new piece were amplified by the next *Variety* bulletin, this one dated May 12. The paper stated that Belasco was paying MacDonald to sit in on *Fanny* rehearsals to help revise the stilted dialogue and "to fuse the lingo into Miss Brice's kind of stage dialect—Yiddish."[46]

Reminiscing about the project, Brice said she knew from the beginning that the production would be a disaster. As she sardonically recalled it:

> Belasco got Willard Mack . . . with a play he [Mack] must have found at the bottom of his trunk.
> Belasco said the play should be about a Jewish girl. So Mack put an "oy" in front of every line and we're in business. He must have looked a long time for the title. He called it *Fanny*. At the first reading I fell asleep. Belasco could see I wasn't enthusiastic. He said: "Don't be discouraged," and told me all he was going to do to the play. Enough had been done to it when it was written. I couldn't back out. I had signed this contract with him.[47]

In 1926, however, she did not give any indication of being apprehensive. Although her daughter, Frances, was only seven at the time, she insisted years later that she remembered her mother's excitement and how "thrilled" she was "to be doing a show with Belasco." Arnstein, too, confirmed his wife's commitment to the project. Certainly not an unimpeachable source, he nevertheless recalled that he tried to dissuade her from going ahead with such a "rotten" play, but she refused to listen to him.[48]

In the remarks she made about Belasco in 1931 after his death—and, granted, the occasion may have colored the recollections—she tried to convey a sense of his power as a director. She remembered a session "one late afternoon" when Belasco had been working since early morning. "His face was drawn, his hand shook from nervous exhaustion, but his eyes "flashed" with "eternal youthfulness." Brice was having difficulty with a particular scene and said that she found the dialogue "impossible." He responded by glaring at her, grabbing the manuscript, pushing her into a chair, and shouting, "Watch me." To her "amazement," the man "who a minute before had looked ready for the hospital," played her part so convincingly that the meaning of the lines suddenly became clear. Brice sat "transfixed," mesmerized by "the inflection of his voice, the mischievous twinkle of his eye and then the masterful sliding from the humorous to the tragic" which were "nothing short of miraculous." Influenced by both his commanding presence and compelling interpretation, Brice repeated the scene and suddenly understood "the transition of moods which he had so superbly demonstrated." Belasco "nodded" his approval and "was again immersed in his own work."[49]

This glowing account simply does not jibe with the one Brice gave almost twenty years later. According to those recollections, Belasco responded quite differently to her efforts. She had "noticed that the curtain scene of the second act was a very dramatic scene" and, after rehearsing it by herself, she was anxious to perform it for him. When she finally "got up and did it," he was furious. As she remembered their confrontation:

> He jumped up and said: "That's the worst thing I ever heard. I could get somebody for fifty dollars a week to do it better than that."
> "Then you should have hired one of them," I told him.
> "Do it again," Mr. Belasco said.
> "Just stop yelling at me," I told him.
> "You stop declaiming, young lady," Belasco said.
> "All right," I said.[50]

She described her repeated attempts to do the scene correctly, ignoring his interruptions and insults. As her frustration turned to anger, she stormed offstage. When fellow cast member John Cromwell tried to calm her, she told him that she was upset because she did not know what Belasco meant by "declaiming." Cromwell explained the term to her and showed her what she was doing wrong. "For the first time," she wrote,

"I knew what straight acting meant. I didn't even learn how to close a door from Belasco. If it wasn't for John Cromwell, I wouldn't have known what he wanted from me."[51] She performed the scene for Belasco once more, using what Cromwell had taught her. Everybody applauded —including "D.B."—and "there was no trouble from then on."

Brice regarded Cromwell's instruction as her dramatic awakening. Before that, she admitted that her acting ability was primitive. "All I knew about acting was doing something with the hands or with the feet," she recalled. "I thought that was it." Although she had never had any trouble conveying the mood of a song, she "didn't know about words without music." Largely because of Cromwell's kindness, however, she felt that she learned "a lot" from her *Fanny* rehearsals. Unfortunately, "it was all wasted on that play." She was dealing with a Belasco who had lost his touch, whose old-fashioned concept of acting no longer worked, and whose script selection left much to be desired. As she put it:

> What I didn't realize was that Belasco was just about finished then, and the things he asked me to do were a little exaggerated. When a comic starts to act, he must always underplay. If he overplays anything dramatic, it becomes silly. You can't go from comedy to tragedy, but from comedy to pathos is all right.
>
> Oh, it was just a terrible play.[52]

In June 1926, Fanny previewed for two weeks in New Jersey, but the show attracted less attention than Belasco's ill health. Reporting on his "simultaneous attack of neuralgia and lumbago," *Variety* also noted that the New York opening of the ill-fated production had been postponed to the fall. In the interim, the indefatigable Brice played two weeks of vaudeville in San Francisco (July 5–10 and 12–17) and two in Los Angeles (July 26–31 and August 2–7). She received very favorable reviews and, encouraged by her West Coast success, returned to the East to prepare for *Fanny*.

After previewing in Baltimore and Washington, *Fanny* opened at New York's Lyceum Theatre on September 21, 1926. It was another dramatic debacle. As *Variety* reported when the show closed eight weeks later, it had been "generally flayed" by the critics, who referred to it irreverently as "What Brice Glory?" "Fanny's Worst Play," and "Rosie of the Rancho." Billed as a "melodramatic comedy in three acts," *Fanny* was almost unanimously panned. Woollcott, now critic for the *New York World*, called it "rubbishy" and said that Belasco and Mack "ought to be ashamed of themselves and each other" for having written it. *Theatre Magazine*'s Hornblow labeled it "an elongated vaudeville sketch" and characterized the plot as being "of the dime-novel order."[53]

The problem with the plot, other than straining credibility, was that it was so obvious it created no suspense.[54] According to *Variety*, there was a "terrible dull first act, with a terrible duller second act and a terrible dullest third act."[55] The supporting characters provided little dramatic interest because they, too, were "dull" and "unbelievable." The dialogue did nothing to enhance the "hackneyed situations" because it was so banal.

Such a play offered Brice "few opportunities to scintillate as a star," and for this, the critics blamed Belasco. *Fanny* had been billed as the piece in which Brice would make her long-awaited dramatic debut, but it was hardly suited to serious acting. There were isolated instances when she emoted, but these seemed forced and totally inconsistent with the "Yiddish burlesque antics" she used for most of her scenes. Belasco had tried to teach her restraint, observed the *New York Telegram*, and had "schooled in her a quietude of demeanor in order to emphasize that she was an actress now, not a gay and reckless hoyden of revues."[56] Yet her best moments were the ones in which she relied on her customary comic artillery. According to Hornblow, only her "broad grins, Jewish mannerisms, and slangy speech" kept the audience from "running out into the street."

Brooks Atkinson reviewed *Fanny* in the September 22 edition of the *New York Times* and joined his fellow critics in panning the play. Unlike his colleagues, however, he wrote perceptively about Brice, contrasting her dramatic ambitions with her real strengths as a performer. Acknowledging that "emotional drama" is "commonly held in higher esteem than comedy," he said that he understood her desire to "abandon base comedy for the pure gold of emotional histrionics." He even credited *Fanny* for giving her "an emotional scene or two" in which she could demonstrate her acting prowess. "Perhaps Miss Brice believes that in such moments her art rises to nobler, exalted inner shrines of the theatrical heaven," he speculated, and then proceeded respectfully to disagree:

> But it cannot rival for a moment the Fannie Brice of the slightly crossed eyes, the broad grin and the comic awkwardness of a gawky east side young lady. Several scenes in which she gets down to her familiar cartooning keep the last act of *Fanny* just this side of boredom. . . . Delightfully vulgarized by her accent and stupendously shrill voice and by her broad grimaces and stiff-jointed bucking and plunging, these episodes reveal Fannie Brice playing confidently

on the home grounds. Most of us are content to see her only at her best. At her best, she is unparalleled.[57]

At her best, Brice was a brilliant comedienne and that was much more than the mere "comic" she thought she was. As Atkinson put it quite clearly, her distinctive comic style not only made her wonderfully amusing, it made her unique. Driven by her desire to become a dramatic star, however, she was still unable to come to terms with her talent and be content with comedy. She wanted respect and acceptance as a serious actress, and the more they seemed to elude her, the greater her determination became.

Despite Belasco's insistence that the show was going to be a hit, it closed in early November, one of the first failures of the 1926–27 season. In an attempt to recoup some of the production costs, *Fanny* was sent on a short-lived tour. It played on what *Variety* called the "subway circuit" until its last performance on January 8, 1927, in Philadelphia. In a letter to *Variety* dated January 7, Brice insisted that the play had done better on the road than *Variety* had indicated in a recent article and objected to the paper's coverage. "I think your wording, 'Miss Brice's disastrous initial legitimate venture,' is hardly fair to me," she wrote. "I'll have to quote Shakespeare in my defense, 'The play's the thing.'"[58]

However much Brice blamed the script, *Fanny* did nothing to enhance her reputation or advance her career. Yet, with characteristic spirit, she moved directly to a new project and returned to California to star in another musical revue. This time, the familiar format was not a success. The *Hollywood Music Box Revue* opened on February 2, 1927, to disappointing reviews. *Variety* called it "a vaudeville show lacking in brilliance and novelty" and reported that even Brice was "handicapped by a lack of new material." Her numbers included "Moving Picture Baby" and "I Want to Be a Ballet Dancer," as well as her "Camille" and "Mme. Pompadour" burlesques. California audiences were familiar with all of them from her previous vaudeville tour.

Only "Make 'Em Laugh," the opening song, was new. Written by Blanche Merrill and Edwin Weber, it showed that Merrill had not lost her ability to produce material well-suited to Brice's comedic talents and also gave Brice the opportunity to comment on the Belasco fiasco. In it she sings about coming West where "it's best" for a rest in the *Music Box Revue* and explains that she has asked her "authoress, Blanche Merrill" to create a "big dramatic scene." She describes her efforts to impress Merrill with her "dramatic stuff," a soft-shoe dance, and operatic singing, and expresses her surprise when Merrill remains unmoved. The songwriter knows her customer too well and, as Brice sings it, responds:

> If you want to knock 'em dead
> Make 'em laugh, Fanny, make 'em laugh!
> Make 'em laugh, Fanny, make 'em laugh!
> All those dramatics and high operatics
> They may be very good
> But you're in Hollywood
> So please, Fanny, make 'em laugh.
> Make 'em laugh, till you double 'em in half
> Even if you have to throw a pie in somebody's face
> Or do a lot of funny falls all over the place
> Everybody in the town knows in your heart
>   you're just a clown
> So make 'em laugh, Fanny, make 'em laugh.[59]

Brice deserves credit for being able to poke fun at herself so openly, especially because she had not totally accepted Merrill's directive. The *Fanny* debacle may have made her feel more comfortable about being "just a clown," but it would soon become obvious that she had not yet given up her dramatic aspirations. She was still not reconciled to her role as a comedienne or comfortable with her uniqueness as a funny woman. Whether she made "'em" laugh or not, moreover, she was increasingly interested in finding a larger audience for her talents. Although she would continue to appear on stage in the coming years, she would focus most of her energy on obtaining work in the two fastest growing media, film and radio. Both offered national exposure and lucrative contracts, as well as the opportunity to participate in dynamic new industries. From 1927 to 1933, however, neither would find Brice and her particular brand of ethnic comedy sufficiently marketable. The "animated newspaper comic strip with a pronounced Jewish flavor" Atkinson so admired would have trouble transferring her distinctive talents to the "silver screen" and the "airwaves." Her efforts to break into those burgeoning entertainment fields would be as frustrating as her attempts to find a suitable stage vehicle had been.

Trying to Reach "the Hillbillies and the *Haute Monde*": 1927–1933

And it is a funny thing, because everything in my life that I ever wanted, if I tried for it, I can say that I got it, but with men, the harder I tried, the harder I flopped.

—FANNY BRICE[1]

In the theater I was always at ease, but in pictures there was the camera following me around like a cop.

—FANNY BRICE[2]

8.

On March 9, 1927, as box office receipts for the *Hollywood Music Box Revue* continued to decline, an interesting item appeared in *Variety*.[3] Film Booking Offices, headed by Joseph P. Kennedy, had placed Fanny Brice under contract for *Clancy's Kosher Wedding*, scheduled to begin production April 4. It was another in a long series of Jewish-Irish jokes which had delighted audiences in burlesque and vaudeville, and were now making a successful transition from stage to screen. Filmgoers had laughed at *Levy and Cohen–The Irish Comedians* as early as 1903, but the success of Anne Nichols's play *Abie's Irish Rose* in 1924 inspired many imitators in the mid-twenties. These included *The Cohens and the Kellys* and *Kosher Kitty Kelly* in 1926, *The Shamrock and the Rose* and *Frisco Sally Levy* in 1927 and, in 1928, the movie version of Nichols's play. Such films treated their ethnic subjects lightly and presented simplistic solutions to serious problems. When Jewish and Irish children fell in love, for example, their parents always objected violently. The couple married anyway, and their families eventually accepted the match.[4] These reconciliations were possible because religious and cultural differences were portrayed as amusing ecentricities and acrimony, like assimilation, was handled humorously.

That is why the next *Variety* article about Brice seems hard to believe. Under the heading "Hoity, Toity Fannie Brice Dramatic Actress Only," the paper reported that she had canceled her F.B.O. contract because she did not want to be a "screen comic." According to *Variety*, a "special role" had been created for her, but when she learned it was a "comedy part," she refused to play it.[5] It is possible that F.B.O. signed her without identifying the picture in which she was to appear. It is equally plausible that she simply changed her mind about making the film. If, however, she actually expected a serious role in a movie with the title *Clancy's Kosher Wedding*, she must have been totally oblivious to the nature of screen stereotyping. Whatever the reason, she informed "the folks" at F.B.O. that "she felt her reputation and standing would be affected [adversely] by appearing in a comedy" and asked to be released from the contract. The film, which *Billboard* described as "another Semitic-Hibernian picture to beat Paramount's *Abie's Irish Rose* to the screen," was made without her and distributed later that year.[6]

Brice continued at the Hollywood Music Box until the end of March, then took the revue to the Biltmore Theatre in Los Angeles for a short engagement. Whatever news might have surfaced about her career was eclipsed by coverage of another event. On May 21, 1927, an unknown young pilot named Charles A. Lindbergh completed the first nonstop solo flight across the Atlantic. His plane, the *Spirit of St. Louis*, touched down at Le Bourget Field in Paris, thirty-three and a half hours after leaving Long Island, New York. The June *Movietone News*, the first sound newsreel to reach theatres across the country, featured the triumphant return of America's newest hero and gave fascinated audiences the opportunity actually to hear him describe his historic flight.[7]

Brice also appeared in the news in June, when the June 3 *New York Times* announced that she had signed a contract to appear in three films "depicting the life of an East Side girl." They would be made under the management of "Asher, Small and Rogers, Hollywood agents," and would be released through First National. The article did not specify titles, directors, or fellow cast members. Instead, it stated that Brice planned to vacation in Europe for the next two months with silent film star Norma Talmadge and would be joined by her two children later in the summer.[8] Nothing was said about Nicky Arnstein, with whom Brice was having marital problems and from whom she was already separated. Although *Variety* noted only Talmadge's June 4 departure, both women left New York shortly after midnight on the ocean liner *Majestic*.

One week after the August 23 execution of anarchists Sacco and Vanzetti, *Variety* published an article headlined "Fannie Brice's Price," which stated that Brice had declined an offer of $6000 a week" in the "picture houses" and was asking "$1000 daily" for her services. As the movie business boomed, many theatres provided live entertainment along with the feature film. In some ways, the shows were like vaudeville. They presented an assortment of acts, generally funny and fast-paced, for the amusement of the patrons. Unlike vaudeville, however, in which the headliner was the star of the bill, the film was preeminent in the picture houses. The stage performers were secondary, and that may have influenced Brice's decision not to accept the job.[9] "Meantime," *Variety* continued, "she is reading several play scripts submitted by different producers who want her to go under contract for another tour in the legit." In addition, "vaude has also beckoned." Nothing was said about the three films for First National, and the implication is that the contract had been canceled. There was no word of it again, either from Brice or from any other source.

She received a great deal of press coverage in September. Virtually none of it dealt with her career plans. Instead, newspapers across the country carried the surprising announcement that on September 12, 1927, Brice had filed for divorce in the Chicago Circuit Court. She had chosen Chicago for two reasons. First, Arnstein was living there, trying to start still another business. This time it was an electric display sign company in partnership with "Big Tim" Murphy, a Chicago "labor leader" whom he had met in prison while Murphy was serving a term for mail theft. Second, Chicago had emerged as the nation's leading divorce center and had already terminated many celebrity marriages.[10]

According to the September 13 issue of the *New York Times*, Brice had requested custody of Frances, eight, and William, six, but did not want alimony. "The charge," the newspaper stated succinctly, "was infidelity," and it marked the first time that plastic surgery had been "responsible for alienating the affections of a husband, for that is what an operation on her nose accomplished, according to Miss Brice." In the bill filed by her lawyer, she actually charged that Arnstein had developed an inferiority complex as a result of her operation. He repeatedly told her that "she was so much more beautiful he was uncomfortable in her presence" and began "seeking the society of other . . . plainer women" because they appealed to him more.[11] "I was not the same Fannie he used to know," she confessed in Chicago.

However ludicrous the explanation may seem, the fact was that Arnstein had been flagrantly unfaithful. Unlike bond theft, adultery was something she could neither countenance nor deny. "Speaking in tones scarcely audible," the *Times* reported, she "alternately laughed and cried as she testified" and received a decree of divorce on September 14. She immediately returned by train to New York and reluctantly posed for photographers at Grand Central Station. The *Times* noted that she looked "tired and worn" and was dressed funereally in "black crepe with a close-fitting black toque, the somberness of her costume being relieved by an Egyptian gold necklace, bracelet and hat ornament." She taxied home where reporters barraged her with questions about her divorce and plans for another marriage. According to the account in the *Times*, "she flashed back, 'Isn't that a silly thing to ask me? How do I know?' Then," trying vainly to conceal her pain, "she made a comic grimace, although her eyes were filling with tears, and said, 'Haven't I had enough?'"[12]

Variety responded skeptically to the public display, doubting the legitimacy of both the sentiment and the suit. A September 21 article quoted knowledgeable "Loopers" who believed that the divorce was simply another Bricean publicity stunt and predicted an equally well publicized reconciliation.[13] The decree was not rescinded, however, and the Arnsteins were never reunited. Years later, Brice wrote that she actually believed Nick would stop the divorce. "Even when the lawyers came to take me to court," she recalled, "I thought Nick would be downstairs to call it off." She hoped he would appear in court to tell the judge: "'Forget it, Judge. My wife and I made a mistake. We're in love. Why, we don't want a divorce.' But he never showed up . . . I was like in another world. . . . All I know is they gave me a bunch of papers to sign, and I signed, and they gave me a copy." She admitted that she had gone after "something" she "really didn't want and got it. I had proved my love for Nick every day for fifteen years. Now I wanted him to prove his love for me."[14] He failed to rise to the challenge, however; and Brice, who knew she cared for him as deeply "as the day [she] first saw him," reluctantly went ahead with the divorce.

Brice recalled that she had been so distraught by the dissolution of her marriage she had been unable to focus on her work for several months. Remembering that unhappy time years later, she wrote:

> I didn't want to go into a show or do anything. People came to me with shows and I tried to tell them I was in no shape to work. I told Flo no that year.

It's funny, when you don't want something, then everybody tries to give it to you. I didn't want to work, but that year [1927], I turned down more offers and better offers than I ever had.[15]

Once she accepted the finality of the decree, she could again concentrate on her career. By the end of October, she had returned to performing with her customary enthusiasm. She was at Keith's in Boston trying out a new vaudeville act by Ballard MacDonald, Jesse Greer, and aspiring impresario Billy Rose. Brice and Rose had met at a New York nightclub he owned and, although initially unimpressed with him, she eventually accepted his offer to create material for her. The *Boston Transcript* reviewed her act very favorably. Stating that she "carried off the honors with a well-chosen medley of old and new," the paper described her as "expressive in every lineament and every gesture," alternating "sly innuendo with mirthful smirk," and rescuing "obvious sob stuff from bathos by restrained and deft handling."[16] From Boston, Brice went to Baltimore (October 31–November 5), Washington, D.C. (November 7–12), and Philadelphia (November 14–19). She returned to New York and opened a three-week engagement at the Palace on November 21. *Variety* reported that her "welcome back impression was little short of sensational" and called her forty minutes on stage "a Bricean triumph," well worth the $3,700 weekly salary she was reportedly being paid.[17]

After some introductory banter, she sang one of her best new songs, Billy Rose's "Sascha (the Passion of the Pasha)." In character as Sascha, she explains how she was traveling through the Orient "like a tourist strictly pleasure bent," when a Arab "named Achmed Hamel" had the nerve to knock her off her camel. He sold her to the Sultan "like a guy would sell a cow" and, much to the displeasure of the rest of the "harem dames," she is "his favorite now." The Sultan spends most of his time "hanging around" her tent and has been "terribly sweet" since she "cooked for him a dinner." As she slyly puts it, "Oh, how he appreciates a little kosher meat." She concludes by delivering what *Variety* considered the "punchline": "Speakin' of the art of sheikin' / Oh the Sultan's wife is a wonderful life / Providing you don't weaken."[18]

As a comedy song, "Sascha" was perfect for Brice. In addition to giving her the kind of incongruous situation with which she liked to work—here, a Jewish girl as a Sultan's wife—it allowed her to be sexy in a completely non-threatening way. For example, after the "kosher meat" double entendre, she sang about how, when they "bill and coo, it's poo-poo-poo-poo-pa-roo-poo." The nonsense syllables, combined with the accent and eye-rolling which inevitably accompanied them, would have robbed the line of any inherent naughtiness. The comedy softened the sexuality and made it safe. Brice could play at being seductive without offending anyone because the punchline reassured her listeners that Sascha had not succumbed to all the temptations of decadent harem life. She was still a nice Jewish girl at heart.

She returned as the quintessential Jewish mother in her next number, a comic monologue called "Mrs. Cohen at the Beach" which soon became one of her most popular routines.[19] The opening lines quickly establish the character and the situation. "Hold onto Mama's dress, Sadie, you shouldn't fall," she cautions in heavily accented English as she shepherds her charges to the beach. "Irving, stop kicking up the sand. Why can't you be a good boy like Sam?" she asks, playing favorites and chastising poor Irving who is warned that he will have to "stay home from the beach" next time. Hen-pecked husband Abe is the next target. "Abe, it's a wonder you wouldn't watch the children once in a while," Mrs. Cohen complains, then asks rhetorically, "Must I do everything?" "Oy, my feet," she moans in response to her own question.

Assuming her role as mother hen, tour guide, and social director, she says, "Come darlings, we'll go over there by the boardwalk. I think there will be a breeze. Follow Mama." They obediently do, and she continues her running commentary on their appearance and behavior. She tells her children to sit down, distributes sand toys, and, with the firmness of a drill sergeant, orders them to play. The siblings immediately squabble and she tries to mediate, her Yiddish accent and inflections adding to the comedy inherent in the situation: "No, darling, the red pail is Sam's. *Nu?* What's the difference, the red pail or the blue pail? Give Irving the shovel. You want the shovel? All right then, give Irving the pail. Go on, dig," she commands, "Dig a hole and bury your father."

Mrs. Cohen's thoughts and moods change rapidly in response to real or imagined dangers and her words create a series of highly amusing scenes. When a loud thunderclap signals an approaching storm, engineering her family's escape becomes the focus of her frenetic activities. They all rush for the streetcar where Mrs. Cohen tries to pass her daughter off as a five-year-old to avoid paying the fare. The dubious conductor protests that the little girl looks older, but her resourceful mother responds, "Can I help it if she worries?"—the line on which the sketch concludes.

As Brice has created her, Mrs. Cohen is a consummate *yente*. She combines all the traits of the type, as it is commonly defined, into one unforgettable characterization. A *yente* is a shrewish woman of low origins and vulgar manners or, more benignly, a gossipy scandal-monger.[20] Mrs. Cohen manages to be both, and her monologue reinforced the stereotypical image of the oppressively close Jewish family with its often ineffectual father and domineering, overprotective mother. Mrs. Cohen's constant carping and complaining, her endless comparisons and criticism, her irrational fears about health and safety, her emphasis on eating, her stinginess and pettiness, her skill at creating guilt and playing martyr, are unattractive characteristics of the Jewish mother as she is frequently portrayed, and Brice incorporates all of them in her interpretation of Mrs. Cohen.

Because she unites two such potentially negative types—the *yente* and the "Jewish Mother"—Mrs. Cohen could have been an extremely unpleasant creation. Portrayed by anyone else, she would have been a vicious caricature, fulfilling the period's unflattering expectations of immigrant behavior and justifying its prejudicial assumptions. As Brice interpreted her, however, she emerged as a character much more innocuous in performance than on paper. Brice's expressive delivery replaced harshness with humor and defused the piece's underlying anti-Semitism. She moved quickly through the monologue, jumping from one idea to another without belaboring any of the points or pausing to allow the audience to contemplate their larger significance. The speed with which her thoughts changed, as well as the high-pitched sweetness of her voice, helped produce a lightness which did a great deal to counteract the oppressive heaviness of the character as she was drawn. Mrs. Cohen often sounded like such a wide-eyed innocent that her comments lost their harsh edge and seemed harmless. The Yiddish accent and expressions she used were so comical that it was difficult to take her, or her insults, very seriously. Moreover, Brice's great warmth softened everything Mrs. Cohen says, even the complaints, and made her sound genuinely maternal. It also made her likeable rather than laughable, and kept the monologue amusing, not offensive. Largely through the force of her own personality, Brice humanized the stereotype and rounded the caricature into a character.

After "Mrs. Cohen," Brice performed "The Song of the Sewing Machine," which *Variety* described as "a gem of a character number."[21] The *Boston Transcript* put it more bluntly: it was "a sob number," "a ghetto version of 'The Song of the Shirt,'" a maudlin nineteenth century ballad championing universal suffrage.[22] She returned to comedy with "all the classic Brice mannerisms" in her standby, "Spring," then became serious again with Cole Porter's "Weren't We Fools?" The song was supposed to reverberate with references to Arnstein and their recent divorce. Such lines as "Weren't we fools to lose each other? / Weren't we fools to say goodbye / Tho' we knew we loved each other / You chose another, so did I," were designed to evoke an emotional response from a sympathetic audience.[23] *Variety* reported that the song was "significantly handled" and that the "strong Arnstein tinge" added an effective "touch of realism."

According to the *New York Telegram*, the audience stopped the show for twenty minutes and "shouted at her" to sing "My Man." This time, the normally obliging Brice did not agree to perform what was obviously a painful selection. Instead, she offered another comic song in dialect, "Is Something the Matter with Otto Kahn?" A prominent New York investment banker and philanthropist, Kahn was an avid patron of the arts. Although he was actively involved in a variety of artistic and theatrical enterprises as backer or board member, his major commitment was to the Metropolitan Opera, where he served as President and Chairman of the Board. Consequently, in this song, Brice posed as an aspiring diva determined to impress Kahn with her talent and puzzled that her attempts to communicate with him have not produced the desired result.

Like so many of her other outstanding comic songs, "Is Something the Matter with Otto Kahn?" combined innocent innuendo with outrageous parody. A newspaper caricature shows an extravagantly outfitted Brice in a jeweled tiara with an enormous feather, a tight sequined gown, and a ridiculously long strand of pearls. She wore almost the same costume three years later when she did the song in the film *Be Yourself*. In the movie, she appears on a tiny proscenium stage and performs a hilarious operatic travesty. She begins with three excruciating trills, during which she grits her teeth, grimaces, and grins at the audience. On the fourth, she jerks her head and flutters her eyelids, then pulls at her cheeks and quickly sticks out her tongue as if she were gagging or swallowing an insect. She launches into her soprano solo with gusto, mugging uproariously as she strains to reach her high notes. She alternates gleeful with disgusted expressions, depending on where the wayward notes go, and when she hits one accurately, smiles with delight at the audience.[24]

The funny faces are in total contrast to the fluttery mannerisms she uses when she is concentrating on playing diva and help to undercut her pretentious pose. Once again, Brice is spoofing high culture and its enthusiasts by becoming an incompetent practitioner. It is not that her voice is so terrible, but the efforts she must expend to produce the desired sounds show that she is striving to be something for which she is really not suited. Like so many of her other comic characters, the dreadful diva struggles so valiantly and is so proud of herself that the audience cares about her, even though she is hopelessly inept.

According to Brice's daughter, Frances, Brice did not approach such characterizations casually. On the contrary, in preparation for this number, she took singing lessons for several weeks. Frances recalled her mother diligently practicing *Tosca* because she believed that she had to be able to do the operatic singing well before she could burlesque it. When she felt comfortable with the kind of performance the parody required, she could then look for aspects of it to exaggerate.[25] Everything about this diva is off just enough to make her seem ridiculous, an unskilled if endearing imitator who could never be mistaken for a legitimate opera singer. When she finishes her unintelligible aria, she strikes a suitably triumphant pose with outstretched arms and upraised chin, ready to bask in the applause from her adoring fans. Instead, she is greeted with laughter as she loses her balance and falls backward through the curtain.

Brice concluded her vaudeville act with "Russian Art." It was another "comedy punch," wrote *Variety*'s Abel, who called her "the iridescent Tiffany in a Palace setting rich, for once, with talent, impressing the more despite the worthy supporting show."[26] The observation is important, not just because it was so laudatory of Brice, but because of what it said, by implication, about vaudeville. By 1927, vaudeville had lost its position as the nation's preeminent entertainment form and had begun a decline from which it would never recover. Other types of live amusement, especially revues and musical comedy, had been stealing its better performers since the late teens, but the combined onslaught of radio, records, and the movies in the mid-twenties contributed far more significantly to its demise.[27] Vaudeville simply could not compete with the new media. Not only were its salaries lower for the majority of performers, but the work was more grueling and reached a much smaller audience. Appearing in two or more live shows a day in week-long engagements along a vaudeville route required far more effort than making a recording, filming a movie, or broadcasting a weekly radio program. As more and more big names left the big-time for big money, the number of vaudeville houses sharply declined and the quality of the programs offered rapidly deteriorated.[28]

In December, noted female impersonator Julian Eltinge declared that vaudeville was "shot to pieces." It would continue, he predicted, "but it has ceased to attract individuals and big names are off the programs."[29] Brice was one of the few "big names" still remaining and as she toured in 1927 and 1928, critics gratefully acknowledged her "drawing ability" as a welcome change from increasingly lackluster programming. Yet one has to question her willingness to continue in a field that so many of her colleagues were deserting. She was being well paid for her efforts, but the work was certainly not as prestigious as it had once been and did nothing to enhance her reputation. In the next three years she would appear in vaudeville five times. She seems to have accepted the engagements as fillers between other jobs, as work with which she felt comfortable and to which she could return when other opportunities proved disappointing.

In her second and third week at the Palace, Brice responded to the audience's insistent demands and added "My Man" to her act. She was astute enough to understand the impact it always had, and her recent divorce had only heightened interest in the song. As *Variety* indicated in its review of her appearance at New York's Riverside Theatre, she performed it as effectively as she had in the past:

> All talk concerned Fannie and sometimes Nick, too. How would she look with her new nose? Wasn't it a shame about Nicky? Would she sing "My Man?"
> She would. She sang it as her first encore, and it gripped the house. She sang it so completely her eyes glistened and whether the emotion was phony or on the level its effect on the audience was something to see.[30]

Variety gave her credit for filling the house to within three rows of capacity and she continued to attract large audiences on tour as a headliner. After New York, she spent two weeks in Chicago where *Variety*'s correspondent welcomed her as "one of the few genuine names left to the Palace and vaudeville, and one of the few whose 'comings' are worth bragging about."[31] He reported that her performance "stopped the show," as it did in her subsequent engagements in San Francisco, Oakland, Los Angeles, Denver, Omaha, Milwaukee, and Kansas City. She concluded her highly successful tour with another appearance at the Palace April 16–21, 1928.

The following week an exciting article appeared in *Variety*. The April 25 edition announced that Brice and Al Jolson were two of the "big star names" awarded movie contracts by Warner Brothers. Jolson would be making his second film, *The Singing Fool*; Brice her first. According to the newspaper, signing her was a coup for Warner Brothers because her fine work for Ziegfeld and Belasco, as well as her considerable experience in vaudeville, gave "her name a drawing power" comparable to Jolson's.[32] Two pages later, the same issue ran a full page ad featuring a sketch of a demure Brice, accompanied by glowing text promising that "added millions" would soon be able to enjoy "the most accomplished comedienne of the legitimate and musical comedy stages" thanks to Warner Brothers and "the medium of the screen."[33]

Brice still did not have the kind of face that Hollywood, in the twenᴄᴇs, loved. Even with her new nose, she was not movie star pretty and, according to *Variety*, "all the pretty faces in the country gravitate Hollywood-way."[34] Brice did not conform to the standards of Hollywood any more than she had met Ziegfeld's exacting requirements for his legions of lovely *Follies* girls. She did not look like delicate Lillian Gish or "America's Sweetheart," Mary Pickford. She had nothing in common with glamorous Gloria Swanson or Greta Garbo. She was too lanky to play feckless flapper roles like pert Clara Bow. But she could sing, and in 1928 Hollywood needed voices. Since the premiere of *The Jazz Singer* in New York on October 6, 1927, the way a performer sounded was as important as his appearance. The first full-length "talking picture" was actually almost all silent except for the songs. Nevertheless, it inaugurated a new era in movie-making and brought an end to many formerly illustrious careers, as speech impediments and incongruous accents were exposed to the merciless microphone. Talent was now "supreme," observed *Variety*, predicting the imminent "fadeaway" of "the beautiful but dumb" stars "of both sexes who have depended upon their faces or vogue with the fans to maintain a spot on the screen."[35]

After one more Palace appearance from April 30 to May 5, Brice prepared for her Hollywood departure. As if to ensure the success of her new career, she had her teeth capped. She confided to gossip columnist and former Shubert press agent Nellie Revell that she had decided to have the "feat of dental engineering performed" based on the reaction to her screen tests and was delighted with the results. Displaying her "synthetic molars," she said, "See, now the Kodak okays me." Accompanied by her children and her cook, Revell reported, she left New York for Hollywood to begin work on her as yet unnamed film.[36] It was still without a title in July when *Theatre Magazine* devoted a full page to Brice, whom it lionized as "one of our Great Character Artists." There were photographs of her in expressive poses for three of her vaudeville numbers ("Russian Art," "Otto Kahn," and "Spring") and text announcing that she was leaving the two-a-day to make a Vitaphone picture for Warner Brothers. *Theatre* predicted that her film would be "as triumphant as Jolson's *Jazz Singer*" and observed that her "art lies in the ease and spontaneity with which she can sway her audience from tears to laughter and back again to tears, all within the span of two or three minutes."[37]

By September, *Variety* was running full page ads for Brice and her movie, which now had as ingenious a title as the one Belasco had chosen for her play. It was called *My Man* and it was said to be "on its way." Lest anyone forget the famous song, an ad in the September 26 edition superimposed Brice's photograph on the sheet music and predicted that the forthcoming film would be "another electrifying hit."[38] In the November 14 issue, an ad promised that *My Man* would "get audiences" because "millions of Fannie's followers are waiting to see and hear her first picture." The famous Belasco and Ziegfeld star would "play upon the whole gamut of emotions, now touching the heart, now tickling the ribs." Naturally, she would also sing "all her old favorites—and many new ones."[39] Two weeks later, a two-page ad for Warner Brothers included *My Man* among "the greatest array of Box Office smash hits in the history of this industry," and the December 5 *Variety* predicted that "Fannie and her following" would fill theatres across the country, beginning with *My Man*'s premiere at Warner Brothers' Theatre on December 21.[40]

Before the film's release, Brice discussed her latest venture in a magazine article chronicling her career. She had developed a "profound interest in the movies," and preferred screen to stage work because it allowed her to use a more "restrained" acting technique: "In the movies you can get ideas over by a look, a gesture, very little action. The entire tempo is more subdued and less tiring than it is on the stage."[41] Such comments contrast markedly with the negative statements she subsequently made. Years later, when she reminisced about her failure in films, she claimed it was because she felt terribly uncomfortable performing on a movie set. Unlike live audiences, with whom she always had a rapport, the camera inhibited her: "Wherever I looked, there is that eye staring at me. Like a peeper. Making pictures is like making love in public," she mused, "you can't be at ease when somebody is watching."[42] As these remarks suggest, Brice's movie career was short-lived and the explanation she gave was the way she rationalized her failure. There were, however, other reasons why she did not succeed as a screen actress. She may not have anticipated them in the fall of 1928, but they quickly became apparent after *My Man*'s release.

In October, when she had completed the film, Brice returned to New York and the Palace for another two-week engagement. The *Times*'s Atkinson wrote that "as usual, Miss Brice is a success and, as usual, she deserves to be," but the tone of his review conveyed his surprise that she was still performing the same vaudeville act. Aside from a spoof on the talkies called "Spoils of Lust" and "a few" ballads, the rest of the numbers had all been done before at the Palace.[43] Brice's reliance on old material indicates that her stage work was not a priority for her at this time. She probably accepted the Palace booking because it was "easy money" for her. With minimal effort, she could perform in a setting with which she was comfortable and be well paid for it. Since she hoped her future lay in Hollywood, she may not have wanted to bother revamping a vaudeville act she thought she would not be using.

My Man, however, did not receive the critical acclaim Brice needed to become a movie star. The "painfully carpentered" script, as one reviewer put it, was partly responsible for the disappointing response. According to *Variety* it was "a succession of thin links to give Miss Brice recurring excuses for her well-known songs." Without those, another critic complained, it would have been "a total loss."[44] *Variety* reported that she sang seven of her "pet numbers" in the following order: "Florodora Baby," "I'm an Indian," "Second Hand Rose," "I'd Rather Be Blue" (new), "My Man" in comic and serious versions, "Spring," and "If You Want the Rainbow" (new). She also performed "Mrs. Cohen at the Beach," which the *New York Times* called her outstanding offering. The songs were as effective as they had always been and the opening night audience responded very positively. In the opinion of Variety's Sid, *My Man* was "about the same as watching a recital by Fannie Brice in all the best things she had ever done. It ought to be good and is."

Paradoxically, however, the songs that saved the movie also revealed Brice's weakness as a film actress. She handled them beautifully, but she did not do as well with the dramatic scenes. Sid put it diplomatically: she was "not entirely at her best when carrying this story, and thirty-seven minutes of these ninety-nine are silent." For roughly one-third of the movie, she could not depend on her voice and had to rely on the techniques of silent movie acting. Although Sid praised her "showmanship" when "leading up to a gag line or delivering a number," he implied that she did not have the requisite skills to sustain the dramatic moments. She simply did not know how to act, and this charge had been leveled against her in both *Why Worry?* and *Fanny*. Equally serious, and this criticism had also been heard before, Sid found her difficult to take in large doses. He compared her to British comedienne Beatrice Lillie in that they were "subject to the same handicap, enough is enough. . . . Each is more at home in a revue where they can come and go with their specialties than when playing a book."[45] In a full-length feature, particularly one with silent segments, her exaggerated mannerisms became monotonous.

There were two other reasons why Sid thought Brice would be a "one-picture star." First, he feared that her "distinct Hebrew clowning" would have limited appeal. Even though she had toured in vaudeville and the *Follies*, her stops had been predominantly in cosmopolitan centers. Movie theatres had already proliferated to the point where they were in smaller, rural "localities" which were apt to "chill" on Brice's brand of ethnic comedy. Second, Sid observed that, in one movie, she performed all the songs she had spent years accumulating. If she used up her best material in *My Man*, what would she do in another picture? "How long would it take Fannie to get as much and as good stuff again?" he wondered, and then answered his own question, "Yars and yars." He also advised her to find new songs if she contemplated future vaudeville engagements, since clinging to "these old favorites" would not endear her to audiences.[46]

All of these observations proved remarkably prescient. In spite of its early success in New York, *My Man* was a failure at box offices across the country. Although it initially attracted audiences in large cities such as Los Angeles, business dropped off dramatically after the first or second week. The film managed to set a new high in its first week at Loew's State in New Orleans, yet reached a new low for the house in its fourth week at the Music Box in Seattle.[47] Most of the engagements were mediocre, but in smaller towns, especially in the Midwest, *My Man* was a disaster. The February 13, 1929, *Variety* reported from Topeka, for example, that "Fanny Brice was flopping at the Grand" in the "first Vitaphone picture to get the razz from Topekans." Brice had "no support" because she was "too apparently trying to do an Al Jolson with her already well known vaude stunts as high spots in too plainly manufactured a story."[48] Another reviewer compared her unfavorably to Jolson, stating that she was "not so sweepingly exuberant and infectious a personality" as he and could not therefore be expected to compensate for a weak vehicle through the sheer force of her performance.

Beyond that, Brice was too Jewish to play well in the hinterlands. The country had just given Republican Herbert Hoover a landslide victory over his Democratic opponent, Governor Al Smith of New York. Smith's Catholicism had been a major issue in the campaign which also focused on immigration, prohibition, and urban corruption. As one New England Protestant expressed it in her diary, the election was "My America against Tammany's. Prairie, Plantation and Everlasting Hills against the Sidewalks of New York."[49] Many shared these narrowly chauvinistic sentiments and could not abide the thought of a Catholic in the White House. Although historians believe that, given the nation's prevailing prosperity, Hoover was probably unbeatable, his margin of victory "demonstrated the pervasiveness of cultural tensions."[50] Religion was as much a factor in Brice's screen failure as it was in Smith's defeat. She was also seen as being "too New York," but in her case, that translated as "too Jewish." The "distinct Hebrew clowning" mentioned by Sid was definitely a disadvantage; it kept her from making a successful transition from stage to screen. Audiences across America could not relate to her Yiddish accent and comic mannerisms, and that was far more serious a problem for her as an aspiring film star than a weak script.

In January and February 1929, Brice still appeared in newspaper advertisements for Warner Brothers, but she was probably no longer under contract to them. When "Warner Bros. Box-Office Stars" filled two pages in the January 9 *Variety*, she had already opened in *Fioretta*, an operetta produced by Earl Carroll, known for his successful series of naughty musical revues. It is unclear exactly when Carroll hired her. As early as November 7, *Variety* had announced that a new Carroll production, financed by a wealthy Philadelphian, was in preparation and by December 5 noted that it had started rehearsing.[51] Neither article mentioned Brice, but she joined the show in time for its five-hour premiere in Baltimore on New Year's Eve.

Variety considered *Fioretta* overlong and underwritten. An opulent spectacle set in eighteenth-century Venice, it was visually beautiful but failed to provide its cast members with a coherent script. *Variety* speculated that Carroll had "signed up everyone available, regardless of whether there was material in the book for them," given them "fancy Italian Renaissance titles," and told them "to strike out for themselves." Some managed to "swim through the two acts and fourteen scenes" without mishap, while others "flounder[ed] in the sea of scenic splendor."[52]

Brice, cast as the Marchesa Vera Di Livio, was among those who floundered. *Variety*'s comments about her suggest that, once again, she was unable to create a believable character without resorting to her customary mannerisms:

> Fannie Brice is all dolled up in 18th century Venetian silks and satins that wholly stifle her style. She just can't get going, and it is only for a brief moment when she, in apparent desperation, lifts her panniered skirt and displays her comic pedals that the audience gets a brief moment of the entertaining Fanny they have been waiting for. For the better part of this long evening, however, her artistry is wasted.[53]

When she had a song that allowed her to create a comic caricature or to tap into deeper reservoirs of feeling, she could be brilliant. When she was playing a dramatic role, however, she was unable to overcome a script's inherent weaknesses. If the material did not suit her style, she could do very little with it and her range as a performer was beginning to seem much more narrow than, understandably, she would want to admit.

After Baltimore, *Fioretta* traveled to Washington D.C., and Philadelphia. By the time it reached New York in February, it had been substantially revised. It was still too long and the story was still subordinate to the spectacular costumes and scenery, but the book was better than it had been in Baltimore. Brice's performance had also improved significantly. In white wig and elaborate gown, she now played the Marchesa with a Yiddish accent and claimed to be the great-granddaughter of the Merchant of Venice. As Robert Garland succinctly observed in the *New York Telegram*, "Fannie Brice is Fannie Brice."[54]

Billy Rose took credit for the changes in her role. According to his recollections, Brice had called him in New York and described *Fioretta* as "a show with a lot of words, and none of them are funny." He immediately left by train for what he incorrectly remembered as Boston and quickly assessed the situation. The problem, as he saw it, was that Carroll, ignoring Brice's talents as a comedienne, was trying to "play her straight." "It's like buying Lindy's and throwing out the bagels and lox." he explained.[55] Rose said he wrote her "a couple of songs" which worked well because they were comic and provided her with material she found congenial.

With Rose's help, Brice was able to salvage her performance, but she could not save the show. In March, the entire company was asked to accept a salary cut. That postponed the inevitable, but not for long. The May 8 *Variety* reported that *Fioretta* would be concluding its fourteen-week engagement on Saturday, May 11, and the June 5 edition listed the production as one of the "Failures of '28–'29."[56] The same issue also noted that Fanny Brice and Billy Rose were on their way to Los Angeles, where Rose had negotiated a contract for her with United Artists. Rose was not simply being altruistic. He had become Brice's third husband in a civil ceremony on February 8 at Manhattan's City Hall and consequently had more than a passing interest in her career.

Although Brice's friends considered the union a mismatch and her children compared the short, stocky Rose unfavorably to their handsome father, the thirty-seven-year-old Brice seemed happy about the marriage. "She told me once," Rose recalled, "that she married Frank White, the barber, because he smelled so good; she married Nick Arnstein because he looked so good; and she married me because I thought so good."[57] Rose may have been physically unappealing, but Brice considered their relationship "stimulating" because they shared a passionate commitment to show business. "I was never bored with Billy," she later reminisced. "The life with him . . . was a different kind of a thing, and of course we had that much in common—our work." Contrasting Rose with Arnstein, she explained, "You see what I found thrilling with Billy was that I was with a man who was creating all the time—doing something. After Nick! Who was just talking and never doing anything."[58]

The June 19 *Variety* reported in its "Hollywood Chatter" column that Brice was still eager for screen success and had two forthcoming features for United Artists.[59] On July 24, the paper announced that the first would be an original story by Warner writer Joseph Jackson called "The Chant." That was a typographical error. The title was actually "The Champ," which subsequently became *Be Yourself* when the film was released the following March.[60] In the parlance of the picture, Brice played another feisty, forthright, forceful "dame." This time, she was nightclub entertainer Fannie Field, inexplicably in love with Jerry Moore, a second rate boxer whose fondness for drinking has diminished his dubious athletic prowess.[61]

The movie opens with Jerry losing badly to his archrival, McCloskey, in a prizefight, after which the scene changes to Field's nightclub. Fannie enters to loud applause and launches into her first number, "When a Woman Loves a Man." Wearing a tight lace gown that clings to her, she struts around, hands on hips, singing and rolling her eyes, smiling broadly and flirting with members of the audience. She does a "Betty Boop" imitation which includes crossing her eyes, puffing out her cheeks, tossing her head from side to side, and grimacing. She finishes to a thunderous ovation and joins Jerry at his table. He is drinking, as usual, and she asks, "Doesn't your elbow ever get tired?" They banter, then Jerry confides in her that he is looking for a new manager because he has just fired his old one, and mutters that fighting is "a racket." Fannie, who has listened sympathetically, looks at him and replies, "So is tennis, but you gotta be sober to play it." When McCloskey tries to take her away with him, the two men almost come to blows. She separates them and, as she prepares for her next song, says to Jerry, "Stick around, I'll be back. Say, listen, lay off those window washers, those (she does another Betty Boop imitation) poop-poop-a-doop-poop-poops." She winds up her arm as if to punch him, grins, and exits.

The scene sets the tone for the rest of the movie in terms of both the dialogue and the characterization. The no-nonsense exchanges in slangy speech are consistent with Brice's presentation of Fannie as tough-talking and street smart. She is a pal, a good sport, and to use her own expression, a "square shooter." She is also warm, perceptive, affectionate, maternal and, as Jerry so gallantly puts it, when she "ain't clownin'," she "ain't bad lookin'." It is as if this comment somehow legitimizes her as the female lead. She may not be gorgeous, but she looks decent enough to have a picture built around her.

The line is revealing because it indicates Hollywood's reluctance to deviate from type. Brice's problem as a film actress was, first of all, that she was not pretty enough to play either a romantic leading lady or a sex goddess. Nor was she sufficiently unattractive to be what one critic called a "gargoyle," a comic grotesque like Marie Dressler or ZaSu Pitts.[62] She fit neither category, and such individuality was not an asset in 1930. Secondly, and this proved as limiting as her looks, she was still too Jewish. Although *Be Yourself* tried to tone down her ethnicity by using a Yiddish accent minimally, Brice's speech was full of Yiddish inflections and expressions. Her brother in the film spoke with a heavy accent, she did three songs in dialect (including one that *Variety* described offensively as "a yid comic number"), and her regular New York accent would have been equally alien in Topeka.[63]

A third problem for Brice in *Be Yourself* was that she had not improved as a dramatic actress. She never knew what to do with her hands, and usually stood with them either resting on her hips or held awkwardly at her sides. She delivered her lines without much variety so that they all sounded remarkably similar. The most animated exhanges were the ones that seemed improvised. When she leaned over the breakfast table and argued with her brother Harry, for example, she was much more expressive because she was probably ad-libbing. As in *My Man*, the best part of the picture was sung, not spoken. The songs gave her an opportunity to show what she could do so well. She had six numbers in all, half of them new, with lyrics by Billy Rose: "When a Woman Loves a Man" (comic and serious versions), "Sascha (the Passion of the Pasha)," "Cooking Breakfast for the One I Love," "Is Something the Matter with Otto Kahn?," "Kicking a Hole in the Sky," and "Spring."[64] In each of them —even the pretentious "Kicking a Hole in the Sky," which was supposedly a musical version of Dante's *Inferno*! —her tremendous warmth and energy were apparent. The *New York Times* praised the "earnestness" and "good nature" she displayed in interpreting her songs.

Be Yourself received reasonably favorable reviews and a barrage of publicity. "Fannie Brice is one of the funniest women in show business!"; "Vimful, vivacious and volcanic! Fannie Brice in a riot of laughter, tears, and adventure"; "Broadway's great favorite: Ziegfeld, Belasco and big-time vaudeville star Fannie Brice in a zippy funful romance of the nightclub and the prize ring" —were all typical of the ads United Artists placed in newspapers.[65] They did not help the picture achieve box office success. Even in New York, *Be Yourself* managed only three weeks at the Rialto in a disappointing engagement characterized by a steep decline in business.[66] In other cities, the runs were shorter and less profitable. The picture set no new lows, but audiences indicated clearly that Brice was not one of their screen favorites.

United Artists responded by dropping her from its roster of stars. She and Billy Rose reacted by filing a $180,000 lawsuit against the corporation for breach of contract. The litigation would drag on for months, but Brice was not preoccupied with its resolution and was already busy with other work. She was one of the lucky Americans for whom unemployment was not a problem. In October 1929, the long period of prosperity in the United States came to an abrupt and startling end with the stock market crash. On Thursday, October 24, over twelve million shares changed hands in a frenzy of selling. Disaster came five days later, on "Black Tuesday," October 29, when, in the words of historian Eric Goldman, "scrambling, yelling traders dumped 16,410,000 shares of stock on the New York Stock Exchange, and the United States refused to believe what it was watching."[67] "WALL STREET LAYS AN EGG," headlined *Variety* on October 30. By the end of the month, stockholders had suffered a paper loss of over $15 billion; by the end of the year, the collapse of all kinds of securities reached the incomprehensible sum of $40 billion.[68]

The financial panic had devastating effects. The Great Depression it triggered was the worst in American history, and would last almost a full decade. By 1931, radio favorites Amos 'n' Andy were joking: "Did you hear about the fellow who registered at the hotel and the clerk said, 'For sleeping or jumping, sir?'" but the nation's desperate situation was far from humorous.[69] By 1932, the number of unemployed had exceeded twelve million, more than five thousand banks and thirty-two thousand businesses had failed, farm prices had fallen to the lowest point in history, and the entire domestic economy seemed to be disintegrating.[70]

Like so many others, Brice lost thousands of dollars in the crash—Billy Rose recalled the amount as "half a million"—but she refused to let the financial disaster interfere with her activities.[71] If anything, the sobering experience fueled her determination to succeed professionally and to seek lucrative contracts on stage, screen, and radio. As early as November 1929, *Variety* reported that she would be appearing at the Los Angeles Orpheum for a week, just before the vaudeville house changed over to "all pictures." According to the paper, after "holding out for six months and $5000," she "gave in" and accepted "$4725."[72] It was a good salary, but could not compare to the $7,500 Beatrice Lillie received for one week's work at the Palace or the $12,000 the Palace would offer Al Jolson, and he would refuse, a few months later.[73] Aside from the fact that Brice may have needed the money, the discrepancy among the figures does make a statement about the relative drawing power of each star and the fact that her perceived value was less than Lillie's or Jolson's.

In its November 23 edition, *Billboard* announced that Brice was preparing to reenter vaudeville and might "play eastward over the circuit."[74] Her willingness to do so suggests, once again, that she had no options. Vaudeville continued its decline—accelerated, no doubt, by the Depression—as more and more houses closed or changed over to pictures, as more and more performers chose work in other fields. In October, *Variety* reported that of the fifteen hundred houses playing vaudeville five years earlier, only three hundred remained and of those, only six were "straight vaude." By the spring of 1930, the Palace would be the last straight vaudeville theatre in the country and it was experiencing difficulties. The May 7 *Variety* reported that the house's gross for the previous week had been the lowest in years because the headlining act, a Cuban orchestra, had played only one week in the United States prior to the Palace.[75] For the Palace to resort to an unknown main attraction, and to have to pay $3,500 for it, was shocking and did not bode well for vaudeville's future. The end was just two years away.

Brice did move "eastward" and on January 25, opened what had been announced as "two Keith weeks at $5000 per" at the Cleveland Palace.[76] She completed only one of them, returning to New York earlier than she had planned, but had a compelling reason for canceling half her Cleveland engagement: she finally had a chance to do a radio show. Since its modest beginning in 1920 with stations in Pittsburgh (KDKA) and Detroit (WWJ), radio had become a vital instrument of communication and entertainment. By 1922, the new industry had expanded to include some five hundred stations in all parts of the country. This number doubled in the following five years, and by 1932 radio had a nationwide audience measured in the millions.[77] The medium offered lucrative contracts for comparatively easy work, and many performers had already made a successful transition from the stage to the "airwaves."

Eager to join the radio ranks, Brice had been signed for three Philco Hours, with the possibility of a weekly series if the programs were successful.[78] The first was to air on Wednesday night, February 5, over WABC's coast-to-coast network. According to the *New York Times*, it promised to feature her songs and "a dialect version of *Romeo and Juliet*."[79] None of the newspapers carried reviews of the broadcast, so it is impossible to discuss Brice's on-air performance as Juliet. She did, however, do the same sketch when she opened at the Palace three days later. This time, her Romeo was comedian Phil Baker and the *Times* found their "Yiddish-English travesty" absolutely "hilarious." Brice waited coyly for Baker on an improvised balcony atop a grand piano. Their romantic rendezvous depended largely on mispronunciation, capitalizing on Brice's flair for dialect and Baker's penchant for zany puns.

The Shakespearean spoof was a hit, but critics expressed surprise that Brice did not present any new songs in her remaining forty-three minutes on stage. They were equally disappointed when she returned to the Palace the following month with another "kitful of old material, all of it known to the Palace fans." *Variety* stated that, unfortunately, "Miss Brice didn't come anywhere near stopping the show" and implied that her continued reliance on a stale act did not speak well for her as an entertainer.[80] It made her seem lazy and unimaginative, as if she were marking time until she could find a better opportunity.

She was not about to find it on the "airwaves," as she soon saw her hopes of winning a radio contract dashed. On Wednesday, March 19, she appeared on her second Philco Hour in a program which included a "Samson and Delilah" sketch in dialect. The negative response to her performance led Philco not only to drop the idea of using her in a series, but even to cancel the third broadcast it had already announced.[81] Brice reluctantly returned to her vaudeville tour, which concluded in Philadelphia on May 16.

She was absent from the newspapers until the end of July when a brief item in *Variety* reported that she would soon star in a new Billy Rose production.[82] By August 6, it had a rehearsal schedule, an opening date in Philadelphia, and a title, *Corned Beef and Roses*, which would eventually be changed to *Sweet and Low*. The show was the first of two revues Rose built around his wife. They would keep her busy for almost two years, but would do nothing to enhance her reputation or advance her career. The material Rose provided was, with few exceptions, undistinguished; instead of using Brice's talents, it only succeeded in revealing her limitations. Apologists might argue that since Rose was the producer, Brice would not have been involved in making critical artistic decisions about the show and would have had no choice but to work with what had been written for her. That seems unlikely, given the many sources alleging both that Rose relied heavily on her judgment as an experienced performer and that she took an active role in the creative process.

Brice herself described her concern with all aspects of the production in an interview she gave in October 1931. She was in Pittsburgh at the time, appearing in *Crazy Quilt*, the second of the two shows:

> "Why I worry more about *Crazy Quilt* than Billy does," she observed the other evening in her dressing room at the Alvin. "If a chorus girl has a little bit of dirt on her gown, or if her makeup isn't on straight, I have a fit. I'm always looking around the stage to see if the line is straight and if the lighting is correct for, after all, it's Billy's show, you know, and I'm Mrs. Billy so that makes it my show, too.
>
> "The trouble is that I'm more interested in seeing the show get over than I am in seeing Fannie Brice get over."[83]

There was more truth to that last statement than Brice, in her desire to sound suitably subservient as "Mrs. Billy," probably realized. So much of the material was so bad, particularly in *Corned Beef and Roses*, that Fanny Brice barely "got over." Several songs and sketches were criticized as being in abominable taste and Brice has to be held at least partially accountable.

Like any performer, Brice was entitled to her failures. To chastise her for the mistakes she made over the course of a long career would be unfair. Yet it does seem that the two years she spent in Rose's revues marked another stagnant period for her, a period in which she worked steadily but did not develop creatively and relied instead on abysmal or all-too-familiar material. This was precisely the point Robert Garland made when he reviewed *Corned Beef and Roses* after its New York opening in November 1930. Garland admired Brice, but his comments were unintentionally damning because they showed that she was coming to be regarded as an entertainer with an increasingly narrow range of talents. After praising her "comedic gifts" and her "infinite capacity for causing two laughs to grow where only one grew before," he observed, "Miss Brice is a limited artiste who is at her best when going through the motions she makes most readily."[84] In *Corned Beef and Roses*, Brice's artistry was not shown to particularly good advantage. At best, her work was amusing. Much of it was mediocre and some of it, apparently, was offensive.

To his credit, Rose had assembled a talented production team for *Corned Beef and Roses* including designer Jo Mielziner, choreographer Busby Berkeley, and writer David Freedman. The music by "Mr. Rose and His Friends" included such effective songs as "Would You Like to Take a Walk?" by Rose, Mort Dixon, and Harry Warren, and "Cheerful Little Earful" by Warren and Ira Gershwin (with some help from Rose). In addition to Brice, the cast featured George Jessel and Hal Skelly, dancers Moss and Fontana, British performer Arthur Treacher, and Hannah Williams as an attractive ingenue. (Williams was engaged to the son of Otto Kahn, who subsequently invested heavily in the show.) Despite its initial promise, however, *Corned Beef and Roses* lacked both coherence and style, and emerged with "neither the lavish opulence of a Ziegfeld show nor the chic naughtiness of an Earl Carroll revue."[85]

The production opened in Philadelphia on October 16, two weeks behind schedule, and, according to *Variety*, received "one of the most consistent critical pannings ever given" in that city. "In fact," the paper reported, "it is generally agreed in Philly that *Corned Beef and Roses* is the dirtiest show ever witnessed here." After thirty good minutes in the first act, it "faded fast" and "had to depend on smut, of which there was plenty." Act I began with a sketch called "Poor Mr. Shufeld" starring Jessel as a movie producer eager to take advantage of the proverbial "casting couch." Brice and Skelly joined him onstage for a song in which they joked about their recent Hollywood flops and announced that they were back on Broadway "at the request of Mr. Zukor, Mr. Warner, Mr. Laemmle, Mr. Schenck, and Mr. Fox."[86]

According to *Variety*, the second act really "plumbed the depths" and Jessel had the distinction of appearing in the "dirtiest bit in the show" as a lecturer with a series of raunchy stereopticon slides. In *Variety*'s uncharacteristically judgmental words, "This wasn't just off color; it was lower class stag smoker stuff, and many a blasé theatregoer was hard put to keep from blushing. Even Jessel was intensely embarrassed."[87] Brice followed in "Babykins," a sketch in which she played a precocious toddler and spoke about sex in baby talk. Although she had previously impersonated a baby in vaudeville, she did so in *Corned Beef and Roses* allegedly out of necessity. According to David Freedman, who wrote the sketch, Rose called him from Philadelphia with a crisis. Brice had just been fitted with a set of false teeth that made her speak with a lisp. Freedman decided to exploit the comic potential of the problem and created a character for whom lisping would be natural. The result was "Babykins," a character that would eventually evolve into Baby Snooks.[88] *Variety* found the scene dirty but extremely funny, and admired Brice's work in "two or three sketches." In terms of songs, however, she had none that "really demonstrat[ed] her abilities."

Corned Beef and Roses closed on October 25, having "nose-dived sensationally" in its second week. After extensive revisions, it opened at New York's 46th Street Theatre on November 17. It had a new title, *Sweet and*

Low; a new co-star, dancer and comedian James Barton, replacing a disaffected Skelly; and several new specialty acts, including the uproarious harmonica-playing "Borrah Minevitch and His Musical Rascals." Publicity for the show advertised Brice as the "world's greatest comedienne," Barton as the "world's greatest eccentric artist," and Jessel as the "world's greatest monologist."[89]

Hyperbole notwithstanding, *Sweet and Low* received only moderately favorable reviews. The critics generally praised Brice, although her work was not uniformly good. Her worst number was a sketch at the end of the first act called "Strictly Unbearable," which burlesqued the popular stage comedy *Strictly Dishonorable.*[90] Even Atkinson, usually a Brice enthusiast, called the travesty tasteless and added that "It had only Miss Brice's mischievous eyes and occasional assumption of the Southern accent to recommend it." Her best offering, not counting the perennially successful "Swan Song and Dance," was a new song, "Overnight," in which the speaker ruefully but realistically acknowledged that the flame of love had cooled and it was now time "to sigh goodbye." Rose's lyrics were trite, but Louis Alter's music was surprisingly affecting and Brice interpreted it sensitively. According to Atkinson, she managed to "inject a genuine touch of simple pathos into a banal Broadway ballad."[91]

Rose continued to tinker with the show during its five-month New York run. Some of Brice's numbers were eventually removed. Others were added, including such old favorites as "Rose of Washington Square" and the inescapable "My Man." In March, several newspaper articles appeared in which she announced that she was tired of "Jewish jingles" and needed a good "coon song" like the ones she used to do when "she was a little girl." She said she wanted a ragtime number, and by mid-month, Billy Rose and Fred Fisher had written one. It was "You Can Buy Kisses but You Can't Buy Love" which she performed effectively in top hat and tails. She also sang "I Wonder Who's Keeping Him Now" in the first act and "I Knew Him before He Was Spanish," with off-key castanets, in the second. Her final appearance was in a serious sketch called "Chinese White," in which she played a cockney maid named Lize who was murdered by Barton's Chang. The *New York Post* compared her histrionics in this scene to the ones she used in the ill-fated *Fanny* and considered them equally unsuccessful.[92]

In spite of the revisions, critics generally found the show lower than it was sweet, and initially it did very poorly in New York. By the third week, the cast had agreed to a 25 percent salary cut in lieu of closing. In January, to stimulate interest in the production, Rose began blitzing the papers with publicity about Brice and her rags-to-riches rise. A story in the *New York American* was typical. Entitled "Fannie Brice Won Stardom in Hard Fight," the article dragged out all the myths about her early years and combined them into a virtually unrecognizable Brice biography, beginning with the following fantasy:

> The career of Fannie Brice, one of the trio of stars of *Sweet and Low*, the revue hit playing at Chanin's Forty-sixth Street Theatre, reads like a chapter out of one of the old rags-to-riches series. Fannie, as she is endearingly called by all who know her, entered upon her professional stage venture in an extraordinary way. She was the perfect tom-boy who loved to amuse herself by singing popular songs to all the newsboys on the Bowery.[93]

A variety theatre manager just happened to hear her sing and asked her to enter one of his amateur night contests. She reluctantly agreed and "that was the turning point in her life." She "literally stopped the show cold, walked off with the meager prize, and embarked upon a stage career" which subsequently brought her "fame, fortune, and a host of admirers."

According to this less than accurate account, Brice bypassed burlesque —which, by now, had become hopelessly sleazy. She immediately became a "star headliner in vaudeville," where her unique talent attracted Ziegfeld's attention. He engaged her for the *Follies*, she "scored an instantaneous hit," and "starred" in several editions of the popular show. She also had "the opportunity to display her ability as a serious actress when she appeared under the Belasco banner" in *Fanny*. As the article's final fabrication, that terrible play has metamorphosed into "one of the pleasantest events in her years on the stage." With her inspiring performance she scored "a personal triumph in a role entirely different from any she had heretofore attempted." Similarly in *Sweet and Low*, lest anyone forget the point of the publicity, Brice shows "she is a real actress" in such powerful scenes as "Chinese White."[94]

These articles, combined with Rose's revisions, did help; business began to improve in February. Nevertheless, the April 22 *Variety* reported that *Sweet and Low* would be closing after a twenty-three-week run that had only recently begun to show a profit. Two weeks later, *Variety* announced that Rose was preparing a new revue called *Crazy Quilt* starring Brice, Phil Baker, and Ted Healy. The show opened on May 19 and the critics agreed that the title was apt. As Atkinson observed, "It is a patchwork affair that scatters the entertainment and seldom puts its best foot forward." *Variety* regarded it more positively as "unpretentious," "intimate," and "entertaining."[95]

Like *Sweet and Low*, *Crazy Quilt* was intended as a showcase for its
"stellar trio" and *Variety* commended Brice for not trying to outshine her
co-stars. Her material was varied, as it had been in the other show, and
it was not equally successful. She made her first appearance in top hat
and tails to sing *Crazy Quilt's* best song, Rose's "I Found a Million Dollar
Baby in a Five and Ten Cent Store," with Baker and Healy. Later in
the run, another of her numbers preceded it, a dialect song by Rodgers
and Hart called "Rest Room Rose," in which she bemoaned her lot as
a washroom attendant. At the opening performance, she did a torch song,
"To Think That We Were Sweethearts (and Now We're Not Even
Friends)." By June, it had been dropped in favor of the more spirited
"I Want to Do a Number with the Boys," in which she expressed her
desire to be an ingenue and dance with the male chorus. She burlesqued
Peter Pan, in Atkinson's words, "in the broadly Jewish style of gleams
and grotesque vulgarity that is the inimitable stuff she can do," but substituted her "Swan Song and Dance" on *Crazy Quilt's* tour. She amused
in "Strictly Unbearable," retained from *Sweet and Low*, but failed to carry
two new numbers which were subsequently dropped. One was a monologue called "Sadie Applegarden for Congress," which Atkinson considered
"witless." He found the other, Dorothy Parker's "Telephone Call," even
worse. In *Variety's* opinion, "it was not so hot, a dash of pathos with too
many appellations to the Almighty."[96] Once again, Brice was trying to
prove herself as a dramatic actress by performing serious material. Once
again, she was not convincing. Atkinson called her anguished "melodra-
matics" no better than "those of the female readers who entertain at church
socials," and perceptively observed: "Miss Brice is a burlesque comic of
the rarest vintage. She should be satisfied with that gift as all her votaries
are."[97] She would not be satisfied with that gift, nor would she come
to terms with it until her work in the *Ziegfeld Follies of 1934* and *1936*.

Variety reported that she sang "I Was a Florodora Baby" and "My
Man" in the finale and continued to do so on the road after *Crazy Quilt*
closed in New York at the end of July. In spite of a salary cut, the show
had run for only eleven weeks, but Rose had planned a tour that would
prove profitable largely because of the "unabashed public hustle" that was
becoming his trademark as a producer.[98] *Crazy Quilt's* route included Pittsburgh, Chicago, Detroit, Kansas City, Los Angeles, and San Francisco,
but it also reached small towns as far south as Texas for a series of "one-
nighters" on the way to, and then back from, the West Coast. The tour
lasted nearly a year and as Rose reminisced years later, "We played whistle
stops that hadn't seen flesh-and-blood entertainment for years."[99] Credit

for much of the show's success, especially in the rural areas, went to Rose's press agent, Ned Alvord, whom *Variety* described as "circusy" and who was responsible for vigorously promoting the production. Apparently, with Rose's blessing, Alvord generated a storm of pre-show publicity that did more to attract audiences than the presence of Fanny Brice in the cast.

Alvord's methods were often devious, if not dishonest. One of his favorite techniques reputedly involved visiting the composing room of a small town newspaper late at night. He would tell the printer that the advertisement for *Crazy Quilt* had been reproduced incorrectly and had to be changed, then substitute the "accurate" version featuring scantily clad chorines and minimal copy. He posted equally titillating—and misleading—signs about town, then visited local leaders to warn them of the immoral production's imminent arrival. They dutifully informed the upright citizens who naturally rushed out to buy tickets. What they saw was *Crazy Quilt*, as one source put it, "the rehashed and refurbished not-very-spicy show."[100]

Largely through Alvord's efforts, the production was banned in Minneapolis. There the irate mayor not only declared it "indecent and obscene," but ordered that the pictures of "nearly nude girls" on the billboard posters be covered with white paper. Suspecting that he had been the victim of what *Variety* termed a "press agent stunt," the mayor's constituents criticized his action, but *Crazy Quilt* benefited from the publicity. The show played for a week in St. Paul where *Variety* estimated that two-thirds of the audience came from Minneapolis and where the "Ned Alvord sex and nudity exploitation campaign" produced a significant increase in ticket sales. When the show left Columbus, Ohio, at the end of April, *Variety* reported that it had set an all-time attendance record with 4,200 at one performance.[101]

Brice never commented publicly on Alvord's tactics, nor did she appear in another Billy Rose production. It is possible that she disapproved of her husband's ruses and Alvord's dirty tricks, but it is far more likely that, at forty, she was simply tired of touring. She also must have wanted desperately to become a radio regular, one of the hundreds of performers with a weekly series, a large following, and a bright future. While she was criss-crossing the country on an exhausting schedule in a mediocre revue, *Variety* reported that "eleven new national stars appeared in the radio firmament," among them Gertrude Berg, the Boswell Sisters, Cab Calloway, Eddie Cantor, Bing Crosby, Guy Lombardo, the Mills Brothers and Walter Winchell.[102] The year 1931 had been "the most prolific starmaker of any of the ten broadcasting years so far," and Brice had not been a beneficiary. Instead, she saw other performers, many of them younger and less experienced, succeed in a field from which, thus far, she had been excluded.

Brice's lack of success in the thriving medium of radio must have troubled her. She was enough of a realist to know that radio was where the large salaries and national audiences now were. During 1932, *Variety* was full of articles about "ether hopefuls" in a "mad scramble" for contracts in a field currently "harder to get in than pictures."[103] "Radio toughest to crash," the August 9 issue announced, yet the following week's edition seemed to compound the problem by informing readers that success in radio was capricious. "Radio stars" were "accidents" that just "happen." Although they were delighted with their "startling public acclaim and acceptance," the new talents were hard pressed to explain their sudden recognition.

Brice's activities for the next eighteen months indicate that she was eager to share in the acclaim and acceptance. From May 1932 until September 1933, she concentrated on obtaining a radio contract and fulfilling her "ethereal ambitions." In its April 19 edition, *Variety* reported that Blanche Merrill was preparing new material for Brice, marking the first time they had worked together since *The Hollywood Music Box Revue*. It is understandable that Brice would have turned to Merrill for help as she had in the past, since the songwriter knew her particular skills so well. This time, however, the formerly fortuitous association did not produce the desired results. Brice appeared with comedian Jack Pearl on the May 22 *WABC Follies of the Air*, but was not asked to perform on subsequent broadcasts. Moreover, Brice and Merrill evidently had no further professional contact.

Brice's relationship with Merrill is puzzling. After their dazzling initial success, the two women worked together only sporadically. Once she returned to the *Ziegfeld Follies*, Brice did not rely exclusively on Merrill for her material, although Merrill continued to supply some of her most effective songs until 1919. In that year, Merrill had a spat with Ziegfeld over her role in the *Follies* and was apparently fired. It is possible that Ziegfeld forbade Brice to have further contact with the songwriter and, since she was then under contract to him, she had to comply. From Ziegfeld, Merrill moved to the Shuberts but had a dispute with them in 1920 over a musical comedy she promised to write but failed to deliver. In 1922, Merrill helped Brice create a new vaudeville act while she waited for her Ziegfeld show to materialize and Brice also performed Merrill material in the *Ziegfeld Follies of 1923* and *The Music Box Revue* in 1924. In her November 1925 *Saturday Evening Post* interview, Brice spoke warmly about Merrill and described their collaboration at length. Yet by the time that article reached the newsstands, the two were no longer working together. As Merrill had explained in a poem *Variety* published the previous May, Brice was now a "Belasco star"; Merrill was just her "Use [sic] to be writer" and "the only one feeling blue." Committed to becoming a serious actress, Brice probably believed that Merrill, with her flair for comedy, could do nothing more to advance her career. After she married Billy Rose, moreover, it is quite possible that he refused to allow collaboration with Merrill because of professional jealousy. About Rose, the fastidious Merrill allegedly remarked, "Ugh! If you ever saw his fingernails—they were black!"[104]

No doubt an extended vacation on the Riviera helped Brice forget her most recent radio failure and her disappointment that Merrill seemed to have lost her touch. The June 7 *Variety* reported that Brice, her children, and friend Beatrice Lillie had already sailed for Paris on the *Ile de France*. Three weeks later, *Variety* informed its readers that Brice would be abroad until Labor Day "when she returns to tackle that radio broadcasting thing again," a clear indication that she had already auditioned. In its July 26 issue, the paper announced that Lucky Strike was considering Brice for its Saturday night show as a replacement for comedian Bert Lahr. According to the August 16 edition, she had several radio offers, including Lucky Strike's, and was also planning to play "some picture house dates she had lined up."

The prospects sounded promising and suggested that in pursuing radio work Brice was moving in the right direction. Two summer milestones corroborated her decision. As she frolicked with friends and family in southern France, two obituaries signaled the end of an era. On July 9, vaudeville died when the Palace, the last remaining straight vaudeville house in the country, changed over to pictures. On July 22, Ziegfeld died suddenly after a heart attack.[105] Both events symbolized the shifting show business scene as surely as did the construction of RKO's mammoth new Radio City Music Hall and RKO's Roxy Theatre. With its elaborate technical facilities, luxurious decor, and extravagant amenities (such as peach-colored mirrors in the powder rooms which cast a flattering glow on the viewer's reflection), Radio City was as much a monument to the dominant new entertainment field as the Palace had been to the old.

When Radio City was completed in December, Brice was experiencing another of her professional "lows." None of her prospects had materialized. She did not get the expected Lucky Strike contract and in the next three months lost at least two others: Chevrolet for NBC and Chesterfield for CBS. The November 29 *Variety* announced that she would be appearing regularly on the Chesterfield show after the first of the year. In its next edition, however, the paper reported that Chesterfield had decided against Brice, even after she brought her original price of $1,500 down to $750 and offered to supply the scripts. The rejection must have been humiliating, and the results of a national poll, published later in the month, showing former stage colleagues Cantor and Jolson among the "twelve best liked air acts" must have added to her discomfiture.[106]

Compounding it still further was the panning she received for her performance in a stage show at New York's Paramount Theatre, one of the many movie theatres offering live entertainment as well as the feature film. She was appearing on the bill with *Undercover Man*, a gangster movie starring George Raft and dealing, ironically, with bond theft. According to *Variety*, the picture was weak, but Brice was worse. She was trying to market herself for radio and was failing because, instead of focusing on what she could do well, she was trying to give audiences what she thought they wanted. In the opinion of *Variety*'s Kauf, she made some extremely poor choices, with the result that she did not "seem to fit," her songs did not work, and her humor did not "click." Her imitation of cartoon character Betty Boop, among others, fell flat and Kauf indignantly implied that Brice was trivializing her talent.[107] At this point she may have wondered if she still had any. Her self-confidence shaken, she returned to radio auditions after an equally disappointing week at the Brooklyn Paramount.

In mid-January, she finally "clicked' with Fleischmann and the J. Walter Thompson agency. *Variety* commented on the positive results of her session and provided an interesting explanation for her succession of recent failures: the interference of Billy Rose. *Variety* quoted representatives from both CBS and NBC who stated that Rose caused Brice to lose the Chesterfield and Chevrolet accounts because of his insistence on directing her. When the networks suggested that she perform her material one way, he "argued that he knew his wife's possibilities and artistic range best and fashioned the audition stanzas to his own viewpoint."[108] Before the Fleischmann test, however, he was persuaded to withhold his advice. Brice benefited, although she did not ultimately get a long-term contract.

In its February 7 issue, *Variety* reported that Brice was contemplating a return to the stage as one of the stars of a new revue Rose planned for the Palace.[109] One week later, that was no longer an option because, at last, she had a job on radio. According to the February 13 *New York World-Telegram*, she was scheduled to join George Olsen's Orchestra on a new series beginning March 4.

Brice finally had a chance to prove that she was a "first-class comedienne," as she put it in an interview, and made her debut for Chase and Sanborn on March 15 at 8:00 P.M. over WFAF.[110] It was not an auspicious beginning. *Variety* was very disappointed with the first program but stressed that the problem was not "due so much to the lack of a click radio personality as the ineptitude of adapting the comedienne's talents for the ether." Drawing on her stage repertoire, she performed "Poor Little Popular Song" (probably the latest version of "Moving Picture Baby"), her standby "Second Hand Rose," and a Cleopatra spoof. Although the songs worked reasonably well, the sketch was not suitable "for mike purposes." According to *Variety*, "Missing was the Brice skill at visual burlesque. As air comedy," therefore, "it couldn't have been productive of anything but an occasional giggle, even to those familiar with the comedienne's style."[111]

Brice had not yet found an effective persona or performance style for radio. It is not surprising that she needed time in which to adjust to the demands of a different medium. She had always relied heavily on physical comedy to carry her routines and, as *Variety* observed, "visual burlesque" simply did not work over a radio microphone. She had to refine her technique so that it would be aurally effective; audiences were going to respond to her solely on the basis of what they heard. The fact that the studio audience could see her complicated the situation, but she had to learn that she could not treat the radio broadcast as a stage performance. As she explained in a May interview in the *New York Times*, she had to remember that she was playing for "a great unseen audience and not the few hundred people gathered to watch the show." Indulging in "a funny grimace or gesture" for the benefit of the "visible audience" only succeeded in offending the "radio listener" who was "not in on the joke." She had to resist the temptation "to extract another laugh by a silly bit of tomfoolery."[112]

The language was stilted, but the message was clear; by May, Brice was well on her way to radio success. In spite of objections that some of her jokes were unsuitable for family audiences, she did well in *Variety's* spring poll of radio popularity. She was not among the twelve national favorites, but she was one of the twelve runner-ups after only two months on the air.[113] In June, she and Olsen's Orchestra had their program extended for another sixteen weeks. By July, *Variety* listed their show as one of radio's outstanding offerings.

In the absence of weekly reviews or scripts, it is impossible to discuss the material Brice used. A blurb in the July 11 *Variety* indicated that she had prepared a burlesque of Mickey Mouse, but had to abandon it after the Walt Disney office refused to permit the parody. One newspaper article praised "My Man," and she undoubtedly performed other songs from her stage repertoire. She presented some of her familiar characters such as Cleopatra, who counters a Prince's objection that "his girl" is "aloof half the time" with the line "Half aloof is better than none."[114] Clearly, that kind of humor, combining punning with dialect, would have been very effective on radio.

In the opinion of the *New York Post*'s Dialist, Cleopatra was more typically Bricean than another character who was, nevertheless, one of the "drollest" on the air. That character was Baby Snooks, described by Dialist as "that much too imaginative child for whom the parlor is infested with lions and rattlesnakes," who is "taken directly from life and knocked just slightly askew as only Fanny Brice can knock it."[115] Snooks, of course, was not Brice's first baby. From time to time in her stage career, she had impersonated a child in songs such as "The Hat," "Moving Picture Baby," and "Rockaway Baby." She was "Babykins" in *Sweet and Low*, but none of these characters was as fully realized as Baby Snooks. The terrible toddler emerged on radio and was the first character Brice developed specifically for that medium. Snooks would make successful stage appearances in the forthcoming *Follies* and, upon Brice's return to radio, would prove to be her most enduring comic creation.

Brice had waited a long time for her radio show and was pleased that it enabled her to "reach the hillbillies and the *haute monde* at the same time."[116] Yet she admitted in an August interview in the *New York Herald Tribune* that was very different in tone from her comments in the *New York Times* that she still preferred entertaining a live audience. When asked if performing for her "concealed public" seemed "a little astral and a little unreal," she answered:

> You said it. It does seem a little spooky. . . . Me, I like to look the customers in the eye, whether they're tossing their hats in the air or sitting on their hands. I like to know what they think about what I am doing. Singing to a million birds you can't see is like being ambushed by the Sioux. Now I know how Braddock felt at Fort Duquesne. You can't alter your tactics to meet conditions when you can't see your foe."[117]

After joking that she judged the success of her broadcasts on the basis of what her children and their friends listened to on Wednesday nights, she said that she planned to leave radio temporarily at the end of September to star in another Billy Rose revue with Phil Baker because she wanted to see "a customer grin again."

Rose's production turned out to be a revival of *Crazy Quilt* which, by October, was touring throughout the Midwest for RKO and Loew. Brice, however, had a better offer and was not in the cast. She had been given the starring role in a posthumous edition of the *Ziegfeld Follies*, produced by the Shuberts and, nominally, by Ziegfeld's widow Billie Burke. In buying the rights to the title "Ziegfeld Follies," the Shuberts were not motivated by any desire to pay homage to their former rival. As enterprising as ever, they sensed that a new *Follies* would have widespread appeal and focused on the profit they intended to make, rather than on the paean they might be perceived as offering the dead impresario.

The Ziegfeld Follies of 1934 opened in Boston on November 7, 1933. In it, Brice proved her newly acquired radio skills had not detracted from her considerable talents as a stage performer. The critics declared that she was "better than ever" in the production and its successor, the *Ziegfeld Follies of 1936*. In what would be her last stage appearances, Brice had the maturity and the material to create some of her most brilliant comic characters. In the process, she provided the definitive examples of Bricean comedy.

"A Burlesque Comic of the Rarest Vintage": The *Ziegfeld Follies* of *1934* and *1936*

> "But I couldn't get excited about anybody because they had money or a title. I never got stuck on myself, so why should I be stuck on anybody else? I can't stand compliments."
>
> —Fanny Brice[1]

> "'Rewolt!' she screams with her wicked eyes crossed."
>
> —Brooks Atkinson, *New York Times*, 31 January 1936[2]

> "Of all the people who make us laugh, we know of no one who is as completely the artist or as unalterably loveable."
>
> —Aaron Stein, *New York Post*, 3 December 1937[3]

9.

When the *Ziegfeld Follies of 1934* previewed in Boston for two weeks in November 1933, the critical consensus was that the show needed work, but Fanny Brice did not. Both *Variety* and the *New York Times* wrote that she dominated the production and predicted that she would help it to a successful New York run. After extensive revisions, cast changes, and engagements in Philadelphia, Washington, Pittsburgh, and Newark, the *Follies* opened at New York's Winter Garden Theatre on January 4.[4] It was, in *Variety's* words, an immediate and surprise "click."[5] Comparisons to previous editions were inevitably made, and there was disagreement over the relative merit of the current version. Some critics said the Shubert production was inferior to any of Ziegfeld's; others thought it was an improvement over all previous *Follies*. Most simply agreed that it was different. "Mr. Ziegfeld might not have recognized it as his own," observed John Mason Brown in the *Evening Post*, "but he would have enjoyed it."[6] Although it lacked "the grandee's unifying touch," Brooks Atkinson explained, it was still extremely entertaining, "lively," "splendidly costumed and lighted."[7] *Time* magazine asserted, "It remembers Ziegfeld only in title and opulent manner," yet found it "fast and funny," with "magnificent sets," "good songs," "flocks of pretty, nimble girls, twittering in and out," and an impressive cast:

> It has . . . little shrugging Willie Howard with his brother Eugene, comedians of, by and for Broadway. It has beauteous Jane Froman and commanding Everett Marshall to sing. It has a pair of Astaire-like dancers in Vilma and Buddy Ebsen. It has an incredible acrobatic child named June Preisser.[8]

Above all, it had Fanny Brice.

With the *Ziegfeld Follies of 1934*, Brice finally achieved a part of her previously elusive goal: she was acclaimed as the star of a successful production. Obviously the *Follies* was not a drama. Like its predecessors, it was a musical revue; but, unlike the others, it appeared to have been built around Brice. Whether or not it was originally intended as a showcase for her talents, that was how it was perceived by the audiences who flocked to see it and were not disappointed by her performance.

Brice received no negative notices. She was hailed as a distinguished comedienne. In part, she was riding a nostalgia wave. She reminded people of a less complicated era in the nation's history, of the period before the First World War, the stock market crash, and the Depression. In 1934, with millions still unemployed, with ominous rumblings coming once again from Germany, it was pleasant to remember simpler times. As so many articles made a point of noting, Brice's career had begun years earlier, even before the *Follies of 1910*. She had outlasted such colleagues as Eva Tanguay who had originally been more famous, but who had been unable to adapt to the changing entertainment industry. She had outlived many others including, of course, Ziegfeld himself. The very idea of mounting a posthumous edition of the *Ziegfeld Follies* imbued the whole project with a certain poignancy from the beginning and Brice's presence in the cast made it that much more intense. Robert Benchley, writing in *The New Yorker*, captured the bittersweet feeling she produced: "And when at the end of the show, she sings 'Rose of Washington Square,' you cry without quite knowing what for."[9] The tears were, presumably, for lost youth, for lost innocence, for lost opportunities, for the past that can never be recaptured, only remembered. Yet watching Brice cavort as she always had must have been comforting, too, because it reinforced a sense of the continuity of theatrical generations and made the audience see that everything did not always have to change for the worse. It was possible to survive the turbulence of the times.

Nostalgia alone, however, was not responsible for Brice's success. She also gave a brilliant performance. She was better than she had ever been in previous appearances under the Ziegfeld banner. With the exception of "Rose of Washington Square" (and even that was not sung in its entirety) her material was new and, for the first time since 1921, it suited her well. Billy Rose once remarked, "Writing for Fanny was a romp. All you had to know was how to fit her."[10] The songs and sketches he helped create for her in the *Ziegfeld Follies of 1934* "fit" her perfectly and enabled her to impersonate a variety of memorable comic characters.

The crucial word here is comic. As she had in the *Follies of 1910, 1911, 1916, 1917,* and *1920,* Brice performed only comedy. She had no serious songs, no dramatic scenes (just a parody of one), and no lugubrious monologues. She must have made this choice deliberately. The Depression may have been partly responsible; even though the nation now had a charismatic leader, Franklin Delano Roosevelt, who had won the presidency in 1932 by promising a "New Deal," including the repeal of Prohibition, economic recovery was slow and audiences still needed an escape from harsh everyday realities. Yet it also seems that Brice had come to terms with her strengths and weaknesses as a performer and was finally willing to accept her limitations. By eschewing maudlin material and concentrating once again on comedy, she demonstrated that she was a vibrant and energetic performer with a captivating stage presence. That, more than the Ziegfeld connection, made her refreshing and relevant.

Brice's first appearance was in "Soul Saving Sadie," a song spoofing evangelist Aimee Semple McPherson. It was not exactly a novel topic. The flamboyant McPherson, whom *Variety* dubbed, "the most sensational showwoman in the world," had penetrated the nation's consciousness in the early twenties with her frequent transcontinental gospel tours and revival meetings, dramatized sermons, robed choirs, orchestra and brass band, and vaudeville-like Sunday night performances. While Brice could have drawn from all of the Aimee lore, she was undoubtedly inspired by the evangelist's recent trip to New York. During the week of September 26,

1933, McPherson had received $5,000 for an appearance at the Capitol Theatre. Covering the event, *Variety* remarked, "She wears a white satin creation—sexy, but Episcopalian."[11] In spite of the publicity, the Capitol lost $20,000 on the engagement.

Brice swept onstage as a McPherson clone, dressed in the evangelist's signature white gown. According to The Skirt in *Variety*, Brice's was long and clinging, made of solid crystal beads. McPherson usually sported a blue cape; Brice had a scarf of jet tipped with ermine.[12] After the audience's ovation, she launched into her fast-paced song, full of references to McPherson and her particular brand of religious racketeering.[13] The first joke was apparent from the opening lines: "I'm in the money riding high / Gather round me little children and I'll tell you why." Soul Saving Sadie is a Jewish evangelist who ballyhoos with a Yiddish accent, and that incongruity instantly produced laughter. She explains how she "read about a person" (pronounced "*poy*son") "named Aimee S. McPherson / Who way out West in the open spaces / Put salvation on a paying basis." She quickly adopted the techniques of Aimee Semple and "opened up a temple" in her neighborhood, Hester Park, where she is now "the biggest thing since Joan of Arc."

Brice's Sadie sounded so Jewish, and the idea of a Jewish evangelist was so improbable, that it made the song much funnier than it would have been based on the lyrics alone. The lyrics provided the appropriate references to McPherson and implied that she was a hypocritical huckster, but they did not attack her directly. Brice did not deliver a vehement denunciation accusing her of sham religiosity or of fleecing the faithful for personal gain. The beauty of the performance was that by becoming Soul Saving Sadie, she reduced Sister Aimee to the level of the ridiculous, and that was her most effective comic weapon. The audience could simultaneously laugh at Sadie, at Brice who was willing to appear so absurd as she played the part, and at McPherson who was obviously the target of the travesty. In true *Follies* tradition, Brice's good-humored interpretation tempered the criticism and kept the characterization from becoming cruel.

Four scenes later, Brice appeared in "Barnyard Theatre, Inc." as Julia, the leading lady of a stock company stuck in the sticks. The opening lines of the sketch quickly establish the situation. The Theatre Manager (Willie Howard) laments to a Constable (Buddy Ebsen) about the lack of business. An irate actress (Eve Arden) deplores the primitive conditions in which she has to perform and rants about the absence of a Ladies' Room. The playwright (Victor Morley) is furious because there is no divan and fears that his play will fail on account of inadequate furniture. When a busload of customers miraculously appears, there is confusion about seats because the theatre really is a barn, complete with audible animals. Everyone is finally settled and the play can begin.

The Manager has already explained that it is "one of them high society dramas. No belching. Just rape and adultery." It is a seduction scene between Rennie (Oliver Wakefield) and Julia (Brice), and the first joke is immediately apparent. Even though they are playing in a barn for an audience of yokels, Rennie and Julia are in elaborate evening dress. (The Skirt described Brice's costume as "white satin, fox trimmed.") They begin to speak and that is the second joke: both use exaggerated British accents which sound especially ludicrous in that setting and are far from the Yiddish dialect the *Follies* audience would have expected from Brice. Rennie and Julia have been lovers; although she is now married to Lord Cecil, he is determined to win her back. The entire scene consists of his efforts to seduce her and her resolution to withstand his assault.

The principal joke of the sketch is that the highfalutin drama it presents is totally inappropriate for a rural audience and a barnyard setting. Animal sounds punctuate the dialogue, an egg drops on Rennie's head, and beer steins are used in lieu of champagne glasses, all serving to undermine Rennie and Julia's exaggerated accents and pretentious behavior. Brice's own flair for physical comedy was ideal in this situation as it complemented the contrast already inherent in the script. While maintaining her upper class affect—in itself, a wonderful surprise for audiences used to her Yiddishisms—she repeatedly used gestures and movements that make Julia seem anything but aristocratic. Such actions as mechanically disrobing at the beginning of the scene, landing clumsily on the floor after an embrace, defending her virtue on the piano stool "so deftly that even the Boston censor laughed and forgave," are comparable to Julia's slipping repeatedly on a banana peel. They happen so swiftly and are so unexpected that they instantly deflate her pretensions to elegance and refinement.

Again and again Julia tries to uphold her honor and retain her dignity against Rennie's determined forays. Brice's behavior not only makes her appear totally undignified but shows what a terrible actress Julia really is. In the process she succeeds in spoofing the British drawing-room comedy.[14] Beyond this, Brice seems to be poking fun at the very idea of presenting summer theatre in barns, a relatively new phenomenon which was not without its obvious disadvantages. Yet, despite the debunking, the mood of the scene remains light. As in the McPherson number, Brice is so willing to appear ridiculous herself and plays Julia with such obvious enjoyment that "Barnyard Theatre, Inc." never loses its sense of fun.

Brice returned next as Baby Snooks and was, as she had so often been for Ziegfeld, a sight gag. The audience reacted with delight when she appeared, enormous hair ribbon aslant, in a short starched dress, ankle socks, and Mary Janes, and announced, "Here I is, Daddy!" in lisping baby talk. Her comic antics produced merriment throughout the scene, largely because she looked so funny. *Time* described her delivering a line, "What did 'oo say?" while "push[ing] out a great idiot face."[15] Photographs show her range of rubber faces with eyes popping and crossing, cavernous mouth stretching in all directions, and a nose with seemingly more than ordinary flexibility. One observer remarked that "her knees and shins and feet are as contrary-minded as is their wont," and they, too, assumed a variety of appropriately infantile positions.

Such grimaces and movements were not merely gratuitous as they had once been. Brice's broad humor created a believable character. Although assuredly audiences were amused by the spectacle of a middle-aged woman parading on stage in a pinafore, Brice played the part convincingly. She looked, sounded, and acted like a bratty toddler and that made the scene work far more than the script did. The situation was simple. Snooks's mother, who speaks with an upper crust accent almost as exaggerated as Julia's, is distressed because she and her equally stuffy husband are "direct lineal descendants of George Washington" and she has actually caught their darling daughter in a lie. Her husband offers to deal with the problem child and summons her for a lecture on honesty. He uses the familiar story of George Washington and his little hatchet so that Snooks may emulate her worthy ancestor.

During the lecture his daughter remains remarkably obtuse. He becomes increasingly exasperated and finally loses his patience when he realizes Snooks has been ignoring him. Threatening to spank her every time she fails to tell the truth, he questions her about the cause of the nursery's broken vase, ink-stained carpet, and smashed window. Snooks answers with one outrageous lie after another, each more far-fetched than the last, as she desperately tries to avoid punishment. When she explains that the window was broken by a lion who jumped through it backwards and killed her, her overwrought father summons his wife. Shouting that he cannot do anything with their incorrigible little liar, he threatens suicide because he is so ashamed of having produced such a child. This outburst prompts his wife to confess that she had a strange experience before Snooks's birth. She recalls being chased across a field by Baron Munchausen, "the direct descendant of the most famous liar in history." Snooks pipes up, "Mommy, I think he caught 'oo," to end the scene.

The sketch is not clever. The dialogue is not witty. What makes "Baby Snooks" so effective is Brice's impersonation of a mischievous toddler. While her father gets more and more excited, she remains so calm and seems so innocent that one cannot help laughing. Even though she uses baby talk for the entire scene, Brice makes it varied and expressive with the result that it does not become cloying. Like her Yiddish accent, it is very funny and works with the physical humor to create a believable, albeit exaggerated, characterization. Brice does not sound like an adult playing a child. She really sounds like a little girl with the requisite obnoxiously lovable, predictably unpredictable behavior. She is far more ebullient and energetic than either of her pedantic parents and that, too, contributes to the convincing childlike quality of her performance. Above all, Brice seems to be enjoying herself so much on stage that the audience cannot help but respond to her enthusiasm.

Brice's next number was her most outstanding offering. Wearing an elegant black velvet gown, she appeared at the end of the first act to sing Rose, MacDonald, and Meyer's "Countess Dubinsky." A reporter asks her to tell him her story and she obliges, speaking slowly with a heavy Russian accent. "I came from Russia, the old Russia, I mean the old old Russia," she explains, and proceeds to sing about her life before the Revolution when "Nicholai and all his princes nibbled nightly on my blintzes." Brice's Russian accent is almost identical to the Yiddish one she customarily used, except that her voice sounds lower and she enunciates more emphatically. It produces the familiar amusing mispronunciations (such as "timbels" for "thimbles") and was probably accompanied by her expressive eye-rolling and grimacing.

The next verse explains why she has fallen so "low"—she is working as a stripper for the Minsky brothers. As she puts it, "The Countess Dubinsky, right down to her skinsky, is working for Minsky now." Billed as "The Vulgar Boatman" and "The Dirty Duchess," she is "shaking those fringes and how!" Brice uses her comical Countess to burlesque burlesque and, in 1934, there was plenty to parody. The popular entertainment form had changed significantly since she last played on the Wheel, largely under the influence of the Minsky Brothers (Billy, Abe, Herbert, and Morton) and the major stock theatres they established in New York in the mid-twenties. As Broadway revues became increasingly revealing, burlesque had to offer more than nudity in order to compete. It needed novelty and found it in the striptease.[16] According to theatre historian Don Wilmeth, the Minskys revolutionized burlesque by making "the strip" the most prominent feature of the show. By the early 1930s, it had brought burlesque to the top of the popular entertainment business, but it was far from being unanimously accepted. In 1931, Billy Minsky opened the Republic Theatre on 42nd Street featuring, as Wilmeth notes, "admittedly dirty burlesque for a Depression audience composed primarily of out of work men."[17] The arrival of burlesque on Broadway had many vociferous critics, appalled by what they perceived as the sleaziness of both the shows and their clientele. Brice's mockery of the Minskys and their methods was therefore timely.

Brice did more than just talk about shaking her fringes; she spoofed the striptease by performing one. The Countess is told she is on "next" and sings three more lines. For these, she drops her Russian accent and sounds like a New York showgirl with a close resemblance to Betty Boop: "I can't show my face, can't go any place / People stop and stare, it's so hard to bear / Everybody knows you left me, it's the talk of the town." The voice is high-pitched and nasal, remarkably different from the one she used earlier. That, however, is only the first surprise. When she finishes her song, the Countess demonstrates her prowess with what *Time* called "a monstrously coy strip-teaser routine." She removes her clothes one by one, beginning with a cape which she drapes over her arm, then unfastens her jeweled shoulder strap so that the front of the dress falls down provocatively. That is just the "teaser," wrote *Variety*. She exits and returns "peeled in the Minsky manner," for a fan dance.[18]

The preemininent practitioner of the fan dance was pert, blonde Sally Rand. In 1933, Rand became the sensation of the Chicago "Century of Progress Exhibition" which had opened in May. As historian Frederick L. Allen put it, "the crowds surged to see her come down the velvet-covered steps with her waving fans (and apparently nothing else) before her and Chicago profited."[19] Attendance records were smashed as Rand was held over through the summer. In 1934, she was equally successful in New York at the Paradise, one of the many nightspots that flourished after the repeal of Prohibition.

According to burlesque queen Ann Corio, the fan dance required as much skill as ballet. The dancer held "two huge ostrich feather fans, one in each hand" and made sure that they were "adroitly placed at all times." "They cover and they reveal at the whim of the dancer," Corio explained, so that "there's always flesh exposed in this dance, but fleetingly." Sally Rand was a "thrilling" performer because she was so graceful, her dance had "true beauty." The conclusion of her act was particularly exciting, Corio recalled, because Rand "would throw up her fans like the statue of Winged Victory" and always "brought the house down with applause."[20]

Brice's fan dance in the *Follies* caused almost as great a stir as Rand's. *Variety* said it was the best dance number she had ever done in her long career and noted that it evoked three distinct reactions from the audience: "the first reaction a positive shock, the second a genuine surprise at the way Fanny shapes up, and the third a real howl at the Brice comedy."[21] If the audience was shocked, it was not just because the fan dance was so risqué. It was also so unexpected. Brice had already changed character once when Countess Dubinsky became a stripteaser and the audience probably thought that would be the extent of the parody. The sight of her on stage, seemingly clad only in earrings and high heels, covering herself with two giant ostrich feather fans, must have been startling.[22]

Brice began her dance to the delighted whoops of the audience. As in all of her comic dance numbers, she used awkwardness to produce an immediate response. Brice was willing to appear ridiculous as a rookie Rand and to deflate fan dancing itself in the process. According to Atkinson, "none of the moral Catos of this town has delivered such a blow to the lascivious mummery of burlesque" as Brice did, but Atkinson's puritanical stance kept him from conveying the great sense of fun with which she performed. Nor did it suggest how effectively she teased the audience members into thinking they might actually get a glimpse of her "skinsky" and then surprised them with her dexterity. One enthusiastic observer wrote: "You must be quick to detect her in any moment when she is not a perfect lady— and you catch yourself off guard admitting to yourself that part of your psyche is still on the Minsky level and that Miss Brice is laughing at you."[23] Each time the fans swooped, creating the illusion of revealing bare skin, Brice adeptly covered herself and grinned at the audience. It responded with cheers and a tremendous ovation when she finished her dance.

Brice returned with Willie Howard in a second act sketch, "Sailor Behave," a spoof of *Sailor Beware*, a popular comedy which had opened at New York's Lyceum Theatre on September 28.[24] *Variety's* Kauf had reviewed that play favorably, even though he thought the story was trite and the dramatic situation mindless. The action takes place in Havana, where "the boys" from a battleship are "on the loose" pursuing "girls" from a nearby cabaret. One of the sailors, Dynamite Jones, "goes after" cabaret girl Billie "Stonewall" Jackson, "whose entire vocabulary, on the subject of sex," Kauf wrote, "consists of the word 'No.'" Dynamite's determination and Billie's virtue are happily rewarded at the end of the play with "ring, wedding bells and all."[25]

The capable cast performed with enthusiasm, but the plot had great potential for parody on which David Freedman was quick to capitalize for the *Ziegfeld Follies of 1934*. Havana became Panama, the battleship a bedroom with a huge circular bed dominating the set. Brice played "Upright Annie" to Howard's "Dynamite Moe," both with heavy Yiddish accents. The situation remained essentially the same, only compressed: Moe is determined to seduce Annie before he sails with the Pacific fleet later that night. Annie, who is so true to her name that she even sleeps standing up, resolves to resist.

Brice and Howard, as Annie and Moe, wisecracked their way through the scene. Their encounter was comical at once because they looked so funny together. Howard was considerably shorter than Brice and both were physically so unlike the romantic leads in the original that they were an immediate sight gag. Second, although the script was little more than a series of one-liners—the verbal equivalent of slapstick comedy—the rapid-fire responses, the Yiddish accent each used, and the puns resulting from the frequent mispronunciations compensated for the dialogue's lack of cleverness. Third, the boisterous physical behavior brought the scene to life. The leers Brice and Howard exchanged, his repeated attempts to tackle her after chasing her around the bed, his tireless efforts to penetrate her tin underwear, the embraces that combined wrestling and gymnastics, made the most of mediocre material. The fact that the scene's abrupt ending left the situation unresolved did not matter because a believable story was hardly the point.

Brice made one more metamorphosis before the end of the show. For her last appearance, she became "Sarah the Sunshine Girl." A neophyte nudist with a Yiddish accent, Sarah sings of her unpleasant experience as a pupil of "Dr. Ludwig Kranz," the director of "a school for nudists located in the Bronx." Embarrassed and uncomfortable, she admits that she is "sunburned all over," "blistered and sore in places the sun never shined on before!" She is also annoyed because she thinks Dr. Kranz has tried to take advantage of his new student. "He don't seem to be on the strict up and up," she wails, complaining that he just wants to ogle her whenever she is undressed. "I personally think he's a snake in the grass," she exclaims, oblivious to the innuendo, and concludes: "When the moon comes over the mountain, I'm Sarah the Sunshine Girl." Aside from the *double entendre*, the line pokes fun at Kate Smith, already a national radio favorite, whose signature song was "When the Moon Comes over the Mountain." Since Smith, a heavyweight in every sense of the word, would have made a most unlikely nudist, the audience undoubtedly found Brice's musical reference to her highly amusing.

"Sarah the Sunshine Girl," however, was not a Kate Smith spoof. It parodied nudism, which had attracted national attention as early as 1929. On Labor Day of that year, a German immigrant named Kurt Barthel organized the first American nudist gathering near Peekskill, New York. The year 1932 saw the establishment of the International Nudist Conference and the publication of the first American nudist journal, *The Nudist*.[26] Newspapers began covering the comings and goings of the "nudies" whenever possible. "The report that a nudist camp had been established anywhere," Frederick Allen observed, "was enough to bring the reporters on a dead run."[27] Clearly, Brice was dealing with a topic of current interest. While her song was hardly biting satire, it succeeded in suggesting that nudists were motivated by more than a desire for healthy bodies unencumbered by clothes. The voyeuristic Dr. Kranz encourages his pupils to return to Nature but, as Sarah indicates, has a different kind of nature in mind. Brice managed to convey the fundamental hypocrisy of the man and, as most people believed, the movement, through sunburnt Sarah's comical saga.

Assessing Brice's performance, Atkinson declared, "Although Miss Brice has been with us for years she has never been more enjoyably funny than she is in the current *Follies*." The unanimous critical opinion was that the six characters she created were among her most outstanding. It is important, at this point, to ask why, to determine what made her work special. For all the hoopla surrounding the revival of the *Follies*, many of the production numbers seemed bland and colorless. It was not simply that they were old-fashioned. They became monotonous, barely indistinguishable from one another and from the hundreds that had preceded them over the years. Betzi Beaton and the *Follies* Girls sang and danced as the *Follies* Girls always had; Everett Marshall performed stirring romantic melodies such as "Water under the Bridge," "Suddenly," "What Is There to Say?" and "Careful with My Heart" with Jane Froman and Patricia Bowman. The Ebsens danced, the Howards joked, the Preissers danced, Don Ross sang, and the audience responded with polite applause. The numbers may have been visually beautiful but tended to go on too long and after a while sounded almost identical.

To use one of Billy Rose's images, Brice stood out like a bagel in a loaf of white bread. From the moment she appeared, she was obviously so different, she immediately captured the audience's attention. She did not look like other women in the cast. She did not sound like anyone else in the show (except, superficially, Willie Howard). She was more colorful and her numbers more interesting on account of the variety of characters she presented, the animation with which she performed, and the warmth she communicated. Part of her success may be attributed to appropriate material, but to place too much emphasis on this is not to do justice to Brice. While her songs and sketches suited her comic style, much of the writing was banal and uninspired. Her animated interpretation transformed the offerings from mediocre to memorable. As Robert Garland put it, she constantly "transcends her material" and causes "two laughs to grow where one is all that could be expected."[28]

Brice created comedy through her skill at visual burlesque. After almost thirty years on the stage, however, she had refined her technique to a point where not all her actions were equally broad. Some, in fact, were extremely subtle. Describing "Countess Dubinsky," an appreciative Garland wrote, "every little movement has a meanness all its own. You must look sharp to catch on to some of them. The lift of a knowing eyebrow. The lift of a protesting knee. The lift of a feather fan. These, and fan dancing is as good as done for."[29]

Such delicacy and control distinguished Brice both from other comedians and from her own earlier work, which tended to be more heavy-handed. It also enabled her to produce a wider range of comic characters because, as her means of differentiating among them became more sophisticated, she could portray their distinctive features more economically. "A cartoonist working in the flesh," as she described herself, her artistry had developed to a point where she could produce more diverse and lifelike cartoons. As one contemporary saw it, "she displays, in the field of caricature, a fine art which is not inferior to any art now to be seen on our stage."[30] Her son, William, compared her to an Olympic athlete in training. "In all her work," he explained, "she was absolutely concentrated and what struck me about her was her range, her ability to move on both sides. . . . When she sang a ballad," he recalled, "it was with such style and grace. Then she would go to a comedic gesture so broad, so physical, but never overdone. Even as a burlesque it had finesse."[31]

In the *Ziegfeld Follies of 1934*, Brice presented six different characters, and the variety was not an insignificant part of her achievement. The audience's delight in her transformation from one number to the next attested to the effectiveness of her overall performance. Having elicited laughter by assuming such disparate identities, she knew how to sustain it. She was a brilliant clown and her comic creations, for all their diversity, had much in common. They depended on slapstick, on surprise, on Brice's willingness to look totally ridiculous in playing them and, above all, on incongruity. Sadie the Jewish evangelist and Sarah the Bronx nudist involved such incongruous pairings, such a reversal of expectations, that just the thought of them was amusing. With Baby Snooks, the idea of an obnoxious four-year-old was not ludicrous, but having a middle-aged woman impersonate her was. That was the joke, and the fact that Brice played Snooks so believably made it even more comical. Putting aristocratic Julia in a barnyard would have been funny enough, but her outrageous behavior made her upper class affectations all the more incongruous. Upright Annie's Yiddish accent was immediately inappropriate and instantly amusing in a Panama setting; the madcap routines Brice performed with the zany Howard transferred the scene to the realm of irresistible lunacy. It made no sense, but that only heightened the comic effect. Finally, however unexpected Brice's sudden transformation into a nimble fan dancer might have been, the joke was on the audience, surprised and delighted by her remarkable dexterity.

Thanks to Brice's outstanding work, the *Ziegfeld Follies of 1934* enjoyed a profitable run and *Variety* named it one of the "Hits of '33–'34."[32] After twenty-three weeks on Broadway, it was finally closing, and the Shuberts planned a cross-country tour. Brice had also received an invitation from Universal Pictures to play herself in their forthcoming movie, *The Great Ziegfeld*; according to the August 7 *Variety*, she was in Hollywood discussing her "sizable part." The following week, however, she was on her way back to New York; the filming had been delayed and she had to prepare for the *Follies* tour. The production was in rehearsal by the end of August. On September 3, it opened at the Grand Opera House in Chicago with "wow trade." It closed two months later, on November 3, after a "smash run."[33]

The Chicago engagement was typical of the entire tour, which subsequently made forty stops in less than five months. The production traveled via the Midwest to California where it played for most of January, then spent much of February in Texas. Moving northeast through Arkansas, Tennessee, Kentucky, and Ohio, the show reached Toronto and Montreal in March. After brief appearances in Providence, Springfield (Massachusetts), and Hartford, the *Follies* concluded its run in New Haven on March 16, 1935. *Variety* reported that it "folded . . . in a blaze of glory with a near-riot being staged by Yale studes."[34]

From March until September Brice was relatively inactive, no doubt relaxing after her grueling performance schedule. In June she returned to radio for one broadcast and appeared as the special attraction on Beatrice Lillie's Borden hour. According to *Variety*, she played "a Bronx mother giving her version of a sweepstake winner," a "natural" for her, then did Snooks and delighted as always with her "hoyden pranks." The same issue also reported that she was "set" for the next edition of the *Follies*, along with Josephine Baker, Harry Richman, and Sophie Tucker.[35] Although work on the production had begun months earlier, this was the first time that Brice's name was publicly linked with it.

The June 19 *Variety* also noted that Brice was "due on the coast shortly" to begin work on *The Great Ziegfeld*.[36] The movie never materialized under Universal's management; it had been an MGM Pictures project since March. It was scheduled for filming in mid-July, but did not actually start until the end of September. Brice, meanwhile, spent July vacationing on Fire Island, and in August *Variety* reported that MGM was paying her $25,000 for four weeks' work. She would be going to Hollywood "shortly," the article continued, because she had to be back in New York by October 20 for *Follies* rehearsals.[37] Accompanied by Ann Pennington, for whom negotiations were still "pending," Brice left New York on September 7. On October 10, instead of working on the *Follies* for the Shuberts, she was recording "My Man" for *The Great Ziegfeld* and could not return to New York until the end of the month.

The filming continued into the early part of 1936. When *The Great Ziegfeld* was finally released in April, it received favorable reviews. *Variety* called it "the last gasp in filmusical entertainment."[38] The *New York Times* described it as "thoroughly Ziegfeldian" but wished that it had included more humorous moments, such as "the briefly narrated but rousingly comic hiring of Fannie Brice."[39] As the movie presents it, Ziegfeld hears of Brice when she is still in burlesque. His accountant urges him to see a promising new talent. Ziegfeld asks, "Is she pretty?" The accountant responds with a typical Hollywood rejoinder, "Shut your eyes and listen—yes. Open them and look—no." Ziegfeld goes to the burlesque show and watches Brice perform Irving Berlin's classic "Yiddle on the Fiddle." It is obviously a dialect song which she sings with a heavy Yiddish accent, as well as tremendous energy and palpable stage presence. Much of the song cannot be heard, however, because Ziegfeld has a conversation which is the focal point of the scene. Brice launches into "Queen of the Jungle" with the burlesque chorines. For this, she affects a British accent and a falsetto, putting the song over with her animated eyes and mobile mouth. Impressed with her work, Ziegfeld visits her dressing room and offers her a job in his *Follies*. She does not believe he is the real Ziegfeld and sends him away after buying his mink coat for forty-five dollars. (She thinks he is an unscrupulous salesman like the one named "Belasco" who has just sold her "silk" stockings made of cheap cotton.) Soon realizing her mistake, she happily signs Ziegfeld's contract.

The scene changes to a *Follies* rehearsal where work is about to begin on "My Man." When Brice arrives in an elaborate costume, Ziegfeld angrily exclaims, "I didn't engage Miss Brice as a showgirl." He rips her dress, as the real impresario supposedly did, and orders the startled Brice to sing. She does, slowly and sorrowfully, as the camera focuses on her tearstained face. Unfortunately, and quite unbelievably, the same camera cuts away from Brice before she is even halfway through her signature song. She remains in the background for the rest of the scene, performing inaudibly, while Ziegfeld confers in the foreground. He nods approvingly at Brice and remarks, "If she can turn on the tears for an audience, she'll be great." With that, the conversation turns to something else and Brice's minor role in the picture ends.[40]

However ancillary she was to the film's success, Brice was acclaimed as the star of the *Ziegfeld Follies of 1936* and dominated that show as completely as she had its predecessor. In fact, when she was forced to drop out of the cast in May on account of illness, the production itself had to close. As it had for the previous edition, publicity emphasized her longevity as a stage performer. An article in the December 29, 1935, *Boston Herald* was typical. Observing that "out of all the shining lights of the first few *Follies* only hers is still bright, out of all those talents only hers has proved adaptable to every succeeding generation, and out of all those personalities only hers was magnetic enough to delight audiences today as much as it did twenty-six years ago," the paper lauded Brice as "not only the *Ziegfeld Follies'* greatest woman comic—but America's."[41]

Although most critics considered the earlier show the better of the two, Brice performed as brilliantly in 1936 as she had in 1934. A Boston reviewer praised her "great comic gifts" and asserted that while "there are not many comedians who have only to walk out before the curtain in order to set the audience laughing before they have uttered a word, Fannie Brice can do it . . . as long as she cares to walk out on any stage, any time, anywhere."[42] She certainly "did it" by walking out on the stage of New York's Winter Garden Theatre when the *Follies* premiered on January 30, after previewing in Boston and Philadelphia. The tension on opening night was high, one journalist reported, because Brice was "the backbone" of the show, "the principal comedienne with a thousand and one laughs in her material," and she had laryngitis. When she came out to sing "He Hasn't a Thing Except Me," her voice audibly cracked on the first line and "performers watching from the wings held their breath." In characteristic fashion, she "took the audience into her confidence, told it about her voice, murmured that she would try again and then went through the number flawlessly." By immediately establishing a rapport with the audience, she succeeded in making an awkward moment work to her advantage.

Variety did not mention the incident, reporting only that on the night before the opening, she "squawked about her throat." As the performance progressed, however, "she forgot all about that and, at the end, the acclaim that was hers almost flattened the most popular of revue comediennes."[43] Brice's laryngitis was apparently legitimate because she was unable to perform at all on February 3 and 4. As a result, the Ziegfeld Follies of 1936 had to close only four days after it had opened. Without Brice, there was simply no show. When she was well enough to return on the 5th, the Follies resumed, but her voice continued to be problematic. The February 12 Variety announced that two of her numbers had been reassigned to others in the cast and that she was unable to appear on the first scheduled broadcast of her new radio series, the Ziegfeld Follies of the Air.[44] She joined the program later in the month, but her performance was a disappointment. The poor review she received from Variety indicated that she had forgotten the lessons she learned about radio in 1933 and failed to project herself appropriately over the airwaves. Calling her "a comedienne without comedy," the newspaper faulted both her material and her delivery. After a "string of wisecracks" that were "unbecoming to a woman," she did a "mildly diverting" Snooks, then "a satire that wasn't satirical on a female platform demon discussing international affairs." She finally sang "I'm an Indian" with "most of the lines either brushed up for radio or shorn of most of their force when divorced from the mimicry that makes this performer stand out behind the footlights."[45]

That negative notice contrasted markedly with the glowing reviews she received for her work in the Ziegfeld Follies of 1936 and suggests that the stage was where she was most comfortable because it suited her physical performance style so much better. Brice had to work at developing the special skills radio required and, although she would soon opt exclusively for that medium, appearing before a live audience came more naturally to her. Certainly in the Ziegfeld Follies of 1936, she was as strong as she had been in 1934 and compensated for that show's generally weaker material. Reviewers called her "gigantically comic," "hilarious," "marvel-ous," and "funnier than ever." The *Follies* was "not as outstanding as one hoped it would be," observed John Mason Brown, but Brice had never been better.[46]

There were no dissenting opinions: critics applauded her distinctive flair for visual burlesque. Burns Mantle wrote, "Some years she can get the songs and some years she can't, but she always has her twisted mouth, her snapping eyes, her eloquent kneecaps and her expressive hips." Brown acknowledged "her famous slice-of-honeydew-melon smile, her delicious mimicry, her occasionally crossing eyes, her flat-footed capers and her knees that often are not on speaking terms with one another."[47] Atkinson, always astute in describing her performances, exclaimed, "Here you will see her up to all sorts of flamboyant Bricean mischief—stretching her mobile mouth a hundred different ways to draw comedy out of her material, rolling those eloquent eyes, fairly engulfing the whole show."[48]

Brice's seven numbers were as varied as they had been in the previous *Follies* and, in some cases, were quite similar to characters she had already created. In addition to another Baby Snooks, her Zuleika in "Fancy Fancy" recalled "Barnyard Theatre"'s Julia and enabled her to use the exaggerated British accent she did so well. In place of her Sally Rand spoof, she had "Modernistic Moe" which mocked Martha Graham and her stark, percussive choreography. She had three other sketches—"The Sweepstakes Ticket," "The Gazooka," and "Amateur Night"—as well as the song with which she made her first appearance, "He Hasn't a Thing Except Me."

Critics were not unanimous in their appreciation of her opening number. Many did not even include it in their reviews. *Variety* observed only that it "amused" the "first-nighters."[49] What made it at all noteworthy was that Brice was spoofing herself and "My Man," the song with which she had so long been identified. She had avoided serious material in the *Ziegfeld Follies of 1934* and continued to do so in 1936, when the country was about to enter the seventh year of the Depression and the world was moving inexorably toward war.

"He Hasn't a Thing Except Me" is a mock-ballad down to the lamppost against which Brice stands when the number begins. Before she starts to sing, the lamppost walks off, a signal that this is not going to be a conventional lover's lament. The lyrics immediately confirm that impression. She refers to the man she adores as "a louse," "nothing you'd want 'round the house," "a rat," "his highness, a pain worse than sinus." She describes his behavior in equally uncomplimentary terms: "The one thing he's mastered / is just getting plastered," "Of money he's got less / than someone who's potless," "His talk isn't flow'ry / it's straight from the Bowery." She explains that she helps out his brother, pays rent for his mother, knows that "somewhere there's a wife," and shrugs, "That's life."

As the music plays softly, she confides in the audience:

> Well, you get the idea. You know I've been singing about this bum for twenty-five years. Sometimes he's called "Oh, my Gawd, I love him so" or "He's just my Bill" or "You made me what I am today," but he's always the same low-life and he's always doing me dirt and I just keep on loving him. Can you imagine if I really ever met a guy like that what I would do to him? Why I'd—it's no use talkin'—that's my type.[50]

According to a stage direction, the conductor disrupts this intimate moment by rapping his baton against his music stand to summon Brice back to character for the final verse. As she sings, she explains that she has struck her perennially mournful pose for money rather than for love. With this cynical revelation, the bogus blues song concludes and the lamppost returns to take a bow with Brice.

One critic called the number "tame," suggesting that Brice did not use her customary comic business to amplify the material. Instead, she must have sung it fairly straight, letting the lyrics convey the humor—something she did not ordinarily do. Judging from the reception, people preferred the exaggerated mannerisms with which she usually accompanied her caricatures to the restraint she demonstrated here. Yet, in that she was spoofing the type of song she had so often performed, her choice was appropriate. The unexpectedly coarse language and the unflattering portrait made the genre suspect because it revealed how contrived such songs really were. In choosing to burlesque them rather than attempting genuinely serious new ones, Brice showed that she had completely embraced comedy. She had finally accepted her identity as an entertainer and, as she demonstrated in 1934, was concentrating on the area in which she excelled.

Four scenes later, she appeared in "The Sweepstakes Ticket," a revised version of the sketch she performed on radio the previous June. She was Norma Shaeffer, a Jewish housewife in the Bronx who is ecstatic when a messenger informs her that she has won the Irish Sweepstakes. Brice returned in "Fancy Fancy" and, as one observer put it, "turns Noel Coward English with a vengeance."[51] She played Zuleika, the bored wife of Sir Henry, who sits in his armchair reading *Punch* while his friend, Sir Robert, valiantly tries to break up his marriage. Zuleika offers to be his mistress, but Sir Robert says he already has one and wants her for his wife. She politely protests, first because divorcing Sir Henry would be too much trouble, then because Sir Robert is "only an Australian" and "it just isn't being done."

Zuleika begins a song full of innocuous contemporary references. She tells Sir Robert she would love him if only he were like "the fancies" she fancies: if he could "rumba like Fred Astaire," or "find that Cecil Beaton savoir faire," or "charm like Noel Coward does / when he says 'How've you been?'" or "make love like Leslie Howard does / when he is on the screen." They exchange a series of flippant remarks, such as Zuleika's question to Sir Robert—"Would you marry a girl if she were as pretty as a picture?"—and his hearty response, "Yes, if she had a good frame!" They dance across the stage together and Sir Robert admits that he would find her more appealing if she dressed like Lady Mountbatten, earned Shirley Temple's salary, had Edna Best's dimples, Marlene Dietrich's legs, and Mae West's curves. He leans over to kiss her, but she burps in his face instead. He pulls away and the number quickly proceeds to its raucous conclusion. When he sniffs her shoulder, she responds, with a Yiddish-accented "Denk you," and the script indicates that "he kicks her in the fanny as they both exit." The affected elegance is effectively exploded as Zuleika and Robert's unexpected behavior takes them on a swift descent from the sublime to the ridiculous.

Brice's next scene featured her as Baby Snooks, now five, in Hollywood, and starring in a movie with Clark Gable (her father), Joan Crawford (her mother), and Greta Garbo (her nursemaid). The harried director tries to explain the dramatic situation to his aspiring Shirley Temple, but she demonstrates remarkable recalcitrance in absorbing it. Her refusal to play her part correctly causes countless complications and misunderstandings, including the one with which the scene ends. An official from the Academy of Motion Picture Arts and Sciences has rushed in to give Snooks a special award for "the most intelligent, spontaneous, and inspired performance of the year." To his surprise, she rejects it and the puzzled official replies, "Just tell me what you want and I'll gladly do it." That line is identical to one of Gable's, which Snooks is supposed to answer by saying, "Awight, stay with Mummy tonight." She responds correctly, startling the official and leaving everyone else speechless. There is nothing clever about this conclusion or, actually, about the entire sketch as it is written. If it succeeded at all, it was on account of Brice's wonderfully amusing performance as Baby Snooks.

Act I closed with another jab at Hollywood in "The Gazooka," described in the program as "a Super-Special Musical Photoplay starring

Ruby Blondell and Bing Powell with a Large Supporting Cast of Featured Players." As the names suggest, the sketch parodied the elaborate movie musicals so popular with Depression audiences—specifically, the "backstage" stories in which the unknown chorine is catapulted to stardom, the struggling young songwriter makes good, and the down-and-out director finally becomes successful.[52] Brice played Ruby Blondell, a delightfully irreverent cross between Ruby Keeler and Joan Blondell, two of Hollywood's most popular screen stars. Bob Hope's Bing Powell made obvious reference to their male counterparts, Bing Crosby and Dick Powell. Spoofing the genre's improbable plots and mindless songs, the sketch moved rapidly to its improbable conclusion—what *Variety* called the "outstanding giggle-inciter." It was a seemingly endless reel of picture credits displayed "in Technique-color on the Widescope Screen." According to Atkinson, the reel became "more laughable" as it continued and succeeded in poking fun at the "grandiose promotion of super-specials from Hollywood."[53]

If "The Gazooka" was the most elaborate of the *Follies* sketches, "Amateur Night" was the weakest. It was reminiscent of the scene Brice had done in the *Ziegfeld Follies of 1923*, only in that one she parodied old-fashioned amateur contests in burlesque and vaudeville houses. This "Amateur Night" was inspired by radio's "Major Bowes" and presented "Major Bones" with his talentless contestants. The script was terrible, but apparently the impersonation of Major Bowes by Hugh O'Connell was excellent and the antics of the amateurs compensated for unfunny lines. *Variety* reported that "girl hillbilly" Judy Canova sang "Music Goes Round" in a distinctive style which included guitar strumming that did not "fit the tune."[54] Eve Arden was effective as a society matron playing the kazoo, with two cymbals hidden under her dress. Brice appeared as Myrtle Oppenshaw, a singer from Amarillo, Texas, who says she first realized she could sing when she listened to the Major's program. He inquires about her previous experience and she describes the instruction she has received. An "Eyetalian" gave her a series of three lessons, a "Roosian" only one. To the Major's dismay, it becomes clear as she talks that what they taught her had nothing to do with music. Abruptly ending the conversation, he encourages her to sing. She obliges and is stopped after only eight bars. The scene concludes with Myrtle and the Major heatedly exchanging insults.

"Without being devastatingly funny," Atkinson explained, "the sketches are neatly written and they are acted in the highest good humor."⁵⁵ That they worked as well as they did is attributable to Brice, for she created five distinct characters and, with them, most of the comedy. Her outstanding offering in the *Ziegfeld Follies of 1936*, however, was a musical number called "Modernistic Moe," which parodied interpretive dancing and its leading practitioner, Martha Graham.⁵⁶ When Graham made her New York debut as an independent artist in 1926, critics praised her graceful lyricism. Yet, within a year, her style had changed dramatically and for the next decade her dances were criticized as stark and ugly. One of her most controversial early compositions was *Revolt*, a dance of protest and social commentary. It was set to the avant-garde music of Arthur Honegger and invariably infuriated its audiences.⁵⁷

Although well known, Graham's dancing was far from winning popular acceptance. It was still considered highbrow, elitist, and bizarre. In spoofing it, then, Brice was working with the kind of material she preferred. She was dealing with a contemporary topic upon which opinion was divided and which was pretentious enough to be effectively parodied. When she appeared as a mock Martha with dark shoulder length hair swept back behind her ears (Graham's hairstyle), wearing Graham's trademark black jersey dress and oversized shoes, crying "Revolt," there was no doubt as to her identity. And when she solemnly began her song, intoning in a heavy Yiddish accent, "My feet are full of splinters / There's water on my knee / A broken down expressionistic dancer / —that's me," she was immediately ridiculous. As in the *Follies* sketches, the writing was not what distinguished this number. Instead, it was the absurdity of the characterization as Brice presented it and the tremendous skill with which she performed. Her incongruous accent and percussive movements worked together to produce an amusing burlesque which reduced Graham and her distinctive choreography to silliness.

Brice continued in the *Follies* on stage and radio until May 8 when she abruptly withdrew from both. The May 13 *Variety* attributed her departure to "arthritis of the legs." The following week's edition amended the diagnosis to "neuritis of the arm" traced to infected teeth.⁵⁸ The painful neurological condition had made Brice extremely uncomfortable for several weeks during which she insisted on appearing in the *Follies* despite a high fever. "I watched her perform with a 103-degree fever," William remarked in a recent interview. "I learned early the meaning of artistic responsibility." He recalled that, exhausted and weak, his mother would lie in bed all day, yet managed to perform with her usual energy at night. Then, totally spent, she would return to bed until the next evening. Her illness finally progressed to a point where those heroic efforts were no longer possible. William said that, aside from administering "alcohol blocks," her doctors could do very little and she was "virtually incapacitated."[59]

The *Follies of the Air*, whose ratings had improved dramatically since the initial broadcast, ran without her until June 6. The *Ziegfeld Follies of 1936*, however, had to close on Saturday, May 9, the day after she left the cast. *Variety* reported that the Shuberts had considered assigning some of her numbers to Eve Arden and having Milton Berle step in "to bolster the comedy end," but abandoned the idea when it was decided that "without Miss Brice, the *Follies* would not do."[60]

On May 20, *Variety* announced that, should the *Follies* tour in the fall, Bobby Clark would replace Brice as the comedy lead. Three months later, the newspaper informed its readers that "dead billing" had "been removed from the canopy of the Winter Garden" and that both Brice and Clark would be featured in the *Follies* "soon resuming."[61] The show finally reopened on Monday, September 14, 1936, and was reviewed even more favorably than the earlier edition. Although much of the material had been retained, there had been several cast changes and the critics applauded the replacements. Most notable among them was Clark, who took over Bob Hope's role as "general utility comic" and was considered much funnier than "the brash Mr. Hope" had been. Josephine Baker was no longer in the show, but stripteaser Gypsy Rose Lee was, and the consensus was that "the Flower of 42nd Street," known for her surprising restraint and elegance, was an improvement.[62] Brice, however, was still largely responsible for the production's success. Happily recovered from her illness, she received nothing but praise for her superlative clowning which was even better than it had been in the spring.

Brice performed the same material, with one addition. She appeared as Mrs. Phoebe Swartz in "Dr. Fradler's Dilemma," a sketch spoofing psychoanalysis. Phoebe, a settlement Gym teacher with a back problem, has mistakenly come to see Dr. Fradler, played by Clark. She thinks he is an orthopedist. He happens to be a psychoanalyst and, as the dialogue reveals, a particularly zany one. He is not interested in his practice, only in playing golf, avoiding his wife and, after he meets Phoebe, seducing his new patient. Since Fradler speaks in non-sequiturs and misinterprets everything Phoebe tells him, much of the scene's humor results from a spiralling series of misunderstandings.

Brice and Clark were at their antic best in their sketches together. Atkinson referred to "that mad Brice-Clark mood that is of the *Follies*." Richard Watts found them magnificent, and observed, "There obviously can be no doubt that here are two of the great comic talents of the American theater."[63] John Mason Brown called them "clowns who know what clowning is all about," declaring, "they are hypnotists in the field of laughter. . . . They know how to make their points and when to reenforce a line by rolling their eyes, twisting up their faces or sending their knees and hands on comic errands."[64]

Although their comic styles were similar, Brice and Clark worked beautifully together. Each enhanced the other's lunacy so that they were complementary, rather than competitive. Yet, however strong his performance, Clark was clearly her supporting player. The *Ziegfeld Follies of 1936* was her show. "Miss Brice is the personification of the *Follies*," Atkinson explained, "And that enterprise is still, to all intents and purposes, the property of Miss Brice. As it was in the old days and will be, Broadway holds, until the title has vanished."[65]

The *Ziegfeld Follies of 1936* closed in New York on December 19 after a profitable eight-week engagement. On December 23, Brice completed her last broadcast for a weekly radio series, the "Revue de Paris," on which she had appeared since September 30. Two days later, she opened with the *Follies* in Pittsburgh, beginning what would prove to be a very successful tour. After a ten-week "high money run" in Chicago, the show traveled to Milwaukee, Des Moines, Kansas City, and St. Louis where *Variety* reported it drew "turnaway business."[66] In April and May, it stopped in Indianapolis, Columbus, Detroit, Toledo, Cleveland, Toronto, Buffalo, Washington, Baltimore, and Richmond, closing with a final performance in Hershey, Pennsylvania, on May 26. One week later, *Variety* listed the *Ziegfeld Follies* as one of only fourteen unqualified "Hits of '36–'37," as opposed to eight "moderate successes" and sixty-eight failures.[67]

The *Ziegfeld Follies of 1936* marked both the apex and the end of Brice's professional stage career. By the end of June, she had arrived in Hollywood to begin work on a series of films for Metro-Goldwyn-Meyer. According to the contract she had signed earlier in the year, her first assignment was to be *As Thousands Cheer*. *Variety* announced that the "top role" in *Molly*, a story MGM had bought for the late Marie Dressler, would most likely follow, adding that "rewriting to fit the Brice character would be necessary." One month later, *Variety* reported that *As Thousands Cheer* had been delayed and that Brice had been reassigned to *Swing Fever*, formerly called *The Ugly Duckling*, in what was now a "one picture deal." The idea of making *Molly* a Brice project had apparently been abandoned. Two months later, when production finally started, the film was again known as *The Ugly Duckling*. According to an article in the September

29 *Variety*, the cast would be "topped" by Judy Garland and Allan Jones and would "also include" Fanny Brice, Reginald Owen, and Lynne Carver.[68]

By November, the movie's title had changed for the third and last time to *Everybody Sing*. When it was released in January 1938, the "filmusical" received favorable reviews for its "fresh ideas" and "corking cast."[69] *Variety* asserted that "if for no other reason than the opportunity afforded Miss Brice to score heavily with her inimitable impressions, the picture is a standout," but the *New York Times* disagreed. Noting that *Everybody Sing* involved so much singing that it would inspire all but the most "fair-minded with a positive hatred of the human larynx," the paper was most critical of "the misuse of Fanny Brice." As the review perceptively observed:

> Nobody has any right to try and foist upon us a cut Brice, robbed of those incomparably subtle touches of vulgarity for which Fanny is noted and widely beloved. As a Russian servant in a mad household of stage people whose waning fortunes are retrieved by Judy Garland (that's the whole story) she sometimes manages by sheer irrepressible genius to be funny, but never Fanny. And it's Fanny we care about.[70]

Whether she was inhibited by the script, the director, or the camera, Brice failed to project her unique personality and talent on screen. If she had anticipated film stardom, she was disappointed once again. She made no movies in 1938, and in January 1939 *Variety* announced that MGM had dropped her from its "player list." She was, however, "still on the payroll" according to "a deal" the studio had made with General Foods to keep her on the "Good News" radio show.[71]

Brice had first appeared on the Metro–Maxwell House Hour, called "Good News of 1938," on November 25, 1937. It was the fourth broadcast of a thus-far unimpressive series, but Brice was instantly successful. "The presence of Fannie Brice at the microphone," wrote Aaron Stein in the *New York Post*, "made all the difference." She offered something the show badly needed and which Stein considered a "solid fundamental of entertainment," namely, "good comedy projected by a consummate artist." She performed two sketches on the program. The first was a dialogue with child star Freddy Bartholomew in which "her speech skidded wildly between Hollywood British and her native Brice." The second was "one of the Baby Snooks masterpieces." Demonstrating an understanding of Brice's ability that few critics, other than Atkinson, ever shared, Stein proceeded to describe the essential characteristic of a Brice performance:

Always it seems as though Miss Brice could never have been more expressive or funnier. There are comedians and comedians, but none with the unfailing artful resources of Fannie Brice, none with such unfalteringly delicate skill in establishing the precisely comic nuance of timing, exaggeration, or distortion.[72]

Brice had managed to adapt her performance technique to the demands of radio. She succeeded in that medium as she never did on film and finally had on stage when she accepted her strengths, and limitations, as an artist. She was not a tremendously versatile talent. Although she could move audiences to tears with an effective ballad, she could not do Ibsen, as she had once hoped, because she was simply not suited for serious drama. When she had appropriate material, she was a brilliant comedienne and one of her greatest assets was her ability to relate to her audience immediately. Stein referred to this quality when he commented on her work in the *Ziegfeld Follies of 1936*, writing, "She seems to be able to give each audience the feeling that it is seeing her and hearing her at her best." A *Boston Transcript* reviewer referred to her as "everybody's friend" and the description was apt.[73] The sentiments she shared in 1925 in "The Feel of the Audience" had not changed at the end of her stage career, except perhaps to have intensified. According to William, she had an "intuitive capacity to communicate with her audience" and believed that, above all else, she had to "move that audience from neutrality into some emotional condition."[74]

In 1934, the weekly magazine *Literary Digest* called Brice "skilled and subtle . . . with an evil talent for sly dissection of all that is fake and preposterous."[75] The observation is provocative, but misses the true spirit of her comedy. She did expose the "fake and preposterous," but in a more open and genial manner than the glib quotation implies. "Sly dissection" does not convey the warmth and ebullience with which she performed, nor does it capture the affection she genuinely seemed to feel for the characters she played. However absurd their poses, she never treated them cruelly and this was possible, in part, because of the nature of the subjects she portrayed. For all of their timeliness, her topics were totally non-threatening. She did not deal with upsetting or controversial events. She once said that she always avoided sex and religion, and it was characteristic of her that whenever she handled anything remotely sexual, she did it in a completely asexual way. The comedy made it innocent and wholly "antiseptic," as *Time* wrote in 1934, so that even a striptease lost its suggestiveness.[76]

Brice's list of taboos, however, went beyond the two she mentioned.

She never alluded to the stock market crash, the Depression, organized crime, the Lindbergh kidnapping, breadlines, Communism, Herbert Hoover, Adolf Hitler, or the Spanish Civil War, to name just a few of the areas she considered off limits. She could present her material without invective or malice because it was sufficiently light. Even a number like "Soul Saving Sadie," which touched upon religious racketeering and hypocrisy on the grand scale, lost its cutting edge because McPherson had become an object of ridicule long before Brice got to her. The song did not tell people anything they did not already know. Moreover, although the references were obviously to Aimee, she was an oblique target. The focus was on Sadie, the clone, as Brice, the clown, played her and this was true for all of Brice's comic portrayals. The character she created was primary. The model, or the supposedly "real" subject, was secondary at best and by the time Brice was finished, it was almost impossible to take the real subject seriously. Countess Dubinsky's fan dance, for example, did not send the *Follies* audience out on the streets to rout Rand or move the Minskys from New York. It made them seem silly and consequently nonthreatening. As with all the subjects she parodied, Brice reduced them to the level of the ridiculous. That was her most effective comic weapon.

Brice's reliance on a perpetual *reductio ad absurdum* makes it difficult to build a case for her as a serious satirist. Atkinson addressed this point when, reflecting upon her performance in the *Ziegfeld Follies of 1934*, he wrote:

> Although some of Miss Brice's material may have satiric implications, if you insist upon looking for them, her good-humored personality is the quality that makes her a heroic entertainer. Her eyes gleam with mischief, she has the clown's wholesome exuberance.[77]

The distinction has to do with what in a literary work would be called tone, the attitude of the author as the reader infers it. Satire, as it is generally defined, ridicules aspects of human behavior and tries to arouse in the reader or observer contempt for its object. Although satire can vary tremendously, the genre is sometimes distinguished from comedy on the grounds that it attempts to correct by ridiculing, while comedy aims simply to evoke amusement, even at the speaker or performer's own expense.[78]

These definitions are helpful in elucidating Brice's comic technique because they clarify what she did not do. First, she was never contemptuous of her subjects. She was never bitter, cynical, or vicious in presenting her material. Second, she never performed with a serious moral purpose, nor did she operate from a sense of moral outrage. The ridiculing in which she reveled did not appear to be aimed at correcting an obvious evil, but existed for its own sake, to delight an audience. One could argue that by caricaturing a person like McPherson, Brice relieved the audience's apprehensions about her and the larger ills she represented and, by so doing, was fulfilling a moral function not unlike the one Aristotle attributed to tragedy. Such reasoning seems as convoluted as a pretentious article which compared the "full flavor of her unique vulgarity" to the "low comedy of Falstaff and Malvolio," then asserted, "It is great comedy in the sense that it observes the two-legged beast called man with cosmic detachment as one cut above the ape but trying harder to improve."[79]

Brice's comic method was almost the antithesis of "cosmic detachment." She could not be totally objective about her subjects because she was playing them on stage. She was the cartoonist, but she was also the cartoon. Her willingness to appear ridiculous in the course of her impersonations succeeded in breaking down any barriers that might have existed between her and her audience. People had to respond to her comedy because she did not hesitate to poke fun at herself. She played the clown agreeably and, at the same time, managed to distance herself from her comic creations. She could portray a character fully, yet stand apart from that character and comment on it by means of revealing winks, smiles, and gestures with which she communicated with the audience. Her ability to do both simultaneously gave her work a special resonance and made the portrait sharper because it was framed by the commentary.

The overwhelming impression that her work makes, however, is of a certain sameness in spite of the variety because, no matter who she was supposed to be, she was always playing Fanny Brice. Her own forceful personality kept bubbling forth, animating and humanizing her characterizations, elevating each to the same zany heights. In the process, she achieved her objective as a performer: to entertain audiences by means of her uproarious antics. The exaggerated gestures and mannerisms, the accents, the satirical references to real people, the character choices themselves, were all a means to that end, not the primary focus. Delighting by amusing was, and that is why Atkinson's description of her as "a burlesque comic of the rarest vintage" was so astute. Brice was indeed a burlesque comic—not burlesque in the sense of a show business form, but burlesque as a genre. According to a standard definition, a burlesque is "any imitation of people or literature which, by distortion, aims to amuse. Its subject matter is sometimes said to be faults rather than vices, and its tone is neither shrill nor savage."[80] Unlike satire which tends to

be harsher, burlesque is designed to arouse amusement rather than contempt, to produce laughter instead of indignation. Its basically cheerful
humor is never bitter or moralistic.[81]

Clearly, that definition applies to Fanny Brice's art. Although, as Atkinson acknowledged, her work was not without satirical implications, it was
fundamentally too good-humored to qualify as satire in the strictest sense.
The affectionate understanding with which she tempered her travesties,
the ebullient enthusiasm with which she performed them, and the absence
of moral indignation to inspire them, precluded satire. Brice's admirers
and the audiences to whom she appealed did not look to her for an evening
of corrosive social commentary. She could be irreverent and outrageous,
but her name meant laughter, hilarious antics, and great fun. Burlesque
enabled Brice to succeed as a popular entertainer who perennially pleased
her audiences; satire, which tends to be more lacerating and, therefore,
more disturbing, probably would have prevented it.

Atkinson frequently refers to Brice's "pronounced Jewish flavor," and
it is tempting to attribute a great deal of significance to ethnicity in discussing her comic style. One could suggest that her willingness to ridicule
herself in the course of an impersonation was the manifestation of her
Jewishness, and that her self-deprecatory manner was deeply rooted in
Jewish humor. Such speculation, however, fails to capture the true spirit
of her comedy because Brice was not fundamentally a Jewish comic. When
she spoke with a Yiddish accent, as she did in much of her stage work,
she used it as a comic contrast to the parts she played. The accent was
a device, a mask like blackface, conducive to comedy because it raised
expectations about the type of behavior to be presented and then made
the character's actual behavior seem wonderfully incongruous. With the
exception of "Mrs. Cohen at the Beach," Brice's routines were only superficially Jewish for the simple reason that her Jewishness was not evidently
something she cared deeply about expressing. She often played to the
prejudices of the period, but affirming or mocking Jewish life and values
was not generally a part of her comic world. To decide that she was a
Jewish comic because she spoke with an accent and poked fun at herself
circumscribes her too narrowly and fails to consider the universality of
her appeal.

Although dialect certainly helped Brice establish her comic identity,
the fact that she was a woman performing broad comedy, an essentially
male field, was far more significant. Brice was not the first funny woman
to reach the stage, nor was she the only woman bold enough to "single"
in vaudeville or musical revues. There were others whose forceful personal-

ities made them headliners, who succeeded in show business without being conventionally beautiful or fulfilling traditional notions of appropriate feminine behavior. Hefty Marie Dressler once commented that all women share the innate desire to be "pretty and nice" rather than "ugly and funny," but won recognition for her own comic skills in vaudeville, musical comedy, and film. Tempestuous Eva Tanguay, inventive Elsie Janis, feisty Irene Franklin, elegant Nora Bayes, lusty Sophie Tucker—among so many others—frequently handled humorous material and impressed audiences with the power of their performances. All were somehow larger than life, able to market their unique talents in a variety of entertainment forms. Yet none of them clowned as broadly as Brice did. None indulged in such outrageous antics so consistently or so effectively. None offered herself as a sight gag with such cheerful good humor, without completely compromising her femininity in the process. Like her friend and colleague Beatrice Lillie—the only other woman whose flair for zany comedy was comparable to Brice's—she played the clown with zest, brilliance, and enthusiasm. She was indeed "a burlesque comic of the rarest vintage" and, before her, the vintage had been predominantly male.

A truly funny woman, Brice broke new ground as an entertainer. Ultimately, however, her consummate skill and professionalism transcended the issue of gender. What distinguished Fanny Brice as a performer was not so much that she was a female clown, but that she was a brilliant clown. She knew that the easiest way to make something laughable was to exaggerate its salient characteristics to the point of absurdity and she was always willing to look ludicrous to achieve her objective. By so doing, she ensured her own survival as a performer and, because ridiculous behavior is always amusing, because it is not subject to quixotic tastes and styles, gave her work a certain timelessness. As *Time* magazine perceptively observed in its review of the *Ziegfeld Follies of 1934*, "She used her kangaroo lollop and wry mouth as trademarks for a great human personality."[82] That humanness allowed her to move beyond the topical and fashion her individual characterizations into creations of great comic resonance.

Conclusion:
"I Knew What I Was
Doing—I Think"

"Fanny Brice—she was great. She could be serious and tear your heart out, or she could make you laugh till your sides ached.

—RAE SAMUELS[1]

"She was a pure character, the strongest human being I've ever known."

—EVERETT FREEMAN[2]

"Any woman who can't say a four-letter word sometimes is deceitful."

—FANNY BRICE[3]

In November 1937 when she rescued the "Good News of 1938" radio show from dismal ratings, Brice had assumed the role she would play—and play exclusively—for the next fourteen years. Until her death in 1951, she would be Baby Snooks, the mischievous moppet whose precocious pranks had delighted audiences in the *Ziegfeld Follies of 1934* and *1936*. Whereas in those shows Snooks had been just one of many Bricean characters, she was now Brice's only comic creation and would serve her well.

Despite her radio success, *Variety* reported in March 1938 that Brice was contemplating a return to the stage. She had received two offers: one from London producer Charles Cochran, who wanted her to star in his new musical revue; the other from General Theatres Corporation for several dates, including at least two weeks at the London Palladium.[4] Brice was interested in both, but ended up accepting neither because MGM still held her under contract and refused to release her. She remained on the radio program throughout its run, broadcasting from New York in April when she had to return there to testify in a lawsuit.

Almost two years earlier, a theatrical agent named Edgar Allen had sued her for $14,250 in fees he claimed she owed him, charging that he had negotiated her starring role in the *Ziegfeld Follies of 1936* and deserved compensation for his services. According to the October 3, 1936, *New York Times*, when Brice appeared in New York Supreme Court for a pre-trial examination, Allen's lawyer asked, "'Isn't it a fact that Allen hired Dave Freedman to write some of the lines in that show for you?'" Glaring at the agent, she responded angrily, "'I could punch him in the nose if he said that.'" Tired of the interrogation, the *Times* reported, "she sighed and remarked: 'I don't see how that man can ask the same question in so many different ways. I wish I could do that with my jokes.'" The case was dismissed and all charges against her dropped following her April 1938 courtroom appearance.[5]

Brice used her trip east as an opportunity to sell her New York apartment and move permanently to California, a sign that her marriage to Billy Rose was about to disintegrate. Never a passionate relationship, it had deteriorated under the pressure of two separate and competitive careers. Rose, determined to make his own name famous, resented being seen as "Mr. Brice." As he told a reporter in Denver, "It's no fun being married to an electric light. Miss Brice is one of the brightest and cleverest stars the stage or screen has ever had, but our careers clash. I have to travel a lot and I want my wife by my side."[6] For Brice, busy with coast-to-coast commitments and cross-country tours, her role as "Mrs. Rose" was the least important one she played. Reminiscing years later about her own experience, she philosophized about the personal price she believed women paid for professional success: "If you have a career, then the career is your life. The hell with anything else. It is the biggest part of you and you can be married, have children, have a husband, but it isn't enough for you because the career is always there in your mind, taking the best out of you which you should give to your husband and kids."[7]

Brice herself admitted that the marriage probably would have lasted had Rose not fallen in love with someone else. That someone was former Olympic swimmer Eleanor Holm Jarrett, whom Rose had hired to star in his *Aquacade*, an aquatic *Ziegfeld Follies* on an even grander scale. The spectacular production was designed to be a major attraction at the 1937 Great Lakes Exposition in Cleveland, another in the glittering series of

World's Fairs that were so popular in the 1930s as an antidote to pervasive Depression gloom.[8] Rose's professional interest in Holm soon developed into romance and an affair that each, though married, did little to conceal. By the fall of 1937, the relationship had attracted considerable notoriety and Rose was skewered in the national press as "Public Heel Number 1." "Billy Rose may have the nation's headlines," Walter Winchell declared, "but Fanny Brice has its heart."[9] The furor continued after the *Aquacade* closed and Rose accompanied Holm, now starring in his *Show of Shows*, on that production's tour.

Brice, who supposedly "hated any show of emotion in public," refused to enter the journalistic fray and maintained a dignified reserve. As Frances later recalled, "Mother didn't say a word. There was never a statement made about it by Mother. It is an amazing thing."[10] She waited until autumn to file for divorce, concentrating instead on her work and on furnishing her new California home in suburban Holmby Hills. When she finally initiated her suit against Rose in Los Angeles, she charged desertion but did not mention his affair with Holm. The decree was granted less than one month later, on October 27, 1938, although under California law it did not become final for a year. As soon as it did, Rose married Eleanor, who had already obtained her own divorce from bandleader Art Jarrett.

A curious mismatch from the beginning, Billy and Eleanor were not destined for happiness together. Their relationship soured predictably and eventually culminated in an acrimonious four-year divorce suit, known in the newspapers as the "War of the Roses." By the time a settlement was announced in January 1954, Rose had paid the woman he once called his "sugar plum candy mouth" $200,000 in cash and $30,000 a month in alimony.[11] He had also spent well over $1 million in legal fees and court costs. Such bitter wrangling contrasted markedly with his relatively uneventful parting from Brice. As Rose later recalled, she sent him a bill for $18,000 a week after his wedding to Eleanor. "I'd forgotten it, but she hadn't. It was for that nine-week salary cut everybody took when *Crazy Quilt* was *Sweet and Low* and I was losing almost ten thousand dollars a week." Nevertheless, Brice and Rose managed to remain on amicable terms and, according to him, saw one another every time he came to California.[12]

More than marking the end of her marriage, the California move symbolized Brice's commitment to comedy and to her new career on radio where she would perform steadily and successfully. Her serious illness in 1936 had left her with a keen awareness of her physical limitations and she greatly preferred appearing on a weekly radio show to the rigors of cross-country touring. She remained on "Good News" (still on Thursday nights at 9:00 p.m. over NBC), and in January 1939, *Variety* included her as one of only five talents "who rose above previous radio levels during 1938."[13] Her popularity grew during the year, although *Variety* occasionally questioned the appropriateness of her material for a family program. In its September 13 review, for example, the newspaper praised the series on which she was one of several regulars, but criticized a "crack about her father not deserving to have children." "Mixing of Katzenjammers with parent psychology," *Variety* warned, "may not only get this comedy segment into hot water, but wash it up as a popular feature."[14]

As Snooks solidified as a character, Brice learned to avoid profundity and profanity so as not to offend her increasingly large audience. The incorrigible child terrorized her household with such stunts as bringing a bees' nest to her mother's club meeting, cutting her father's fishing line into little pieces, ripping the fur off her mother's coat, putting marbles in the piano, and applying stripes of shoe polish to her little brother so that he would look like a zebra. Brice, however, maintained that Snooks was "a good sweet kid at heart." Discussing her creation in a 1946 interview, she explained:

> She's got a lot of high spirits and loves good clean fun, but she is never vicious or mean, and if she is, it's all the fault of my script writers. I am always struggling with them they shouldn't picture Snooks like such a little brat. She should be true to life. But in Hollywood, you have to exaggerate. Everything is exaggerated.[15]

The exaggeration apparently extended to a fictionalized account of Brice's life in the movie *Rose of Washington Square*, which appeared in the spring of 1939. Hollywood may have spurned her services as an actress, but had no qualms about exploiting her biography, particularly its more melodramatic aspects. The Twentieth Century-Fox film starred Alice Faye, Al Jolson, and Tyrone Power and focused on Brice's tumultuous relationship with ex-husband Arnstein. According to the *New York Times*, it told "the story of the loyal Ziegfeld star who married a thief and a confidence man, stuck by him through his disgrace and poured all her love and faith into the song 'My Man' which she sobbed out each night from the Ziegfeld stage." Noting that "Miss Faye doesn't resemble Fannie Brice; she doesn't sing 'My Man' as well either," the reviewer wryly observed, "If she did, it would have been just too coincidental."[16] It was coincidental enough for Brice, who decided to sue Twentieth Century-Fox, Faye, Jolson, and Power in July. Charging defamation of character, unauthorized use of her life story, and invasion of privacy, she asked for $750,000 in damages. When the suit was finally settled out of court in December 1940, Brice received $30,000.

Meanwhile, "Good News" resumed in September 1939 after a summer hiatus. Although MGM no longer had any connection with the series, its format remained unchanged. The hour-long program featured variety acts in its first half and "dramatizations" in its second. Baby Snooks appeared each week with Daddy Hanley Stafford and received favorable reviews, but the show itself was not doing well. Overlong and lacking focus, it was almost canceled in December. Instead, largely because of Snooks's popularity, the weekly broadcast was cut to thirty minutes beginning in March 1940.[17] The elimination of half an hour of air time helped, but did not solve the program's problems. *Variety* wrote that it was still "a revue in need of a sock" and that the exchange between Snooks and Daddy "represented the show's only scoring moments."[18]

By the fall, the program was known simply as "Maxwell House Coffee Time" and had been streamlined. The half-hour broadcast was now divided equally between Brice as Baby Snooks and comic monologuist Frank Morgan. In March 1941, *Time* observed that Brice had "cooed, gurgled and whined her way to a berth in radio" and, with Morgan's help, now attracted an audience estimated at 15 million.[19] Their uneasy partnership lasted until 1944, when both emerged with their own shows. Brice's "The Baby Snooks Show" for Post Toasties, began in September on Sunday nights from 6:30 to 7:00 P.M. over CBS. She tried to introduce a new character, Irma Potts, a "trustful shopgirl with a protruding lower lip and a slight lisp," but Irma could not compete with Snooks, who remained the uncontested star.[20]

Snooks's career almost ended in July 1945 when Brice suffered a serious heart attack and was hospitalized for several weeks. By the fall, she had recovered sufficiently to resume her radio show, now for Sanka Coffee. She continued with Sanka and Snooks during the 1946–47 season, moving to Friday nights at 8:00 P.M. According to the September *Cosmopolitan*, the program was sent to 154 stations of the CBS network and had an audience of more than fourteen million. Brice received $6,500 each week and, by *Cosmopolitan*'s calculations, had earned close to $2 million since Snooks's debut.[21]

The profitable series continued until 1948 when Brice went off the air during a highly publicized contract dispute. It was a period of upheaval in the radio industry, caused by fierce competition from the latest technological marvel to arrive on the show business scene: television. Many performers saw their salaries shrink drastically, but accepted the reduction as necessary for radio's survival. Brice, however, refused the new terms. Told that she would be receiving only $3,000 for each broadcast, she would not take the cut and stayed off the air for a year. "She had made up her mind not to go on," reminisced Everett Freeman, the writer and director of her program, "and wrong or right, that was it."[22] She used the time productively, beginning the autobiography she would not live to complete. In a November 1949 newspaper article, she called the experience of reminiscing about her life "amazing." "It's like being psychoanalyzed," she explained. "There were days when I felt very sad. And days when I felt very happy."[23]

Presumably the resumption of "The Baby Snooks Show" the following week pleased her. She was heard regularly on Tuesday nights from 8:30 to 9:00 p.m. over NBC and, according to Freeman, "she was immediately in the first ten most popular programs." Although she had moved to a new network, she had not changed her characterization of Snooks. Nor had she lost her huge national audience, which never seemed to tire of the impossible child. Snooks continued happily wreaking havoc until May 24, 1951, when the fifty-nine-year-old Brice suffered a cerebral hemorrhage. She died five days later, never having regained consciousness. That night, instead of the program on which she was scheduled to appear, NBC broadcast a musical tribute preceded by a short eulogy. Hanley Stafford, her long-suffering "Daddy," said simply, "We have lost a very real, a very warm, a very wonderful woman."[24]

Her funeral on May 31 received extensive press coverage. The *New York Times* reported that a crowd of more than two thousand people, predominantly middle-aged women, stood outside Hollywood's Temple Israel and wept as the short service was broadcast over loudspeakers. They listened as George Jessel, one of Hollywood's favorite eulogists, called her "a great artist" capable of playing "life's fullest emotional part." They heard the rabbi praise her as "an entertainer with a great heart who brought so much joy to the human heart."[25]

That Brice managed to move people for so many years was a tribute to her dedication and tenacity, as well as to her talent. A show business survivor, she took pride in having spanned theatrical generations so successfully. On one occasion, as she enthusiastically recalled her stage career, she provided a reasonably accurate summary of her diverse activities:

Listen, kid! I've done everything in the theater except marry a property man. I've been a soubrette in burlesque and I've accompanied stereopticon slides.

I've acted for Belasco and I've laid 'em out in rows at the Palace. I've doubled as an alligator; I've worked for the Shuberts; and I've been joined to Billy Rose in the holy bonds. I've painted the house boards and I've been fired by George M. Cohan. I've played in London before the King and in Oil City before miners with lanterns in their caps. . . . So what is it you'd like to know?[26]

Her ability to transfer her talents and continue for so long on radio is particularly impressive given her theatrical performance style. Her reliance on visual burlesque would not have made her a natural for the new medium and it is not surprising that Baby Snooks was the character who ensured her success. Brice said she decided to dispense with the rest of her repertoire and concentrate on Snooks when she realized that she would be subject to less rigorous censorship if she played a baby. As she explained in her memoirs:

You know the way they have to go over your script for censorship? I found out when I was doing "Mrs. Cohen at the Beach." We'd be ready to rehearse and they'd say: "You can't do this, you can't do that. This will offend and that will not sound nice." And I knew this couldn't happen with a baby. Because what can you write about a child that has to be censored?[27]

According to *Variety*'s reviews of some of Brice's early Snooks broadcasts, it was indeed possible to write about a child in a risqué and potentially offensive fashion. Yet, once Brice accepted certain limitations, taste was no longer an issue. Snooks provided wholesome entertainment, good clean fun in a family time slot, and endeared herself to audiences for fourteen years.

Brice's comment, however, is too simplistic an interpretation. Although she may have been oblivious to them, and it is quite possible that she was, there were other compelling reasons why Snooks would have been Brice's obvious choice for radio. First, of all her comic creations, Snooks was the only one who did not require an accent of any kind. Brice mimicked a child's speech pattern but even that, she believed, was only minimally exaggerated. She said she was a convincing "Schnooks," as she always pronounced it, because she kept her voice as natural as possible. "Most kiddie mimics," she stated in an interview, "go for the higher octaves and start screeching till it gets on your nerves. To me, Baby Schnooks is real. I don't burlesque her. I'm sincere when I'm talkin' Schnooks. I don't have any grownup thoughts in my mind."[28] She became the character and played her fully, without relying on the gestures and mannerisms that accompanied her stage performances and, as she quickly learned, would not work on radio.

By abandoning her Yiddish accent, she freed herself from her reliance on visual burlesque. Instead, she had to depend on the script to create the dramatic situation and on her own convincing impersonation to sustain it. That is probably why she was said to have avoided improvising on radio. Unlike her stage performance, which always had a quality of spontaneity, Brice did not deviate from her radio script. She needed it to communicate to the radio audience what she had been able to convey on stage through her mugging and gestures: the total absurdity of the situation.

Second, it was not simply that dialect comedy demanded physical behavior. The accent itself was no longer appropriate and was probably part of the "something wrong"[29] Brice sensed but could not articulate. In the late 1930s, there was a marked upsurge in anti-Semitism, both nationally and globally. Nazi atrocities may have been physically confined to Europe, but the noisome effects of Hitler's mad propaganda were felt throughout the United States. A variety of hate groups had become alarmingly prominent in the country, fueled by the Depression, fervent opposition to Roosevelt, fears of coming change, and the spectacle of European turmoil.[30] Even Brice, admittedly uninformed about world events, could not have failed to realize that a Yiddish accent was probably not the best way to win a national following. "Schnooks" ensured a much wider appeal. Many Americans hated Jews, but only the most misanthropic disliked children.

Third, in playing a little girl, Brice may have been tapping into a mass belief that women are the dumber, more childlike sex. As an informative study of male-female vaudeville teams has recently suggested, the image of women as either "dumbbells" or "kids" had a long history on stage and screen. Those stereotypes were still popular in the thirties when women were frequently portrayed on film as society madcaps or little girls. Between 1935 and 1938, the leading box office star, male or female, was Shirley Temple.[31] With her dauntless optimism and saccharine personality, Temple was an important cultural symbol for a country still reeling from the Depression. By becoming Snooks, as innocently bad as Temple was good, Brice was not only spoofing the legitimate child star, but was pushing the notion of woman as little girl to its most absurd extreme. It is unlikely that Brice was aware of the sociological implications of her impersonation, but that is probably why her character took such an immediate hold on the national consciousness.

In Baby Snooks, moreover, Brice seems to have found a congenial character, one that she could create by drawing upon her own childlike qualities. Although this is something that cannot be documented, there was a certain ingenuousness to Brice that she never lost. Friends always spoke of her warmth, energy, vitality, and enthusiasm for life, as well as her lack of inhibition and complete naturalness. A longtime acquaintance allegedly remarked, "Fannie is herself all the time. She can't help being herself. There isn't an ounce of pose or affectation in her makeup." Her son, William, emphasized her "aliveness" and said that she talked with an almost "confrontational candor." Reminiscing about her forthrightness, Everett Freeman explained, "She could speak only in truths. Truth is often shocking, but Fanny knew no other way. She devastated some of the most sensitive men of this generation with things she said in their presence."[32] Such comments suggest that Brice would have been very comfortable with Snooks for fourteen years and even she implied that she did not have to stretch too far to play the role. She boasted in 1941, "I could do Snooks blind. I don't have to work into it. It's part of me. It's like stealing money to get paid for it."[33]

It is ironic that Brice, who had worked steadily for so long, died just as she was contemplating retirement. Many obituaries reprinted something she had told an interviewer a few months earlier: she was "tired of fighting to stay on top." "Radio doesn't have the excitement of the theatre," she explained, "and television and movies are too much work." She had considered returning to the stage as late as April 1945 when she admitted, "I miss the theatre, but I won't come back unless someone comes along with material that would be startlingly new, not an imitation of 'My Man.' It has to be very, very good."[34] Her heart attack three months later precluded that option and she returned to her weekly radio program.

Billy Rose maintained that Brice could easily have created a career on what he called "the big picture tube," but believed that "she couldn't be bothered any more." As he recalled in 1963, she had told him that "she felt like loafing for a change."[35] It is more likely that she feared television would reveal the absurdity of a middle-aged woman masquerading as a terrible toddler. According to Eddie Cantor in his biography, *Take My Life*, "She felt that television was her enemy. On radio the Baby Snooks character was convincing, on stage for a scene it was great. Fanny felt it wouldn't work on television, she thought she looked old."[36]

Since it is a visual medium, television could not have concealed the incongruity of a "Grandmother Snooks," as *Newsweek* put it in 1946.[37] On the radio, however, she could carry on as Snooks in the minds of her audience. As long as she sounded appropriately infantile, her real appearance was irrelevant. "I'd look at this woman," Freeman fondly remembered, "seeing this dignified lady in the best clothes, the height of fashion. . . . She'd nod and leave me. And when she went out in front of all those people," he marveled, "she was suddenly a little child, clothes and coiffure and high heels forgotten."[38] Radio preserved the illusion in a way that television, with its merciless video closeups, never could have.

Brice always sounded somewhat condescending in talking about her radio series, as if she were tacitly acknowledging the superiority of her stage performances. It was not simply that radio was a less demanding medium. It was that the work itself was less complex, less resonant, less universal in its implications. Brice became Baby Snooks so completely that the character took on a life of its own. There was no distance between Brice and her comic creation, as there had been on the stage, and that was because of the nature of radio itself. When she played Baby Snooks on stage, she looked ridiculous. The audience could see that she was not really a little girl and that was part of the joke. On radio, however, even though the listeners knew that Brice was a woman in her fifties, they obviously could not see her. The impersonation was so convincing they might even forget that they were not hearing an impish child. With Snooks, moreover, there were no surprises, except the continual surprise at how freshly she was presented. Aside from the ingenuity Brice brought to her mischiefmaking, the format of the broadcasts remained constant, even to the ear-splitting "WAAAAAAAHHHH" with which they invariably ended. Since "The Baby Snooks Show" was a radio "sit-com," the title character never changed and the impossible situation she always created was the focus of each program.

In Brice's best stage work, on the other hand, the emphasis was on the character and her incongruous behavior. Brice's antics always pointed to the discrepancy between the character's perception of herself and the way she appeared to others. The audience's awareness of that disparity made the character seem ridiculous, and Brice's hilarious actions always heightened the comic effect. Yet, ultimately, it was Brice's willingness to play the clown herself that humanized the caricatures and kept them from becoming cruel. The fact that she could both identify with and comment on the character allowed the audience to laugh at her and, at the same time, to see the larger significance of her comic creations.

One of Brice's many admirers observed, "We had in her one of the great comic artists of our time, with an instinctive sense of what was funny, who seemed entirely uninhibited, letting herself appear awkward or ungainly or foolish so long as she was creating her characters."[39] On the stage, Brice was a character comedienne creating a series of animated comic types. On radio, she was a comedienne playing one consistent character. To both, she brought the uncompromising honesty with which she said she approached her life. In the memoirs she planned to fashion into an autobiography, she reflected:

> When I think back, I know I was the same person at all times. Right from the beginning, from the minute I could think, I know my brain worked the same way and I wanted the same things. And I was never ashamed of myself. I was practically raised in a saloon, and I never had any feeling about that. I guess I knew it was better to be honest. If you are honest, it makes the sailing so much easier. The most dangerous thing in the world is not to be honest. I think you can only get in trouble. You are either something or you are not.[40]

Brice's forceful statements are incredibly ironic, given the way she has been posthumously portrayed. Her own early efforts to alter the facts of her life pale in comparison with her family's attempt to picture her as the epitome of gentility and refinement. According to "the tasteful legend" Brice became, her California days were spent with family and friends, to whom she was devoted, and whose homes she delighted in decorating. She had a natural flair for interior design and the exquisite furnishings she invariably chose reflected her innate aesthetic sense. She was knowledgeable about fine art and antiques, painted as a hobby, and encouraged son William to pursue an artistic career. With daughter Frances, she shared her love of beautiful objects and expensive clothes. "Mother was always very elegant," Frances recalled in a magazine interview. "Almost every day when I was a child she was having a fitting for something. Mother liked Falkenstein suits. She bought at Carnegie and Mainbocher. We went to Europe every summer and she ordered at Worth and Patou, too. She spotted Norell early." She was also "a connoisseur of jewelry," Frances asserted, and enjoyed selecting unusual items such as "a Russian necklace set with diamonds and Oriental pearls."[41]

Magnificently dressed, coiffed, and groomed, Brice was indeed a handsome woman of impeccable taste. Yet, however much her family might choose to emphasize her elegance and refinement, that is far too simplistic an image for such a dynamic and complex personality. Norman Katkov, whom Brice's family subsequently engaged as her biographer, described his subject as "this woman who had sat like a queen and could talk like a truck driver." Adding "maybe she could have taught the driver a few things," he observed, "nobody had the flair for downright earthiness that Fanny Brice was blessed with. She didn't just swear, she created her own language."[42] His book presented Brice as tough-talking and hard-driving, a woman who never forgot where she came from and often spoke with a bluntness verging on insensitivity. He also showed her as warm, dedicated, compassionate, and gifted, but his account was far from the sanitized portrait her children had envisioned. According to one source, it so upset them that Ray Stark, Frances's husband, pulled the book from circulation, allegedly paying $50,000 to have the plates destroyed.[43]

William Brice admitted recently that the family may have "overreacted" to Katkov's book, but remembered its publication as having been "very painful." "By temperament," he explained, "my sister and I are not inclined to be public about our personal lives" and "we were particularly concerned about anything written about our father." Frances had unhappy childhood memories of reading newspaper accounts of Arnstein's trial and incarceration, of seeing photographs of him behind bars, and wanted to shield her children from similar traumatic experiences. An artist himself, William was in the difficult position of having to enforce "creative censorship" because the "protectionist instinct" was so strong. "Beyond that," he continued, "our own experience of our mother was key. . . . There's a lot we don't know about, but what we did know was so extraordinary. It was clear that this was an extraordinary person, larger than life in every way." Reflecting on their disenchantment with Katkov's portrait, he added, "perhaps we had fantasized that there would be a book as extraordinary as she was."[44]

Also complicating a contemporary assessment of Brice is the inevitable association with Barbra Streisand. An extremely talented performer in her own right, Streisand played Brice on stage and screen in *Funny Girl*, as well as in its film sequel *Funny Lady*. Many people, therefore, remember Brice's performances through Streisand's—that is, they confuse the real Brice with Streisand's interpretation of the character Fanny Brice in a fictionalized account of her life. Aside from the fact that the film presents a rags-to-riches version of Brice's career and ignores such unpleasant biographical episodes as her first marriage, Streisand projects a persona that is quite different from Brice's. Despite the obvious similarities—two poor Jewish girls from New York, neither one conventionally beautiful, but both with strong voices, expressive hands, and dramatic aspirations—Streisand lacks the warmth that critics always attributed to Brice. Her presence is compelling, but cold. It is not surprising that she reportedly prefers the isolation of the recording studio and the film set to performing live. Brice, on the other hand, loved appearing on stage and thrived on the electric communication she believed took place between performer and audience. Even after she moved exclusively to radio, she still needed a live audience for her broadcasts. According to director Freeman, she was always flat and lifeless in rehearsals, but "something happened" when she went on. "She just needed that audience in front of her and she was trouping."[45] Although the gifted Streisand has a flair for comedy, she does not play the clown with Brice's wonderful zaniness, abandon, or brilliance.

Brice did not scrupulously document her own life and career. She worked too hard and enjoyed socializing too much to have taken the time to keep scrapbooks or diaries. According to William, she left "very little." Since her memoirs are currently unavailable for scrutiny, there is virtually no primary source material on which to rely and one has, at best, tantalizing glimpses of the woman behind the public persona. Who was Fanny Brice, really? A consummate professional and a dedicated artist, she has been called the least temperamental of all the female vaudeville headliners and a performer who always seemed like everyone's best friend. A single parent and a working mother, she tried hard to remain close to her children in spite of the many separations required by her arduous cross-country tours. William stated recently that he really did not get to know her until he was sixteen. "My childhood memories are very vague," he explained, because "with my mother away forty-four weeks a year, I was essentially brought up by nurses and governesses."[46] Nevertheless, as older children they spent more time with her, going to movies together between matinee and evening performances in New York and joining her on the road during vacations. "We spent Christmas in every big city in the country," Frances recalled. We always hoped to hit Los Angeles where it was warm, but it never happened."[47] When Frances and William returned to New York, Brice pleased them by sending presents from different cities along her route. "Mother had charge accounts in every good store and shop in the country," Frances reminisced. "She loved to shop, for us as much as for herself, and we were always getting gifts: from Kansas City and Cleveland and Pittsburgh and Chicago and Seattle and everywhere."[48]

Devoted to her children, loyal to her friends, ambitious, pragmatic, and forthright, the real Brice still remains elusive. Given the revealing statements she made about the price women pay for success, one wonders about her own inner resources, her ability to triumph over adversity, personal pain, and loneliness. She had a long-standing relationship with a man named Roger Davis, whom she met in 1916 when he was in the chorus of the *Ziegfeld Follies*. According to an article in the June 14, 1931,

New York Herald Tribune, Davis appeared in three more *Follies* with Brice, traveled to Europe with her and Norma Talmadge in 1927, and performed in the vaudeville act with which she toured in 1927-28.[49] He subsequently played minor roles in *Sweet and Low*, *Crazy Quilt*, and the *Ziegfeld Follies of 1936*.

Although Brice apparently valued Davis's companionship more than his acting ability, there was nothing sexual about their relationship. He was variously described as her mascot, stooge, and social guide. The *Tribune* reported that "she has a bad memory for names and Davis guides her through the intricacies of large parties with constant nudges and sly whispers that enable her to identify other guests." William characterized him as "my mother's dear and close friend, an amazing and humorous man who never managed to succeed in show business on his own." "In a room," he recalled, "Roger was hilarious. On the stage, he was frozen." According to William, Davis lived with the Brices "for a while" and always traveled with Fanny on the road where "he kept her company and watched out for her." "One had a sense, though," William reflected, "of his being not quite a real person, of his being like a jester."[50] It is interesting to note as well that whatever influence Davis may have had, Brice does not mention him at all in her reminiscences.

However unique a personality Brice may have been, she was also not untypical of her generation, the many other children of immigrants who turned to show business and fulfilled the American dream. Ambitious and determined, indefatigable and tenacious, she deserved the accolades she won. Yet for a long time, she was uncomfortable with her identity as a performer and struggled to become a serious actress on stage and screen, a role for which she was unsuited. Undervaluing her gift for comedy, she sought recognition instead in what she perceived as more legitimate entertainment forms. Having worked her way up in the show business hierarchy from burlesque to the *Ziegfeld Follies* to vaudeville, she believed that starring in her own dramatic production or motion picture would validate her talent and bring her respectability, and she endured countless disappointments in her quest to reach this goal. To Brice as an ethnic outsider, respectability was terribly important; it meant acceptance by the dominant culture she so much wanted to be a part of. Her self-mockery, her repeated attempts to fictionalize her past, her plastic surgery all stemmed from the same desire for approval, the same need for approbation, the same wish to be loved by her audiences.

Brice finally achieved greatness as a performer when she realized that her wonderful comic creations made her special, when she accepted her role as a brilliant clown. A woman working in a traditionally male field, Brice was a major comic figure and her important contribution to American show business cannot be minimized. Frances once remarked, "Mother was a comic but she was never a nut."[51] She was, more accurately, a comic genius whose lunatic creations inspired endless delight.

In what would have been the conclusion of her planned autobiography, Brice reflected:

> I wanted to call my book, *I Knew What I Was Doing—I Think*, because whatever happened to me in my life was not a surprise when it happened.
>
> I made most things happen for me, and if they were good, I worked to get them. If they were bad, I worked just as hard for that.
>
> But I am not sorry. I will tell anybody that, and it is the truth. I lived the way I wanted to live and never did what people said I should do or advised me to do. And I want my children to do the same. Let the world know you as you are, not as you think you should be, because sooner or later, if you are posing, you will forget the pose, and then where are you?[52]

Brice's comic brilliance enabled her to simultaneously assume and reveal the poses of her characters. That she did so with warmth, good humor, and understanding gave her best performances their most distinctive quality: their humanity.

William Brice said recently that he would like his mother to be remembered as "the great artist she was."[53] That is an honorable request. Fanny Brice was a gifted performer and a genuinely funny woman who deserves her special place in the history of American popular entertainment.

Notes

The following abbreviations are used to indicate frequently cited collections.

BR   Harris Collection, John Hay Library, Brown University
BRTC   Billy Rose Theatre Collection, New York Public Library at Lincoln Center, Astor, Lenox and Tilden Foundations
BU   Resource Center, School of Public Communication, Boston University
HTC   Harvard Theatre Collection, Harvard College Library
MCNY Theatre and Music Collection, Museum of the City of New York
MD   Special Collections, Music Division, New York Public Library at Lincoln Center
PC   Private Collection
SA   Shubert Archive, Lyceum Theatre, New York
WI   Wisconsin Center for Film and Theater Research, Archive of the University of Wisconsin and the State Historical Society, Madison, Wisconsin

Introduction

1. Brooks Atkinson, "Crazy Quilt," *New York Times*, 20 May 1931, 28:4; George Cukor quoted by Norman Katkov, *The Fabulous Fanny* (New York: Alfred A. Knopf, 1953), p. 163.
2. Katkov, p. viii.
3. Telephone interview with William Brice, 1 August 1988.
4. I have not included Brice's many nightclub engagements in this study.

1. The Early Years

1. Fanny Brice, quoted by Katkov, p. 16.
2. Carolyn Saul, quoted by Katkov, p. 33.
3. Fanny Brice as told to Palma Wayne, "Fannie of the *Follies*," Part 1, *Cosmopolitan*, February 1936, p. 20.
4. Ibid., p. 22.
5. *Variety*, 30 December 1905, p. 11
6. "Fannie of the *Follies*," Part 1, pp. 22–23.
7. Ibid., p. 23.
8. Ibid., pp. 23 and 138.
9. Ibid., p. 138.
10. Allan Nevins and Henry Steele Commager, *A Pocket History of the United States* (1942; rpt. New York: Washington Square Press, Pocket Books, 1981), p. 341.

11. Milton Hindus, "An East Side Anthology," in *The Lower East Side: Portal to American Life (1870–1924)* (New York: Jewish Museum, 1966), p. 15.

12. Nevins and Commager, p. 341.

13. Ronald Sanders, *The Lower East Side* (New York: Dover, 1979), p. 1; Jenna Weissman Joselit, *Our Gang: Jewish Crime and the New York Jewish Community, 1900–1940* (Bloomington: Indiana University Press, 1983), p. 160.

14. John T. Cunningham, *Newark* (Newark: New Jersey Historical Society, 1966), p. 276

15. Carolyn Saul, quoted by Katkov, pp. 16–17.

16. Ibid., pp. 20 and 26.

17. Eric F. Goldman, *Rendezvous with Destiny: A History of Modern American Reform* (New York: Vintage Books, Random House, 1956), p. 43.

18. Nevins and Commager, pp. 330–31.

19. Goldman, p. 43.

20. According to the Newark City Directories, neither Charles nor Rose Borach ever owned more than one saloon at any given time. No Borach appears in the Directory for 1895–96 and the 1896–97 Directory seems to have erred in listing two Charles Borachs, one a waiter with a home at 110 William Street, the other a bartender with a home at 110 Washington Street. From the year ending in May 1898 to the year ending in May 1900, Borach is included as the owner of a saloon at 49 Rankin Street. For the next three years, he has one at 26 Lafayette Street, in the center of the city's industrial district. The last listing for this location is in the 1902–03 Directory. Borach's name does not appear the following year and the 1904–05 Directory lists him as a laborer with a house at 212 1/2 Camden Street.

21. Fanny Brice, quoted by Katkov, p. 25.

22. Ibid., p. 17.

23. Ibid., p. 17.

24. Katkov, pp. 26–28.

25. Ibid., pp. 28–29.

26. Unidentified newspaper clipping, Fanny Brice file, New Jersey Room, Newark Public Library.

27. "Fannie of the *Follies*," Part 1, pp. 20–21.

28. Ibid., p. 21.

29. Ibid., pp. 21–22.

30. Lew Brice, quoted by Katkov, pp. 3 and 11–12.

31. Ibid., p. 8.

32. John F. Kasson, *Amusing the Million: Coney Island at the Turn of the Century* (New York: Hill and Wang, 1978), p. 38.

33. Ibid. p. 39.

34. "Fannie of the *Follies*," Part 1, p. 21.

35. Lew Brice, quoted by Katkov, p. 7.

36. Carolyn Saul, quoted by Katkov, pp. 19–25; Irving Howe, *World of Our Fathers* (New York: Simon & Schuster, 1976), p. 560.

37. Lew Brice says that his sister was fourteen when she entered the contest and, with an October 1891 birthdate, Fanny would have been fourteen in 1906. Moreover, the song Brice remembers singing, "When You Know You're Not Forgotten by the Girl You Can't Forget," was published in 1906.

38. *Variety*, 13 January 1906, p. 9.

39. "Fannie Brice and Her Adventures," *New York Dramatic Mirror*, 22 April 1914, p. 20.

40. Fannie Brice, "The Feel of the Audience," *Saturday Evening Post*, 21 November 1925, p. 10.

41. David Ewen, *All the Years of American Popular Music* (Englewood Cliffs, New Jersey: Prentice-Hall, 1977), p. 108; Sigmund Spaeth, *History of Popular Music in America* (New York: Random House, 1948), p. 252.

42. Ed Gardenier and J. Fred Helf, "When You Know You're Not Forgotten by the Girl You Can't Forget" (Helf and Hager, 1906), MD.

43. Bryan, Kendis and Paley, "Cheer Up Mary" (New York: Cooper, Kendis & Paley Music Pub. Co., 1906), MCNY.

44. Russel B. Nye, *The Unembarrassed Muse: The Popular Arts in America* (New York: Dial Press, 1970), p. 317.

45. Lew Brice, quoted by Katkov, p. 11. In the 22 April 1914 *New York Dramatic Mirror* and "Fannie of the Follies," Part 1, p. 138, Brice says the amount she won was thirty to forty dollars.

46. "The Feel of the Audience," p. 10.

47. Ibid., p. 10.

48. "Fannie Brice Gives an Audience," *New York Herald Tribune*, 14 August 1938, Fanny Brice file, HTC.

49. Russell Lynes, *The Lively Audience: A Social History of the Visual and Performing Arts in America, 1890–1950* (New York: Harper & Row, 1985), p. 148.

50. Brooks Atkinson, *Broadway*, rev. ed. (New York: Macmillan, 1974), p. 11.

51. Fanny Brice, "'I'm Baby Snooks, You Know,'" *New York Globe*, 8 May 1938, p. 3.

52. In "Fannie of the *Follies*," Part 1, p. 138, Brice states that the nickelodeon was on the corner of 83rd Street and Second (as opposed to Third) Avenue. Neither block as it currently exists gives a clue as to which one might have housed a theatre.

53. "Fannie of the *Follies*," Part 1, p. 138.

54. Ewen, p. 114.

55. Gerald M. Bordman, *The Oxford Companion to American Theatre* (New York: Oxford University Press, 1984), p. 670.

56. "Fannie of the *Follies*," Part 1, p. 138.

57. Fanny Brice, quoted by Katkov, p. 37.

58. Bernard Sobel, *Burleycue: An Underground History of Burlesque Days* (New York: Farrar & Rinehart, 1931), p. 146.

59. "Fannie of the *Follies*," Part 1, p. 138.

60. Sobel, p. 146.

61. "Fannie of the *Follies*," Part 1, p. 138.

62. Fanny Brice, quoted by Katkov, pp. 38 and 39.

63. William Weaver, *Duse: A Biography* (New York: Harcourt Brace Jovanovich, 1984), pp. 20–21.

64. Fanny Brice, quoted by Katkov, p. 39.

65. *Theatre Magazine*, September 1907, p. x. The *New York Dramatic Mirror's* Theatrical Roster for 1907–08 (7 September 1907, p. 3) listed a "Fannie Bradshaw" as a cast member of *The Time, the Place, and the Girl*. According to Frances Brice Stark in a 4 May 1982 telephone interview, her mother never used the name "Fannie Bradshaw."

66. Fanny Brice, quoted by Katkov, p. 40.

67. "Fannie Brice Gives an Audience," Fanny Brice file, HTC.

68. "Fannie of the *Follies*," Part 1, p. 138.

69. "Fannie Brice and Her Adventures," p. 20.

70. *New York Dramatic Mirror*, 8 November 1905, p. 11.

71. "Fannie Brice and Her Adventures," p. 20. In a 1923 interview, Brice said that the production in which she played an alligator was *The Ballad Girl*. Lewis's company had opened in Hazelton, Pennsylvania, with that show, which was so bad that "business got worse and worse." According to these recollections, the company was "so rotten the little towns didn't want us even before they'd seen us. They'd heard about *The Ballad Girl*." Believing that "there's only one thing left to do and that's to give 'em drama," James O'Neill turned in desperation to *The Royal Slave*.

The source for this account is Ashton Stevens in *Actorviews* (Chicago: Covici-McGee, 1923), pp. 221–26, reproduced in *Selected Vaudeville Criticism*, edited by Anthony Slide (Metuchen, New Jersey: Scarecrow Press, 1988), pp. 38–40.

72. Garrett H. Leverton, "Introduction," *The Great Diamond Robbery and Other Recent Melodramas* (Princeton, New Jersey: Princeton University Press, 1940), pp. x–xi.

73. "Fannie Brice and Her Adventures," p. 20.

2. A "College Girl" on the Wheel

1. Ann Corio, with Joseph DiMona, *This Was Burlesque* (New York: Grosset & Dunlap, 1968), p. 39.

2. "Fannie of the *Follies*," Part 1, p. 138.

3. Don B. Wilmeth, *Variety Entertainment and Outdoor Amusements: A Reference Guide* (Westport, Connecticut: Greenwood Press, 1982), p. 153.

4. *Variety*, 12 May 1906, p. 4.

5. Irving Zeidman, *The American Burlesque Show* (New York: Hawthorn Books, 1967), p. 53.

6. *Variety*, 9 June 1906, p. 4.

7. Sobel, *Burleycue*, pp. 144–46.

8. *Variety*, 26 December 1908, p. 12.

9. "Fannie Brice and Her Adventures," p. 20; *New York Mirror*, unidentified clipping, Hurtig and Seamon file, BRTC.

10. Sobel, p. 147.

11. "Fannie of the *Follies*," Part 1, p. 138.

12. Sobel, p. 149.

13. Ibid., p. 149.

14. "The Feel of the Audience," p. 181.

15. After its opening week in Washington, D.C., from 24 to 31 August 1907, the *Transatlantic Burlesquers*' stops included Chicago (September 15–21), Milwaukee (23–28), Chicago (September 29–October 5), Detroit (6–12), Toledo (13–19), Cleveland (21–26), Buffalo (28–November 2), Rochester (4–9), Albany (11–13), Holyoke (14– 16), Boston (18–23), Brooklyn (25–30), New York City (December 2–7), Philadelphia (9–14), Scranton (19–21), Newark (23–28), New York City (December 30–January 4), Providence (6–11), Boston (13– 18), Springfield (20–22), Albany (23–25), Brooklyn (27–February 1 and 3–8), Scranton (10–12), Reading (13–15), Philadelphia (17–22), Baltimore (24–29), Washington (March 2–7), Pittsburgh (9–14), Cincinnati (22–28), Birmingham (30–April 4), New Orleans (5–11), Kansas City (19–25), St. Louis (26–May 2), Chicago (3–9), and Milwaukee, where it closed on 16 May 1908 (according to weekly route listings in the *New York Clipper* and *Dramatic Mirror*).

16. *Variety*, 16 January 1909, p. 16; *Variety*, 26 December 1908, p. 12.

17. Maurice Zolotow, "Baby Snooks," Part 2, *Cosmopolitan*, October 1946, p. 51.

18. *New York Clipper*, 26 December 1908, p. 1136; *Variety*, 26 December 1908, p. 12.

19. *Variety*, 26 December 1908, p. 12.

20. Ibid., p. 12; *Springfield Daily News*, 9 February 1909, p. 7. According to the *New York Clipper*, *The Girls from Happyland*'s route was as follows: Birmingham (August 30–September 5, 1908), New Orleans (6–12), Memphis (14–19), Kansas City (21–26), St. Louis (27–October 3), Chicago (4–10), Milwaukee (11–17), Chicago (18–24), Cleveland (26–31), Buffalo (November 2–7), Rochester (9–14), Toronto (16–21), Montreal (23–28), Albany (30–December 2), Holyoke (3–5), Boston (7–12), Brooklyn (14–19), New York City (21–26), Philadelphia (28–January 2), Newark (4–9), Hoboken (10–16), New York City (18–23), Providence (25–30), Boston (February 1–6), Springfield (8–10), Albany (11–13), New York City (15–20), Brooklyn (22–March 6), Philadelphia (8–13), Baltimore (15–20), Washington (22–27), Pittsburgh (29–April 3), Columbus (5–10), Toledo (11–17), Detroit (18–24), Chicago (26–May 1), Cincinnati (2–8).

21. "The Feel of the Audience," p. 181.

22. *Variety*, 13 November 1909, p. 6.

23. *Variety*, 4 September 1909, p. 17.

24. Both programs are in The Billy Rose Theatre Collection.

25. *Variety*, 4 September 1909, p. 17. According to the *New York Clipper* (26 February 1910, p. 58), Brice's songs included "Music Man"; the "O.I.C. Quartette" number with Clara Hendrix (Nanie), Willie Weston (young McFadden), and Andrew Toombes (young Schmitz); and "The Girls [sic] with the Diamond Dress."

26. Unidentified clipping fragment, Brice file, BRTC.

27. *Variety*, 11 October 1909, p. 25.

28. Unidentified clipping, Brice file, BRTC.

29. Fanny Brice, quoted by Katkov, p. 50.

30. Ibid., p. 50.

31. Sobel, p. 50.

32. Howe, *World of Our Fathers*, p. 562.

33. Abel Green and Joe Laurie, Jr., *Show Biz from Vaude to Video* (New York: Henry Holt, 1951), p. 9.

34. Bram Dijkstra, *Idols of Perversity: Fantasies of Feminine Evil in Fin-de-Siècle Culture* (New York: Oxford University Press, 1986), p. 396.

35. Stephen Burge Johnson, *The Roof Gardens of Broadway Theatres, 1883–1942* (Ann Arbor, Michigan: UMI Research Press, 1985) p. 122.

36. Green and Laurie, p. 9.

37. *Variety*, 24 April 1909, p. 4.

38. Edgar Leslie and Irving Berlin, "Sadie Salome, Go Home!" (New York: Ted Snyder Co., 1909), PC.

39. Paul A. Distler, "The Rise and Fall of the Racial Comics in American Vaudeville" (Ph.D. diss., Tulane University, 1963), p. 28.

40. Sanders, *The Lower East Side*, p. 4.

41. Ibid., p. 4.

42. Irving Howe, "The Lower East Side: Symbol and Fact," in *The Lower East Side: Portal to American Life (1870–1924)*, edited by Allon Schoener (New York: Jewish Museum, 1966), p. 11.

43. Howe, *World of Our Fathers*, p. 402.

44. *New York Dramatic Mirror*: Frey, 20 January 1906, p. 23; Mooney, 3 February

1906, p. 18; Steward, 16 June 1906, p. 18; Gilday and Fox, 15 August 1905; Hall, 10 October 1908, p. 19; Russell, 27 July 1907, p. 10.

45. *New York Dramatic Mirror*: Fields, 20 September 1907, p. 17; Gold, 30 January 1909, p. 9; Russell, 13 July 1907, p. 10; Shaw, 10 July 1909, p. 19; Woods, 27 March 1909.

46. "Fannie of the *Follies*," Part 1, p. 138.

47. Fanny Brice, quoted by Katkov, pp. 50–51.

48. Lynes, *The Lively Audience*, p. 104.

49. Robert C. Toll, "Fanny Brice," in *Notable American Women: The Modern Period*, edited by Barbara Sicherman and Carol H. Green with Ilene Kantrov and Harriette Walker (Cambridge, Massachusetts: Belknap Press of Harvard University Press, 1980), p. 107.

3. The Ziegfeld Connection

1. "The Feel of the Audience," p. 181.

2. Eddie Cantor, quoted by Katkov, p. 59.

3. "The Feel of the Audience," pp. 10 and 181.

4. Ibid., p. 181.

5. Correspondence between J. J. Shubert and Stanley Sharpe about *The Whirl of Society*: Shubert to Sharpe, 18 and 23 September 1912; Sharpe to Shubert, 1 October 1912; File 102–A (1), SA.

6. "The Feel of the Audience," p. 181.

7. *Variety*, 11 October 1909, p. 25.

8. Unidentified clipping fragment, Brice file, BRTC.

9. *Springfield Daily News*, 15 February 1910, p. 5.

10. Zolotow, "Baby Snooks," Part 2, p. 124.

11. Fanny Brice, quoted by Katkov, p. 57.

12. The Columbia's seating capacity was estimated at eighteen hundred, with approximately seven hundred seats on the main floor, two balconies, and six boxes (*New York Dramatic Mirror*, 15 January 1910, p. 20).

13. *New York Clipper*, 7 May 1910, p. 319.

14. Ibid., p. 319.

15. Randolph Carter, *The World of Flo Ziegfeld* (London: Paul Elek, 1972), p. 169.

16. Ziegfeld called the first edition of his celebrated series the *Follies of 1907* and did not add his name to the title until 1912. Annual editions were produced through 1925. There were *Ziegfeld Follies of 1927* and *1931*, and Ziegfeld toured a show known on Broadway as *No Foolin'* as the *Ziegfeld Follies of 1926*. After his death, the Shuberts bought the rights to the name and staged successful editions in 1934, 1936 (both with Brice) and 1943. A production in 1957 was short-lived.

17. Katkov, p. 61; Sobel, *Burleycue*, p. 150.

18. Sobel, p. 150.

19. Fanny Brice, quoted by Katkov, p. 62; "Fannie of the *Follies*," Part 1, p. 139.

20. "Fannie of the *Follies*," Part 1, p. 139.

21. *New York Herald Tribune*, 14 August 1938, Brice file, HTC.

22. Christine Hamilton, "The Rise of Fannie Brice," Part ?, *Moving Picture Stories*, fragment, Brice file, BRTC.

23. Ibid.

24. Florenz Ziegfeld, "Stars in the Making," *Theatre Magazine*, November 1926, p. 9.

25. "Fannie of the *Follies*," Part 1, p. 139.

26. Fanny Brice, quoted by Katkov, p. 64. In the July 1927 *Theatre Magazine* (p. 34), Brice stated that she wore out twenty contracts that way. "When I came back to the office for a twenty-first copy of it, the stenographer said, 'We know, you needn't say you lost it. We know you wore it out showing it.'"

27. "Fannie of the *Follies*," Part 1, p. 139.

28. Ibid., p. 139.

29. Ibid., p. 139.

30. Johnson, p. 105.

31. Atkinson, *Broadway*, pp. 12–17.

32. "Fannie of the *Follies*," Part 1, p. 139.

33. Will Marion Cook and Joe Jordan, "Lovie Joe" (New York: Harry Von Tilzer Publishing Co., 1910), MD.

34. "Fannie of the *Follies*," Part 1, p. 139.

35. Ibid., p. 139.

36. Ibid., p. 139.

37. In her essay "Blacks in Vaudeville: Broadway and Beyond," Helen Armstead-Johnson states that Brice introduced "Lovie Joe," her hit song in the *Follies of 1910*, in "brown face" (in *American Popular Entertainment*, edited by Myron Matlaw [Westport, Connecticut: Greenwood Press, 1979], p. 83). I have found absolutely no pictorial or written evidence to support this allegation! The only time Brice appeared in blackface was in a number she performed with Eddie Cantor in the *Ziegfeld Follies of 1917*.

38. George Jean Nathan, quoted by Carter, p. 91.

39. J. Lawrence Toole, "'Girls and Laughter—That's What the Public Wants,' says Florenz Ziegfeld," *San Francisco Examiner*, 16 April 1911, Sunday Magazine Section.

40. Unidentified clipping fragment, Brice file, BRTC.

41. *New York Herald Tribune*, 14 August 1938, Brice file, HTC.

42. Zolotow, "Baby Snooks," Part 1, p. 170.

43. Hamilton, "Rise of Fannie Brice," 5 February 1929, p. 11, BRTC.

44. *New York Herald Tribune*, 14 August 1938, Brice file, HTC.

45. Toole, *San Francisco Examiner*, 16 April 1911.

46. "Fannie of the *Follies*," Part 1, p. 139.

47. *Variety*, 25 June 1910, p. 15.

48. *Variety*, 25 June 1910, p. 17.

49. Ibid., p. 15.

50. Ibid., p. 15. The others were "Don't Take a Girl to Coney," "Sweet Kitty Bellairs," and "Kidland."

51. *New York Times*, 21 June 1910, 9:1; *New York Dramatic Mirror*, 2 July 1910, p. 10; *New York Clipper*, 25 June 1910, p. 485.

52. Cook and Jordan, "Lovie Joe."

53. "Fannie of the *Follies*," Part 2, *Cosmopolitan*, March 1936, p. 48.

54. *New York Dramatic Mirror*, 2 July 1910, p. 10.

55. *Variety*, 14 January 1911, p. 4. Unfortunately, the quality of this important picture is too poor to allow it to be reproduced in this book.

56. Ibid., p. 4. In its 14 January 1911 issue, the *Clipper* ran the same text with a different photograph. Much less expressive than the one in *Variety*, the *Clipper*'s shows Brice looking very serious in a wide-brimmed hat.

57. Caricature of Fanny Brice in the *Follies of 1910*, HTC.

58. *Variety*, 14 January 1911, p. 4.

59. Unidentified clipping fragments, Brice file, BRTC.

60. *Follies of 1910* programs: Broadway Theatre, Brooklyn, week of 2 January 1911, MCNY; Tremont Theatre, Boston, week of 23 January, HTC.

61. *Washington Post*, 27 December 1910, p. 10.

62. "Fannie of the *Follies*," Part 2, p. 49.

63. Undated clipping fragment, *Washington Star*, Brice file, BRTC.

64. Unidentified clipping fragment, Brice file, BRTC.

65. Ibid.

66. *Los Angeles Times*, 9 May 1911, II:5.

67. "Fannie of the *Follies*," Part 2, p. 49.

68. *Variety*, 24 June 1911, p. 9.

69. *Variety*, 1 July 1911, p. 20.

70. Ibid., p. 20.

71. Unidentified clipping fragment, Brice file, BRTC.

72. Irving Berlin, "Doggone That Chilly Man" (New York: Ted Snyder Co., 1911), MCNY.

73. Vincent Bryan and Irving Berlin, "Ephraham Played upon the Piano" (New York: Ted Snyder Co., 1911), MD.

74. Thyra Samter, "Listen if You Would Hear the Sad Story of Fanny's Life," *Chicago Tribune*, undated clipping fragment, Brice file, BRTC.

75. Ibid.

76. Ibid.

77. *Variety*, 8 July 1911, p. 17.

78. *Chicago Daily Tribune*, 5 September 1911, p. 10; *St. Louis Post-Dispatch*, 6 November 1911, p. 8; *Cleveland Press*, 28 November 1911, p. 4; *Detroit News*, 5 December 1911, p. 11.

79. *New York Dramatic Mirror*, 13 March 1912, p. 14.

80. *Springfield Daily News*, 23 February 1912, p. 8.

81. *Springfield Daily News*, 15 February 1912, p. 11. Again, poor picture quality precludes reproduction in this book. It is interesting to note that in many publicity shots, Brice looks demure, serious, and almost ethereal. For example, in a *Redbook* series of "Photographic Art Studies," there is a romanticized Brice gazing off into the distance. Her head is cocked slightly, resting against the back of the chair on which she sits. One hand reaches delicately across her chest and brushes her chin with a large flower (*Redbook*, 17 October 1911, p. 989).

82. *Washington Post*, 27 February 1912, p. 5.

83. "Fannie of the *Follies*," Part 2, p. 108.

84. Ibid., p. 108.

85. Ibid., p. 108. Katkov does not discuss this breach at all. Instead, he quotes Eddie Cantor who states, incorrectly, "Except for one year, Fanny was in every *Follies* from 1910–1923" (p. 76). This is not true. Brice did not appear in the *Ziegfeld Follies of 1912, 1913, 1914, 1915, 1918, 1919* or *1922*.

4. Dramatic Doldrums

1. Fanny Brice, quoted by Katkov, p. 88.

2. *Variety*, 27 June 1913, p. 20.

3. "Recalling Provincetown's Cultural Moment," *Boston Globe*, 17 June 1987, p. 78.

4. Goldman, *Rendezvous with Destiny*, pp. 173–74.

5. Lynes, p. 271.

6. Ibid., p. 91.

7. Marjorie Rosen, *Popcorn Venus: Women, Movies and the American Dream* (New York: Coward McCann, 1971), p. 59.

8. Goldman, p. 175.

9. "Fannie of the *Follies*, Part 2, p. 108.

10. Some sources claim that Arnstein was Norwegian. His son, William Brice, says he was "part-Norwegian," but asserts that he knows virtually nothing else about his father's background.

11. Katkov, p. 82.

12. Carolyn Saul, quoted by Katkov, p. 97.

13. Fanny Brice, quoted by Katkov, p. 115.

14. Frederick L. Collins, "The Private Life of Baby Snooks," *Liberty*, Winter 1972 (originally published in *Liberty*, 20 August, 1938), p. 66, Brice file, BRTC.

15. Fanny Brice, quoted by Katkov, p. 89.

16. Ibid., p. 195.

17. Nicky Arnstein, quoted by Katkov, p. 195.

18. Fanny Brice, quoted by Katkov, p. 136. That pragmatic attitude helps to explain a comment Katharine Hepburn allegedly made about Brice. As Katkov relates it, Hepburn stated, "Fanny had a kind of peasant quality in her honesty to her work. The theater was what she did, as the butcher cuts meat and the tailor mends clothes. One didn't talk or think about one's work. One did it" (Katkov, p. 117). In a 1982 telephone conversation with me, however, Hepburn's personal secretary maintained that the actress did not know Brice and never discussed her with Norman Katkov.

19. *New York Clipper*, 27 April 1912, p. 12; *Variety*, 27 April 1912, p. 14.

20. Brice headlined at the New Brighton, July 1–6; at Keith's Union Square, July 15–20; at Morrison's, July 29–August 3; at Proctor's Fifth Avenue, August 5–10; and at Proctor's Newark, August 12–17.

21. *New York Clipper*, 10 August 1912, p. 7.

22. *Variety*, 9 August 1912; *New York Clipper*, 10 August 1912, p. 7.

23. For example, *Chicago Sunday Tribune*, 15 September 1912, II:2.

24. Michael Freedland, *Jolson* (New York: Stein & Day, 1972), p. 54.

25. Some accounts put the chorus at eighty. Either way, it was a big show.

26. The runway was supposedly inspired by the apron Max Reinhardt used in *Sumurun*, produced in conjunction with the Shuberts, at New York's Casino Theatre earlier in the year.

27. *Chicago Evening Post*, 4 September 1912; *Chicago Examiner*, 4 September 1912, p. 8; *Chicago Record Herald*, 5 September 1912; *Chicago Evening American*, 4 September 1912—all in *The Whirl of Society* scrapbook, BRTC.

28. *Chicago Tribune*, 5 September 1912, p. 10.

29. Edward Madden and Jean Schwartz, "Fol de Rol dol Doi" (New York and Detroit: Jerome H. Remick & Co., 1912), BR.

30. *Chicago Tribune*, 15 September 1912, p. 3.

31. *Detroit News*, 26 October 1912, p. 10.

32. Unidentified clipping fragment, 15 September 1912, Brice file, BRTC.

33. Unidentified clipping fragment, Brice file, BRTC.

34. Nellie Revell to J.J. Shubert from Kansas City, 19 September 1912, File 426J, SA.

35. Stanley Sharpe to J.J. Shubert from Kansas City, 16 September 1912, File 102–A, SA.

36. Letter from J.J. Shubert to Stanley Sharpe, 23 October 1912, File 102–A, SA.

37. Night letter from Nellie Revell in Baltimore to J.J. Shubert, 18 November 1912, File 426J, SA.

38. Letter from J.J. Shubert to Stanley Sharpe in Montreal, 30 December 1912, File 102–A, SA.

39. *The Honeymoon Express* program, p. 11, MCNY.

40. *New York Times*, 7 February 1913, 11:1.

41. *Variety*, 14 February 1913, p. 18.

42. *New York Clipper*, 15 February 1913.

43. *Variety*, 4 April 1913, p. 21.

44. *Variety*, 2 May 1913, p. 19.

45. *New York Dramatic Mirror*, 30 April 1913, p. 6.

46. *Variety*, 9 May 1913, p. 13.

47. *Variety*, 16 May 1913, p. 16.

48. *Variety*, 27 June 1913, p. 20.

49. Ibid., p. 20.

50. *Variety*, 15 August 1913, p. 4.

51. "Our London Letter" (dated 9 August), *New York Clipper*, 23 August 1913, p. 4.

52. "Our London Letter" (dated 16 August), *New York Clipper*, 30 August 1913, p. 4.

53. *Variety*, 14 February 1913, p. 4.

54. *Variety*, 24 January 1913, p. 4.

55. "Fannie of the *Follies*," Part 3, *Cosmopolitan*, April 1936, p. 64.

56. "The Feel of the Audience," p. 86.

57. "Fannie of the *Follies*," Part 3, p. 64.

58. "The Real Spider," *The Era*, 20 August 1913, p. 20.

59. *London Times*, 27 October 1913, p. 12.

60. *Variety*, 31 October 1913, p. 4; "Our London Letter" (dated 1 November), *New York Clipper*, 22 November 1913, p. 26.

61. *The Era*, 3 December 1913, p. 27.

62. *Variety*, 31 January 1914, p. 4.

63. *Variety*, 16 January 1914, p. 21.

64. *New York Dramatic Mirror*, 25 February 1914, p. 23. A comparison of that spurious photograph with the picture accompanying Brice's 22 April 1914 interview in the same paper (p. 20) is particularly revealing. The poses, hairstyles, dresses—even the long strand of pearls—are very similar, but the faces themselves are totally different. Unfortunately, poor picture quality makes it impossible to reproduce these important pictures here.

65. "Here's Somebody Who Will Wake You Up! Fannie Brice, the Character Comedienne," spurious Brice photograph, 1914, Brice file, BRTC.

66. Joe Laurie, Jr., *Vaudeville: From the Honky-tonks to the Palace* (New York: Henry Holt, 1953), p. 482.

67. *Variety*, 27 February 1914, p. 19.

68. *New York Clipper*, 7 March 1914, p. 9.

69. Unidentified clipping fragment, 11 March 1914, Brice file, BRTC.

70. Johnson, pp. 84, 105–06.

71. *Variety*, 22 May 1914, pp. 29–30.

72. *Variety*, 5 June 1914, p. 16.

73. *Variety*, 10 July 1914, p. 14.

74. *Variety*, 17 July 1914, p. 4.

75. *Variety*, 17 July 1914, p. 4; *Variety*, 28 August 1914, p. 14, lists Brice in "Bills Next Week" as opening on 31 August at Brooklyn's Orpheum; according to the 4 September 1914 issue, p. 14, she would appear at the Colonial beginning 7 September.

76. *Brooklyn Eagle*, undated clipping, Brice file, BRTC.

77. Blanche Merrill, "We Take Our Hats Off to You, Mr. Wilson!" (New York: Leo Feist, Inc., 1914), MCNY.

78. *Variety*, 3 October 1914, p. 7.

79. *Variety*, 19 October 1914, Brice file, BRTC.

80. *Variety*, 14 November 1914, p. 8.

81. Unidentified clipping, 1 November 1914, Brice file, BRTC.

82. *Theatre Magazine*, December 1914, p. 281.

83. *Louisville Post*, 25 November 1914, Brice file, BRTC.

84. *Variety*, 5 December 1914, p. 19; *New York Dramatic Mirror*, 9 December 1914, p. 19.

85. *New York Star*, 30 December 1914, Brice file, BRTC.

86. *Variety*, 9 January 1915, p. 9.

87. *New York Clipper*, 6 February 1915, p. 8, *Variety*, 6 February 1915, p. 18; *New York Dramatic Mirror*, 10 February 1915, p. 17.

88. L. Wolfe Gilbert and S. R. Henry, "By Heck" (New York: Jos. W. Stern & Co., 1915), PC.

89. L. Wolfe Gilbert and Malvin M. Franklin, "Mosha from Nova Scotia" (New York: Jos. W. Stern & Co., 1915), BR.

90. *New York Dramatic Mirror*, 16 December 1914, p. 29; *Variety*, 25 December 1914, p. 140.

91. *Detroit News*, 16 February 1915, p. 9.

92. Sophie Tucker with Dorothy Giles, *Some of These Days: The Autobiography of Sophie Tucker* (Garden City, New York: Doubleday, Doran, 1945), p. 268.

93. *New York Clipper*, 29 May 1915, p. 3.

94. *New York Clipper*, 26 June 1915, p. 3.

95. *Variety*, 25 June 1915, p. 4.

96. New Brighton, Brighton Beach, July 19–24; Morrison's Rockaway Beach, August 16–21; New Brighton, August 23–28.

97. *New York Dramatic Mirror*, 7 July 1915, pp. 17 and 18.

98. *New York Dramatic Mirror*, 21 July 1915, p. 6; 11 August 1915, p. 16; 28 August 1915, p. 15.

99. "The Feel of the Audience," p. 182.

100. Mary B. Mullett, "Still in Her Twenties She Has Won Fame and Fortune as Songwriter," unidentified Boston newspaper, 11 February 1917, BU.

101. "Successful Women Songwriters," *Library Digest*, 13 October 1917, p. 88.

102. *New York Clipper*, 11 September 1915, p. 12; *New York Dramatic Mirror*, 15 September 1915, p. 18.

103. *Variety*, 10 September 1915, p. 13.

104. *Variety*, 15 October 1915, p. 15.

105. *New York Dramatic Mirror*, 23 October 1915, p. 15.

106. *New York Dramatic Mirror*, 28 April 1915, p. 8.

107. *Nobody Home* program note, Princess Theatre (Chicago), p. 12 *Nobody Home* file, BRTC.

108. *New York Dramatic Mirror*, 13 November 1915, p. 6.

109. *Baltimore Sun*, 9 November 1915, p. 5; clipping fragments, *Pittsburgh Leader*, 16 November 1915, Brice file, BRTC; *Chicago Tribune*, 1 December 1915, II:3.

110. Schuyler Greene, Harry B. Smith, Otto Motzan and Jerome Kern, "Any Old Night Is a Wonderful Night," MD; Schuyler Greene and Jerome Kern, "The Magic Melody" (New York: Day & Hunter, 1915), HTC.

111. *Variety*, 31 December 1915, p. 5; *New York Clipper*, 1 January 1916, p. 7.

112. *New York Clipper*, 12 February 1916, p. 12.

113. *New York Dramatic Mirror*, 19 February 1916, p. 17.

114. *Variety*, 11 February 1916, p. 18.

115. *San Francisco Examiner*, 17 April 1916, p. 8.

5. "A Cartoonist Working in the Flesh"

1. "At the Baltimore Theatres This Week," *Baltimore Sun*, 27 March 1917.

2. Fanny Brice, quoted by Norman Katkov, p. 205.

3. *Variety*, 5 May 1916, pp. 3 and 11.

4. *New York Telegraph*, 4 May 1916, Brice file, BRTC.

5. "Fannie of the Follies," Part 3, p. 65.

6. Ibid., p. 65.

7. *Billboard*, 17 June 1916, pp. 4 and 11.

8. *New York Times*, 13 June 1916, 9:1.

9. *Variety*, 16 June 1916, p. 13.

10. *New York Herald*, *Ziegfeld Follies of 1916* file, HTC.

11. *New York Clipper*, 17 June 1916, p. 7.

12. *New York Times*, 13 June 1916, 9:1.

13. *Brooklyn Citizen*, 13 June 1916, *Ziegfeld Follies of 1916* file, HTC.

14. Barbara Naomi Cohen, "The Dance Direction of Ned Wayburn: Selected Topics in Musical Staging, 1901–1925" (Ph.D. diss., New York University, 1980), p. 93.

15. *New York Times*, 13 June 1916, 9:1.

16. Gene Buck and Dave Stamper, "Nijinsky" (New York: Day & Hunter, 1916), MD.

17. *Variety*, 16 June 1916, p. 13.

18. Rosen, *Popcorn Venus*, p. 60.

19. "The Feel of the Audience," p. 185.

20. Ibid., p. 185.

21. John De Koven, "Follies Favorites Imitate Stars of the Moving Picture World," *Cleveland Leader*, 25 June 1916, Magazine Section, p. 5.

22. Ibid., p. 5.

23. "The Feel of the Audience," p. 185.

24. *New York Evening Journal*, 13 June 1916, and *New York Evening Sun*, undated clipping, Wayburn Scrapbook MWEZ + n.c. 21064, BRTC; *Brooklyn Citizen*, 13 June 1916, and *New York Herald*, undated clipping, *Ziegfeld Follies of 1916* file, HTC.

25. *Variety*, 16 June 1916, p. 13.

26. "The Feel of the Audience," p. 182.

27. Ibid., p. 182.

28. Frances Stark told me that her mother "mimicked dancing throughout her career." Brice herself explained why ballet had inspired so many of her songs: "It is so very difficult to become a ballet dancer and it is so universally and rightly accepted

as a criterion of a girl's grace, that it lends itself to satire" ("The Feel of the Audience," p. 182). That is an interesting comment, given the problems she had with dancing early in her career.

29. "The Feel of the Audience," pp. 181–82.

30. Ibid., p. 182.

31. Ibid., pp. 184–85.

32. Fanny Brice, quoted by Katkov, p. 205.

33. *Be Yourself,* based on Joseph Jackson's story, "The Champ," directed by Thornton Freeland, produced by Joseph M. Schenck, United Artists, 1930.

34. "At the Baltimore Theatres This Week," *Baltimore Sun,* 27 March 1917. Between the beginning of its tour on 18 September 1916 and its conclusion on 31 March 1917, the *Ziegfeld Follies of 1916* played in Boston, Philadelphia, Pittsburgh, Cleveland, Detroit, Chicago, St. Louis, Cincinnati, Indianapolis, Columbus, Washington, D.C., and Baltimore.

35. *Variety,* 4 May 1917, p. 4.

36. *Variety,* 15 June 1917, p. 18.

37. *New York Clipper,* 20 June 1917, p. 20.

38. *Variety,* 15 June 1917, p. 18.

39. According to a *Ziegfeld Follies* program, 27 April 1917, *Ziegfeld Follies of 1917* file, MCNY.

40. Walter LaFeber, Richard Polenberg, and Nancy Woloch, *The American Century: A History of the United States since the 1890s,* 3d ed. (New York: Alfred A. Knopf, 1986), p. 117.

41. *New York Times,* 13 June 1917, 11:1.

42. *New York Times,* 13 June 1917, 11:1; *Variety,* 15 June 1917, p. 18; *New York Evening Sun,* 13 June 1917 and *New York Telegraph,* Wayburn Scrapbook, MWEZ + n.c. 21065, BRTC; *New York Tribune,* 13 June 1917, *Ziegfeld Follies of 1917* file, HTC.

43. According to a *Ziegfeld Follies of 1917* program, MCNY.

44. *New York Evening Telegram,* 13 June 1917, Wayburn Scrapbook, MWEZ + n.c. 21065, BRTC.

45. *Variety,* 15 June 1917, p. 18.

46. Walter Terry, *The Dance in America* (New York: Harper & Bros., 1956), p. 53.

47. Blanche Merrill and Leo Edwards, "Egyptian," in *Fanny Brice's Comedy Songs,* MD.

48. *New York Globe and Commercial Advertiser,* 13 June 1917, Wayburn Scrapbook, BRTC.

49. *New York Times,* 17 June 1917, VIII:5:1.

6. Disappointments, Debacles, and "That Immortal Song"

1. Fanny Brice, quoted by Katkov, p. 209.

2. *New York World,* reviewing the *Ziegfeld Follies of 1921,* quoted by Katkov, p. 140.

3. "Fannie of the *Follies,*" Part 3, p. 101.

4. Ibid., p. 101.

5. Brice was starring in the *Music Box Revue* at the time and was accused of unfairly obtaining a part in the show for the warden's stepdaughter so that Arnstein would receive preferential treatment in jail (*Variety,* 4 February 1925, p. 1).

6. Katkov, p. 150.

7. Zolotow, Part 1, p. 169.

8. *Variety*, 15 March 1918, p. 1; 3 May 1918, p. 13.

9. Unidentified clipping fragment, *Potash and Perlmutter* file, MCNY. The two previous shows were *Potash and Perlmutter* (1913) by Montague Glass and Charles Klein and *Potash and Perlmutter in Society* (1915) by Glass and Roi C. Megrue. Subsequent productions included Glass and Goodman's *His Honor, Abe Potash* (1919) and *Partners Again* (1922). In addition, there were three Potash and Perlmutter films with Alexander Carr and George Sidney: *Potash and Perlmutter* (1923), *Partners Again* (1923), *In Hollywood with Potash and Perlmutter* (1924).

10. Edward D. Coleman, *The Jew in English Drama: An Annotated Bibliography* (1943), quoted by Ellen Schiff, *From Stereotype to Metaphor: The Jew in Contemporary Drama* (Albany: State University of New York Press, 1982), p. 29.

11. Alexander Carr and Barney Bernard, "The Humor of the Jewish Character," *Theatre Magazine*, March 1914, p. 136.

12. Schiff, p. 29; Edwin Bronner, *Encyclopedia of the American Theatre, 1900–1975* (San Diego: A. S. Barnes, 1980), p. 71.

13. Unidentified clipping fragment, *Potash and Perlmutter* file, MCNY.

14. *Variety*, 21 June 1918, p. 1.

15. *Washington Star* quoted by *Variety*, 2 August 1918, p. 13; *Washington Post*, 30 July 1918, p. 4; *Variety*, 2 August 1918, p. 13.

16. *Variety*, 16 August 1918, p. 13.

17. Edgar Leslie, Al Piantadosi, and Halsey Mohr, "I'm a Yiddish Cowboy (Tough Guy Levi)" (New York: Ted S. Barron, 1908), HTC; "Solomon Cohen, Indian Chief," mentioned by the *New York Dramatic Mirror*, 5 February 1910, p. 21.

18. Blanche Merrill and Leo Edwards, "I'm an Indian," in *Fanny Brice's Comedy Songs*, MD.

19. *New York Evening World, New York Tribune*, 24 August 1918, *Why Worry?* file, MCNY.

20. The *Journal's* was the only favorable review.

21. *New York Herald*, 24 August 1918, *Why Worry?* file, MCNY.

22. Brooks McNamara, *American Popular Entertainments: Jokes, Monologues, Bits, and Sketches* (New York: Performing Arts Journal Publications, 1983), p. 101.

23. *Variety*, 30 August 1918, p. 19.

24. *New York Evening World*, 24 August 1918, *Why Worry?* file MCNY.

25. *New York Tribune*, 24 August 1918, *Why Worry?* file, MCNY.

26. Joe Smith, quoted by Bill Smith, *The Vaudevillians* (New York: Macmillan, 1976), p. 244.

27. *Variety*, 20 September 1918, p. 1.

28. *Variety*, 4 October 1918, p. 6.

29. In July, Arnstein's wife, Carrie, had filed an alienation suit against Brice for more than one hundred thousand dollars. Arnstein managed to settle it out of court for fifteen hundred and, in October, married Brice.

30. *Variety*, 29 November 1918, p. 6.

31. Geoffrey Perrett, *America in the Twenties* (New York: Simon & Schuster, 1982), p. 15.

32. *Midnight Frolic* program, MCNY.

33. Johnson, p. 146.

34. *Variety*, 2 August 1932, p. 43.

35. The *Midnight Frolic* ran until May 1921, but was never the same after the Prohibition Enforcement Act went into effect on 16 January 1920. Congress had passed it on 28 October 1919.

36. *Variety*, 17 May 1918, p. 5.

37. Johnson, p. 152.
38. *Variety*, 13 December 1918, p. 15.
39. *Theatre Magazine*, March 1919, p. 176.
40. *Variety*, 13 December 1918, p. 15.
41. Telegram quoted by Katkov, p. 102.
42. *Variety*, 25 July 1919, p. 5.
43. Fanny Brice, quoted by Katkov, p. 101.
44. *Variety*, 10 October 1919, p.17.
45. Ibid., p. 17.
46. Ibid., p. 17.
47. Unidentified clipping fragments, Brice file, BRTC.
48. LaFeber, Polenberg and Woloch, p. 158.
49. *New York Times*, 21 February 1920, quoted by Katkov, p. 112.
50. Fanny Brice, quoted by Katkov, pp. 114–15.
51. *Variety*, 19 March 1920, p. 15.
52. Ballard MacDonald and James F. Hanley, "Rose of Washington Square" (New York: Shapiro, Bernstein & Co., 1920), MCNY.
53. Spaeth, *A History of Popular Music in America*, p. 427.
54. MacDonald and Hanley, "Rose of Washington Square," MCNY.
55. *Variety*, 19 March 1920, p. 15.
56. *New York Times*, 23 June 1920, 14:1.
57. Unidentified clipping, *Ziegfeld Follies of 1920* file, HTC.
58. Ibid.
59. *Variety*, 25 June 1920, p. 15.
60. Lois W. Banner, *American Beauty: A Social History through Two Centuries of the American Idea, Ideal, and Image of the Beautiful Woman* (New York: Alfred A. Knopf, 1983), p. 181.
61. Ibid., p. 182.
62. Ballard MacDonald and Harry Carroll, "I Was a Florodora Baby" (New York: Shapiro, Bernstein & Co., 1920), MCNY.
63. *Variety*, 20 March 1921, "Chicago News."
64. *Variety*, 8 April 1920, p. 14.
65. *Billboard*, 19 February 1921, p. 26.
66. Katkov, p. 134.
67. Fanny Brice, quoted by Katkov, p. 135.
68. *Vanity Fair*, October 1920, Brice file, MCNY.
69. *Theatre Magazine*, November 1921, Brice file, BRTC.
70. Unidentified clipping, *Ziegfeld Follies of 1921* scrapbook, MWEZ + n.c. 22360, BRTC.
71. *Variety*, 24 June 1921, p. 17.
72. Grant Clarke and James F. Hanley, "Second Hand Rose" (New York: Shapiro, Bernstein & Co., 1921), MCNY. As with all the *Ziegfeld Follies*, the show changed during the run. By October, when the *Ziegfeld Follies of 1921* reached Boston, the order of the numbers was different in both acts. Most notably, in Act II, "Spring" had replaced "Allay Up" and "My Man" had moved to a more climactic position as scene eight. (It had originally been scene three, preceding both "Off to the Country" and "Allay Up.")
73. Unidentified clipping, *Ziegfeld Follies of 1921* scrapbook, MWEZ + n.c. 20425, BRTC.
74. Blanche Merrill and Leo Edwards, "I'm a Hieland Lassie," in *Fanny Brice's Comedy Songs*, MD.
75. "Fannie of the *Follies*," Part 2, pp. 107–08.

76. Channing Pollock, *Harvest of My Years: An Autobiography* (New York: Bobbs-Merrill, 1943), p. 224.

77. Perrett, p. 215.

78. Stanley Green, *The Great Clowns of Broadway* (New York: Oxford University Press, 1984), p. 11.

79. "Fannie of the *Follies*," Part 3, p. 101.

80. Pollock, p. 223.

81. Albert Willemetz and Jacque Charles (paroles), Maurice Yvain (musique), English lyrics by Channing Pollock, "Mon Homme (My Man)" (Paris: Francis Salabert, 1920; New York: Leo Feist, Inc., 1921), MCNY.

82. Katkov, pp. 137–39.

83. "Fannie of the *Follies*," Part 3, p. 101.

84. Fanny Brice, quoted by Katkov, p. 139.

85. *Boston Globe*, 4 October 1921, p. 8.

86. *Variety*, 21 April 1922, p. 13; *Variety*, 5 May 1922, p. 4.

87. Blanche Merrill (supposedly by Fanny Brice), "When I was with the *Follies*," *Variety*, 9 June 1922, p. 19.

88. *Variety*, 16 June 1922, p. 10.

89. Ibid., p. 18.

90. Ibid., p. 18.

91. Lynes, p. 276.

92. Ibid., p. 276.

93. *Variety*, 23 June 1927, p. 17.

94. *Variety*, 25 August 1917, p. 12.

95. *Variety*, 8 September 1922 and 15 September 1922.

96. *Billboard*, 4 November 1922, p. 14. Brice's vaudeville engagements were as follows: October 30–November 4, Palace; November 6–11, Orpheum, Brooklyn; November 20–25, Riverside; November 27–December 2, Keith's Boston; December 4–9, Orpheum, Brooklyn; December 11–16, Maryland, Baltimore.

97. *Variety*, 15 December 1922, p. 14.

98. *Billboard*, 30 June 1923, p. 32.

99. *New York Times*, 27 February 1923, p. 10; *Billboard*, 3 March 1923, p. 14.

100. *Billboard*, 14 April, 21 April, and 26 May 1923, p. 14.

101. *Variety*, 16 July 1923, p. 35.

102. *Variety*, 13 September 1923, p. 13.

103. *Variety*, 10 November 1922, p. 10; Kalmar, Ruby, Friend and Downing, "The Sheik of Avenue B," on *The Original Funny Girl: Fanny Brice Sings the Songs She Made Famous*, Audio Fidelity AFLP 707.

7. Plastic Surgery for the Stage

1. *New York Times*, 15 August 1923, p. 10.

2. *New York Times*, 2 August 1923, p. 10.

3. *New York Times*, 3 August 1923, p. 1ff.

4. *New York Times*, 15 August 1923, p. 10.

5. *New York Times*, 16 August 1923, p. 2. The "team" consisted of Chicago's Dr. Schireson, assisted by Dr. Edward J. Porteous of Atlantic City.

6. Ibid., p. 14.

7. Oscar Handlin, *A Pictorial History of Immigration* (New York: Crown, 1972), p. 281.

8. Nevins and Commager, p. 411.

9. Ibid., p. 411.

10. *Variety*, 30 August 1923, p. 4.

11. *Variety*, 8 November 1923, p. 4.

12. *Billboard*, 5 January 1924, p. 18.

13. Fanny Brice, quoted by Katkov, p. 142.

14. Karl K. Kitchen, unidentified clipping fragment from Boston newspaper, probably the *Herald*, Brice file, BU.

15. Ibid.

16. Ibid.

17. *New York Times*, 22 October 1923, p. 17. The show opened in October because the *Ziegfeld Follies of 1922*, which had premiered in June of that year, had not toured, and spent the entire season in New York. Ziegfeld decided to send that show on tour in the fall of 1923 and to open a new edition of the *Follies* for New York audiences.

18. *Theatre Magazine*, clipping in *Ziegfeld Follies of 1923* file, HTC.

19. *Variety*, 25 October 1923, p. 17.

20. Unidentified clipping, 22 October 1923, *Ziegfeld Follies of 1923* file, HTC; *Variety*, 25 October 1923, p. 17. The other scene Skig enjoyed involved Bert and Betty Wheeler.

21. Benton Ley and Lee David, "The Fool" (New York: M. Witmark & Sons, 1923), HTC; Lew Brown and James F. Hanley, "Lonesome Cinderella" (New York: Shapiro, Bernstein & Co., Inc., 1923), HTC.

22. *New York Times*, 22 October 1923, p. 17.

23. Roswell Dague, *Oakland* (Calif.) *Tribune*, 16 December 1923, *Ziegfeld Follies of 1923* file, HTC.

24. "The News of Motion Pictures," *New York Herald Tribune*, 11 November 1923, *Ziegfeld Follies of 1923* file, HTC.

25. Blanche Merrill and Leo Edwards, "Russian Art," in *Fanny Brice's Comedy Songs*, MD.

26. Gene Buck and Maurice Yvain, "Mary Rose" (New York: Harms, Inc., 1921), MCNY.

27. *New York Times*, 6 February 1924, p. 29. David W. Sullivan and Wilen W. Easterday, stockbrokers, each received a two-year sentence without fine. Norman S. Bowler, a Washington attorney, was fined $5,000 and sentenced to two years in the penitentiary.

28. *Variety*, 14 May 1924, p. 5

29. *Variety*, 27 August 1924, p. 12.

30. *New York Times*, 2 December 1924, 23:3; *Variety*, 3 December 1924, p. 16.

31. Green, p. 12.

32. Unidentified clipping, *Music Box Revue* file, MCNY.

33. Green, p. 12.

34. Fanny Brice, quoted by Katkov, p. 244; Blanche Merrill and Leo Edwards, "Poor Little Moving Picture Baby," in *Fanny Brice's Comedy Songs*, MD.

35. Unidentified clipping, *Music Box Revue* file, MCNY.

36. *Variety*, 14 January 1925, p. 44; Katkov, p. 167.

37. The other investors were Earle Booth, Everett Butterfield (the director), Donald Gallagher, James Gleason and Richard Tabor (the authors), and Lee Shubert.

38. *Boston Globe*, 26 May 1925, p. 10.

39. Katherine Lyons, "Comedienne-Producer Says Idleness Makes Folks Nervous," 29 May 1925, *Boston Herald*, Brice file, BU.

40. *New York Times*, 2 May 1925, p. 12.

41. *Variety*, 6 May 1925, p. 22.

42. Atkinson, *Broadway*, p. 45.

43. "'The Final Curtain—David Belasco, Dean of the American Stage Passes' by Fannie Brice, Foremost American Jewish Comedienne." The article appeared in a number of newspapers, including the *Kansas City Chronicle* and the *Jewish Times*, MWEZ + n.c. 25505, BRTC.

44. Blanche Merrill wished Brice well in a column she wrote for *Variety*, 13 May 1925, p. 4:

> Our greatest comedienne! Now a Belasco star!
> I can imagine, Fanny, just how thrilled you are.
> I'm now your "Use to be writer"—I'm the only one feeling blue
> 'Cause oh, the very joy it was just to write for you.
> Here's to you! Happiness and success!
> And here's to the old song,
> Your little authoress.

45. *Variety*, 31 March 1926, p. 20.

46. *Variety*, 12 May 1926, p. 40.

47. Fanny Brice, quoted by Katkov, p. 178.

48. Telephone interview with Frances Stark, 4 May 1982; Nicky Arnstein, quoted by Katkov, p. 177.

49. "The Final Curtain," BRTC.

50. Fanny Brice, quoted by Katkov, p. 179.

51. Ibid., p. 180.

52. Ibid., p. 181.

53. Woollcott's and Hornblow's reviews are in the *Fanny* file, MCNY.

54. My comments on *Fanny* are based on a reading of the script on file under "Drama Promptbooks and Typescripts" (NCOF +), BRTC.

55. *Variety*, 29 September 1926, p. 46.

56. *New York Telegram*, 22 September 1926, *Fanny* file, MCNY.

57. *New York Times*, 22 September 1926, 30:1.

58. *Variety*, 12 January 1927, p. 37. The publicity photographs for *Fanny* include one in which Brice's nose has obviously been reduced in size. There is no evidence, however, that this picture was actually used in articles or advertisements about the show.

59. Blanche Merrill and Edwin Weber, "Make 'Em Laugh," in *Fanny Brice's Comedy Songs*, MD.

8. Trying to Reach "the Hillbillies and the *Haute Monde*"

1. Fanny Brice, quoted by Katkov, p. 184.

2. Ibid., p. 208.

3. According to *Variety*, 23 March 1927, p. 43, Brice's show operated at a loss almost from the start.

4. Lester D. Friedman, *Hollywood's Image of the Jew* (New York: Frederick Ungar, 1981), p. 31.

5. *Variety*, 20 March 1927, p. 29.

6. *Billboard*, 28 May 1927, p. 32.

7. Robert Oberfirst, *You Ain't Heard Nothin' Yet* (San Diego: A. S. Barnes, 1980), p. 196.

8. *New York Times*, 3 June 1927, p. 25.

9. *Variety*, 31 August 1927, p. 29.

10. *Variety*, 18 January 1928, pp. 25 and 31.

11. *New York Times*, 13 September 1927, p. 3.

12. *New York Times*, 16 September 1927, p. 7.

13. *Variety*, 21 September 1927, p. 29.

14. Fanny Brice, quoted by Katkov, pp. 193, 195–96.

15. Ibid., p. 193.

16. *Boston Transcript*, 25 October 1927, Brice file, HTC.

17. *Variety*, 23 November 1927, p. 38.

18. Billy Rose, "Sascha (the Passion of the Pasha)" (New York: William Rose, Inc., 1930). I found the lyrics in a United Artists publicity release for *Be Yourself*, WI.

19. "Mrs. Cohen at the Beach," on *The Original Funny Girl: Fanny Brice Sings the Songs She Made Famous* (Audio Fidelity AFLP 707, 1964); originally recorded December 1927.

20. Leo Rosten, *The Joys of Yiddish* (New York: Simon & Schuster, 1968), p. 429.

21. *Variety*, 23 November 1927, p. 38.

22. *Boston Transcript*, 25 October 1927, Brice file, HTC.

23. Cole Porter, "Weren't We Fools?" (New York: Harms, Inc., 1927), HTC.

24. I am assuming that the song Brice sings in *Be Yourself* is "Otto Kahn."

25. Telephone conversation with Frances Stark, 4 May 1982.

26. *Variety*, 23 November 1927, p. 38.

27. Wilmeth, *Variety Entertainment and Outdoor Amusements*, p. 134.

28. According to *Variety*, 25 May 1927, p. 25, there were only fourteen "big-time" (two-a-day) houses left in the country, whereas there had been forty-four in 1924. Keith-Albee had eight in the East; the Orpheum Circuit had six in the West.

29. *Variety*, 27 December 1927, p. 25.

30. *Variety*, 14 December 1927, p. 39.

31. *Variety*, 28 December 1927, p. 50.

32. *Variety*, 25 April 1928, p. 13.

33. Ibid., p. 15.

34. *Variety*, 21 August 1929, p. 48.

35. *Variety*, 28 November 1928, p. 1.

36. *Variety*, 9 May 1928.

37. *Theatre Magazine*, July 1928, p. 25.

38. *Variety*, 26 September 1928, p. 22.

39. *Variety*, 14 November 1928, p. 23.

40. *Variety*, 5 December 1928, p. 17.

41. "Fannie Brice Tells Her Story," unidentified magazine clipping, Brice file, BRTC.

42. Fanny Brice, quoted by Katkov, pp. 207–08.

43. *New York Times*, 30 October 1928, 27:3.

44. Unidentified clipping, Brice file, BRTC.

45. *Variety*, 26 December 1928, p. 11.

46. Ibid., p. 11.

47. According to *Variety*, 6 February 1929, pp. 10 and 26, the picture's grosses were as follows at Warner Brothers in Los Angeles: week of 29 December, $34,000; 5 January, $24,000; 12 January, $11,500; 29 January, $20,000 (a slight increase). "My Man" did not do nearly that well in Seattle, grossing $13,000 for the week of 29 December; 5 January, $10,000; 12 January, $7,000; and 19 January, only $4,250.

48. *Variety*, 13 February 1929, p. 10.

49. LaFeber, Polenberg, and Woloch, p. 156.

50. Ibid., p. 156.

51. *Variety*, 5 December 1928, p. 45.

52. *Variety*, 6 January 1929, p. 63.

53. Ibid., p. 63.

54. *New York Telegram*, 6 February 1929, *Fioretta* file, MCNY.

55. Billy Rose, quoted by Katkov, p. 214.

56. *Variety*, 8 May 1929, p. 48.

57. Billy Rose, quoted by Katkov, p. 215.

58. Fanny Brice, quoted by Katkov, pp. 212–13.

59. *Variety*, 19 June 1929, p. 35.

60. In August 1929, while Brice was involved in filming *Be Yourself*, a movie called *Nightclub* was released. According to *Variety*, it was Paramount's "first talker feature made in Astoria, Long Island" and was a "nonentity, a mess of miscellaneous ends of a revue broken into by shots to ladies' room and coat rack" (14 August, p. 31). The *New York Times* noted that it made no attempt to tell a story, but did portray "stage luminaries doing their turn in a nightclub." Among them was Brice, who sang "Sascha (the Passion of the Pasha)." According to *Variety*, that "comedy number" was the best part of the picture.

It is unclear exactly when *Nightclub* was made, although *Variety* stated that it had been "on the shelf" for "about a year." That would have meant it was filmed in the fall of 1928 when Brice was in New York after completing *My Man* and would have had time to have participated in the project.

61. My comments on *Be Yourself* are based on the version I saw. I did not have a script.

62. Molly Haskell, *From Reverence to Rape* (New York: Penguin Books, 1974), p. 63.

63. *Variety*, 12 March 1930, p. 21.

64. Unfortunately, "Sascha" was cut from the copy of the film I screened, so I did not see Brice perform it. All the publicity for *Be Yourself* indicates that she sang it and photographs show her in a costume identical to the one she used for "Sascha" on stage.

65. *Variety*, 23 April 1930, p. 38 and 7 May 1930, p. 28.

66. *Variety*, 2 April 1930.

67. Goldman, p. 248; Nevins and Commager, p. 414.

68. Nevins and Commager, p. 414.

69. Goldman, p. 248.

70. Nevins and Commager, p. 416.

71. Billy Rose, quoted by Katkov, p. 226.

72. *Variety*, 13 November 1929, p. 45.

73. *Variety*, 23 October 1929, p. 1; 10 September 1930, p. 40.

74. *Billboard*, 23 November 1929, p. 3.

75. *Variety*, 7 May 1930, p. 49.

76. *Variety*, 22 January 1930, p. 34.

77. Charles Hamm, *Yesterdays: Popular Song In America* (New York: W. W. Norton, 1983), p. 337.

78. To my knowledge, no one else has linked Brice to the Philco Hours (1930). The year of her first radio broadcast is usually given as 1933 when she was heard on a series with George Olsen's Orchestra.

79. *New York Times*, 2 February 1930, VIII, p. 16.

80. *Variety*, 19 March 1930, p. 46.

81. Brice filed a lawsuit against Erwin-Wasey, the agency producing the program, for breach of contract in January 1931. In April 1932, she was awarded $1,000.

82. *Variety*, 6 August 1930, p. 63.

83. *Pittsburgh Post-Gazette*, 1 October 1931, p. 6. Brice also served as costume designer for the show.

84. *New York Telegram, Sweet and Low* file, MCNY.

85. Stephen Nelson, *"Only a Paper Moon": The Theatre of Billy Rose* (Ann Arbor, Michigan: UMI Research Press, 1987), p. 15.

86. *Variety*, 22 October 1930, p. 71.

87. Ibid., p. 71.

88. Green, p. 14. As colorful as Freedman's story is, it contradicts *Variety*'s report in May 1936 that Brice was seriously ill with a painful neurological condition caused by infected teeth (see chapter 9).

89. *Sweet and Low*, assorted clippings, MCNY.

90. *Strictly Dishonorable* by Preston Sturges was one of the most popular comedies of 1929. It starred Muriel Kirkland and Tullio Carminati.

91. *New York Times*, 18 November 1930, 28:5.

92. *New York Post*, 13 December 1930, Brice file, HTC.

93. *New York American*, 11 January 1931, Brice file, MWEZ + n.c. 25505, BRTC.

94. Ibid.

95. *Variety*, 27 May 1931, p. 94.

96. Ibid., p. 94.

97. *New York Times*, 20 May 1931, 28:4.

98. Nelson, p. 19.

99. Billy Rose, quoted by Katkov, p. 232.

100. Earl Conrad, *Billy Rose: Manhattan Primitive* (Cleveland: World, 1968), p. 89.

101. *Variety*, 16 February 1932, p. 67.

102. *Variety*, 26 January 1932, pp. 1 and 34.

103. *Variety*, 27 September 1932, p. 1.

104. Telephone interview with Julia Wille (age 79), Merrill's "third cousin once removed," 21 July 1986. Merrill, understandably, had professional aspirations of her own. Shortly after parting with Brice, she left New York for Hollywood and movie work. Unfortunately, haunted by the label "the schoolteacher from Astoria," she did not find great success and eventually returned to New York. According to *Variety*, Merrill began writing for Belle Baker, Irene Ricordo, and Lillian Shaw. She tried, and failed, to create suitable radio material for Brice and drifted into retirement in the early 1930s. She came to live with her sister in Jackson Heights, New York, and spent much of her time at the horseraces. Although she did not die until 1966, at seventy-one, her show business career ended almost thirty years earlier. She wrote no memoirs and kept no scrapbooks. Whatever papers and photographs she left were destroyed following her sister's death in 1972. Sadly, there is no primary source material and remarkably little information currently available about one of America's first prolific female songwriters.

105. *Variety*, 16 August 1932, p. 23. According to the obituary in *Variety* (26 July 1932, p. 37), Ziegfeld had survived a bout with pneumonia. On the advice of his doctors, he went to New Mexico for further recovery in its dry climate. He soon became ill with pleurisy and hurried to Los Angeles, where he died following a heart attack.

106. *Variety*, 27 December 1932, pp. 1, 32, 35.

107. *Variety*, 6 December 1932, p. 13.

108. *Variety*, 24 January 1933, p. 33.

109. *Variety*, 7 February 1933, p. 43.

110. *New York World Telegram*, 13 February 1933, Brice file, BRTC.

111. *Variety*, 21 March 1933, p. 36.

112. *New York Times*, 21 May 1933, VIII, 4:6.

113. According to *Variety*, 16 May 1933, p. 39, the twelve national radio favorites were: 1. Eddie Cantor (Chase and Sanborn Coffee); 2. Jack Pearl (Baron Munchausen —Lucky Strike); 3. Ed Wynn (Texaco Fire Chief): 4. Rudy Vallee Varieties (Fleischmann's Yeast); 5. Burns and Allen—Lombardo Orchestra (Robert Burns Cigars); 6. Amos 'n' Andy (Pepsodent); 7. Myrt and Marge (Wrigley's Gum); 8. Maxwell House Showboat (Maxwell House Coffee); 9. Ben Bernie (Blue Ribbon Malt); 10. Stoopnagle and Budd (Pontiac); 11. Jack Benny (Chevrolet); and 12 Kate Smith (La Palina Cigars).

114. *Variety*, 11 July 1933, p. 44; *New York Post*, 14 September 1933, Brice file, BRTC.

115. *New York Post*, 14 September 1933, Brice file, BRTC.

116. *New York Herald Tribune*, 6 August 1933, Brice file, MCNY.

117. Ibid.

9. "A Burlesque Comic of the Rarest Vintage"

1. Fanny Brice, quoted by Katkov, p. 151.

2. *New York Times*, 31 January 1936, 17:2.

3. *New York Post*, 3 December 1937, Brice file, BRTC.

4. The show played in Philadelphia for the weeks of November 21 and 28; in Washington D.C., December 4; Pittsburgh, December 11. It was off for the week of December 18 and in Newark December 25.

The production had changed directors and this necessitated additional rehearsals. Bobby Connolly, the original director, severed his connection with the *Follies* after Pittsburgh, allegedly because of "interference from the Shubert office." John Murray Anderson took charge during the week of 18 December (*Variety*, 26 December 1933, p. 45).

Brice filed a lawsuit against Lee Shubert in January 1934 on account of the extra week in Newark. She claimed that she was only supposed to rehearse for four weeks because she had a club date in Chicago. She was forced to cancel that booking and demanded compensation. They reached an out-of-court settlement.

5. *Variety*, 9 January 1934, p. 44.

6. John Mason Brown, undated review, *Ziegfeld Follies of 1934* file, MCNY.

7. *New York Times*, 5 January 1934, 24:3.

8. *Time*, 15 January 1934, p. 40.

9. Robert Benchley, "The 'Follies' and Others," *The New Yorker*, 13 January 1934, *Ziegfeld Follies of 1934* file, MCNY.

10. Billy Rose, quoted by Katkov, p. 202.

11. Green and Laurie, *Show Biz*, p. 469.

12. *Variety*, 9 January 1934, p. 50.

13. All my comments about the *Ziegfeld Follies of 1934* are based on two sources. First, I listened to a recording of the show, taped in New Haven on 16 March 1935, on file at Lincoln Center's Rodgers and Hammerstein Archives of Recorded Sound. Unfortunately, the quality of the tape was quite poor, making portions of it almost incomprehensible. Second, I read a copy of the script on file at the Shubert Archive.

Although it seems to be an early draft rather than a definitive version, it was invaluable because it gave me something concrete to analyze.

14. Noel Coward provided two particularly good models: *Private Lives*, a hit when it opened in New York in 1931 starring the playwright and Gertrude Lawrence; and, in 1933, *Design for Living*, in which he appeared with the Lunts.

15. *Time*, 15 January 1934, p. 40.

16. Wilmeth, p. 155.

17. Ibid., p. 155.

18. *Time*, 15 January 1934, p. 40; *Variety*, 14 November 1933, p. 48.

19. Frederick Lewis Allen, *Since Yesterday* (1940; rpt. New York: Bantam Books, 1965), p. 99.

20. Corio, *This Was Burlesque*, p. 99.

21. *Variety*, 14 November 1933, p. 48

22. She was wearing a flesh-colored body stocking.

23. Unidentified clipping, Brice file, BRTC.

24. Written and directed by Kenyon Nicolson and Arthur Sircom, *Sailor Beware* starred Audrey Christie and Bruce MacFarlane.

25. *Variety*, 3 October 1933, p. 50.

26. "Nudism," *Encyclopedia Americana* (Danbury, Connecticut: Grolier, 1983), Vol. 20, p. 536.

27. Allen, p. 70.

28. Robert Garland, *Ziegfeld Follies of 1934* review, *Ziegfeld Follies of 1934* file, MCNY.

29. Ibid.

30. Unidentified clipping fragment, Brice file, BRTC.

31. Telephone interview with William Brice, 1 August 1988.

32. *Variety*, 5 June 1934, p. 51.

33. *Variety*, 6 November 1934.

34. *Variety*, 20 March 1935, p. 51.

35. Richman and Tucker did not appear in the *Ziegfeld Follies of 1936*.

36. *Variety*, 19 June 1935.

37. *Variety*, 28 August 1935, p. 2.

38. *Variety*, 15 April 1936, p. 16.

39. *New York Times*, 9 April 1936, 21:2.

40. Brice fared better than Ann Pennington and Gilda Gray, who were cut from the film completely.

41. *Boston Herald*, 29 December 1935, *Ziegfeld Follies of 1936* file, HTC.

42. Elinor Hughes, *Boston Herald*, *Ziegfeld Follies of 1936* file, HTC.

43. *Variety*, 5 February 1936, p. 56.

44. For Colgate-Palmolive-Peet on Saturday at 8:00 p.m. over WABC.

45. *Variety*, 4 March 1936, p. 52.

46. John Mason Brown, *Ziegfeld Follies of 1936* review, *Ziegfeld Follies of 1936* file, MCNY.

47. Burns Mantle, *New York Daily News* and John Mason Brown, *Ziegfeld Follies of 1936* reviews, *Ziegfeld Follies of 1936* file, MCNY.

48. *New York Times*, 31 January 1936, 17:2.

49. *Variety*, 5 February 1936, p. 56.

50. All specific references to and quotations from 1936 *Ziegfeld Follies* songs and sketches are based on the script I read at the Shubert Archive. Like the 1934 *Ziegfeld Follies* material on file there, the *Ziegfeld Follies of 1936* script is probably just a draft, rather than a final version.

51. Unidentified clipping, Brice file, BRTC.

52. Gerald Mast, *A Short History of the Movies*, 4th ed. (New York: Macmillan, 1986), p. 229.

53. *New York Times*, 31 January 1936, 17:2.

54. *Variety*, 5 February 1936, p. 56.

55. *New York Times*, 31 January 1936, 17:2.

56. It is tempting to ascribe the song's origin to *Vanity Fair* because, in its December 1934 issue, the magazine staged an "Impossible Interview" between Sally Rand and Martha Graham. The cartoon shows a pink and white Rand, blond curls cascading over her arched back, standing sexily with two huge pink feather fans placed strategically over her body. She smiles warmly at the audience as an ashen-faced Graham seems oblivious to all but her own movements. She wears a long red gown which clings to her as she strikes an angular pose, but the severity of the position and her somber expression make her totally asexual. The accompanying text has the two engaged in a less-than-friendly conversation which Rand begins by saying: "Hello, Martha. Still doing the same old intellectual striptease?" When Graham haughtily tries to ignore her, Rand insists that they are in the "same racket. . . . Just a couple of little girls trying to wriggle along." Graham disagrees, explaining that her dancing is "modern-classical-imaginative" and urges Rand to learn to "bare her soul." Rand refuses, saying, "I got to keep something covered."

57. "Martha Graham," *Encyclopaedia Britannica* (Chicago: Encyclopaedia Britannica, 1975), Vol. VIII, p. 264.

58. *Variety*, 13 May 1936. She subsequently had all her teeth extracted.

59. Telephone interview with William Brice, 1 August 1988.

60. *Variety*, 13 May 1936, p. 55.

61. *Variety*, 19 August 1936, p. 46.

62. *New York Times*, 15 September 1936, 37:1; Richard Watts, Jr., *New York Herald Tribune*, 16 September 1936, p. 22, *Ziegfeld Follies of 1936* file, MCNY.

63. Watts, *New York Herald Tribune*, p. 22.

64. John Mason Brown, *Ziegfeld Follies of 1936* review, *Ziegfeld Follies of 1936* file, MCNY.

65. *New York Times*, 15 September 1936, 37:1.

66. *Variety*, 3 March 1937.

67. The other "hits" were: *The Women, You Can't Take It with You, Yes, My Darling Daughter, Tovarich, Stage Door, Tonight at 8:30, Room Service, Wingless Victory, The Show Is On, High Tor, Brother Rat, Having a Wonderful Time, Babes in Arms* (*Variety*, 2 June 1937, p. 56).

68. *Variety*, 30 June 1937, p. 3; 28 July 1937, p. 6; 29 September 1937, p. 9.

69. *Variety*, 26 January 1938, p. 14.

70. *New York Times*, 11 March 1938, 15:3.

71. *Variety*, 25 January 1939, p. 6.

72. Aaron Stein, *New York Post*, 3 December 1937, Brice file, BRTC.

73. Stein, unidentified clipping, 8 October 1936, Brice file, BRTC; *Boston Transcript*, 31 December 1936, *Ziegfeld Follies of 1936* file, HTC.

74. Telephone interview with William Brice, 1 August 1988.

75. *Literary Digest* 117, 2 June 1934, p. 20.

76. *Time*, 15 January 1934, p. 40.

77. *New York Times*, 21 January 1934, X:1:1.

78. Sylvan Barnet, Morton Berman, and William Burto, *The Study of Literature* (Boston: Little, Brown, 1960), p. 334.

79. Unidentified clipping, Brice file, BRTC.

80. Barnet, Berman and Burto, p. 270.

81. Wilmeth, p. 155.
82. *Time*, 15 January 1934, p. 40.

Conclusion

1. Rae Samuels, quoted by Bill Smith in *The Vaudevillians*, p. 192.
2. Everett Freeman, quoted by Katkov, p. 284.
3. Fanny Brice, quoted by Frances Stark in "Life with Mother," interview Eugenia Sheppard, *New York Herald Tribune*, 22 March 1964, Brice file, BRTC.
4. *Variety*, 9 March 1938, p. 59.
5. *New York Times*, 3 October 1936, p. 21.
6. Billy Rose, quoted by Katkov, p. 273.
7. Fanny Brice, quoted by Katkov, p. 241.
8. Nelson, p. 63.
9. Ibid., p. 79.
10. Frances Stark, quoted by Katkov, p. 271.
11. Nelson, p. 68.
12. Billy Rose, quoted by Katkov, p. 275.
13. *Variety*, 11 January 1939, pp 1 and 24.
14. *Variety*, 13 September 1939, p. 29.
15. Zolotow, Part 1, p. 168.
16. *New York Times*, 6 May 1939, 21:2.
17. It was still heard on Thursday nights at 9:00 over NBC.
18. *Variety*, 13 March 1940, p. 30.
19. *Time*, 10 March 1941, p. 42.
20. *Time*, 2 October 1944, p. 56.
21. Zolotow, Part 1, p. 25.
22. Everett Freeman, quoted by Katkov, p. 285.
23. Unidentified clipping, November 1949, Brice file, BRTC.
24. Arthur F. Wertheim, *Radio Comedy* (New York: Oxford University Pre 1979), p. 376.
25. *New York Times*, 1 June 1951, p. 26.
26. *Time*, 2 October 1944, p. 56, quoting a 1933 newspaper interview, Bri file, MCNY.
27. Fanny Brice, quoted by Katkov, p. 245.
28. Zolotow, Part 1, p. 168.
29. Katkov, p. 245.
30. Nevins and Commager, p. 422
31. Shirley L. Staples, "From 'Barney's Courtship' to Burns and Allen: Male Female Comedy Teams in American Vaudeville, 1865–1932" (Ph.D. diss., Tufts Uni versity, 1981), pp. 395–96.
32. Zolotow, Part 1, p. 170; telephone interview with William Brice, 1 Augus 1988; Freeman, quoted by Katkov, p. 284.
33. *Time*, 10 March 1941, p. 42.
34. Irving Spiegel, "Having to Do with Baby Snooks," *New York Times*, 22 April 1945, Brice file, HTC.
35. "A Girl Named Fanny," *McCall's*, September 1963, p. 19, Brice file, BRTC.
36. Eddie Cantor, with Jane K. Ardmore, *Take My Life* (New York: Doubleday, 1957), p. 46.
37. *Newsweek*, 27 March 1946, p. 60.

38. Freeman, quoted by Katkov, p. 290.
39. Gilbert Seldes, *The Public Arts* (New York: Simon & Schuster, 1956), p. 74.
40. Fanny Brice, quoted by Katkov, p. 330.
41. Frances Stark in "Life with Mother," *New York Herald Tribune*, 22 March 1964, Brice file, BRTC.
42. Katkov, p. viii.
43. Shaun Considine, *Barbra Streisand* (New York: Dell, 1985), p. 58.
44. Telephone interview with William Brice, 1 August 1988.
45. Freeman, quoted by Katkov, p. 290.
46. Telephone interview with William Brice, 1 August 1988.
47. Frances Stark in "Life with Mother."
48. Frances Stark quoted by Katkov, p. 262.
49. *New York Herald Tribune*, 14 June 1931, Brice file, BRTC.
50. Telephone interview with William Brice, 1 August 1988.
51. Frances Stark in "Life with Mother."
52. Fanny Brice, quoted by Katkov, p. 337.
53. Telephone interview with William Brice, 1 August 1988.

Bibliography

Articles

The following list includes all important articles consulted, with the exception of the many reviews of Brice's performances throughout her career. (See "Newspapers and Periodicals" for additional explanation.)

Atkinson, Brooks. "Salute to Low Comedy." *New York Times*, 21 January 1934, X:1: 1.

"Brat's Birthday." *Time*, 10 March 1941, p. 42.

Brice, Fannie. "The Feel of the Audience." *Saturday Evening Post*, 21 November 1925, pp. 10, 181–82, 185–86.

———. "Clothes Are a Big Thing in My Life." *Theatre Magazine*, April 1929, p. 30.

———. "'The Final Curtain—David Belasco, Dean of the American Stage Passes' by Fannie Brice, Foremost American Jewish Comedienne." Billy Rose Theatre Collection at Lincoln Center, Scrapbook MWEZ xxx n.d. 25, 505.

Brice, Fanny, as told to Palma Wayne. "Fannie of the *Follies*." Part 1, *Cosmopolitan*, February 1936, pp. 20–23, 138–39; Part 2, March 1936, pp. 46–49, 106–108; Part 3, April 1936, pp. 64–65, 101–102.

Carr, Alexander and Bernard, Barney. "The Humor of the Jewish Character." *Theatre Magazine*, March 1914, pp. 136–44.

"The Clown Extraordinary of American Musical Comedy: Fannie Brice in the *Ziegfeld Follies of 1934*," Photographs from the Orchestra by Remie Lohse. *Stage*, January 1934, pp. 26–27.

Collins, Frederick L. "The Private Life of Baby Snooks." *Liberty*, 20 August 1938. Reprint. *Liberty*, Winter 1972, pp. 66–68.

De Koven, John. "Follies Favorites Imitate Stars of the Moving Picture World." *Cleveland Leader*, 25 June 1916, Magazine Section, p. 5.

"Fannie Brice and Her Adventures." *New York Dramatic Mirror*, 22 April 1914, p. 20.

"Fannie of the *Follies*—Five Good Reasons Why Fannie Brice Stops the Winter Garden Show Every Night." *Stage*, March 1936, p. 51.

"A Girl Named Fanny." *McCall's*, September 1963, Fanny Brice file, Billy Rose Theatre Collection at Lincoln Center.

"Grandmother Snooks." *Newsweek*, 27 March 1946, p. 60.

Hamilton, Christine. "The Rise of Fannie Brice," in four parts. *Moving Picture Stories* (1929) Fanny Brice File, Billy Rose Theatre Collection at Lincoln Center.

Hardy, Camille. "Martha Graham: Mythmaker." *Ballet News*, March 1984, pp. 11–16.

"The Homes of American Stage Celebrities." *Theatre Magazine*, September 1928, p. 59.

Hymer, John B. "De Sloamey Dance." *Variety*, 1 August 1908, p. 7.

"'I'm Baby Snooks You Know'—Fanny Brice Gives Her Own Lively Story of Her Rise from New York's Ghetto to the Forefront of Stage, Screen and Radio." *New York Globe*, 8 May 1938, p. 3.

"In the Halls—Acts That Sit Well on the Pinnacle of Vaudeville." *Theatre Magazine*, February 1923, p. 43.

"In Support of the Moonstruck." *Literary Digest*, 2 June 1934, p. 20.

Kutner, Nanette. "If You Were Daughter to Baby Snooks." *Good Housekeeping*, March 1943, pp. 38, 168.

Laurie, Joe, Jr. "Vaudeville's Ideal Bill." *New York Times Magazine*, 15 May 1949, pp. 24–25.

"Mingling Laughs and Tears." *New York Times*, 21 May 1933, VIII:4:6.

"The Nickelodeons," *Variety*, 14 December 1907, p. 33.

"100% Irma." *Time*, 2 October 1944, p. 56.

"Photographic Art Studies." *Redbook*, 17 October 1911, p. 989.

"Popular Leading Women in New Roles." *Theatre Magazine*, November 1921, p. 310.

"Recalling Provincetown's Cultural Moment." *Boston Globe*, 17 June 1987, pp. 77–78.

Rose, Billy. "A Girl Named Fanny." *McCall's*, September 1963, pp. 52, 190–91.

Royle, E. M. "The Vaudeville Theatre." *Scribner's*, October 1899, Vaudeville file, Harvard Theatre Collection.

Spiegel, Irving. "Having to Do with Baby Snooks." *New York Times*, 22 April 1945.

Stark, Frances Brice. "Life with Mother." Interview with Eugenia Sheppard, *New York Herald Tribune*, 22 March 1964.

"Successful Women Songwriters." *Literary Digest*, 13 October 1917, pp. 87–91.

Toole, J. Lawrence. "'Girls and Laughter—That's What the Public Wants,' Says Florenz Ziegfeld." *San Francisco Examiner*, 16 April 1911, Magazine Section.

Ziegfeld, Florenz, Jr. "Stars in the Making." *Theatre Magazine*, November 1926, p. 9.

Zolotow, Maurice, "Baby Snooks." Part 1, *Cosmopolitan*, September 1946, pp. 25, 168–72; Part 2, October 1946, pp. 50–51, 124–26.

Books and Manuscripts

Allen, Frederick Lewis. *Only Yesterday: An Informal History of the Nineteen-Twenties.* 1931. Reprint. New York: Harper & Row, 1964.

———. *Since Yesterday: The Nineteen-Thirties in America. September 3, 1929–September 3, 1939.* 1940. Reprint. New York: Bantam Books, 1965.

Altman, Sig. *The Comic Image of the Jew.* Rutherford, New Jersey: Fairleigh Dickinson University Press, 1971.

Armstead-Johnson, Helen. "Blacks in Vaudeville: Broadway and Beyond." In *American Popular Entertainment*, edited by Myron Matlaw. Westport, Connecticut: Greenwood Press, 1979.

Atkinson, Brooks. *Broadway.* New York: Macmillan, 1974.

Banner, Lois W. *American Beauty: A Social History through Two Centuries of the American Idea, Ideal, and Image of the Beautiful Woman.* New York: Alfred A. Knopf, 1983.

Barber, Rowland. *The Night They Raided Minsky's: A Fanciful Expedition to the Lost Atlantis of Show Business.* New York: Simon & Schuster, 1960.

Barnet, Sylvan; Berman, Morton; and Burto, William. *The Study of Literature: A Handbook of Critical Essays and Terms.* Boston: Little, Brown, 1960.

Bennett, Clarence. "A Royal Slave." In *The Great Diamond Robbery and Other Recent*

Melodramas, edited by Garrett H. Leverton. Princeton, New Jersey: Princeton University Press, 1940.

Berlin, Edward A. *Ragtime: A Musical and Cultural History*. Berkeley: University of California Press, 1980.

Blesh, Rudi, and Janis, Harriet. *They All Played Ragtime: The True Story of an American Music*. 1950. Reprint. New York: Oak Publications, 1971.

Blum, Daniel. *A Pictorial History of the American Theatre, 100 Years—1860–1960*. New York: Crown, 1960.

Bogle, Donald. *Toms, Coons, Mulattoes, Mammies and Bucks: An Interpretive History of Blacks in American Films*. New York: Viking, 1973.

Bordman, Gerald. *American Musical Theatre: A Chronicle*. New York: Oxford University Press, 1978.

"Brice, Fanny," In *Current Biography*, edited by Anna Rothe. New York: H. W. Wilson, 1947.

"Brice, Fanny." In *Dictionary of American Biography, Supplement Five: 1951–1955*, edited by John A. Garraty. New York: Charles Scribner's Sons, 1957.

"Brice, Fanny." In *Who's Who in the Theatre*, 11th ed., edited by John Parker. New York: Pitman, 1952.

Bronner, Edwin. *Encyclopedia of the American Theatre: 1900–1975*. San Diego: A. S. Barnes, 1980.

Burke, Billie, with Cameron Shipp. *With a Feather on My Nose*. New York: Appleton-Century Crofts, 1949.

Burton, Jack. *In Memoriam—Old Time Show Biz*. New York: Vantage Press, 1965.

Busch, Niven, Jr. "Firesign." In *Twenty-One Americans*. New York: Doubleday, 1930.

Caffin, Caroline. *Vaudeville*. New York: Mitchell Kennerley, 1914.

Cantor, Eddie. *Ziegfeld—The Great Glorifier*. New York: A. King, 1934.

Cantor, Eddie, with Jane K. Ardmore. *Take My Life*. New York: Doubleday, 1957.

Carter, Randolph. *The World of Flo Ziegfeld*. London: Paul Elek, 1972.

Churchill, Allen. *The Great White Way*. New York: E. P. Dutton, 1962.

Cohen, Barbara Naomi. "The Dance Direction of Ned Wayburn: Selected Topics in Musical Staging, 1901–1923." Ph.D. dissertation, New York University, 1980.

Conrad, Earl. *Billy Rose: Manhattan Primitive*. Cleveland: World, 1968.

Corio, Ann, with Joseph DiMona. *This Was Burlesque*. New York: Grosset & Dunlap, 1968.

Cunningham, John T. *Newark*. Newark, New Jersey: New Jersey Historical Society, 1966.

Day, Donald. *Will Rogers: A Biography*. New York: David McKay, 1962.

Dijkstra, Bram. *Idols of Perversity: Fantasies of Feminine Evil in Fin-de-Siècle Culture*. New York: Oxford University Press, 1986.

DiMeglio, John E. *Vaudeville U.S.A.* Bowling Green, Ohio: Bowling Green University Popular Press, 1973.

Distler, Paul A. "The Rise and Fall of the Racial Comics in American Vaudeville." Ph.D. dissertation, Tulane University, 1963.

Dunning, John. *Tune in Yesterday—the Ultimate Encyclopedia of Old-Time Radio*. Englewood Cliffs, New Jersey; Prentice-Hall, 1976.

Erenberg, Lewis A. *Steppin' Out: New York Nightlife and the Transformation of American Culture, 1890–1930*. Westport, Connecticut: Greenwood Press, 1981.

Erens, Patricia. *The Jew In American Cinema*. Bloomington, Indiana: Indiana University Press, 1984.

Ewen, David. *Great Men of American Popular Song*. Englewood Cliffs, New Jersey: Prentice-Hall, 1970.

————. *All the Years of American Popular Music*. Englewood Cliffs, New Jersey: Prentice-Hall, 1977.

Farnsworth, Marjorie. *The Ziegfeld Follies: A History in Text and Pictures*. New York: G. P. Putnam's Sons, 1956.

Fido, Martin, *Oscar Wilde*. New York: Viking Press, 1973.

Fields, W. C., with commentary by Ronald J. Fields. *By Himself*. New York: Warner Paperback Library, 1974.

Freedland, Michael. *Jolson*. New York: Stein & Day, 1972.

Friedman, Lester D. *Hollywood's Image of the Jew*. New York: Frederick Ungar, 1982.

Fussell, Betty Harper. *Mabel, Hollywood's First I Don't-Care Girl*. New York: Ticknor & Fields, 1982.

Gilbert, Douglas. *American Vaudeville—Its Life and Times*. 1940. Reprint. New York, Dover, 1968.

Goldman, Eric F. *Rendezvous with Destiny: A History of Modern American Reform*. Revised edition, abridged by the author. New York: Vintage Books, Random House, 1956.

Graham, Martha. *The Notebooks of Martha Graham*. New York: Harcourt Brace Jovanovich, 1973.

"Graham, Martha." In *The New Encyclopaedia Britannica*, in 30 volumes. Chicago: Encyclopaedia Britannica, 1975. VIII, 264.

Green, Abel and Laurie, Joe, Jr. *Show Biz from Vaude to Video*. New York: Henry Holt, 1951.

Green, Stanley. *Ring Bells! Sing Songs! Broadway Musicals of the 1930s*. New Rochelle, New York: Arlington House, 1971.

————. *The Great Clowns of Broadway*. New York: Oxford University Press, 1984.

Hamm, Charles. *Yesterdays: Popular Song in America*. New York: W. W. Norton, 1983.

Handlin, Oscar. *The Uprooted*. 1951. Revised edition. Boston: Little, Brown, 1973.

————. *A Pictorial History of Immigration*. New York: Crown, 1972.

Harmon, Jim. *The Great Radio Comedians*. Garden City, New York: Doubleday, 1970.

Haskell, Molly. *From Reverence to Rape: The Treatment of Women in the Movies*. New York: Penguin Books, 1974.

Higham, Charles. *Ziegfeld*. Chicago: Henry Regnery, 1972.

Hindus, Milton. "An East Side Anthology." In *The Lower East Side: Portal to American Life (1870–1924)*, edited by Allon Schoener. New York: Jewish Museum, 1966.

Howe, Irving. "The Lower East Side: Symbol and Fact." In *The Lower East Side: Portal to American Life (1870–1924)*, edited by Allon Schoener. New York: Jewish Museum, 1966.

————. *World of Our Fathers: The Journey of the East European Jews to America and the Life They Found and Made*. New York: Simon & Schuster, 1976.

Jessel, George. *Elegy in Manhattan*. New York: Holt, Rinehart & Winston, 1961.

Johnson, Stephen Burge. *The Roof Gardens of Broadway Theatres, 1883–1942*. Ann Arbor, Michigan: UMI Research Press, 1985.

Joselit, Jenna Weissman. *Our Gang: Jewish Crime and the New York Jewish Community, 1900–1940*. Bloomington, Indiana: Indiana University Press, 1983.

Kasson, John F. *Amusing the Million: Coney Island at the Turn of the Century*. New York: Hill & Wang, American Century Series, 1978.

Katkov, Norman. *The Fabulous Fanny: The Story of Fanny Brice*. New York: Alfred A. Knopf, 1953.

Kinkle, Roger D. *The Complete Encyclopedia of Popular Music and Jazz, 1900–1950*. New York: Arlington House, 1974.

Krasovskaya, Vera. *Nijinsky*, translated by John E. Bowlt. New York: Macmillan, 1979.

LaFeber, Walter; Polenberg, Richard; and Woloch, Nancy. *The American Century: A History of the United States since the 1890s*, 3rd ed. New York: Alfred A. Knopf, 1986.

Lahr, John. *Notes on a Cowardly Lion*. New York; Ballantine Books, 1969.

Laurie, Joe, Jr. *Vaudeville: From the Honky-tonks to the Palace*. New York: Henry Holt, 1953.

Levy, Lester S. *Give Me Yesterday: American History in Song, 1890–1920*. Norman, Oklahoma: University of Oklahoma Press, 1975.

Lynes, Russell. *The Lively Audience: A Social History of the Visual and Performing Arts in America, 1890–1950*. New York: Harper & Row, 1985.

Mantle, Burns and Sherwood, Garrison P. *The Best Plays of 1899–1909 and the Yearbook of the Drama in America*. Philadelphia: Blakiston, 1944.

Marks, Edward B., as told to Abbott J. Leibling. *They All Sang: From Tony Pastor to Rudy Vallee*. New York: Viking Press, 1934.

Mast, Gerald. *A Short History of the Movies*, 4th ed. New York: Macmillan, 1986.

Mattfield, Julius. *Variety Music Cavalcade: Musical-Historical Review 1620–1969, A Chronology of Vocal and Instrumental Music Popular in the United States*. Englewood Cliffs, New Jersey: Prentice-Hall, 1971.

McLean, Albert F. *American Vaudeville as Ritual*. Lexington, Kentucky: University of Kentucky Press, 1965.

McLoughlin, William G. "Aimee Semple McPherson." In *Notable American Women 1607–1950: A Biographical Dictionary*, edited by Edward T. James, Janet Wilson James, and Paul S. Boyer. Cambridge, Massachusetts: Belknap Press of Harvard University Press, 1971. II, 477–80.

McNamara, Brooks, editor. *American Popular Entertainments: Jokes, Monologues, Bits, and Sketches*. New York: Performing Arts Journal Publications, 1983.

Mistinguett. *Mistinguett, Queen of the Paris Night*, translated by Lucienne Hill. London: Paul Elek, 1954.

Moody, Richard. *Ned Harrigan: From Corlear's Hook to Herald Square*. Chicago: Nelson-Hall, 1980.

Mordden, Ethan. *Better Foot Forward: The History of the American Musical Theatre*. New York: Grossman, Division of Viking Press, 1976.

———. *Movie Star: A Look at the Women Who Made Hollywood*. New York: St. Martin's Press, 1983.

Nelson, Stephen. *"Only a Paper Moon": The Theatre of Billy Rose*. Ann Arbor, Michigan: UMI Research Press, 1987.

Nevins, Allan and Commager, Henry Steele. *A Pocket History of the United States*, 7th ed. New York: Washington Square Press, Pocket Books, 1981.

Nijinska, Bronislava. *Early Memoirs*, translated and edited by Irina Nijinska and Jean Rawlinson. New York: Holt, Rinehart & Winston, 1981.

Norman, Charles M. "May Irwin." *Notable American Women 1607–1950: A Biographical Dictionary*, edited by Edward T. James, Janet Wilson James, and Paul S. Boyer. Cambridge, Massachusetts: Belknap Press of Harvard University Press, 1971. II, 257–58.

Norton, Elliot. *Broadway Down East*. Boston: Boston Public Library, 1978.

Novotny, Ann. *Strangers at the Door: Ellis Island, Castle Garden and the Great Migration to America*. Riverside, Connecticut: Chatham Press, 1971.

"Nudism." In *Encyclopedia Americana*. Danbury, Connecticut: Grolier, 1983. XX, 536.

Nye, Russell B. *The Unembarrassed Muse: The Popular Arts in America*. New York: Dial Press, 1970.

Oberfirst, Robert. *You Ain't Heard Nothin' Yet*. San Diego: A. S. Barnes, 1980.

Oliver, Donald, editor. *The Greatest Revue Sketches*. New York: Avon Books, 1982.

Perrett, Geoffrey. *America in the Twenties: A History*. New York: Simon & Schuster, 1982.

Pollock, Channing. *Harvest of My Years: An Autobiography*. New York: Bobbs-Merrill, 1943.

Rosen, Marjorie. *Popcorn Venus: Women, Movies and the American Dream*. New York: Coward McCann, 1978.

Rosten, Leo. *The Joys of Yiddish*. New York: Simon & Schuster, 1968.

Rourke, Constance. *American Humor: A Study of the National Character*. 1931. Reprint. New York: Harcourt Brace Jovanovich, 1959.

Sanders, Ronald (text) and Gillon, Edward V., Jr. (photographs). *The Lower East Side: A Guide to Its Jewish Past with 99 New Photographs*. New York: Dover, 1979.

Sandler, Martin W. *This Was America*. Boston: Little, Brown, 1980.

Schiff, Ellen. *From Stereotype to Metaphor: The Jew in Contemporary Drama*. Albany, New York: State University of New York Press, 1982.

Seldes, Gilbert. *The Public Arts*. New York: Simon & Schuster, 1956.

————. *The Seven Lively Arts*. 1924. Reprint, New York: Sagamore Press, 1957.

Shelton, Suzanne, *Divine Dancer: A Biography of Ruth St. Denis*. Garden City, New York: Doubleday, 1981.

Sklare, Marshall. *America's Jews*. New York: Random House, 1971.

Slide, Anthony, editor. *Selected Vaudeville Criticism*. Metuchen, N.J.: Scarecrow Press, 1988.

Smith, Bill. *The Vaudevillians*, New York: Macmillan, 1976.

Snyder, Frederick E. "American Vaudeville—Theatre in a Package." Ph.D. dissertation, Yale University, 1970.

Sobel, Bernard. *Burleycue; An Underground History of Burlesque Days*. New York: Farrar & Rinehart, 1931.

————. *Broadway Heartbeat: Memoirs of a Press Agent*. New York: Hermitage House, 1953.

————. *A Pictorial History of Vaudeville*. New York: Citadel Press, 1961.

Sochen, June. "Fanny Brice and Sophie Tucker: Blending the Particular with the Universal." In *From Hester Street to Hollywood: The Jewish-American Stage and Screen*, edited by Sarah Blacher Cohen. Bloomington, Indiana: Indiana University Press, 1983.

Spaeth, Sigmund. *A History of Popular Music in America*. New York: Random House, 1948.

Spitzer, Marion. *The Palace*. New York: Atheneum, 1969.

Staples, Shirley L. "From 'Barney's Courtship' to Burns and Allen: Male-Female Comedy Teams in American Vaudeville." Ph.D. dissertation, Tufts University, 1981.

Stearns, Marshall and Jean. *Jazz Dance: The Story of American Vernacular Dance*. New York: Macmillan, 1968.

Terry, Walter. *The Dance in America*. New York: Harper & Bros., 1956.

Toll, Robert C. *On with the Show: The First Century of Show Business in America*. New York: Oxford University Press, 1976.

————. "Fanny Brice." In *Notable American Women: The Modern Period (A Biographical Dictionary)*, edited by Barbara Sicherman and Carol Hurd Green with Ilene Kantrov and Harriette Walker. Cambridge, Massachusetts: Belknap Press of Harvard University Press, pp. 107–08.

Tucker, Sophie, with Dorothy Giles. *Some of These Days: The Autobiography of Sophie Tucker*. Garden City, New York: Doubleday, Doran, 1945.

Weaver, William. *Duse: A Biography*. New York: Harcourt Brace Jovanovich, 1984.

Wertheim, Arthur F. *Radio Comedy*. New York: Oxford University Press, 1979.
Wilders, Alice. *American Popular Song, The Great Innovators; 1900–1950*. New York: Oxford University Press, 1982.
Wilmeth, Don B. *Variety Entertainment and Outdoor Amusements: A Reference Guide*. Westport, Connecticut: Greenwood Press, 1982.
Young, William C. "Fanny Brice." In *Famous Actors and Actresses on the American Stage*. New York: R. R. Bowker, 1975.
Zeidman, Irving. *The American Burlesque Show*. New York: Hawthorn Books, 1967.
Ziegfeld, Patricia. *The Ziegfelds' Girl*. Boston: Little, Brown, 1964.

Interviews

Brice, William. Telephone interview, 1 August 1988.
Stark, Frances Brice. Telephone interview, 4 May 1982.
Wille, Julia (Blanche Merrill's "third cousin, once removed"). Telephone interview, 21 July 1986.

Clipping, Personality and Production File

These files on individuals, shows, and theatres included interviews, reviews, news items, promotional articles, programs, and iconographic material—all of which were extremely useful in reconstructing Brice's career. The following collections have been invaluable sources of information about Fanny Brice and the larger theatrical scene:

Billy Rose Theatre Collection, New York Public Library at Lincoln Center, Astor, Lenox and Tilden Foundations. All Fanny Brice files (including items in Cage File); all files on productions in which Brice appeared (listed individually by show title in card catalogue); all photographs filed by show title, including Van Damm Collection and White Studio Key Sheet Codes; all files on relevant personalities (such as Ray Dooley, Hurtig and Seamon, Willie Weston, and the like); all material in appropriate general categories (such as Vaudeville: programmes, U.S.). It should be noted that there are several scrapbooks in which clippings about Brice appear. These are not her own, if indeed she kept any, and if significant Brice memorabilia still exists, it is not housed here.

Harvard Theatre Collection, Harvard College Library, Cambridge, Massachusetts. Fanny Brice file; files on the *Ziegfeld Follies* in which Brice appeared (and which played in Boston); photographs; some information on vaudeville.

Theatre and Music Collection, Museum of the City of New York. Fanny Brice file; all files on productions in which Brice appeared in New York; files on related personalities and shows (such as *Potash and Perlmutter*).

Resource Center, School of Public Communication, Boston University. Small Brice file; clippings on productions in which Brice appeared in Boston. All clippings are from the *Boston Herald Traveler*'s morgue.

Shubert Archive, Lyceum Theatre, New York. Very little material specifically on Brice. Files on *The Honeymoon Express* and *The Whirl of Society*, including revealing Shubert correspondence with references to Brice. Limited material on the Shubert *Ziegfeld Follies of 1934* and *1936*, including portions of a draft for each show's script. Although fragmentary, these scripts were extremely helpful in reconstructing Brice's role in each production.

Wisconsin Center for Film and Theater Research, Archive of the University of

Wisconsin and the State Historical Society, Madison, Wisconsin. Assorted Brice photographs, with a large number from *Be Yourself* (1930).

Other collections providing information included:

Actor's Equity Theatre Collection, Robert Wagner Labor Archives, Bobst Library, New York University. Small Brice file.

Municipal Archives, Department of Records and Infomation Services, 5 Chambers Street, New York. Brice's birth certificate; New York Census and Directory information.

National Center for Jewish Film, Brandeis University, Waltham, Massachusetts. Some early Edison films, valuable for their depiction of Jews in vaudeville.

New Jersey Room, Newark Public Library, Newark, New Jersey. Small Brice file; Newark Census and Directory information.

New York Historical Society Library, 1 Central Park West, New York. New York Census and Directory information.

Newspapers and Periodicals

The reviews on which I relied for information about Brice's appearances in burlesque, vaudeville, musical comedy, drama, film, the *Ziegfeld Follies*, on records and radio, were so numerous that I have not listed them individually. Documenting Brice's career, however, would have been impossible without them and without the following publications in which they regularly appeared.

Billboard. On microfilm at the Boston Public Library.

New York Clipper. Limited run at the Harvard Theatre Collection; on microfilm at the Billy Rose Theatre Collection.

New York Dramatic Mirror (1909–1917; became *Dramatic Mirror* 1918–1922). Limited run at the Harvard Theatre Collection; on microfilm at the Billy Rose Theatre Collection.

The Era (London). Bound volumes in the Boston Public Library's Microtext Division, restricted use (very fragile).

Theatre Magazine (or *The Theatre*). Harvard Theatre Collection.

New York Times. Film and theatre reviews were very helpful; Personal Name Index simplified process of locating articles about Brice.

Variety. Since *Variety* is not indexed, I read it cover to cover, beginning with the first issue (16 December 1905) and continuing until after Brice's death in 1951. This laborious process enabled me to chronicle her career year by year, verifying her activities with reasonable certainty.

Whenever possible, I followed Brice's shows and vaudeville engagements along their routes by checking the listings published in the *New York Clipper*, *New York Dramatic Mirror* and/or *Variety*. Once I determined the cities in which a given production played, I was then able to look for reviews and commentary about Brice's performance in local newspapers on microfilm at the Boston Public Library and at Harvard's Lamont Library.

Films, Recordings, and Scripts

Be Yourself (1930), United Artists. Obtained from Budget Films, Los Angeles, California.

Everybody Sing (1938), MGM. Screened on cable television.

Fanny Brice — Helen Morgan. Rare Originals by Two Legendary Pioneers of Theatre and

Tin Pan Alley. RCA Victor LPV 561. Rodgers and Hammerstein Archives of Recorded Sound at Lincoln Center *LRX5528. (Includes "I'd Rather Be Blue over You," "My Man," "Second Hand Rose," "Becky Is Back in the Ballet," "Mrs. Cohen at the Beach," "The Song of the Sewing Machine.")

Glass, Montague and Goodman, Jules E. *Why Worry?* (1918). Musical Comedies, Restricted Material #1867, Billy Rose Theatre Collection.

———. *Partners Again - A Comedy in Three Acts (1920)*. Drama Promptbooks and Typescripts, NCOF +, Billy Rose Theatre Collection.

Great Personalities of Broadway - The Original Great Performances. RCA Camden CAL 745 (1963). Rodgers and Hammerstein Archives of Recorded Sound. (Includes "My Man," recorded 15 November 1921.)

The Great Ziegfeld (1936), MGM. Obtained from Films, Inc., New York.

The Great Ziegfeld — Original Soundtrack Recording. Classic International Filmusicals, C.I.F. 3005.

"The Honeymoon Express" (fragment). LC NCOF + p.v. 450, Billy Rose Theatre Collection.

Legends of the Musical Stage — Outstanding Performances from 1929 to 1931: Ethel Merman, Nick Lucas, Al Jolson, Marilyn Miller, Eddie Cantor, Sophie Tucker, Fanny Brice, Harry Richman. Take Two Records, TT 104. (Includes "I Was a Florodora Baby," 1929.)

Mack, Willard and Belasco, David. *Fanny*. Drama Promptbooks and Typescripts, NCOF +, Billy Rose Theatre Collection.

The Original Funny Girl: Fanny Brice Sings the Songs She Made Famous. Audio Fidelity AFLP 707. (Includes "Oy, How I Hate That Fellow Nathan," "My Man," "When a Woman Loves a Man," "I'm an Indian," "The Sheik of Avenue B," "If You Want the Rainbow," "I'd Rather Be Blue," "Mrs. Cohen at the Beach," "Second Hand Rose," "Becky Is Back in the Ballet," "Cooking Breakfast for the One I Love.")

The Original Torch Singers: Fanny Brice, Ruth Etting, Libby Holman, Helen Morgan, 1928–1935. Take Two Records, TT 207. (Includes two versions of "My Man" and "Second Hand Rose," all originally recorded in 1928.)

Ziegfeld Follies of 1934, with Fanny Brice and Willie and Eugene Howard. Two sound tape reels (2 hours and 23 minutes). Complete show in two acts recorded live at the Shubert Theatre, New Haven, Connecticut, 16 March 1935. Rodgers and Hammerstein Archives of Recorded Sound *LT- 10 3580- 3581.

Ziegfeld Follies of 1934 and *1936*. Script fragments, presumably of an early draft; they do not appear to be part of a finished version. Shubert Archive.

The Ziegfeld Follies (1946), MGM. Obtained from Films, Inc., New York.

Song Listing

Lincoln Center's Special Collections, Music Division, yielded an anthology of songs created for Brice by Blanche Merrill. The volume, published in 1939, does not indicate the original publication or performance dates of the compositions:

Fanny Brice's Comedy Songs: A Collection of Original Comedy Songs as Introduced and Featured by Fanny Brice in Many of the Famous Ziegfeld Follies. Lyrics by Blanche Merrill, Music by Leo Edwards and Edwin Weber. pub: Mills Music Inc., 1939. Folio File: JPB 79- 2 408. Contains, in the following order: "Make 'Em Laugh," "I'm an Indian," "I'm a Hieland Lassie," "Russian Art," "I'm a Little Butterfly," "Egyptian," "Spring," "I'm Bad," "The Dance of the

Rake," "Pavlowa," "Ain't That Always the Way," "If We Could Only Take Their Word," "Poor Little Moving Picture Baby."

I am grateful to a private collector for making his copies of "By Heck," "Poor Pauline," and "Sadie Salome, Go Home!" available to me. Each of the other songs mentioned in this study may be found in at least one of the following collections: Harris Collection, John Hay Library, Brown University; Harvard Theatre Collection; Music Division, Library of Congress; Theatre and Music Collection, Museum of the City of New York; Special Collections, Music Division, New York Public Library at Lincoln Center; Shubert Archive.

Index